101
HARLEY-DAVIDSON
PERFORMANCE PROJECTS
FOR EVOLUTION BIG TWINS AND SPORTSTERS

KENNA LOVE AND KIP WOODRING

MBI Publishing Company

First published in 1998 by MBI Publishing Company, 729 Prospect Avenue, PO Box 1, Osceola, WI 54020-0001 USA

The information in this book is true and complete to the best of our knowledge. All recommendations are made without any guarantee on the part of the author or Publisher, who also disclaim any liability incurred in connection with the use of this data or specific details.

We recognize that some words, model names and designations, for example, mentioned herein are the property of the trademark holder. We use them for identification purposes only. This is not an official publication.

MBI Publishing Company books are also available at discounts in bulk quantity for industrial or sales-promotional use. For details write to Special Sales Manager at Motorbooks International Wholesalers & Distributors, 729 Prospect Avenue, PO Box 1, Osceola, WI 54020-0001 USA.

Text by Kip Woodring
Photography by Kenna Love

Edited by Lee Klancher
Designed by Katie L. Sonmor

Library of Congress Cataloging-in Publication Data
Woodring, Kip.
    101 Harley-Davidson performance projects: how to modify your Evo in a weekend/Kip Woodring & Kenna Love.
        p. cm.
        Includes index.
    ISBN 0-7603-0370-3 (pbk.:alk. paper)
    1. Harley-Davidson motorcycle—Customizing. 2. Harley-Davidson motorcycle—Performance. I. Love, Kenna. II. Title.
    TL448.H3W66   1998
    629.28'775—dc21

On the front cover: There's nothing more distinct than that trademark Harley rumble, and performance projects center around the engine. This RevTech engine is the ultimate in streetable performance for your Evo. *Kenna Love*

On the frontispiece: You may not think about it that way, but the heart of your beast is the oil pump. Keep it happy and pumping—or else. *Kenna Love*

On the title page: Keeping your Big Twin at maximum steam entails more than big-bore cylinders, open pipes, and trick heads—regular maintenance needs to be part of the program as well. *Kenna Love*

On the back cover: To reach the pinnacle of performance, you'll need a bike that works on all fronts, from exhaust and carburetion to braking and handling. *Kenna Love*

Printed in Hong Kong through World Print, Ltd.

CONTENTS

ACKNOWLEDGMENTS

It's patently obvious that a book like this doesn't spring forth from thin air. A lot of folks have helped to make this one possible, but to thank them all individually would take a book in itself. So, consider this the "highlights reel," and forgive any errors of omission.

First, I must thank my wife Susan who just knew it would be a good thing; then there's my co-author Kenna ("you shoot the light, not the subject"), and Motorbooks senior editor Lee Klancher, who were pretty sure but . . . I can't forget Greg Field for keeping me on track and not too word happy, as well as Motorbook's editorial assistsant Tracy Snyder for minding my Ps and Qs. Tom Heffron, the graphic artist for making the book illustrations come alive, and Katie Sonmor for making it come togeth-er. Everyone at MBI Publishing, for taking the shot and doing the job in an extraordinary situation, deserves a pat on the back for their efforts.

Without South Coast Harley-Davidson, especially Jeff, John, Charlie, and Tom, it would all have come to nothing. Steve Davies at Custom Chrome was instrumental and a life saver. . . since most of the goodies shown in between these covers came courtesy of him and his fine company. I've got to thank Ken Thurm of KT Components, Mel at Rivera Engineering, and Todd at Race Tech, . . . even if they were beginning to wonder if they'd ever see the result in print.

Thanks are also due to Mary and Sandy Ruthman and Dave at Hi-Tech Custom for supplying parts to photograph.

Of course, I want to praise my friends and morale officers Kevin and Amy, and probably 64 other people from at least two dozen outfits, (including "those who shall go un-named" at The Motor Company) who must take comfort in the fact they did their bit to help in anonymity. Perhaps it's they, like most of the unsung heroes in the Harley-Davidson universe, who best of all prove the knowledge and assistance resulting in this book are their own reward. To thank you, one and all, is my only reward to you. Hopefully, it's enough to know that everyone involved has my undying gratitude, including, naturally, you, the reader.

—Kip Woodring

INTRODUCTION

One of the charms of the Evolution engine is that it can easily—in some cases, drastically—be improved upon by you, the owner. Whether you intend to do it yourself or want to know what should be done as you turn your baby over to someone else for the work, this book offers insights into those improvements.

This book is not intended to be a substitute for a shop manual. There is no better source for step-by-step processes than one of those. But a shop manual is a very limited linear tool when you think about it. Manuals, good ones at least, tell you how, often when, sometimes even where, but rarely what or why.

That's where this book comes in. It will provide insights into the modifications that get the most from your Evo. You'll learn why Evos shouldn't really be revved past 8,000 rpm, why you should swap out your oil pump for the 1998 version, and so on. This book won't dwell too extensively on the how—that's where a shop manual shines—but will definitely tell you why and (usually) what part will do the trick. Speaking of tricks, the book also provides the slick little moves that the manual doesn't cover.

While this book will allow a person with limited wrenching experience to modify (or understand how to modify) their Harley, everyone should come away with something to make the cost of this humble volume worthwhile. Maybe learning to change a cam bearing when you change a cam saves you the grief and aggravation of a premature $2,500 rebuild. Maybe learning a logical approach to carb jetting turns a bucking, snarling beast into a well-mannered rocket ship. Perhaps a gearing change makes life easier for you and your ride. If so, the book has fulfilled its purpose—saving time, headaches, and money.

Although the engine is the star performer in this book, the supporting cast—chassis, suspension, drive-train, brakes, electrical systems, and more—are given plenty of air time. In fact, these crucial cast members should probably receive top billing, since no one does these things quite like Harley-Davidson. Whether they're Wide Glide forks, Fat Bob gas tanks, or Softail frames, they're different. Sometimes the differences arise from a genuine, reasonable adherence to proven concepts; sometimes they arise just from crass marketing ploys or reasons of style. Nevertheless, this book will offer logical suggestions and multiple options to help you make these systems perform their best.

This book does not propose to comment from a style standpoint. Beauty is, as they say, in the eye of the beholder (but the beholder still wants to add his or her "personal touch" to the machine, so there's a whole chapter about the rudiments of that game). If there's more than one way to skin a cat, there's surely more than one way to spruce up a Hog. One of the main functions of the personal touches section is to make you aware of that.

One of the most important purposes of this book is to help you find answers, maybe to questions you didn't know existed. Whether your answer is finally found on page 87, down at your dealer, or in the mind of your riding buddies, you have to know enough to ask the questions. At least the book may keep you from making rookie mistakes in matters mechanical; at best it'll make you a lifelong student.

And, yes, if all this is too philosophical for you, there's some "how to" inside as well! It is usually aimed at informing you of any quicker, better, or easier method of performing a given task that the shop manual somehow managed to overlook or, more importantly, where the shop manual fears to tread—namely installing aftermarket goodies the factory doesn't want to admit to. See, between you, me, and the fence post, between the tires and the tops of the mirrors, there's nothing you can't get for or do to a Harley. All it takes is imagination and money.

If you've got the imagination, you also realize, just because something's possible doesn't mean it's a good idea. If you have money, spend it wisely because not everything is a good value. The best plan, you'll usually find, is to respect the imagination and money of the aftermarket minds and bodies, expending bunches of both to cater to a need. If a given company *really* builds a better mousetrap, something that corrects a defect or improves a function (and more companies do that every day), that's where the value and true worth lie. If it also happens to look great, even better! You'll find many of these kinds of projects in the book (and hints about how to recognize which are worthwhile and which are not).

Performance is an intriguing word, with many meanings. For some it's all about horsepower. Others consider fuel efficiency and a general lack of distractions as the highest form of performance. Even the achievement of a two-fingered pull on a clutch that won't slip means it performs within its parameters. Suspension that won't allow wallowing, wiggles, or washout is true high performance in its own right. You see where this is headed, right? These "performance projects" will all improve your scoot, in a wide variety of ways.

To use this book to help point the way, try reading the "Basics" section just for fun. It's kind of a behind-the-scenes look at the reality behind the myths of these motors and a general primer for a specific project. It's also intended to offer you an edge when the parts counter person hits you with the perennial questions about make, model, and year. If you're ahead of the curve on details, you may jump right into the swirl of suggestions and specifics for most areas of the motorcycle. If all you really care to deal with are the routine requirements of regular maintenance, that information is here. If you want to jump into major projects for the engine, chassis, drivetrain, electrical stuff, or simply learn about bolting up a luggage rack, there's some insight to be had in these pages.

But, at its core, this book, like your Harley, is meant to be used for *enjoyment*, as well as information and insight. So should you find yourself snowed in, laid up, unable to ride, or with a bike in pieces until UPS shows up with *the* doodad that is on back order, relax, sit back, flop this puppy open to any page you like, and take a short cruise that will help you improve your bike's performance.

UNDERSTANDING THE INFORMATION BOXES

At the beginning of each project you'll find a list of topics. This is a guide to assist you in having all the "right stuff" to complete the project. It is sincerely hoped that you'll get a good idea of what you're up against and what you'll need in the way of time, tools, talent, and so on.

Most of the list is self-explanatory, but in case you're curious, "Tab" is a ball-park expense figure, expressed in dollar signs, each of which roughly represents $100. The oldest joke in the book, this one included, is that "H-D" really stands for Hundreds of Dollars . . . not Harley-Davidson. Now you know why.

"Talent" is represented by a star rating. One star means any warm body with the inkling to tinker can do it. Two stars means the project requires some mechanical experience and ability. Three stars means you should be comfortable working on more complex assemblies, such as top ends, clutches, and so on. Four stars means preparation, training, and practice are required; these projects are not for novices.

"Tools" lists what you need to do the job at hand. For simple projects, every tool is listed by size and type. For more complex projects, the assumption is that the reader has the basics covered (see the "Tools" section of "Basics" for specific listings). In these advanced projects, tools may be listed by general categories (sets of combination wrenches, sockets, etc.) but not by size. Special tools, however, will always be listed specifically.

"Tip" lists a slick trick that will make the project easier, the gems of knowledge that the shop manual doesn't include and your buddies don't know or forget to tell you.

"Performance Gain" is pretty self-explanatory. What you get for your money is found right here.

"Complementary Modifications" will offer some trick bits and alterations that will help you get the most out of the project. In some cases, these might be other projects that work well.

Go from there!

SECTION ONE
BASICS

The notion that you must be prepared is not unique to Boy Scouts. If you intend to become mechanically intimate with your Evo, there are certain principles you need to know, and prepare for in advance, both physically and mentally. Parts, tools, numbers, and more are covered here, giving you a good base to begin with before embarking on your high-performance voyage.

The Lowdown on Replacement Parts

It's fairly common knowledge that all Harley-Davidsons are 97 percent American-made as they come off the assembly line. This is absolutely true. It is equally true that what H-D refers to as parts and accessories division (P&A) replacement parts are nothing like American-made. They can and do come from wherever Harley can get them, from Singapore to West Germany. So the rods that were in the motor when the factory assembled it were "U.S. of A.," but the set you bought when you blew up the motor are (gasp!) Japanese.

Unless you're sure you can do better for your dollar, the motto "make mine genuine" is the best rule to follow. H-D's quality and cost control for functional parts is second to none, so it's always the safe bet. Nonfunctional parts and accessories (chrome doodads, decorations, decals, etc.) aren't subject to that motto. Do what you like. So if the factory doesn't make it well enough or doesn't make it at all . . . my best advice:

Get power producing parts from folks who know how to build those parts. Don't skimp on dollars; you'll get what you pay for.

Get shiny stuff from those who can dazzle you with their capabilities.

Spend a dollar on maintenance before you spend a dime on anything else, and buy junk from junkyards, okay?

As a final note, be sure to use the proper fastener. Sticking in any old bolt that fits the slot can cost you big. Bolts are made in specific grades; if you don't thoroughly understand the cryptic markings on 'em, go down to the dealership, suck up the cost, and get the bolt the factory specified.

Tools

Throughout this book you'll find advice on specific tools you'll need to do a specific job. That won't help much if you do something to your scoot that's not in the book or (and believe it, this happens a lot) goes beyond the scope of the specific job you started out to do. Tool acquisition can become a project in itself for some, a never-ending quest for the latest gadget that will help you get the job done, even if you never get around to the job in the first place. It's a "be prepared" game, so consider these broad guidelines.

Shop Manual

This is the first tool you should buy. It'll tell you the specifics about your bike, stuff that this book doesn't have space to include and basic, simple things that you really need to know.

Buy it and use it. Dollar for dollar, it's the best tool out there. In fact, owning two or three (perhaps the factory manual and aftermarket versions) is a good way to be extra sure a process or specification is correct. If the majority of sources agree, it's gotta be right, right?

Tools for Your Shop

Obviously, it makes more sense to buy tools in complete kits than piece by piece. If you need much more than one or two of the individual items, hit Sears (1-800-948-8800) or the local Tool Mart and go for a set that's a little more extensive than you think you need. You may need the extras more extensively than you think.

MMI REQUIRED HARLEY-DAVIDSON TOOL LIST

Description	Size drive
Quick release ratchet	1/4-in drive
1 1/2-in extension bar	1/4-in drive
3-in extension bar	1/4-in drive
5/8-in 6-point spark plug socket	3/8-in drive
13/16-in 6-point spark plug socket	3/8-in drive
Quick release ratchet	3/8-in drive
3-in extension bar	3/8-in drive
6-in extension bar	3/8-in drive
3/8-in to 1/4-in adapter	
Fluke multitester	
Safety glasses	
Rally toolbox	
Tire irons (2)	
Universal spoke wrench	
Valve stem remover	
Scientific calculator	
Metric thread pitch gauge	
U.S. thread pitch gauge	
6-in adjustable wrench	
6 3/4-in pliers with wire cutting slot	
6-in long-nose pliers	
7-in adjustable joint pliers	
Phillips screwdriver #0	
Phillips screwdriver #1	
Phillips screwdriver #2	
Phillips screwdriver #3	
3/16x4-in screwdriver	
1/4x6-in screwdriver	
20-Piece hex key set	
3/8x4 1/2-in center punch	
5/32x5-in pin punch	
3/8x4 1/2-in prick punch	
6-Piece impact driver set	
16 oz. ball-peen hammer	
36-blade master feeler gauge	
Tire gauge	
3/16-in 12-point standard socket	1/4-in drive
7/32-in 12-point standard socket	1/4-in drive
1/4-in 12-point standard socket	1/4-in drive
9/32-in 12-point standard socket	1/4-in drive
5/16-in 12-point standard socket	1/4-in drive
11/32-in 12-point standard socket	1/4-in drive
3/8-in 12-point standard socket	1/4-in drive
7/16-in 12-point standard socket	1/4-in drive
1/2-in 12-point standard socket	1/4-in drive
9/16-in 12-point standard socket	1/4-in drive
3/8-in 12-point standard socket	3/8-in drive
7/16-in 12-point standard socket	3/8-in drive
1/2-in 12-point standard socket	3/8-in drive
9/16-in 12-point standard socket	3/8-in drive
5/8-in 12-point standard socket	3/8-in drive
11/16-in 12-point standard socket	3/8-in drive
3/4-in 12-point standard socket	3/8-in drive
13/16-in 12-point standard socket	3/8-in drive
3/8-in 6-point deep socket	3/8-in drive
7/16-in 6-point deep socket	3/8-in drive
1/2-in 6-point deep socket	3/8-in drive
9/16-in 6-point deep socket	3/8-in drive
5/8-in 6-point deep socket	3/8-in drive
11/16-in 6-point deep socket	3/8-in drive
3/4-in 6-point deep socket	3/8-in drive
13/16-in 6-point deep socket	3/8-in drive
7/8-in 6-point deep socket	3/8-in drive
5/32-in hex bit socket	3/8-in drive
3/16-in hex bit socket	3/8-in drive
7/32-in hex bit socket	3/8-in drive
1/4-in hex bit socket	3/8-in drive
5/16-in hex bit socket	3/8-in drive
3/8-in hex bit socket	3/8-in drive
3/8-in 6-point standard socket	1/2-in drive
7/16-in 6-point standard socket	1/2-in drive
1/2-in 6-point standard socket	1/2-in drive
9/16-in 6-point standard socket	1/2-in drive
5/8-in 6-point standard socket	1/2-in drive
11/16-in 6-point standard socket	1/2-in drive
3/4-in 6-point standard socket	1/2-in drive
13/16-in 6-point standard socket	1/2-in drive
7/8-in 6-point standard socket	1/2-in drive
15/16-in 6-point standard socket	1/2-in drive
1-in 6-point standard socket	1/2-in drive
1 1/16-in 6-point standard socket	1/2-in drive
1 1/8-in 6-point standard socket	1/2-in drive
1 1/4-in 6-point standard socket	1/2-in drive
1/2-in to 3/8-in adapter	1/2-in drive
Quick release ratchet	1/2-in drive
3-in extension bar	1/2-in drive
6-in extension bar	1/2-in drive
1/4-in combination wrench	
5/16-in combination wrench	
11/32-in combination wrench	
3/8-in combination wrench	
7/16-in combination wrench	
1/2-in combination wrench	
9/16-in combination wrench	
5/8-in combination wrench	
11/16-in combination wrench	
3/4-in combination wrench	
13/16-in combination wrench	
7/8-in combination wrench	
15/16-in combination wrench	
1 1/16-in combination wrench	
13 Piece balldriver hex key set	
Dead blow hammer	
7 1/2-in needlenose Vise Grips pliers	
Wire cutter	
Channel locks	
Convertible retaining ring pliers	
Double-point scriber (2)	
Single-point scriber	
6-wire spark plug gauge	

ADDITIONAL HAND TOOLS

Screwdriver sets
- Posi-drive #1, 2, 3, 4
- Angle driver (for carb adjustment)

Pliers Sets
- Sidecut
- Channel lock
- Hose clamp crimpers

3/8-in T-Handle

3/8-in Air Ratchet

3/8-in drive Allen Sockets
- Straight and ball sockets (short and long)
- 3/16-in to 3/8-in
- Long 5 mm

Crows Foot Set
- 3/8-in to 1 1/8-in

Torx driver Bit Set
- Up to and including #40 and #45

Torque Adapter Set
- 3/8-in to 3/4-in
- 1/2-in extension sets
- 2-in to 12-in straight

Hand Impact driver and Bits

Air Impact Wrenches
- 3/8-in and 1/2-in

Torque Wrenches (click type)
- 3/8-in to 288-in lb
- 3/8-in to 75-in lb
- 1/2-in to 288-in lb

Line Wrenches
- 1/4-in, 5/16-in, 3/8-in, 7/8-in

Crescent Wrenches
- 10-in and 12-in

Complete Set of Metal Files
- File handles
- Thread files
- Jewelers' files

Feeler Gauge (flat and wire type)

SPECIALTY TOOLS

Transmission and drive
- Sprocket lock links
- Clutch spring compressors
- Clutch hub puller
- Primary bearing remover and installer
- Main drive gear and bearing
- Remover and installer
- Main drive gear cross plate (1991–on XL)
- All needle bearing installers
- Main drive gear locknut wrench

Miscellaneous
- Safety glasses
- Drill bits (numbered, lettered, and fractional—all sizes to 1/2-in)
- Chemicals (contact cleaner, etc.)
- Hacksaw
- Assorted blades
- Tap and die set
- 1/2-in pneumatic drill
- Bolt cutters
- Automatic center punch
- Pop rivet gun
- Shop towels
- Flashlight
- Heavy vice

Facility
- Air compressor vehicle lifts
- Bench grinder
- Parts washer
- Carburetor cleaner
- Oil disposal system
- Tire changer
- Vehicle wash bay
- Pressure washer
- Shop vac
- Arbor press
- Hydraulic press
- Drill press
- Sunnen hone
- Lathe
- Boring bar
- Exhaust system

Electrical
- Digital multimeter (10-amp scale, 00-milliamp scale)
- Battery charger
- Ignition jumper with condenser (as per service manual)
- Kent Mooer Terminal Kit (H-D #39448-3)
- Soldering iron
- Timing light
- Hydrometer (small Yuasa)
- Mity-Vac kit
- Charging system and battery
- Load tester
- Jumper leads (24-in long)
- Inductive ammeter, 3 each (14 gauge with

30-amp clips)
- CB test set (H-D #39448)
- Test light

Engine
- Valve guide tools
- Guide drivers
- Guide and seal installers
- Reams and flex hones
- Seat cutter/grinder
- Sprocket shaft bearing installer
- Cam gear gauge pin sets
- Small hole gauges
- Rocker bushing ream
- Telescoping gauges
- Blind hole puller
- Piston pin retaining ring installer
- Cam bearing installers
- 6-in machinist square
- Connecting rod clamping tool
- Die grinder and bits
- Stethoscope
- Piston pin bushing tool
- Pinion gear puller and collars
- Crank seal installer (H-D #39361)
- Pin bushing ream
- Crankcase main bearing
- Lapping tool
- Sprocket shaft installer (H-D #97225-55A)
- Piston ring compressor
- Valve spring compressor
- Flywheel rebuilding fixture
- Dial calipers
- Timing plug (H-D #96295-65D)
- Flywheel truing stand
- Micrometer set 1-in to 4-in
(in 0.0001-in increments)
- Dial bore gage

Chassis
- Wheel bearing remover and installer
- Inclinometer
- Power brake bleeder
- Vehicle alignment bars
- Cleveblock spreader
- Wheel bearing packer
- Small scissor jack
- Fork bushing and seal installers
- Wheel truing stand
- Plumb bob
- Steering head bearing installer
- Spoke wrench
- Rear axle alignment tools
- Rear swingarm assembly tool
- Valve core tool
- 24-in bungee cords (qty 6)
- Belt tension gauge (H-D #35381)
- Shock absorber spanner
- Pointer for front fork
- Adjustment
- Dial indicator set
- Vise Grip mount (flexible shaft)
- No-loss pressure gauge (H-D #34633)
- Long punch for FLT
- 6-in dial vernier caliper

The tool list shown is what is required by the Motorcycle Mechanics Institute (MMI). If it's good enough for a trained mechanic, it's good enough for you.

And don't forget the "expendable" tools such as:
- Rags
- Bearing grease
- Hand cleaner
- Drain pan
- Funnel
- Single-edged razor blades
- Old coffee cans or plastic jugs
- Sealable plastic baggies and film canisters
- Marking pen
- Wood blocks and short 2x4s
- Work gloves
- Safety glasses

The list runs to whatever length you need to feel comfortable and safe for the job at hand.

So much for standard tools. It's naive to believe you can get any major work done on an Evo without resorting to tools designed for that specific job. That's where so-called "special" tools come in. The two best sources for these are Kent-Moore and Jim's, both accessible through your dealer. You'll find the need for primary side tools first, such as a clutch puller or mainshaft socket, so you should budget for these. Other special tools, get only as and if you need them, but always before you have to use them. Just remember it's better to have it and not need it than need it and not have it. There's nothing more irritating than to be stuck for lack of a tool.

TOOLS TO TAKE
You bought that new Hog to ride, right? Well, on the road in the middle of nowhere is generally when you first discover Harleys don't come with tool kits. And the ones they'd like to sell you cost a bundle and usually don't come with everything you need. What to do? Build it, buy it, beg it, borrow it, or ride with someone who drags this stuff along. One way or the other, you're going to want each of these tools with you if ride long enough.
- Wrenches: 3/8-, 7/16-, 1/2-, 9/16-, 5/8-, and 11/16-inch open end; 6- and 10-inch adjustable crescents; full ("key-ring" style) Allen set; Torx bit set; spark plug wrench and driver; and small Vise Grips (tapered tip is best)
- Screwdrivers: Phillips and straight-tip
(preferably a reversible, double-ended type)
- Pliers: small needle nose and 6-inch
standard (or, optionally, 8-inch channel-lock type)
- Safety wire: 16-18-gauge stainless
- Small tire repair kit: CO_2 type with patches or

"plugs"; another option is an aerosol "sealer" or an " engine pump" patch/inflator kit
• Small battery hydrometer
• "Pocket" multimeter or voltmeter
• Black laundry marker and, optionally, type correction "white out"
• Tape: small roll of electrical and a small roll of duct
• Impact driver: "vessel type" with assorted tips
• Hammer with shortened or removable handle
• Small file (with one "grade" of "cut" on each side) or, optionally, an emery board and a piece of sand paper
• Hacksaw blade
• Two rags
• Small tube of liquid gasket
• Small container of grease
• Small can of chain/cable lube
• Spare spark plugs
• Feeler gauge
• Spare bulbs
• Chain master link (or repair kit)
• Small assortment of fasteners
• Roll of 16–18-gauge insulated electrical wire
• Three small alligator clips
• Anything else you can carry and use for your particular needs.

VEHICLE IDENTIFICATION NUMBERS (VIN)

Once you've acquired your new or used H-D, you may want to know a little bit more about it. If it's been modified beyond all recognition, you especially might have need to figure out how the beast started life. That's what this chart is intended to help you with. The current system that Harley uses for its federally mandated 17-digit VIN numbers dates from 1981, so I've thrown in the last of the Iron Sportster VIN numbers. The 80-cubic-inch Shovelhead was still on the scene back then as well, and those VIN numbers are shown because of the overlap in model codes. Because H-D built Shovelheads and Evos side by side in 1984, you could get a little confused—unless you read this chart.

The H-D VIN System

All 1981–on Harley VIN numbers start with "1HD" followed by a series of codes that reveal model, displacement, and other information, followed by a serial number. Following the "1 HD" is a one-digit class code ("1" denoting engines under 1,000 cc and "4" denoting engines over 1,000 cc). Next comes a two-letter model code. Information on interpreting the model codes follows in a subsection for each model grouping. After the model code is a one-letter engine code (H = 1,000 cc, M = 883 cc, N = 1,100 cc, P = 1,200 cc, L = 1,340 cc carbureted, and R = 1,340 cc fuel injected). After the engine code is a special one-digit "introduction date" code (1 = regular introduction, 2 = midyear, 3 = California model, and 4 = special edition). This is followed by a second "internal" number or digit that is meaningless to anyone outside the factory; it can be anything from 0-9, or even X. Then comes a one-letter year code (B = 1981, C = 1982, D = 1983, E = 1984, F = 1985, G = 1986, H = 1987, J = 1988, K = 1989, L = 1990, M = 1991, N = 1992, P = 1993, R = 1994, S = 1995, T = 1996, V = 1997, W = 1998, and so on). The last code before the serial number is a one-letter code for the assembly plant (Y = York, K = Kansas City). Thus, code 1HD1EKL10FY122386 denotes 1985 FXRP serial number 122386.

Sportster Model Codes
CA = XLH (iron-barrel)
CAM = 883
CAN = 1100
CAP = 1200

In addition to a full set of standard hand tools, H-D likes you to employ a series of special tools for specific tasks. These tools, made by Kent-Moore, are available from your dealer. Jim's in Camarillo, California, can supply improved versions. One of the more useful special tools for an owner is a clutch-hub puller like the Jim's version shown on the left. It works on all versions of the Big Twin clutch and will also remove the alternator rotor and motor sprocket. Of course, that tool won't help much unless you can compress the diaphragm spring. Use the tool on the right for that little chore. With proper adapters, these tools will also work on Evo Sportsters. Since alternator and clutch work are the most common of the uncommon chores an owner may want to tackle, these items should be in the toolbox of any long-term Evo owner.

CB = XLS
CC = XLX
CD = XR1000
CE = Hugger
CF = Deluxe
CG = 1200 Custom
CH = 1200 Sport

FX/FL (Swingarm) Model Codes
AA = FLH80
AB = FLH80 Police
AC = FLH80 Shrine
AD = FLH Classic
AH = FLH80 Police/Deluxe
AK = FLHS80
AL = FLH80 Shrine/Deluxe
BA = FXE
BB = FXEF
BC = FXS
BD = FXB
BE = FXWG
BF = FXSB

FXR Model Codes
EA = FXR
EB = FXRS
EC = FXRT
ED = FXRP with windshield
EF = FXRP with fairing
EG = FXRS-SP
EH = FXRD
EK = FXRP California police
EM = Convertible

FLT Model Codes
DA = FLHTP with windshield
DB = FLT-C

DC = FLHT (1982–1983)
DD = FLHT(1984–1985 and 1995–on)
DE = FLHT with sidecar
DF = FLHTP with fairing
DG = FLHTP Shrine
DJ = FLHTC
DP = FLHTC-U
FA = FLHS
FD = FLHR Road King
FB = FLHR-I
FC = FLHTCU-I
FF = FLHTC-I
FG = FLHTCU-I with sidecar
FL = Shrine
FP = FLTR
FR = FLHRC-I
FS = FLTR-I

Softail FL Model Codes
BJL = FLSTC Heritage
BML = FLSTF Fat Boy
BNL = FLSTN Nostalgia
BRL = FLSTS Heritage Springer

Softail FX Model Codes
BLL = FXSTS Springer
BKL = FXSTC Custom
BHL = FXST
BPL = FXSTSB Bad Boy

Dyna Model Codes
GA = FXDD Daytona
GB = FXDS Sturgis
GC = FXDC Custom
GD = FXDL Low Rider
GE = FXDWG Wide Glide
GG = FXDS Convertible

Assorted pullers and extractors are the next item on the agenda if you plan to work on the transmission. This tool is used for removing and replacing the inner race of the gearbox mainshaft. You simply cannot do the job without it.

But to get even that far, you'll need a 1 7/8-inch socket like the one in the upper left corner of the photo to remove the countershaft nut on Big Twins. If you're working on a four-speed Sportster, you'll need a different hub puller and a spring compressor for the clutch.

Harleys use a number of bushings and needle bearings that occasionally need attention, and these are the kinds of tools you attend with. Top to bottom are a rocker arm bushing remover, a cam bearing remover, a cam bearing installer, the tiny but useful tappet alignment tool, and the cam bushing reamer.

Here we have a piston pin (wrist pin) bushing tool, which is indispensable if for removing and installing new bushes without taking the rods out of the cases. Its helper, comprising the two pieces to its right, is the piston pin keeper (circlip) tool.

When the valvetrain needs help, you can help yourself to these: the ubiquitous valve spring compressor and installation tools for new shoulderless valve guides.

And what do you do when it's necessary to remove the engine? A proper engine stand like one of these is a necessity. Actually, the top stand is for Sportsters, the middle one for five-speed Big Twin transmissions, and the bottom one for tall Big Twins.

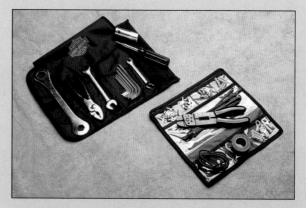

Let's not forget the chassis. A tool like this one makes removing and replacing tapered bearings in the wheels and the steering head of the frame a breeze. Add a few different sizes of split collars to that handle, and you can remove and replace the Timken bearings in both Big Twins and Sportsters engine cases as well. The thing to remember is that this is just a basic sample of the world of special tools. If you do more involved work, you'll get more involved with tools. These tools aren't cheap, so if you'll only need them once, it may not be cost-effective to own them.

If you've just got to have genuine Harley tools to take with you on long rides, here are a couple that are worthwhile. The Universal Wire Repair Kit (#91936-96) will help with the kinds of problems that, these days, are responsible for 80 percent of the stuff that stops the ride. For the other 15 percent, get a Deluxe Tire Repair Kit (#91901-84A, not shown), and just so you aren't totally insecure the remaining 5 percent of the time, order the factory tool kit (#94435-82D), complete with H-D logo and chrome wrenches.

Don't forget that some of the most important tools come in tubes or cans rather than drawers or boxes. Keep your Hog long enough and take reasonable care of it, and you'll find you need and use virtually everything you see here—and then some!

Replacing fasteners is not nearly as simply as you might think. Be sure that the bolt you install is not only the same size but the same strength as the factory unit. Although the markings on the head of a fastener give a good indication of its strength, the other method of ensuring quality is to buy from a reputable supplier. Truth be told, many shops stock hardware from whoever has the best price and presume it is safe—you shouldn't. Instead, insist on genuine factory hardware, which comes in plastic bags so you can be reasonably certain it's been checked by the same people who built your motorcycle.

SIMPLE MAINTENANCE

Evolution Harleys don't really ask much from you. You don't have to adjust valves, synchronize carburetors, or mess with electrical system settings. In fact, one of the great charms of Evos is this lack of maintenance. It's pretty basic. Those basics, however, are key to getting the most from your machine. Before you swap to those trick custom wheels, you should understand wheel bearing preload. Prior to slamming on those radical exhaust pipes, you should think about blocked access to the tranny drain plug. Want that fancy oil pump cover? You should know that it'll have to come back off every time you access the oil pump. Take care of the bottom line and you'll be ready to move up to bigger things!

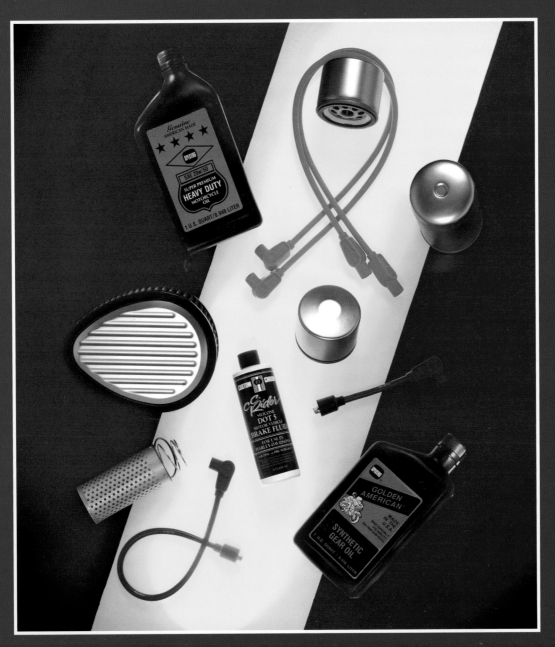

SIMPLE MAINTENANCE

PROJECT 1 • PERFORMING THE 10,000 MILE SERVICE

 Time: 4 to 8 hours

 Tools: All your regular hand tools, Allen and Torx bits, an impact driver, a wheel bearing packer tool (optional), a torque wrench, a fish scale, a tappet screen plug tool (or equivalent), and other odds and ends (see chart)

 Talent: 👤👤

 Tab: $

 Tinware: See chart

 Tip: Warm motor for draining fluids; then cool motor for the rest

PERFORMANCE GAIN: About 60,000 miles over the life of the motorcycle (maybe more)

COMPLEMENTARY MODIFICATION: Allen- or hex-head aftermarket tappet plugs or screw-type (rather than pinch-type) hose clamps

The secret of a long and happy life for you and yours is regular maintenance. You want to make your Hog run like the wind? Start with regular maintenance.

This project is a bit different from the others, in that it is not one single project but a group of them. The rest of this section includes most of the major tasks that you will need to do to perform at each 10,000-mile service.

A 10,000-mile service entails checking, lubing, adjusting, and freshening essentially all of the minor systems on your Harley-Davidson. Routine maintenance of an H-D can be broken down into three rough categories: minor (every 2,500 miles), major (every 5,000 miles), and chassis (every 10,000 miles).

A minor service amounts to a glorified oil change and relatively thorough inspection. A major service extends to changing all powerplant fluids and actual lubing and adjustment of all kinds of stuff. But all this is mere prelude to the subject of this project, a chassis service—otherwise known as a "10K."

The key point of this project is that to consistently repeat your 10,000-mile service. The bald fact is a 10K is typically the only attention paid to "out-of-sight out-of-mind" stuff like wheel bearings, steering bearings, fork, and brake fluid.

1 A full service on a Harley is the main thing you must learn to master if you intend to keep your motorcycle acting its best. It involves every major area of the machine. You will see more in-depth procedures for certain specific tasks throughout this book; the core of so-called routine maintenance lies in the "big picture" provided by a correct and complete service. Unfortunately, many of the most important chores are the tedious ones involved in keeping the chassis happy. For instance, starting at the front of the bike, changing the fork oil.

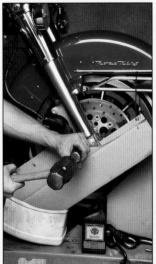

2 Once you have the bike secured, locate the drain screw, and build a cardboard chute to the dump pan, you may find the need for an impact driver. Once the screw has been removed, allow enough time for the oil to drain completely—usually until no more fluid will drip.

3 To save time and effort, don't bother to remove the caps bolts on top of the fork tubes. Simply use an oil can and a piece of rubber tubing with a modified cap from a Bic pen (or the equivalent) fixed to the end. Pour the measured amount of fluid into the oil can, screw the Bic pen adapter into the fork drain hole, and pump the oil in. Replace the drain screw quickly once the adapter has been removed, to minimize any fluid losses.

Bear in mind that, on infrequently ridden machines, a 10K can take years to get around to. This is not an ideal scenario. Too many vital components wind up suspect, if not downright unsafe. Thus using mileage intervals as a guide to frequency can steer you wrong. A good alternative would be to do it once each riding sea-

4 While you've got that oil can handy, if need be, you can fill it with brake fluid and "back bleed" the front brake. Since air wants to move up not down, this procedure can be much more effective than conventional techniques. Attach the tubing to the brake bleeder, remove the master cylinder lid and rubber gasket, crack the bleeder, and pump slowly.

5 Of course, you want to check the brake pads. You should eyeball the pads before every ride, but remove the caliper to double-check them during a full service. Make sure the little nubbin on the pad carrier is in good shape as well. When you reassemble things, clean everything up, apply lube to the brake pins, and apply blue Loctite blue to the mounting bolts.

6 Don't forget to torque the caliper bolts, slider caps, and axle nuts for the front wheel to the specs in your shop manual after you remove them for service.

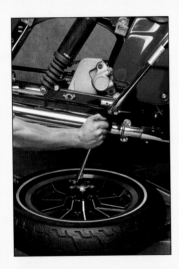  

7 Once the wheel is off (front and rear will both be done), you need to service the wheel bearings. Pull the old seal out with a screwdriver, pull the bearing out, and inspect the race that remains in the wheel. Any scratches, wear marks, or "waves" in the surface of the race are cause for replacement, especially if the bearing itself has similar matching marks. Wheel bearings are sold as race and bearing sets for good reason. Don't be tempted to throw a new bearing in there against an old or damaged race.

8 Whether the old bearing passes muster or a new one must replace it, you need to pack grease in between the individual rollers. The best way is with an automotive bearing packer tool. You lay the bearing on, pump the tool, and bingo, a properly lubricated bearing. Doing the same job by hand takes, first and foremost, clean hands, and a lot more patience. That said, if you are particular enough to do it right, hand packing is perfectly acceptable.

9 The bearing tool removes and installs the race. Use it to pop out the old race. Then clean the race seat in the wheel thoroughly and set the two halves of the installer in place in the race. Insert the tool handle, and pound away until the sound you hear changes from a ringing noise to a dull flat clack sound. Check the race you've just installed against one of the originals to ensure that it's properly "bottomed out" in the wheel.

son begins, whether you put on 10,000 miles or not. Of course, if you put on 30,000 miles a season, you're going to have to service it more often.

Another option is to do your services based on the condition of your bike. For example, check your oil every other time you fill the bike with gas. Oil's pretty honest. If it looks clean and smells okay, it probably is. On the other hand, regardless of time or miles since the last change, if the oil is dark, muddy, or stinky, it's telling you loud and clear it's time for a change.

This logic works for chassis service as well. Most of us wear out a back tire (and rear brake pads) at about 10,000-mile intervals, give or take. So, when the tire gets renewed, do the rest of the chassis service at the same time. If you subscribe to the notion that "anything worth doing is worth overdoing," you cannot go wrong here.

Intended as a guide, in conjunction with the shop manual, the following list of goodies is what it generally takes to do a complete chassis service on a Harley. Since it's broken down by task, you can perform all or part as you need to. A couple of things to be aware of, however, are the fact that some late models (1995 and newer) no longer use a rear axle cotter pin, and that the grease zerk listed is standard on most 1994 and newer models, except Dynas. Installing the zerk in the steering head of your machine, if it doesn't have one already, is a great "update" and saves time and effort when it comes time to service the steering bearings. Once fitted with a grease zerk, you no longer need to disassemble the fork to perform this routine service.

What you do need to do is use the latest factory bearing grease (#99857-97) when you service a steering head equipped with a zerk. Otherwise you'll have a big messy glob of grease seeping from the bottom of the neck out onto the lower triple tree. The factory's new grease is too "stiff" to leak out like that.

A complete 10,000-mile service by a trained technician for a bike under warranty, done at a dealer, observing the suggested flat rate times established by the factory, using air tools, takes anywhere from 3.8 hours for a Sportster to 5.5 hours for a full-dresser. These times do not factor in removing all the extra stuff you've bolted on (or intend to) and certainly don't deal with a bike that's out of warranty and has 3 inches of crud all over it when it's time to work on it. It also doesn't figure in stripped fasteners, using hand tools, and other real-world factors. Just the same, the chart lists a comfortable range of time for you to perform each task involved. You may be faster or slower, but figure out what your time is worth relative to the professional labor rates in your neighborhood ($45–$85 per hour) and decide who's going to do it. Don't forget, you have to have (and use) special tools for a 10K too.

10 New bearings can mean new pre-load measurements. Older Evos used center spacers of different specific lengths to obtain the necessary 0.0004 to 0.0018-inch figure. Those are obsolete, and the latest iteration is a standard spacer and various thicknesses of shims, as shown. Endplay is checked by torquing the rear axle to 60–65 foot-pounds and then using a dial indicator mounted (usually) on the swingarm to check endplay. To adjust endplay, you need to add, subtract, or use different thicknesses of shims.

11 Once the wheel's off, you may be tempted to do other things like inspect the rear pulley for rock damage and road grunge, which may be packed into the bottoms of the teeth. Even if the pulley is in fine shape, that chrome cover you've been thinking about can go on now, or if you happen to need a new pulley due to wear (or a desire for different gearing, or any reason at all), use quality replacement fasteners, blue Loctite (if the fasteners don't come equipped with their own thread locker), and a torque wrench. Also, be aware that dropping from a 70-tooth to a 61-tooth rear pulley on Softails requires use of thin-headed bolts for the belt guard, or they'll scrape.

12 Removing a brake disc is generally a pain. They do wear out and get damaged, however; so if yours is beyond minimum thinness (marked on the disc) or you've got a bent one pulsing back through the lever or pedal under light application, it's time to replace the disc. Or you may just want a new polished disc or a floater? Go for it! Use heat to soften the thread sealant on the original fasteners before you try to remove them. You can break an alarming number of tools on these bolts if you try to remove them using brute strength only. Just don't think the bolt has to be red hot; too warm to touch will do nicely. Wear protective gloves and use that impact wrench.

13 Adjusting neck bearings on a dresser can make a monkey out of the best of us. Most models aren't this much grief, but this adjustment is important so gut it out, even if it means removing the fairing and using a hammer in close proximity to expensive pieces. Late models (except Dynas) have incorporated a grease zerk in the steering head to make lubing the steering bearing a little easier, and it's a good idea to upgrade to this setup on early Evos. You'll need a drill, a tap, and a zerk, and it'll take an extra 30 to 45 minutes to install, but it's worth it. Springers should have their bearings serviced and adjusted twice as often as the others. The weight, rigidity, and anti-dive geometry of that famous fork is murder on steering neck bearings.

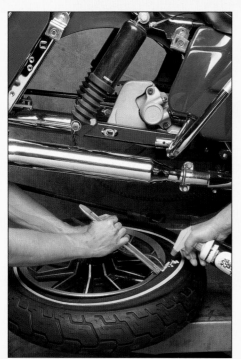

14 Okay, now that you've spent half a day on the front end and wheels, you may as well deal with tires. Yes, it is possible to change a tire by hand, but a quality tire changer is less likely to damage your rims. If you're stuck somewhere with a flat on tubeless, cast wheels, the easiest way to deal with it is to use tire plugs (not a sanctioned repair, you understand) and one of those air pumps that inflates the tire by using the engine as a compressor. Harley conveniently offers a kit (#91901-84A) that has the pump, tire irons, patches, and plugs. Get one before your next trek across the hinterlands.

15 For some reason (probably safety and liability), Harley persists in sliding the rear axle in from the right (pipe) side to the left. This can be a real pain if the muffler blocks removal of the axle. You can either remove the muffler or compress or remove the shock to gain clearance every time you do this, or you can get smart and flip the axle end for end. Just be sure you have it torqued properly.

16 After you've been through the service, by the book, from (steering) stem to stern, it's a good idea to double-check alignment after the bike's back on deck, and preferably with some weight in the saddle. Measure with a rod that has a tiny O-ring or rubber band around it to mark your measurement and one end bent 90 degrees for a clear reference. From the center of the swingarm pivot to the center of the rear axle, check for the same distance—exactly—on both sides of the machine. If the measurement is shorter on one side, adjust each side an equal amount, but in opposite directions, until the measurements are the same. Once straight, move the wheel back exactly the same number of turns on the adjusters until belt tension is correct.

17 If you've done a thorough job so far, keep it up! Not only should you lube all the pivot points that have a zerk (like this one), but you should pull apart things like the shifter on forward controls (especially for aftermarket sets) and hand grease them. Also lube the handlebar under the throttle tube, the pivot pins for the control levers, and the hinges on flip-up seats, to name a few. It's safe to say that any pivot point, zerk fitting or no, needs to be greased now and then.

PERFORMING THE 10,000-MILE SERVICE

10,000-MILE SERVICE CHART
(Use With Shop Manual)

*The item is recommended but not always necessary.

Service Task	Big Twin Parts	Sportster Parts	Tools Required	Time
Change oil	One oil filter: #63805-80A black filter (#63812-90 for Dynas), or one #63796-77A chrome filter (#63813-90 for Dynas) Four quarts of #99816-SP 20/50 motor oil (motorcycle or synthetic oil)	One oil filter: #63805-80A black filter or #63796-77A chrome filter Three quarts of #99816-SP 20/50 motor oil	Shop manual, oil dump pan, plastic trash sack, oil filter wrench, screwdriver, clean rags, drain plug "spanner"	0.4–0.8 hour
Service air filter	*K&N replacement element	*K&N replacement element	*K&N air filter oil, soap and water, air cleaner removal "spanner" or Allen wrenches, *electric fan for drying filter	0.3–0.6 hour
Clean tappet screen	none needed	none needed	Tappet plug tool or modified coin, toothbrush, mild solvent	0.3–0.5 hour
Change primary fluid	New 739A or equivalent drain plug Appropriate inspection gasket: #60567-90A oval inspection gasket (long primary) or #34906-85 square inspection gasket (short primary) Two quarts of H-D primary fluid	New 739A or equivalent drain plug O-ring(s) for inspection cover and screws (1991 and later): one #11188, one #11187, and two to four #11171 Sport transmission fluid	Teflon sealant for drain plugs	0.2–0.4 hour
Change gear oil	One quart of #99892-84 (or 85/140 equivalent) transmission lube	One quart of #99896-88 Sport transmission/primary lube	Replacement drain plug and/or washer, appropriate drain plug removal "spanner" or Allen wrench	0.3–0.6 hour
Adjust drive belt	*#511 axle cotter pin (as/if required)	*#511 axle cotter pin (as/if required)	Motorcycle lift or jackstand, belt tension tool (#40006-85) or 45-degree "twist" technique, chain lube (as required), axle nut wrench, pliers, tape measure or H-D belt align tool, swingarm adjuster wrench	0.1–0.3 hour
Lubricate levers,	none needed	none needed	Dri-Slide or chain lube, grease gun with	0.8–1.2 hours

25

Service Task	Big Twin Parts	Sportster Parts	Tools Required	Time
pedals, and cables			flex neck, needle-nose pliers, grease	
Check brake pads	none needed	none needed	Small flashlight, skinny screwdriver, good eyes	0.1–0.6 hour
Check brake fluid	none needed	none needed	Appropriate screwdriver or wrench, appropriate DOT 5 brake fluid, master cylinder gasket (as required)	0.1–0.2 hour
Check brake lines and calipers	none needed	none needed	Brake joint "banjo" washers (as required), caliper or master cylinder seals (as required), oil hose (as required), double-loop zip ties (as required), appropriate line "pinch" clamp or mini-hose clamp (as required)	0.1–0.3 hour
Check enricher (choke) cable	none needed	none needed	Strong fingers or pliers (use light touch with pliers)	0.1–0.2 hour
Check fuel valve and lines	Fuel line (as required), fuel valve seal washer (as required), pinch or screw clamps (as required), new mounting grommets, rubbers	Fuel line (as required), fuel valve seal washer (as required), pinch or screw clamps (as required), new mounting grommets, rubbers	Vise-Grips	0.1–0.2 hour
Clean fuel tank filter	none needed	none needed	Compressed air to back flush through fuel line or wrench to remove valve, fuel can to drain into, fuel line clamps	0.3–0.6 hour
Check tire wear and pressure	none needed	none needed	Tire gauge, coin, compressed air with tire chuck, tweezers, needle-nosed pliers	0.1–0.2 hour
Check wheel spokes	none needed	none needed	Appropriate spoke wrench, spokes and nipples (as required), dial indicator, and a good ear	0.2–0.8 hour
Check mag wheels and service wheel bearings front and rear (all wheel types)	Four #47519-83A wheel seals *One #511 axle cotter pin (substitute #510 R-clip) #9052 wheel bearings (if/as required)	Four #47519-83A wheel seals *One #511 axle cotter pin (substitute #510 R-clip) #9052 wheel bearings (if/as required)	Good eye, *wheel bearing grease "packer" tool, screwdriver or wheel seal removal tool, *wheel bearing removal/installer tool (#33071-73 and 33416-80)	1.5–3.5 hours
Service front fork fluid and steering bearings	*One #50972-75 Zerk grease fitting (if/as required)	*One #50972-75 Zerk grease fitting (if/as required)	Fish scale, stand or lift, appropriate wrenches, Mity-Vac tool, grease, grease	0.8–1.6 hours (longer on older dressers)

Service Task	Big Twin Parts	Sportster Parts	Tools Required	Time
	One or two pints #99884-80 fork oil	One pint #99884-80 fork oil	gun, *bearing removal/installation tool	
Check electrical system	Appropriate bulbs, connectors, wire, electrical tape, shrink tubing, solder, soldering iron, zip ties (all as required)	Appropriate bulbs, connectors, wire, electrical tape, shrink tubing, solder, soldering iron, zip ties (all as required)	Contact cleaner, electrical connector-stripper tool, *multimeter, *test lamp	0.3–0.8 hour
Check cruise control	none needed	none needed	Shop manual and test ride	0.5–1.0 hour
Service battery	none needed	none needed	Distilled water, hydrometer, voltmeter, load tester, small flashlight, eye dropper or ear syringe	0.3–0.9 hour
Replace spark plugs	Two #32311-83A spark plugs or two #32326-91 Screamin' Eagle plugs	Two #32317-86A spark plugs or two #32320-91 Screamin' Eagle plugs	Magnifying glass and light, B120 chemtool (aerosol cleaner), emery board, gappingtool, appropriate spark plug socket wrench or ratchet, anti-seize compound, proprietary plug cleaner	0.2 hour (longer on twin-plug heads, XL1200S)
Adjust shocks	none needed	none needed	Shock adjusting tool (as required), lift, obese buddy	0.1-0.4 hour
Check air suspension	none needed	none needed	Appropriate wrenches, soap-and-water solution, low-pressure hand pump with built-in gauge	0.1-0.4 hour
Torque engine mounts	none needed	none needed	Appropriate wrenches and sockets, torque wrench	0.5–1.0 hour
Torque fasteners	none needed	none needed	Appropriate wrenches and sockets, torque wrench, Allen and Torx bits	0.5–1.0 hour
Lube hinges, latches, locks	none needed	none needed	Dri-Slide, chain lube, 3-in-1 oil, Teflon spray, oil, grease	0.3–0.6 hour
Set ignition timing or VOES	*Two 8/32x5/8-inch screws Two #8 washers or two #8699 rivets	none needed	Clear plastic timing-hole plug, appropriate timing light ("dial back"-type preferred), *3/16-inch hose (as required), anti-seize compound, screwdriver, silicone sealant, *rivet gun	0.3–0.6 hour
Set engine idle	Miscellaneous "helpers": *clip-type zip-tie #10074, *double-loop zip-tie #10081, *h/bar clip #10073, *hose clamps #10014 (fuel) and #10080 (oil)	none needed	Long, skinny Phillips screwdriver, good ear or accurate tach	0.1 hour

Time: Less than 1 hour

Tools: 3/8-, 7/16-, 1/2-, and 9/16-inch wrenches and Dri-Slide aerosol chain lube (or equivalent)

Talent: 👤

Tab: $

Tinware: Maybe a tin pan and some extra rags to catch any messy drippings

Tip: The object of the game is to keep dirt and grit from ruining, not just the all-important "feel" of these control cables, but the cables themselves; do this as often as you change oil

PERFORMANCE GAIN: Cleaner, crisper shifts and a longer lasting, smoother functioning clutch and throttle; also, less carpal tunnel over the long run

COMPLEMENTARY MODIFICATION: "Reduced reach" clutch (and brake) levers, as fitted to 1993 and later models, really do help, especially for stubby-fingered folk; stainless cables need more of this kind of attention (and adjustments) than stockers do because the sheath compresses more yet is less flexible

1 Begin by loosening the jam nut on the adjuster. Run the adjuster sleeve in until you have just enough slack to pull the cable down and are free of the metal elbow. Lube the cable. Use Dri-Slide, aerosol chain lube, or Tri-Flow (Teflon in a spray can). The little plastic tube that comes with the aerosol stuff and the needle that comes with the Dri-Slide may not be absolutely necessary, but they sure do make the job easier and cleaner. Then apply copious amounts of the lubricant of your choice at the joint between the wire and the sheath.

4 Lube the cable with Dri-Slide, chain lube, or the equivalent.

Some very early motorcycles didn't use cables. Clutches were foot-operated, there was no front brake to worry about, and throttles could be controlled by anything from Heim-jointed articulated rods to a simple lever. Then a guy named Bowden came along. His cable, consisting of several single strands of wire woven into a flexible steel wire, then sheathed in an outer housing of flat spiral-wound metal with a covering of black plastic (in the early days it was cloth), was elegantly simple and very effective. The Bowden control cable offered precise, reliable control and asked only for occasional adjustment and lubrication. Somebody must've been impressed because today this type of control cable is used universally in the motorcycle industry. Some are Teflon lined, some use a special process to weave the individual strands into an extra-flexible control wire, and some use exotic sheathing, like woven stainless steel or Kevlar. Still, that's about as high tech as it gets for this essentially perfected design. Aside from being a bit more heavy-duty than others, Harley's cables are no different.

Unfortunately, too many of us take the performance of these critical components for granted. Why is it that a control cable is so often ignored until it's dry, cracked, worn, kinked, frayed, out of adjustment, or just out of luck? It seems that the only time these lowly, reliable servants get the attention they deserve is at the point of mutiny, when they switch from offering you absolute control to trying to wrestle control from you. It shouldn't come to that, you know. Cables should be maintained as rigorously and regularly as any other part of the drivetrain—and more often than most.

THROTTLE CABLES

The most intimate control on your Harley is the throttle. Makes sense when you think about it. What other single item does more to connect you with the capabilities of the bike? Subtly or abruptly, gently or

2 Once the lubrication phase is complete, adjust freeplay. You can do it just like the shop manual says, but do yourself a favor before you get that far. Pull the air cleaner cover and peer down the carb throat as you open the throttle. Look to make sure the accelerator pump is working (and no fires, please!), but mostly you should verify that the throttle plate (butterfly) is opening all the way. You'd be surprised at how many poor-running Harleys simply aren't getting 100-percent throttle. Make your base adjustments accordingly, then set freeplay.

3 Pull the rubber boot up to expose the clutch adjuster and then loosen the jam nut. Remember, this is lube and adjust cables, not clutches, so if you choose not to mark the original position of the adjuster halves, you may wind up doing both. Anyway, back off the adjuster until you have the amount of freeplay at the lever you desire. The factory setting has the engagement point out toward your fingertips, which is tough for folks with stubby fingers. Don't get nuts here, but be aware that you can increase freeplay a bit to get the lever slightly closer to the grip.

5 After lubing the cable, lube the adjuster with anti-seize. Arguably the most overlooked item in a service, the clutch cable adjuster is hollow and, therefore, brittle. Let it corrode, and when you try to use it, it snaps!

6 Button everything up at the adjuster, and then dose the lever pivot with lube. Yes, H-D uses a Teflon pin at the pivot, making for less wear and tear and a smooth pull. No, that isn't a substitute for proper lubrication of the wire strands and the sheath. Get plenty of slippery stuff between the two, and keep the Teflon pin clean and slippery too.

brutally, moderately or massively, it is your telegraph to total mastery of motion. Keep the messages loud and clear.

You can do that very simply by keeping the little devils properly adjusted and copiously lubricated. A dry, ratchet-like twist at the right grip is hardly conducive to a sense of control, let alone mastery. Repeat after me: "Lube and adjust. Lube and adjust. Lube and adjust."

CLUTCH CABLES

The difference in feel between a lubed cable and a dry one is even more pronounced where clutch cables are concerned. A he-man, two-fisted pull at the lever has gone the way of the dodo bird on Evo Harleys. Besides, in stop-and-go traffic, you want to do just that, as smoothly and effortlessly as possible.

Since Evos were introduced, the materials and design of factory clutch cables have changed. The original design used a conventional "barrel" at the lever end with two fiddley teflon "top hats" to smooth the pull. These "arm over the tranny" cables used until 1988 were "dry" cables on Big Twins. The 1988 and later cables used an eyelet or ring-type end with a huge teflon button and, due to the redesigned release mechanism, were "wet" cables, lubed partly by tranny oil, like on Sportsters. Needless to say, the dry cable design, while convenient to change, takes a lot more lubing. It's also more obvious when it's worn out. A two-fisted pull even after lubing—the sheathing compressed at either lever, and/or abraded clear through anywhere along it's length—is suspect. Nineteen eighty-eight and newer cables are much harder to check for wear. The sheathing is a heavy, stiff nylon that doesn't compress, and the eyelet never frays to warn you of imminent breakage. If the sheath is cracked, replace it; otherwise, keep it lubed, and it may last the life of the machine.

SIMPLE MAINTENANCE

PROJECT 3 • CHANGING ENGINE OIL

Time: 1/2 to 1 hour (10 or 15 minutes, with a little practice)

Tools: Standard screwdriver for the clamp on the drain hose, 3/4-inch socket or wrench for the drain plug, piece of cardboard to make a temporary oil "chute," and drain pan

Talent:

Tab: $

Tinware: 3–4 quarts of motor oil, new oil filter, and clean rags or towels

Tip: Consider using a good synthetic motorcycle oil

PERFORMANCE GAIN: Increased engine reliability

COMPLEMENTARY MODIFICATION: Convert to synthetic oil; install a "no-mess" oil drain kit

Frequent oil changes can triple the life of an air-cooled motor. Remember oil actually does most of the work that coolant does in a water-cooled engine, and that kind of heat wears it out quickly. Change it often because oil is definitely cheaper than engine parts.

If it's hard for you to get motivated for those few minutes, think about this: At 6,000 rpms a four-stroke engine is enduring 50 explosions every second in every cylinder. The crank turns 100 times a second, and the piston and rod are screaming up and down slamming to a complete halt and reversing direction almost instantaneously at twice the rate. The unsung hero in all this boogying is oil.

The other valiant one is the oil filter. Dramatic increases in engine life are the result of the superior materials used in the construction of the newer motors, vast improvements in the additive packages in modern multigrade oils (the dead dinosaur parts haven't changed), and the perfection and inclusion of good quality oil filters.

The details of filter ratings are pretty involved and include percentages of various sized particles that a

1 Over the [...] Harley ha[...] variety of oil [...] designs, any of which [...] better than no filter [...] That said, the old-fa[...] drop-in filters ("hors[...] in Harley-speak) are [...] for their ability to pl[...] tappet filter screen. [...] pleated-paper upgra[...] much better option [...] row, far right).

2 Even Harley-Davidson offers an "inexpensive" line of oil filters called "Classic Motor Parts." Nothing much is inherently wrong with them, as long as you don't own a fuel-injected FL. (They won't fit those because of a dimensional difference from the genuine Harley filter that causes interference with the stator lead wire coming out of the crankcase.) Just the same, as you can see in the photo, these H-D/Buell filters are generically constructed with internal plates using six holes. The genuine filter has only four. There are likely to be other related design details that set this filter apart from the genuine article. The $2 difference in the retail price isn't the only difference. Be aware.

3 The world [...] um lubric[...] changing rap[...] for the better. New s[...] oils are giving petro[...] based oils, even Ha[...] real run for the mor[...] Traditional mentaliti[...] have a hard time wi[...] facts, but nonetheles[...] they're true. The sy[...] blended with proper [...] and quantities of ad[...] for use in motorcycl[...] especially the uniqu[...] ments of Harley eng[...] the way of the futur[...] those who want thei[...] to have long and h[...] futures, while those [...] in the past are cond[...] to—ahem!—rebui[...]

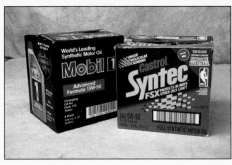

given filter can stop. The interesting thing is that a 25-micron filter will take out many particles much smaller than 25 microns, so the ratings are pretty conservative.

Then there is the issue of "correct" filters to use as replacements for factory specified full-flow filters. Make no mistake, even if they look identical, two filters can function in a completely different fashion. The filter for a Buick V-6 turbo motor will screw right on an Evo, but no way should you take a chance on a filter designed for a water-cooled, plain-bearing, wet-sump auto engine with 50 to 60 pounds of hot oil pressure.

Factory filters are made by Purolator to H-D specs, and Fram #6022 is also good for Harley motors. Beyond that you are on your own and at risk.

5 Dynas and 1993 and later FLTs use a sump (oil pan) rather than an oil tank. The sump has two plugs, but only one is for motor oil. The drain plug for the motor oil is always the plug farthest towards the front of the machine. The other drain plug is for the transmission. Oil should be drained warm, not hot, into a suitable drain pan. Once it's all in the pan, it's not a bad idea to drag a magnet though the stuff to see if there's any serious contamination. If the drained oil has a metallic color but the magnet doesn't find much of anything, you may have nonferrous contaminate problems like aluminum or brass. Anything you find in the oil made it past the filter. If there are larger chunks or lots of material, cut the old filter in two and unfold the element for inspection.

4 Harley's with oil tanks—Softails, Sportsters, and early FLT models and FXRs—have either a drain plug in the tank itself or a hose like the one you see peeking below the frame tubes here. Softails have a little metal tab on the frame to clip the plug out of the way between oil changes. Avoid bending this tab too often or too much or it might snap off. Sportsters have the end of their hose clamped to a boss on the frame below the battery box.

7 About every fourth or fifth oil change, start the engine *after* filling up with oil but *before* you mount the new filter. Let it idle until the sludgy black oil coming from the filter boss starts to turn clean (or until about 1 quart has pumped into the drain pan), then shut off the motor and top off the oil tank/sump to the proper level. Ninety percent of the time, you'll see the oil start to run clean before you've used a full quart, but either way you've flushed out the cupful of crap that stays in the cases. Old timers call this a "5-quart oil change," and it was the only way to get over 100,000 miles out of a bottom end on a Big Twin—until proper oil filters came into use or unless you tapped the cases for a crank drain plug. Modern filters have removed most of the problems, but you'll still be surprised at what you find in a high-mileage motor if a 5-quart change has never been done.

6 If you want to be safe, take a long pencil-shaped magnet, stick it in the filler hole, and drag the oil tank or sump before you fill up with oil. If you find anything suspicious, you've got more than an oil change to deal with. Most likely, you'll find nothing to worry about, so pour in that fresh fluid.

8 Oil filter wrenches are handy, but the specific type you use is strictly a matter of personal taste. The type of filter shouldn't be. Actually, the standard factory oil filter for Evos traps down to 25 microns, but the Twin Cam Big Twin has a 10-micron filter. Using the Twin Cam filter on your Evo—it's a bolt-on swap—is a highly recommended upgrade.

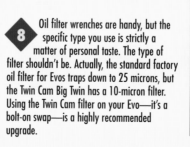

SIMPLE MAINTENANCE

PROJECT 4 • CHANGING TRANSMISSION AND PRIMARY FLUID

Time: 1/2 to 1 hour

Tools: All the standard stuff plus the specific items listed below

Talent: 👤

Tab: S

Tinware: Primary inspection gasket, drain plug washer or O-ring, and Teflon sealant (as required)

Tip: Some Big Twins have an exhaust pipe right in the way of the tranny drain plug; you may be able to work around it by modifying the drain plug removal tool so that you needn't remove the exhaust; just loosen it a bit and sneak in

PERFORMANCE GAIN: Added longevity for the primary chain and the gears in the box; clean fluid actually adds to the shift quality, and changing often is the best way to get another 100,000 miles out of a tranny that already had its first 100,000 when you bought it

COMPLEMENTARY MODIFICATION: Convert to synthetic oil

1 Sportsters use the same fluid for both transmission and primary lubrication. Changing, as per the manual, is pretty much a snap. Big Twins are not as easy. Softails and pre-1993 FLTs and FXRs often have an exhaust pipe right in front of the little drain plug at the bottom of the tranny end cover. You can loosen and swing away, or remove the offending pipe, as shown in this photo, or make up a special tool to snake around the pipe. A wobbler extension, with the appropriate Allen or Torx bit brazed onto an old socket will usually do the trick. Some folks also use a Mity-Vac with a small diameter hose stuck down the filler hole to suck the gear oil out. This is not the most effective way to get the last drop, but since most contaminants in the gearbox wind up in the bottom of the box, this method will work once and a while. Sooner or later, however, you'll have to do it right.

Most foreign motorcycles use one oil for everything. Yeah, multigrade motor oil for not only the engine but the transmission, clutch, and any thing else they've got stuffed in there. This smacks heavily of "convenient" engineering. All these components have a different job to do and different stresses to deal with while they do it. How can one fluid fit all? Well, the answer is it doesn't, so Harley-Davidson, in sharp contrast, uses specific lubricants for specific jobs. Big Twins have three kinds:

Engine oil that is specially formulated for roller-bearing engines and has never complied with automotive API ratings because they are optimized for oils designed for plain-bearing engines.

Gear oil that has additives to bolster its film strength, since gears push round and round more than they slide up and down like pistons and rings. Plus gear oil doesn't circulate like motor oil, so its job is to keep metal from metal under extreme pressure and humongous heat.

Primary lube, which has two jobs—keeping the clutch moist and happy and the primary soaked and rust free. To do that it must be a fairly thin, watery fluid that slips into every nook and cranny but not so slippery that the clutch won't work.

Sportsters get the motor oil, same as the Big Twins, but since XLs are of so-called unit construction (wherein the same cases hold engine and gear bits), the trans and the clutch—pardon the expression—"pool" their resources.

CHANGING TRANSMISSION OIL ON A BIG TWIN

The process is straightforward enough, and here's what you'll need for Big Twins:
- 1/2 quart of transmission lube (check your manual)
- 3/8-inch Allen (for removing the filler plug)
- 3/16-inch Allen for the drain plug on early models

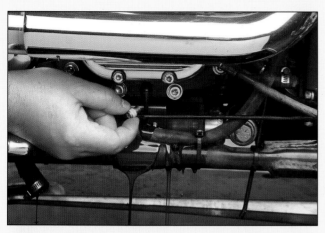

2 This is the infamous #739A drain plug. It's used for both the tranny drain and the primary drain on most Big Twins, and it's been through a couple of changes over the years. The early plug has an Allen head, and frankly, the magnetic tip had a tendency to come loose, sometimes falling into the motor. Second, the plug is a fine thread going into aluminum, therefore, a prime candidate for getting stuck in its hole or stripping out. It's a fine plan to have at least one new one of these on hand during fluids changes. The latest version is a Torx head, with a secure magnet and Teflon on the threads so finger tight and half a twist will keep it secure and hassle-free.

3 Filling the transmission requires a small funnel and a little patience. Big Twins with five-speed boxes take exactly 16 ounces to fill (if completely drained). Four-speed Big Twins take a pint and a half, and Sportsters with four gears take a pint and a half as well. Five-speed XLs use a full quart (32 ounces) of gear lube, but tradition has it that you simply hold a four-speed Sporty straight up and fill until oil runs out the check screw on the primary (that's the one about a third of the way up, with a fiber washer under a Phillips head).

* #T-40 Torx for drain plugs on late models
* Dump container
* Rags

Since there's little rocket science involved in this, use the procedures in the shop manual. One thing that's not covered there is the interference of the exhaust pipe. On several models the stock pipe inhibits access to the drain plug. Aftermarket pipes can create this same problem on any model. You can either loosen the pipe every time you change gearbox fluid, use a "turkey baster" or similar suction tool to suck the fluid out the filler hole, or braze the Allen/Torx bit you need for removal on to a small swivel socket, add an extension to the ratchet, and try to sneak past the pipe with that.

BIG TWIN PRIMARY LUBE CHANGE

Here's what you'll need to change the primary lube on your Big Twin:

* 1–2 quarts of primary chaincase lube (check your manual)
* #T-27 Torx to remove the inspection cover screws (late models)
* 5/32-inch Allen to remove the inspection cover screws (early models)
* Derby cover O-ring (#25416-84)—just in case
* 3/16-inch Allen wrench for early-model drain plugs
* #T-40 Torx wrench, for late-model drain plugs
* Inspection gasket #60567-90A (long primary, oval-shaped) or #34906-85A (short primary, D-shaped). Long primary models include Softails and Dynas; short primary models are used on FLT/FXRs
* Dump container
* Rags

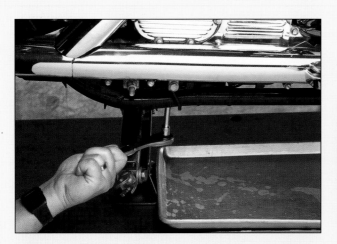

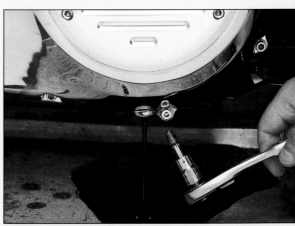

4 FLT's and Dyna's gear oil drains from a sump plug. The tip here is that once the plug is loosened with a socket, unscrew it by hand while keeping a slight upwards pressure on this vertical plug. That way you don't get hot oil all over your hands as you snatch the plug away to drain the gear oil. Of course, you could always wear gloves.

5 Primary fluid is easily drained on all models. Just keep that extra #73S plug handy and check for metallic fuzz on the original. Those magnets help prevent a lot of potential mischief in there, so the least you can do is help out with thorough cleaning during changes. Watching drain plug fuzz may n be an Olympic sport anytime soon, but it's the best early warning system on the engine. A certain amount of growth is normal, but if the plug goes from a little fu to long hair between routine changes, you need to unbutton the primary case for close inspection.

Some primary drain plugs are located in the inner primary housing (such as 1984–1985 FLTs), but most are identical to the tranny drain plug in appearance and are located in the lowest part of the outer primary cover. The shop manual tells you where yours is and how to drain the fluid but not what to do if the plug decides to strip out. If yours won't come out, try a heat gun on the surrounding aluminum first, then an Easy-Out; lastly remove the whole primary cover and "back" the plug out from the inside with a pair of Vise Grips on the magnetic tip, or a drill. Go easy. Older drain plugs can have loose magnets as it is, so plan on replacing the whole plug once you've fought it out.

The factory has changed their mind a few times over the years as to exactly how much fluid you need in the primary. Keep in mind, however, that the object of the exercise is to keep the chain wet, not to see if your derby O-ring will leak. Long primaries typically use a quart and a half, short ones a single quart. Check your manual or your dealer if in doubt.

Note: Early FXRs and FLTs may have a 7/8-inch tranny drain plug and a 13/16-inch oil drain plug. Double-check what's actually on your bike before you assume too much.

SPORTSTER TRANSMISSION/PRIMARY FLUID CHANGE

Here's what you need:
- 1 quart of Sport-Trans Fluid
- #T-27 Torx to remove the inspection cover screws on 1994 and later five-speed models
- Phillips screwdriver to remove the check screw on four-speed and early five-speed models
- 3/4-inch socket or wrench to remove the drain plug
- New O-ring (#11105) for the drain plug—just in case
- Dump container
- Rags

6 The debate rages over exactly how much fluid goes into a Big Twin primary. Even your service manual might be in error on the subject. The factory has changed its mind a couple of times, and there are service bulletins to prove it. From 1990—on, long primaries (Dynas and Softails) are fine with 32 ounces (1 quart), while short primary models (FLTs and FXRs) call for 38 to 44 ounces. The 1984 to 1989 models typically use 1 1/2 quarts, regardless of primary length. The key is to keep the primary chain wet without drowning the clutch, and you can vary things as much as 6 to 8 ounces without making much difference. You can check with the dealer for any specific deviations peculiar to your bike. Clean fluid makes as much difference as the amount, so change it regularly, checking to ensure that the derby cover is flat and marked so it goes back on exactly as it came off. Even a new derby O-ring won't seal a warped cover.

Until 1994, the "correct level" of transmission/primary fluid in Sportsters was determined by filling slowly until it ran out the level screw hole in the primary. Nice and simple if the bike was sitting straight up. When the Sportster finally got its first derby cover in 1994, the process suddenly resembled that used on Big Twins. Not to worry. You need precisely a pint and a half in a four-speed and exactly a quart in a five-speed no matter which way it's installed and checked (as long as it doesn't leak). It's all in the shop manual, but the manual makes it seem a little more complicated than it is.

It's also worth mentioning that a whole lot of folks have changed the fasteners on the inspection covers and check screw on Sportsters, so double-check what's actually on your bike before you assume too much.

SIMPLE MAINTENANCE
PROJECT 5 • SERVICING AIR CLEANERS

 Time: 1/2 to 1 hour

 Tools: Allen wrench to remove air cleaner cover

 Talent: ∮

 Tab: $

 Tinware: Compressed air to blow filth from the filter

 Tip: If the stock unit is too filthy to be reused, upgrade to a K&N element as a replacement; better yet, upgrade to a Free-Flow air cleaner

 PERFORMANCE GAIN: None from keeping the factory set-up clean, but it prevents a loaded-up filter from causing lousy gas mileage, increased engine wear, and power loss

COMPLEMENTARY MODIFICATION: Machines equipped with CV carbs need more inlet area than the stock plastic backing plate offers, but you can cut and drill the outside perimeter to achieve this; California models with a solenoid-operated "trap door" benefit from its removal (for "off-road" use only, of course)

1 If you haven't decided to switch to a high-flow air cleaner, you'd better plan on taking good care of the factory one, especially if you have a California model. Aside from that nice chrome cover, federal- and California-version air cleaners are substantially different.

Air cleaners on Evos actually have two jobs, the obvious filtering of our nasty atmosphere before it gets inside the combustion chamber and the not-so-obvious silencing of intake noise. Even older models with the giant "Ham Can" air cleaners are designed with these two objectives in mind. The problem arises when you realize that you've got a big-inch V-twin trying to breathe through a soda straw! Later models from the 1990s literally have less area to inhale with than a Briggs & Stratton lawn mower motor does.

If you decide to leave the stock air cleaner in place, your only hope for decent performance is to keep the air cleaner serviced for maximum efficiency. Ham Can models use a green foam filter element; round and oval cleaners use pleated paper. All of them plug up fairly quickly. All could filter better.

One of the simplest and best favors you can do yourself and your engine is to upgrade to replacement-style K&N filter elements. These elements not only filter more efficiently right out of the box, they breathe better used and dirty than factory elements do brand-new and clean.

If you can't get your Hog over the hills these days because it acts asthmatic, dive right on that air box cleaning. If fuel mileage has fallen off 10 percent or so lately, unclog the filter. The 1992 and later Big Twins and all five-speed Sportsters also suffer from oil-mist accumulation in the air cleaner. When ridden hard, these machines require a filter service every few hundred miles. That can mean every week for some people. You can't do much about it either, if you stick with the stock air cleaner arrangement.

The simple specifics are in the shop manual, but they fail to mention the potential frequency (wonder why?). Plus this little irritation is liable to show up on the road not in the garage, so the easy thing is to keep the appropriate tool for removing the cleaner cover and a small spray can of filter cleaner on the bike at all times.

2 On the California models fitted with stock CV carbs, check the electric solenoid frequently because it can be responsible for a host of mysterious maladies, like sluggish performance, unwillingness to rev, and misfires. The little trap door at the bottom of the backing plate is supposed to open 90 degrees when the engine is started and close again when the engine is shut off. If the solenoid misbehaves, the door won't open properly. Sometimes the solenoid can short against a cylinder fin, or moisture gets in the plug, creating havoc. More often, it's the plunger that mechanically controls the trap door. Occasionally, it's a bit of debris that gets stuck in the door and prevents it from fully opening. Don't trust it. Check it!

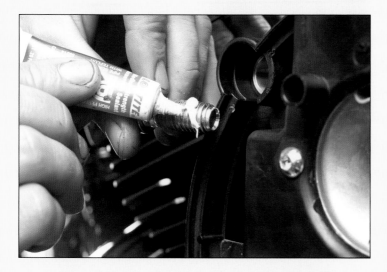

3 The stock filters can only be cleaned by blowing the dirt out of the paper pleats with (low) air pressure. Once you can no longer see daylight through them (hopefully before), throw them away. Foam-type elements are cleanable in soap and water. To dry them, just hang 'em over a fan or put them in the sun, but don't blast holes in them with an air hose. K&N makes a pricey replacement filter that, unless physically damaged, can be cleaned and reused indefinitely. Clean or replace your air filter about as often as you change engine oil. Whenever the breather bolts come off, make sure to apply sealant to the threads when you put them back on.

4 The three trapped screens holding the back plate to the carburetor should be torqued carefully. If they are too tight, the inserts in the plastic back plate will pull loose.

SIMPLE MAINTENANCE

PROJECT 6 • CHOOSING, READING, AND REPLACING SPARK PLUGS

Time: 10 minutes

Tools: Spark plug wrench, magnifying glass, gapping tool, and flashlight

Talent:

Tab: $

Tinware: Protective gloves (if you're going to read hot plugs), aerosol cleaner, eye protection, and anti-seize compound for the threads

Tip: Platinum-tipped plugs allow car guys to get 100,000 miles between tune-ups; think what they can do for you

PERFORMANCE GAIN: Improved starting, throttle response, and fuel efficiency

COMPLEMENTARY MODIFICATION: "Degreeing" spark plugs is nice, if not necessary; simply, to degree a plug is to shim the body so that when installed and properly torqued, the open end gap faces the incoming charge of fuel and air mixture, which requires shims, available from automotive race shops, a felt pen to mark desired location, and a little patience

1 Look at the photo of the 5R6A. This plug came out of a 30th Anniversary fuel-injected Ultra and has 514 miles on it. You are looking at a perfect "burn." If your jetting is right, your plugs will look like this.

The moment you start modifying your motor, you should consider the effects on spark. The stock spark plug is fine for a stock engine, but with literally hundreds of choices, it should be an absolutely routine thing to fine-tune spark plugs to the motor. Everything that's done to the motor affects the spark plug. That includes running it until the spark plug wears out.

HOT OR COLD?

The words *hot* or *cold* when used to describe spark plugs are confusing, since most often you use hot plugs in a cold engine (low power and operating temperatures) and cold plugs in a hot engine (high power and operating temperatures). What those terms really refer to is the spark plug's ability to conduct heat out of the combustion chamber. Combustion temperature is not affected by a hot or cold spark plug. Spark plugs are thermal surfers, riding the waves of heat between the 600-degree F

(Fahrenheit) temperature at which fouling occurs and the 1,750-degree F temperature at which pre-ignition occurs. That may not sound too tough, with 1,000 degrees F to play in, but high-performance parts and air cooling cut the margins a lot finer than you'd think. The secret is to maintain optimal combustion temperatures, which stock or hot-rod, all else perfect, should hover at or below 1,400 degrees F. But how do you select a spark plug that can manage it based on your engine's state of tune?

The heat range is "right" if it keeps temperatures normal in the rpm range it's to function in and won't foul the rest of the time. That's perhaps an oversimplification but true all the same. Stock Harley engines aren't exactly overstressed, and their specific output (horsepower per cubic inch of engine size) is well below the level where spark plug choice becomes a tough decision. Hence, they are equipped with a spark plug that's not strained sucking relatively low levels of heat from the combustion chamber—under all circumstances. Bump power levels up, and the situation changes dramatically. Using the stock spark plug may result in pinging or dieseling. These are clear indications a "colder" plug is needed to suck the heat out quicker and stabilize the operating temperature.

TAKIN' THE HEAT

Before we get too much further, you should be aware of two things. First, not all manufacturers have a direct equivalent in another manufacturer's line-up. Sure, you can almost always get close, but sometimes close just isn't close enough.

Second, even in the same manufacturer's line-up, the heat-range difference between one specific type and number and the next closest one may not be close at all. Few manufacturers go to the trouble of showing you the differences, great and small, that can mean everything to a successful engine build. If they all did, life would sure be simpler. To demonstrate this, look at this heat-range bar graph that Champion uses for its racing plugs. You can't fail to notice that an N4 is considerably hotter than an N3, while an N2 isn't all that much colder. Likewise, N3s and N4s seem to be equivalent to N3Gs and N4Gs, respectively, but an N2 and an N2G aren't.

So bear in mind that heat range alone isn't the only criteria for proper plug selection. The materials the plug is made of and the electrode (tip) design are important as well.

TIP TIPS

There are five fundamental types of spark plug tip designs. Well, maybe five and a half. The only ones we're concerned with as Harley tuners are the (conventional) L-gap, the (competition) J-Gap, the (projected tip) Y-gap, and the G-gap (which is really one and a half types).

The L-gap is your basic sparker. A Harley #4, for instance, has this tip, which has a side electrode that extends over the center electrode.

The J-gap isn't that much different, with a side electrode extending only halfway over the center, yet this subtle change in design makes a noticeable difference in performance. The J-gap requires less voltage to fire at high rpm, resists fouling because more of the center electrode is exposed, and is less likely to short out or "crud up" with particulates. This is a good example of small details making a big difference.

The Y-gap works well in hemi, dome, or wedge combustion chambers, where its projected tip has room to work. The tip gets cooled by the incoming charge at high speeds yet runs hotter at lower speeds; therefore, it's hard to foul, but heat-range characteristics differ from other plugs. Not surprisingly, these are Evo plugs, working well, as they do even with aftermarket heads. But they aren't the best choice for blower motors or mega-compression fuelers.

G-gap actually means "gold palladium," but for the purposes of this book all precious metal sparkers are included in this category (and a half) whether gold, silver, platinum, or green kryptonite. The common bond may be the exotic materials, but the common (and important) characteristic is this group typically takes a mere fraction of the voltage to fire that the others require. They are far more thermally conductive and, because of that, compliant. Meaning that if you can afford 'em, they should jump right to the top of your ignition wish list—especially if they offer longer life into the bargain, like platinum-tipped plugs do. Platinum doesn't burn or erode nearly as fast as conventional tip materials, so the all-important gap remains sharp-edged and constant in both senses of the terms. (Race tuners may not like them, but they go through plugs like popcorn anyway, so longevity is irrelevant to them.)

READ 'EM AND WEEP

The way to know, ultimately, if you've got the right plug is to go straight to the source and read your own. It's not that difficult, but it does take practice. To oversimplify, if you know what the tip of a "known right" plug looks like, then however much your plug looks different, it's that much wrong.

Every service manual worth owning will teach you about proper gap, correct torque, and using anti-seize on the threads—in short, the required maintenance of a spark plug. Most will also have a chart, often in color, to show you what plugs should and shouldn't look like after use. The thing is, these charts show extreme cases, so they're not worth diddly for tuning purposes. The ability to recognize the subtleties makes the tuner a tuner. The first rule is that it's virtually impossible to learn anything from a plug unless the engine has been cut clean at operating temperature and at exactly the engine speed you are concerned with. If you back off, or worse, let the bike idle, you have ruined the reading.

A clean tip means just that. It's not necessarily too lean, unless the insulator nose is blistered. Look for signs of melting on the electrode edges too. Any sharp edge will get hot first, and it will show first on the edges. Burned and pitted electrodes usually indicate too hot a plug not too lean a mixture. You will also learn, if you look, that the faint light spots on the electrodes at the side of the gap are an important clue as to the health of the ignition system. When the spot shrinks, fades, gets ragged around the edges, or if the size of the spot on the side electrode no longer matches the one on the center electrode (or vice-versa), the spark is literally fading away.

SIMPLE MAINTENANCE
PROJECT 7 • CHECKING AND TENSIONING YOUR DRIVE BELT

 Time: 1/2 hour

 Tools: Belt tension tool (or fish scale), possibly a pair of needle-nosed pliers or an awl—depending on whether or not there's debris in the belt

 Talent:

 Tab: $

 Tinware: Unofficially, a properly aligned, cleaned, and tensioned belt that squeaks can be quieted considerably with the occasional shot of Armor-All, which keeps the belt lookin' good too

 Tip: While keeping track of belt tension is a good plan, the real value of routine inspections is to avoid having some nail, rock, or piece of glass damage the thing to the point of failure because you didn't know it was in there sawing and cutting away; belts are so tough that if you catch a problem early and remove it carefully, it usually won't wreck the belt

PERFORMANCE GAIN: Fifty percent more life in the belt if it's adjusted properly and kept clean

COMPLEMENTARY MODIFICATION: Make sure, especially on dresser models, that the lower belt guard doesn't turn into the lower belt assassin; keep them close to, but not interfering with, the belt, particularly any edges

1 If you don't have the factory tool or just can't figure out how to use a fish scale to adjust your belt's tension, try this instead. Grasp the belt with your thumb and two forefingers at about 1 1/2 inches back from where it exits the bottom of the primary case. Now twist the belt back and forth on its axis. You should feel serious resistance to this twisting at about a 45-degree angle from flat. If you can twist your belt more like 90 degrees with just a thumb and two fingers, it's too loose. If it feels tighter than a bow string at only 25 to 30 degrees of twist, it's too tight. This may not be the "rocket science" method, but it's pretty accurate just the same.

If your Harley suffers leakage in the primary drive area, the first thing to check is belt tension. What is proper tension? Well, using the factory tool (#H-D 35381), hook the belt like a fish in between the pulleys and check that 10 pounds of force results in 5/16–3/8 inch of deflection in the belt, as seen through the little window in the bottom belt guard.

A belt that's too tight can cause problems far worse than oil leaks, including pulley splines stripping out. Also, belts don't like being bent into a radius of less than 3 inches or having their direction of rotation reversed once they've gotten used to it. If you can keep from cutting them or poking gaping holes in them with road debris, they will last for 70,000 to 90,000 miles. But they aren't immortal. These modern belts are so good, so durable, so tough, and so proven, they are virtually ignored by the majority of riders. Let's be honest; some of the belts out

there are 10 to 12 years old or more. Do you trust oil or tires that old? Checking the belt regularly for damage and wear is a necessary part of getting the best out of them.

In the old days, you could look at the fan belt on an automobile and easily tell at a glance if it was shot. The tell-tale signs were cracking in the rubber, frayed edges, a scrubbed and kind of burnt look on the sides where it ran through the pulleys, and hey, they even squeaked! By contrast, modern automotive belts have one, and only one, remotely reliable indicator of wear: When they are new, the top edge of the belt rides high on the flange on its pulley; when it settles to below flush on the flange—like the sun slowly sinks in the west—it's done for. To some degree, it's like that with the Harley drive belt. The trouble is it's much harder to detect or recognize because a Harley-Davidson drive belt appears to sit down in the pulley,

2 Look closely now. Aside from the familiar belt damage, like punctures, splits, cuts, and so on, there's this one, caused by a plastic lower belt guard getting cock-eyed and going unnoticed. This belt died in less than 4,000 miles. It looks okay from the edges, but it has no teeth in the load-bearing middle. There's more than one way to wear out a belt!

even when new. It's also covered up with belt guards.

Just the same, if you were to look at a cross section of the belt's tooth pattern, relative to its counterpart in the pulley, you'd see that, when new, the belt tooth doesn't bottom out. When broken in, it might, slightly. When worn out, it will—excessively! Once this stage is reached, the teeth on the belt begin to get pulled out by their root, where they attach to the cords on the outside edge of the thing.

Sometimes you can spot this early on by looking for a series of hairline cracks or wrinkles on the tips of the teeth running parallel to the run of the belt. Belts with just a few wrinkles can be considered sort of, well, middle-aged. But if the wrinkles extend from the top to the bottom of the teeth clear to the outside edge of the belt, it's all over. Keep riding on that one and you're gonna wind up toothless.

SIMPLE MAINTENANCE
PROJECT 8 • REPLACING BRAKE PADS

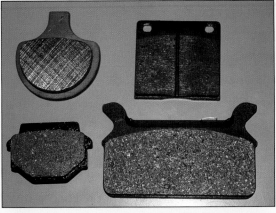

Time: 1/2 to 1 hour

Tools: Screwdrivers, wrenches, and some 12-point sockets for older models and Torx bits and Allen wrenches for newer models

Talent:

Tab: S

Tinware: Brake pads, shims (if required), aerosol brake cleaner, and special lube for the brake pins and caliper bolts

Tip: Typically rear brake pads on Harleys wear at about the same rate as the back tire, thus it's wise to plan on replacing pads when you replace rubber; fronts, both tires and brake pads, seem to last two to three times as long no matter how hard you hammer them

PERFORMANCE GAIN: Shorter, safer, straighter stops, with no squeaks or leaks

COMPLEMENTARY MODIFICATION: If top-shelf brakes are the straight man for stopping stories, it's tires that deliver the punch lines; actually, traction loss isn't funny, so if you match the abilities of these two partners in the stop game, you'll avoid being the butt of cruel jokes

Brake pads have a hard life. They have to work hot or cold, wet or dry, with various amounts of talent and pressure at the lever. Different road surfaces and rubber compounds on the tires don't make it any easier either. When you give even a moment's thought to all that they must work through, it probably makes you nervous. Yet every time you ride, probably without much thought at all, you bet your life on little silver-dollar-sized chunks of mysterious materials clamped against whirling metal Frisbees to keep you safe and healthy in an environment that more often than not isn't. Now that I've got your attention, here's a quick study in "my pad or yours?"

First, there are *sintered* pads with the friction material sort of "pressure cooked" onto the backing plate. The sintered pads include things like copper and graphite, compounded with up to six other materials (even on occasion, ceramics) in their recipe. Next, there are *resin* pads, which, much like you'd imagine, have the "stuff" glued to the metal part of the pad. This "stuff" is mostly compounds of reinforced fibers, including Kevlar or steel and bits of copper (for semi-

1 Ignore the shapes and sizes, it is the material that needs examining here. A Brembo pad for the rear of a 1995 Buell S2 is in the lower left corner. Look closely at the differences in compound, relative to the sintered front H-D Dunlopad above it. The square SBS units for GMA calipers in the upper right corner appear to have less metal in them than the Brembo or Dunlopad, and the EBC version, lower right, for the back brake of a dresser, is the most metallic of the group. There's no way to be certain how all this translates into performance on the street, but the high metal content is an indicator of wet-weather performance, disc abrasion, and initial "bite."

2 Greater thickness may merely mean "harder to install" and not "longer lasting." The pad on the far left at least covers more area of the metal with pad material. The one next to it would appear to be a lot less endowed, yet both types stop you efficiently and effectively. It's how they go about it that differs. One may not really perform until it's nearly red hot; the other may bite hard stone cold then fade as the heat comes on. Which works for you depends on whether you commute to work in all kinds of weather or charge down twisty mountain roads, repeatedly, and only in the middle of summer.

3 Whatever you do, don't let it come to this. By the time you can hear metal-to-metal screeching, you've jeopardized your safety and damaged the brake disc. It's not a question of whether you can afford to replace worn brake pads—you can't afford not to! Fortunately, it couldn't be much easier. Undo a couple of bolts, lift the caliper clear, and fish the old pads out. Gently spread the brake piston with a screwdriver, fit the new ones (complete with abutment shims where necessary), and remount the caliper. There's not much to the time-honored "bedding" or burnishing of new brakes these days. More often than not, you'll be best off just using them as you intended when you bought them. Unless, of course, the instructions that came with your particular pads say differently.

metallic pads), brass, carbon, and (believe it or not) rubber thrown in the mix.

Both types often use insulating "shields" to prevent too much heat transfer from the disc, and therein lies a tale. See, it's not how much friction is created but how it is controlled from one minute to the next that really matters. All the variables mentioned at the beginning of this article demand an engineered "indifference," if you will, on the part of your brakes to ensure consistent behavior regardless of speed, temperature, or road conditions.

The challenge in building a street pad is in making it consistent (there's that word again) enough to be most things to most people. At any rate, the search goes on. The factory has been messing with pad compounds and disc materials for years with varying degrees of success. So has the aftermarket industry, in an effort to provide consistency in performance, longer pad and disc life, easy installation, and a price most of us can afford. This leads most of us to consider alternatives such as Ferodo, Vesrah, SBS, EBC, or others. None of these is necessarily a poor choice, but, be it hereby known, all are slightly different. And none (including stockers) come with a guarantee of "perfection." It's hard enough to describe the characteristics of brake pads ("feel," for example) let alone measure them in the real world. And there are now so many different pad compounds for so many different specific purposes that choosing the right one can be rather bewildering. The easy way to cope is to ask yourself what precisely you value in brake performance. And with a little diligence you can effectively tune the brake to suit your riding style.

Just ask yourself: What about "feel"? Are shorter-than-average stopping distances crucial to your riding style or environment? Will you give up a little sheer stopping power in order to avoid replacing expensive worn-out rear discs constantly? Or, for that matter, what about pads that don't chew up the disc but are themselves destroyed at a prodigious rate? At what speeds do you do most of your heavy braking? Daily commuting in city traffic or Sundays flying down mountain roads at warp speed? Should you be able to lock the wheel? If so, in the rain or just when? And which wheel are we talking about, front or rear? We all know 80 percent or better of stopping power is really the province of the front wheel, yet in certain situations the rear's 20 percent can save the day. Harleys, with their generous wheelbase, actually resist too much forward weight transfer in hard stops, therefore making their oversized rear brake more useful than most. In the Buell world you may even consider running two different types of pads—one for the nasty front brake and one for the numb rear.

From all this you should also gather that choice of brake pads is an important enough subject that you should have questions of your own—lots of them—and they should be asked as if your life depends on the answers. Consider the following admittedly general characteristics when it's time to replace these lifesavers.

PERFORMANCE

Stock—Very consistent behavior from cold to 400 degrees. Minimal to moderate fade. Quick recovery. "Wooden" feel but still the standard by which the others must be judged.

Vesrah—Somewhat erratic at higher temps. Moderate fade. Have been known to crack under extreme use. Feel is indifferent. Fine for street use, but racers need not apply.

Ferodo—Justly renowned. Very consistent. No fade. Decent to good feel. Many compounds available, so be aware.

EBC—Good consistency. No fade as such, but they typically need to be not too cold and not too hot to give their best. Instant good feel, but increasingly sensitive with speed and temperature.

SBS—Mr. Consistent. Can leave deposits on discs.

WEAR (AND FIT)

Stock—Hard to beat for fit and durability; the base line for disc wear also.

Vesrah—Like iron, but only fair to fit. As easy on the disc as stockers.

Ferodo—The downside of these pads is their relatively high wear and only average fit. Depending on compound, they can be hard on the disc.

EBC—Wear isn't much above average, but they are thicker than standard, leading to the biggest problem, fit. They are very gentle to the disc, with something like half the wear rate of standard.

SBS—These are very long wearing with no real fit problems. They also baby the disc.

EXPENSE AND VALUE

As a general rule, any part that can save your neck is worth whatever it costs. However, prices do vary and it always pays to be an astute shopper. Enough said.

Remember, we have not come with drink, but to make you thirst. Think for yourself and shop so you can stop without dropping.

P.S. Dunlopads are available for Buells now as well. There is virtually no Buell time on them, but a lot of Harley time. They are of the sintered category and are quiet, consistent, and long wearing. There's plenty of feel, and they stop as well as the stockers, or slightly better. On the street, they work very well.

SIMPLE MAINTENANCE
PROJECT 9 • TIMING YOUR ENGINE

 Time: 1/2 to 1 hour

 Tools: Clear plastic timing plug, timing light, and screwdriver

 Talent: ††

 Tab: 0 to $

 Tinware: A plastic bag to stick over the timing light if you choose not to use a timing plug and perhaps a little bright white or yellow paint to highlight timing marks

 Tip: See Project 89: Mapping Your Ignition Curve

 PERFORMANCE GAIN: Sharp running and starting, added engine reliability, and a lot less "pinging"

COMPLEMENTARY MODIFICATION: You could install an aftermarket device called an "E-Z Time" that eliminates a lot of running back and forth during this process

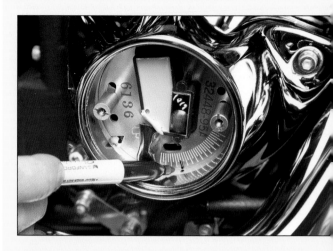

1 Here's where the adjustments are made. Each of the tiny hash marks stampe[d] in the base plate represents 1.5 degrees. Whether you choose to stay with fa[c]tory settings or experiment, it's a good idea to "mark the spot" with a scribe, touch of paint, or, as here, a black Sharpie felt-tip pen.

They say that most good things in life come to us as a result of "luck and timing." Well, when it comes to your Harley's ignition, the last thing you want to do is leave the timing to luck.

The shop manual, as always, will tell you how to go about checking and adjusting ignition timing, but as usual, it's a little light on background and details. A lot of folks set timing "by the book" for years and never knew what timing really is, or does. For instance:

Advance means that ignition occurs at some point in time before the piston reaches top dead center (TDC) on the combustion stroke. The interval between ignition and TDC is expressed in degrees of crankshaft rotation, and that interval represents the amount the spark is advanced. If the spark happens sooner, more degrees ahead of TDC, it is more advanced. Twenty degrees before top dead center (BTDC) is more advanced than 10 degrees BTDC. Ignition advance generally starts at some small amount, say 5 to 10 degrees, then increases with engine speed, the idea being that as turbulence in the combustion chamber increases with speed, it affects the amount of time available for burning the fuel-air charge. At some speed, generally 2,500 to 3,000 rpm in an Evo engine, this turbulence offsets the reduced burn time. At that point, the spark advance required becomes nearly constant, up to the highest engine speed.

The name of the game is efficient combustion. When you think about it, in this particular degree range, near the top of the rotation, there's relatively little vertical movement. But once that piston rolls over the top, it picks up speed like the first drop on a roller coaster. So combustion must occur late enough in the rotation to ensure the mixture is totally compressed but early enough to use all the force in the power stroke.

That's why it's crucial to take the time to set your ignition timing carefully and precisely. Each engine requires its own specific setting to give its best. For instance, on many twin-plug setups, since combustion is more efficient and less time is required to burn the mixture, less advance is required, meaning you can time the spark later in rotation by retarding timing and still get a complete burn.

This attention to timing pays off in ways that may not be immediately apparent. See, besides the obvious benefit of good performance, proper timing helps ensure optimum fuel mileage and a lack of fuel "fussiness" and its attendant pinging and dieseling, and last but not least, the engine runs cooler and

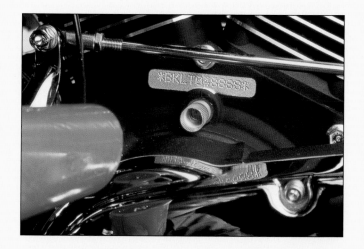

2 The timing hole has a range of about 8 degrees from the back to the front. If you set timing to occur in the center of the hole, that leaves 4 degrees of advance or retard that you can see, to play with. In timing terms, stock full-advance timing puts the line (to 1995) or the dots (1996—on) smack in the middle of the hole. When the ignition timing is retarded, the line/dots show up more toward the front of the timing hole. When the ignition timing is advanced, the line or dots show up more toward the rear of the timing hole.

3 If any adjustment is required (a big "if" these days), allow for it by loosening the pillar bolts with a screwdriver, leaving a slight "drag" on the ignition plate. If it's too loose and you're trying to do this single-handed, vibration will move the timing around while you're running from one side of the bike to the other to check and adjust it.

4 Make any movements slowly and in small steps. Keep an eye on those little hash marks on the timer plate (each mark is about 1.5 degrees), relative to your felt pen markings, and you can set very close to correct. When you're done, verify the timing with a light and adjust as necessary. Don't forget, if final adjustment is different than your original setting, mark the new timing with your felt-tip pen.

therefore lasts longer. It's almost an axiom that an advance in ignition timing may help power a little, but it will increase heat a whole lot, which is not a great tradeoff in an air-cooled engine. Wouldn't you trade a tenth or two at the strip for 20,000 more miles on the road? Retarding the timing from its factory setting is an age-old method of preventing detonation and preignition when you're stuck with a tankful of low-grade fuel. By the way, anybody know where to find high-grade fuel these days?

The factory ignition setting, in many ways, is a compromise. The evidence of this is as close as the Screamin' Eagle catalog. Here you find ignition modules and coils that The Motor Company admits will improve performance. These improvements come from different advance curves and stronger spark energy, but what about full advance timing? Even aftermarket ignitions with adjustable curves and rev limiters tend to go along with the factory recommendation for maximum ignition timing.

Maximum timing (full advance) is determined by the overall operating efficiency of the engine. For instance, on Big Twins full advance is 35 degrees, while XL models with their shorter stroke and different combustion chamber shape require 40 degrees. Some of the high-output four-cylinder, four-valve, water-cooled, foreign competition require as little as 17 degrees of full advance. Yes, the service manual shows specifications for late models (and HDI) that are 20 degrees for Big Twins and 30 degrees for XLs. Don't let this confuse you. What's really happening is that when you "shoot" the timing with a timing light at a given rpm, you are seeing the percentage of full advance that the module allows at the specific rpm you test. Welcome to the age of electronics.

But never mind all that. The thing to remember is that a major change in combustion efficiency will often require a change in full-advance ignition timing. Bear in mind, a major change in this case would be more in the nature of installing four-valve heads or a turbo. Milling 0.050 inch off the stock heads, even having the heads flowed, probably won't require a radical readjustment in timing. Fine tuning the timing is a good idea, just the same, and a 2- to 3-degree change can make a difference, even on a stock machine. Now that you know about good timing—good luck!

SIMPLE MAINTENANCE
PROJECT 10 • ADJUSTING YOUR CLUTCH

  Time: 15 to 20 minutes

 Tools: Allen or Torx wrenches, 1/2- and 9/16-inch sockets, screwdriver

 Talent:

 Tab: 0-$

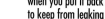 **Tinware:** New derby cover O-ring, sealing washers for the cover screws

 Tip: Mark the derby cover (on Big Twins) when you remove it so it goes back on in the same position; *do not* overtighten the thing when you put it back on; all it takes is finger tight and a half turn to keep from leaking

PERFORMANCE GAIN: Clean shifts, extended life for the clutch plates, and improved feel and action at the lever; you can find neutral sitting still too

COMPLEMENTARY MODIFICATION: See "Drivetrain" projects

1 First, you must loosen the clutch cable. The 1984 to 1986 models have an arm over the top of the gearbox, and you do all cable maneuvers from there. Later models have an internal ramp mechanism, and the cable features a midway adjuster (shown) to adjust for tension.

Big mileage on Big Twins with little routine maintenance and adjustment can leave you feeling like your tranny doesn't seem to shift gears as easily as before. But don't panic; the problem's not likely to be your gearbox. Look instead at your clutch. More often than not, a clutch that's out of adjustment, usually accompanied by a bone-dry cable, can be the cause of faulty or erratic shifts. It's sneaky because it's a series of minor long-term changes you don't notice until they catch up with you. By this time, you've overlooked the basic simple stuff and start sweating major items. Don't. Just take a few minutes and deal with the culprit.

Before you begin, support the bike in a level position to keep the transmission fluid in the primary case where it belongs. As with any repair procedure, disconnect your battery before you start the job.

The first step is to totally slacken the clutch cable by loosening the cable jam nut and threaded cable end adjuster until no threads are visible. After loosening the cable adjuster, check for freeplay by pulling the clutch lever. Lube the cable. Next, using a 5/32-inch hex-head wrench, remove the three screws that hold the derby

cover in place. Do yourself a favor and mark the original location of the derby cover with a felt pen or something before you remove it from the motor. The cover must be returned to its original position to avoid improper seating and leakage. While it's off, find a flat surface, like glass, and lay the derby on it face down. If you can see daylight between the screw holes, can get a 0.10-inch feeler gauge under the lip, or if it rocks around, it's not flat at the sealing surface. Get a new one. Next, use a deep well socket to loosen the 1/16-inch jam nut.

To return the clutch plates to a neutral position, use a 7/32-inch hex wrench to complete these steps in order:
- Tighten the center adjusting screw to separate the clutch plates.
- Loosen and back out the center adjusting screw.
- Screw the center adjusting screw back in until it bottoms out (do not overtighten).
- Back out the center adjusting screw one-half to one full turn.

While holding the center adjusting screw in position, torque the jam nut to 6 to 10 foot-pounds. Make sure that the center adjustment screw doesn't move, or you will need to redo the steps just completed.

Adjust the clutch cable adjuster for 1/16 to 1/8 inch of freeplay at the clutch lever. Squeeze the clutch lever three or four times to reseat the balls in the ramps. Tighten the cable jam nut at the adjuster. Before replacing the derby cover, check the level of the fluid in the primary housing and add fluid if needed. The upper level of fluid should just cover the bottom edge of the clutch plates and basket. After applying anti-seize to the derby cover screws, remount the cover to the position marked and insert the screws.

A few notes: If you happen to own a 1990 model that was made early in the model year and this procedure doesn't get the tranny to shift clean and smooth with no engagement grief, you might just have bad ramps on the operating mechanism. Check with your dealer, but if you turn out to have 13-degree ramps instead of 18-degree ramps, you'll need to update. It was an experiment the factory tried very briefly, and it didn't work. All models before and after have the good ramps. One visual way to tell is if the edges of the three ball bearing grooves almost touch. If so—bad ramps. If you can get your pinky in the spaces between the grooves, you're fine. Any problem is somewhere else.

You can help the throw-out bearing live longer on 1991 and earlier models by using the latest version of the clutch pushrod end, #37069-90, with an oil slinger on its end that helps a lot. Last but not least, if you have the older two-piece clutch adjuster, update that as well to #37090-90A. You'll be glad you did.

2 Sportsters, Buells, and Big Twins since 1990 have the same adjustment sequence and essentially the same hardware. Adjust with the center screw

3 After adjusting, don't forget to tighten the jam nut!

4 The tricky thing about a clutch adjustment is getting both the freeplay at the clutch lever and the engagement point. To get your clutch adjusted perfectly, you will have to adjust, check both freeplay and engagement, and readjust until you get it right.

FUEL AND EXHAUST

Nothing else makes as much difference to the overall performance of an Evo as the proper selection of components for two simple systems—intake and exhaust. Simple isn't always easy, unfortunately, and there are as many ways to do it wrong as right. Make no mistake, getting it wrong on a Harley motor just about cancels out any inherent advantages of the big V-twins. You can spend a fortune and wind up with something that doesn't work as well as the stock setup. You can spend very little by comparison to correctly correct certain inherent flaws and get more than you bargained for. It's a synergistic situation. Increasing airflow both in and out of the engine in a balanced fashion is the name of the game. Play that game well, and you can increase both torque and horsepower by anywhere from 50 to 100 percent just by changing the stock configuration from what the government wants to what the engine needs. One rule of the game is to avoid wasting too much time trying to out-guess the proven winners. This section describes some of those winners (in both categories) and shows you how to spot one on your own as well.

FUEL AND EXHAUST

PROJECT 11 • INSTALLING A SCREAMIN' EAGLE AIR CLEANER

 Time: 1 to 2 hours

 Tools: Allens, combination wrenches, screwdrivers, and diagonal cutters

 Talent: ♟♟

 Tab: $-$$

 Tinware: The air cleaner, the required breather manifold (chrome "horseshoe") for 1990 and newer Big Twin models; for 1992 Big Twins, a head insert kit and a new carb-to-manifold rubber/gasket; and for 1984–1989 Big Twins, a #20946-88A high-performance intake manifold kit is highly recommended; Sportsters and Buells will get the job done very nicely with the Screamin' Eagle air cleaner

 Tip: The factory never made a high-flow air cleaner kit specifically for California models with all their extra smog hoses. If you have a California bike, remove all the smog hoses along with the canister, cap the small vent line to the manifold/carb with a #27079-84 vent port plug and don't bother to plumb the breather line into the new air cleaner. Stick a small breather K&N filter on the end of the hose and route it out of the way somewhere. Also, don't forget the overflow hose for the carb's float bowl. Late models have a real short one, about 2 inches long. Replace it with a longer one (#27369-76) and route it to the ground—not the hot engine

 PERFORMANCE GAIN: More horsepower, better throttle response

COMPLEMENTARY MODIFICATION: Exhaust system, rejet the carb, and add a deep K&N filter element (Evos love this)

1 The path of least resistance (in more ways than one) for a Sportster owner to add power is H-D's own Screamin' Eagle air cleaner kit. It's simple to install, relatively inexpensive, and very hard to beat overall.

2 Big Twins, Buells, and even Sportsters can use the 8-inch round version of the Screamin' Eagle as well. What's really accomplished by these filter kits, round or oval, is ridding yourself of the incredibly restrictive stock backing plate and increasing the air intake potential via the flat Screamin' Eagle backing plate and pleated K&N filter element. These kits flow air as well as no air cleaner at all.

It's no big secret that the first thing most of us do to a Harley is put an exhaust on it that lets it sound like a Harley. But if that's all you do, you haven't finished the job. A good set of pipes may get you 3 to 4 extra horses. Almost any decent air cleaner, and the stock one doesn't qualify, will gain you 3 to 4 horsepower as well. If you put the two together, however, you can expect 10 to 12 horsepower.

Truth is, this isn't as much an endorsement of aftermarket air cleaners as an indictment of the stock one. Have you ever looked at the inlet area on the factory plastic backing plate? Federal (49-state) versions have a small rectangular orifice that is all of 3 square inches

in area. The California models' cocked-up plate is even worse. In the midst of the rectangle is a solenoid-operated trapdoor that further restricts the already strangled air supply to the engine. It's not really a design H-D wants, but the government's requirements for a quiet intake force them to do it that way.

If you want to pick up some cheap horsepower, take a hard look at the factory's very own Screamin' Eagle line of "off-road" air cleaners. These, dollar for dollar, are impossible to beat. The kits consist of a flat-backed aluminum plate, a pleated cloth K&N filter element, a small plastic venturi, and some assorted hardware. And they allow reuse of the standard chrome cover, whether oval for Sportsters or round for Big Twins.

The instructions that come with any Screamin' Eagle kit are clear and concise, and you'd do well to follow them to the letter when installation time rolls around. There is one thing though—California models with their attendant smog can and hoses aren't covered in the instructions, and rejetting recommendations are left to your imagination.

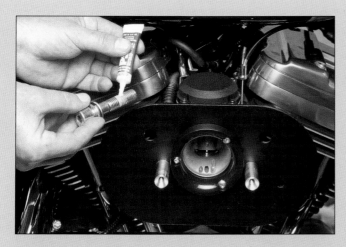

3 The kits all come with useful instructions. Some things are left unsaid, however. The biggy is the lack of commentary on California models and what to do with the various smog canister hoses. Well, plug anything that leaks air into the intake tract, and vent everything else to the atmosphere, to oversimplify a bit. And be sure to seal the vent bolts on head breathers with PST or Teflon tape. Just remember, an air cleaner's first job is to clean the air it lets into the engine. Think that way during the installation, and performance will take care of itself.

4 Big Twins built after 1992 require an adapter to use the Screamin' Eagle air cleaner. The 1992 models use adapter #29304-92, and everything else uses #29310-93, or something like the setup you see in the photo. Some folks don't care for the "chrome horseshoe" the factory offers, so they opt for an aftermarket adapter that runs under the carb, behind the air cleaner. These adapters can be pretty unobtrusive, and they also address part of the oil carryover problem that some head-breather models suffer from.

5 Regardless of your personal choice of adapter, it's not a good plan to route the vent line back into the air cleaner. It's asking for the suction of the carb to draw oil in, which makes a mess the engine doesn't like to run on anyway. Better to vent to a little K&N breather filter.

6 Speaking of better, Zipper's Performance offers a deep-filter upgrade for both oval and round cleaner kits. Dyno testing has shown that while true the Screamin' Eagle air cleaner flows like none at all, and a 2-incH-Deep K&N flows like a velocity stack, as in 5 to 10 percent more air than no filter at all. But don't get caught in a downpour with the deep filter! The stock cover doesn't completely cover a deep filter. If you use the deeper filter, plan on frequent cleaning and dry rides.

Time: 1/2 to 1 hour

Tools: Depends on the specific carb, but tiny screwdrivers and a small adjustable wrench usually get the job done

Talent: ▮

Tab: 0-S

Tinware: Extra smaller-sized jets for each circuit of the carb, but mostly the low-speed and mid-range; you'll also need extra O-rings and gaskets for any orifice you have to open up to change jets

Tip: Don't use so-called adjustable jets; remember to revert to sea-level jetting when you get back down there

PERFORMANCE GAIN: Minimize loss of performance above 3,000 feet

COMPLEMENTARY MODIFICATION: A high-flow air cleaner is nearly mandatory

1 When you're just passing through high country, shutting down the low-speed mixture screw might get you through. If it's set at 1 1/2 to 2 turns at sea level, 3/4 to 1 might be more like it a 7,000 to 9000 feet. If the screw alone won't do, you'll need to drop a size on the low-speed (pilot, intermediate) jet first and perhaps on the high speed (main).

So, you've got the ol' iron horse running like a freight train. Starts instantly, pulls clean, and runs sharp all the way to the redline. It gets good gas mileage to boot. Everything is great—until you take a ride up a mountain. As you rise in altitude, engine power steadily declines until at the top your trusty steed is wheezing and coughing like an asthmatic mule.

If your bike is jetted a little on the rich side at lower altitudes, it may not run at all at high altitudes. If you happen to be the proud owner of a late-model Harley (1996 or newer), you may discover that problems caused by ultra-lean factory jetting actually are reduced if you live, say, in Denver.

Install a high-performance carb, like an S&S Shorty, QwikSilver, or Mikuni HSR42, and you get a whole new set of variables to deal with—all because of one simple law of physics. Namely, that for every 1,000-foot increase in altitude there is a 3-percent drop in power. Which means that 10,000 feet, a stock 50-horsepower Big Twin is making a lousy 35—if the carb is jetted perfectly for its height. What's up with this anyway?

Well, stock CV carbs cope better than most because of their ability to compensate for altitude. The QwikSilver carb is able to perform this trick also. Does that mean you can just slam one of these mixers on your sled and forget it? Not likely. Short visits to mountaintops excepted, if you plan on riding high for more than a week or so, you should plan on rejetting.

THE BASICS

At sea level barometric air pressure is about 30 inches of mercury or, if you prefer, 15 pounds per square inch (psi). Up to altitudes of, say, 10,000 feet, that pressure will drop about an inch for every 1,000 feet, so at 6,000 feet you've got 24 inches of mercury and 20 percent less air available. The engine is 20 percent less powerful. Thing is, the loss in power can be more than 20 percent, perhaps far more, if you don't jet—you guessed it—roughly 20 percent leaner. Therefore, if the incremental percentage of flow between one jet and another is 5 percent, you need to drop to a jet three or four sizes smaller to restore the fuel-air balance. Less air is available, so you need less fuel to get the same ratio. That's the name of that tune. If you don't have any idea what the differences in flow are between one jet and another (by the same carb manufacturer), call and ask. You can't always judge flow rates by jet sizes. Mikuni, for example, uses several different main jet designs, some rated (and marked) by the size of the hole in the jet, some rated by flow, and none interchangeable.

THE STOCK CV CARBS

As a guide (since there's no way for me to know what cam, pipe, and air cleaner you're using), it's best to verify the existing jet sizes (markings) and drop one size on the main and pilot for anything over 3,000 feet. The needle that controls things from roughly 2,500 to 4,000 rpm is not adjustable and may need to be changed for another. As crazy as it may sound, usually the safest bet for non-California bikes at altitude is to swap to the California-model needle for the same year and model as yours. Compulsive types might find a better choice in the needle chart shown elsewhere in this section. Once the tuning is in the ballpark, the best thing to do to verify your choice is to check the engine on an exhaust gas analyzer (EGA) before you take too much for granted. Fuel mileage and engine temperature are pretty good checks as well.

S&S SHORTY (SUPER E AND G)

These carbs don't have a conventional mid-range circuit, so there's only two jets to deal with, the low-speed jet (or in S&S lingo, the "intermediate jet") and the main jet. At much over 3,000 feet, drop a jet size on both. The tricky thing is what to do above 3,000 feet. It may take three sizes smaller from the sea-level jetting to get a Shorty to run worth a darn at 5,000 feet, but it will be too lean if you drop down in altitude 1,000 feet. At 8,000 feet or higher, you may not be able to find a jet that's perfect. One size is too lean; the next closest is too rich. It's the nature of large-bore butterfly carbs. There's a lot of airflow but not a lot of air velocity, at least at low engine speeds. It makes these carbs extra tricky to jet for high altitude.

MIKUNI HS40, HSR42, AND HSR45

These carbs are just the opposite of an S&S. They are slide-type carbs with no butterfly at all, and they have not only fuel jets but air jets for every operating range of the carb from idle to wide open. This complexity bodes well for proper jetting potential but almost locks you into using an EGA to get it right. The one-size-smaller-jet-at-3,000-feet rule still holds, but it holds rather tenuously where these carbs are concerned. You can get much closer to "spot on" with a Mikuni but not without making a concerted effort—and buying lots of jets.

QWIKSILVER (ALL NON-CALIFORNIA SMOG COMPLIANT CARB MODELS)

The QwikSilver is unique in its use of a shaved, adjustable rod as the metering device for virtually the entire operating range of the carb. The range of "tuneability" on one of these rods, if it's correct at sea level, will take you to 6,000 feet or more by a simple adjustment of the existing rod. Much above that the rod may need to be replaced with a "leaner" one, but these carbs are internally "pressure balanced" and, therefore, altitude compensating. Chances are this carb will work as well as any of the others and as well as can be expected by tuning the rod that's in it. And nothing, but *nothing* (well, maybe a bike equipped with turbocharger or supercharger) will run worth a darn at 10,000 feet; there's just not enough air.

PROJECT 13 • TUNING YOUR STOCK CV CARB

Time: 1 to 1 1/2 hours

Tools: Phillips screwdriver; flat-blade screwdriver; 1/2-, 9/16-, 5/8-inch wrenches; and possibly a drill

Talent:

Tab: 0-$

Tinware: None

Tip: If measured fuel economy decreases by much more than 10 percent, you're either having way too much fun with the throttle or you've overdone it on jetting

! PERFORMANCE GAIN: A noticeable increase in mid-range power (especially torque) and smoother running at the expense of about a 10-percent decrease in fuel mileage

COMPLEMENTARY MODIFICATION: Use this information to complement what you've already done; nothing makes a package come together like pin-sharp carburetion

1 Once the air cleaner is out of the way, pop the carb off its rubber spigot and drill the little plug that covers the low-speed mixture screw. If the adjustment screw on a given carb is located on the air-cleaner side of the carb body, it meters air; if on the engine side, it meters fuel. So the low-speed screw on a CV carb actually adjusts the amount of fuel to be mixed with the air at idle to 1/4 throttle—place where you spend a surprising amount of riding time. No wonder the EPA wants set lean.

You want to improve the performance of your Milwaukee-built scoot? Then uncorking the stock Keihin carb is pretty much a necessary evil. Oops! Let's be more specific, the CV Keihin. Unfortunately, the earlier butterfly Keihin used on Big Twins from 1984 to 1989 and Sportsters for 1986 and 1987 can only be considered adequate for stock or near-stock applications, and that's being pretty generous. With proper care and feeding, the CV, on the other hand, can be made to perform as well (or better) than most name-brand aftermarket carbs at a fraction of the cost, all the while offering some fringe benefits the others struggle to match or can't provide at all. Most of the aftermarket carbs sell performance not economy, and that's because they are usually hard-pressed to match, let alone exceed, the economy levels on a CV Keihin. Likewise, for all intents and purposes, the aftermarket carbs (except the Edelbrock/QwikSilver)

don't offer the ability to compensate automatically for changes in altitude. The CV also offers truly excellent throttle response, particularly at low engine speeds, when compared to other 40-millimeter and larger carbs.

All these qualities are desirable, yet in stock trim the CV still leaves some things to be desired. Here's how to make it the best it can be without making major changes:

Start with the low-speed mixture screw. The initial low-speed mixture setting on your "tamper-proof" carburetor may be anywhere from screwed down tight to falling out. To set the mixture right, you've got to gain access to the screw by removing the welch plug (you never heard me say this!).

Once the low-speed mixture is properly adjusted, your motorcycle will run significantly better and much smoother when started cold.

2 Setting the low-speed screw is something of a dark art, unless you have an exhaust-gas analyzer. If not, adjust it until the engine is idling properly, and then run the screw in (clockwise) in increments of 1/8 turn, with a 5-second pause between each increment to let the idle stabilize, until the engine starts to not want to idle smoothly and drops rpm. Then run the screw back out 1/8 turn at a time, with the 5-second pause between each, and when the idle comes back up, as smooth and as high as it will get, back the screw out 1/8 turn more and stop right there. Set the idle speed (850 to 950 rpm) with the idle adjuster. Snap the throttle open and shut again as rapidly as you can. If you've got it right, the bike will not bog or cough and will drop right back to idle speed.

3 The three wise men of carburetion: low-speed (idle) jet on the left, jet needle in the middle, and high-speed (main) jet on the right. Ninety-five times out of 100 you will not need to mess with the main jet to cure EPA leanness. The low-speed jet can be swapped for a 45 or 48 (if gas mileage isn't important), or the needle can be swapped. Almost never all three.

4 The other player is the slide, or more accurately, the vacuum piston assembly. While lots of sources talk about drilling out the vacuum port in the slide for quicker response, it's an option to be approached with caution because it's too easy to overdo. The rubber diaphragm, on the other hand, should never be modified or even touched if you can help it. Otherwise, you might tear it—something like this one. Check the diaphragm often for pinholes or tears and replace them the minute they don't rise to the occasion.

FUEL AND EXHAUST
PROJECT 14 • CHOOSING A JET KIT

 Time: 1 to 2 hours

 Tools: A drill and regular hand tools are all you normally need; the kits come with drill bits and any other specific extras they require

 Talent:

 Tab: $-$$

 Tinware: Carb-to-manifold seal (#27002-89), float bowl O-ring (#27577-92) in case you tear the old ones, a couple of float bowl screws (#27579-88A), and top screws (#27129-88) because you almost always bugger the old ones getting them out

 Tip: Be certain that the kit of your choice will work with the other choices you've made

PERFORMANCE GAIN: More mid-range power (typically)

COMPLEMENTARY MODIFICATION: Free-flowing air cleaner and aftermarket exhaust

1 It seems everybody has a different notion of the best way to get rid of the EPA-induced "Keihin cough" that plagues late-model CV carbs. Take jet needles for instance. We have four shown here, two from the same outfit, yet all are different. The aftermarket needles are adjustable, via a series of clip grooves at the top and shims, like the one below the clip on the Thunder Slide version (at left). That's more than you can say for the stock needle (third from left). What thickens the plot is the thickness of the needle before the taper begins. The length and diameter of this dimension is the major factor in idle to 1/4 throttle. A fatter needle means a leaner mixture in this rev range, so it seems strange that the Yost needle, on the right, appears to have the largest beginning diameter.

Here's a typical scenario: You put a new exhaust pipe on the beast, slap a main jet two sizes larger than stock in there, and it results in absolutely no appreciable increase in peak power and horrific gas mileage.

Same scene, act two: Install a cam, and you've got to have a larger main jet (again); maybe swap to a "fat" idle jet one or two sizes larger than stock, and it has to run better than ever, right Wally? *Not*, Beav!

Act three, different scene: Got the double-throw-down, hot-rod air cleaner. Short of a turbo, this puppy will stuff air in that motor like a bandit stuffs money in a sack. For sure, you gotta rejet way fat to cover that program. Well, guess again. And unless you have access to a long deserted road, a Dyno, or an EGA, guessing is exactly what you're doing. It makes far more sense to use a well-developed jet kit than waste time, fuel, and horsepower.

But, since even the pros have different notions of what works (and the differences in their kits tell part of the story), your part is to figure out what you really want the kit for. As you will see, some kits are "tuning" kits for race bikes, and some are simple "bolt-ins" that only fix a lean spot. In no particular order, here's a run down on some of the jet kits out there, complete with certain insights into their suitability for your Harley, whatever state of tune it's in.

THE THUNDERSLIDE KIT FROM DYNO JET

These kits are for basically stock Big Twin and Sportster engines. The correct Thunderslide kit works very well indeed on Big Twins with aftermarket air cleaners, carburetors, and exhaust systems but not so well on cammed Big Twins. Sportsters and Buells are less a certainty.

These kits are simply not built to make horsepower, only to correct factory jetting and improve throttle response. Generally, that's exactly how it works out within the parameters of the kit. However, using a kit designed for a near-stock Sporty may not do much good

2 The Yost needle begins to make sense when you look at the needle's counterpart, the needle jet, alias "spray bar," "nozzle," "emulsion tube," and other dandy slang terms. The H-D jet is easy to spot because it has hex flats on the base. The Dynojet design, on the left, has fewer bleed holes, only two, to be exact, drilled into the body and removes with a screwdriver. Yost, creator of the so-called Power Tube, buys into the screwdriver removal part but diverges sharply from there on. His jet is peppered with tiny bleed holes, and though you can't see it in the photo, all three of these things have minutely different bores. Meaning, since the needles are supposed to work in conjunction with their respective jets, both items differ in design philosophy from manufacturer to manufacturer.

3 Philosophies about slide springs also differ. The longer, slightly stronger one on the left is the stocker. Many jet kit makers provide a weaker one, like the Dynojet unit on the right, figuring to help out throttle response. While this is a necessity with the Thunder Slide kit's ultra light slide, it's of questionable value with the factory version. If you get too crazy with lightening the spring, you may get a surging effect at cruise. The slide may "float" on every little impulse, and if the spring is too light, it can't dampen that effect. Apparently, some kit companies agree, and those makers don't offer a spring with their kit.

on a Buell. Exhaust scavenging is far different, cam timing is more radical, and the patented, silent Helmholtz design air box doesn't restrict as much on a Buell.

DYNO JET KIT WITHOUT THE SLIDE

Dyno Jet lists kits for both the S1 Lightning and the S2 Thunderbolt as well as "regular" Harley kits. Buell kits are notably different from Harley versions, but again the point is to correct EPA flaws in mildly uncorked motors. The only "race" kit offered is for 883s with disabled accelerator pumps.

"CLONE" KITS

Several companies make jets and needles for the stock carbs on Harleys. The accuracy of the "knock off" needle tapers and needle jet drillings are not guaranteed accurate. This is a classic case of both "buyer beware" and "you get what you pay for." Plus, too often these kits come with more choices than solutions, as if they're trying to kill all the birds with one rock.

Choose the wrong needle out of the selection, and you're going nowhere, slow. Your particular bike may run well with one of these installed, but don't bet on it. Spend the money for original equipment manufacturer (OEM) carb parts.

FACTORY IRON KIT

The Factory Iron Kit takes a slightly different tack in that it doesn't include a different needle jet. Rather it treats that function as a constant and uses a different taper on the needle, much the same as both Buell and Harley do. The instructions also stress the need to hold that needle steady and provide useful tips on exactly how to do just that. Good advice for any tuner. Well made, the Factory Iron Kit doesn't include a different spring either, but the precious needle it does provide is made of titanium. Buell kits weren't available when this book went to press, but they'll likely be on the market by the time you read this.

YOST MASTER KIT

Ah, simplicity! This kit makes changes pretty much right where they needs to go—to the midrange circuit—by including both needle and needle jet and not much else. This kit works (see Project 15: Installing a Jet Kit).

YOST RACER KIT

As the name implies, the racer kit is for folks who race and have time to tune accordingly. Although components are outwardly similar to those in the Master kit, the Race kit is really a tuner's kit, and both needle and jet are different from those in the company's Master kit.

Prior to 1996, one could guess at an alternative factory jet needle and come up with decent results. But that simple $10 solution doesn't always work on 1996 and newer bikes. With their new low-volume accelerator pumps and reworked internal passages, these 1996-style CVs run smog clean but not always horsepower crisp—especially, and particularly, if they are highly modified in the traditional manner. Still, the most amazing fact to emerge from all this is the growing awareness that unless you've built a real monster motor, one that makes in excess of 100 rear-wheel horsepower, you can buy a jet kit for $75 to $140 and get as much from the CV as a $500 hot-rod carb will give—especially at anything over 3,000 feet of altitude. No guess, just fact. Rather than start from scratch, eliminate most of the guesswork, and go with a jet kit for your jet.

FUEL AND EXHAUST

PROJECT 15 • INSTALLING A JET KIT

 Time: 3 1/2 hours

 Tools: Shop manual, small screwdriver, drill, 8-millimeter wrench, 1/2- and 9/16-inch wrenches and sockets, Allen wrenches, Phillips screwdriver, and clean rags

 Talent:

 Tab: $$$

 Tinware: Yost CV40 Master Kit (or alternative jet kit of your choice)

 Tip: Be patient and gentle when putting the rubber diaphragm on the slide; gently push down on the slide with your finger and go *very* slowly as you replace the carb top; if all else fails, set the slide in place, lay the diaphragm in place as best you can, and go have a cup of coffee or two—when you come back the diaphragm should have dried out some, settled down a bit, and you can finish without pinching it

! PERFORMANCE GAIN: Look at the dyno charts

COMPLEMENTARY MODIFICATION: High-performance exhaust and aftermarket air cleaner

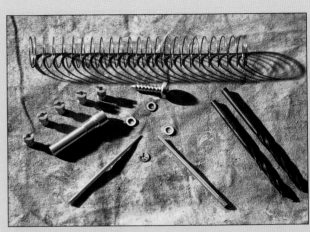

 1 Good things really do come in small packages. These are the components of the Yost CV40 Master Kit, which is designed to "master" the ultra-lean mid-range of the stock 1996 and newer Harleys. The heart of the kit is the fully adjustable jet needle and its mate, the amazing, better atomizing, needle jet, perhaps better known as the Power Tube. Yost recommends parking a #45 pilot jet in that tube. If you can't find one, you can very cautiously use a standard #77 jet drill to make the stocker a little larger. The operative word is "little." Don't overdo it, and do it carefully, or you'll wind up with a junk jet or fouled spark plugs. The brass the jet is made of is soft enough and the sizes are close enough that you can do it by hand.

New 1996 and later models are hampered by super lean fuel jetting to comply with ever-more-stringent emissions standards. In standard trim this means you're saddled with excessive warm-up times and, worse, a lot of coughing and spitting.

In the past, the Screamin' Eagle air cleaner kit and a set of Harley's off-road mufflers would pretty much do the trick. These simple add-ons would uncork the V-twin engine enough to make a real difference at the throttle. But from 1996–on, The Motor Company has been forced to run the CV carb even leaner than before. That's not as easy to work around as it used to be either. The latest carbs are more sophisticated than those of just a few years ago.

Enter the new Yost CV40 Master Kit. Like other aftermarket jets kits, this completely adjustable kit fixes what was wrong in the first place, a lean mid-range. No amount of low-speed jetting changes or high-speed jetting

changes address what happens in between these two extremes. And it's there, at half throttle, that this lean condition is most pronounced. Thank you, EPA. To get the most from your Harley's CV, this must be corrected. It's the cure for the common cough. Yes, it's more money initially than a couple of jets, but after months of poor gas mileage, you may feel this kit and others like it are a bargain after all. If nothing else, it eliminates guesswork and constant fiddling.

First, install the mufflers as the enclosed instructions tell you to. It's a no-brainer beyond remembering to use a dab of silicone sealant on the ends of the headers to prevent exhaust leaks.

Once that's done and before you put the air cleaner on, install the Yost kit.

It's almost too easy. Begin by removing and draining the carb float bowl, then take out the stock main jet and jet holder and install the Yost power tube, complete with the #175 main jet included in the kit. Now, replace the stock low-speed (pilot) jet

2 The first thing you notice when comparing a standard factory needle jet to the Power Tube is that the Power Tube has a bunch more holes in it. This allows better "bleed" as the fuel is siphoned up by vacuum. The fuel atomizes better, and throttle response, not to mention power, is vastly improved. However, as simple as it looks, don't try this at home kids, as the precise location and diameter of the holes is critical to the performance of the part.

3 Yost also recommends enlarging the vacuum port at the bottom of the slide and provides the drill bit to do it with. This trick is mostly to improve throttle response and should be considered recommended, but optional. If you do it, be cautious of this modification. And, *never* drill the port any larger than the 1/8-inch size Yost provides. The reason—if you mess this up, the motorcycle will have a pronounced erratic surging or "hunting" feel at what should be steady cruising rpm. And a new replacement throttle slide isn't exactly cheap either.

with a #45. Once done, screw it all back in place. Reinstall the float bowl.

Next, moving to the top of the carb, it's necessary to pop the lid off, so you may as well unplug the carb from its rubber manifold. There are actually five screws to remove, the four in the lid and one on the throttle cable side. Lift the lid slowly and remove the spring, white plastic needle retainer, stock needle, and the throttle slide.

Then, simply drop the new Yost needle into the slide. Unless you know better, leave the needle clip located in the middle groove of the needle. Trust it, it's set rich enough to do the trick on most models, as delivered. Now, you can put the lid back on. Plug the carb back in the rubber manifold, check throttle operation, and test-start the bike. That's it! The whole operation takes just a few minutes.

Finally, it's time to mount the new air cleaner. This is simple on 49-state models, but there are a couple of things you do differently on a California bike, as mentioned in project 11.

WHAT A JET KIT DOES FOR YOU

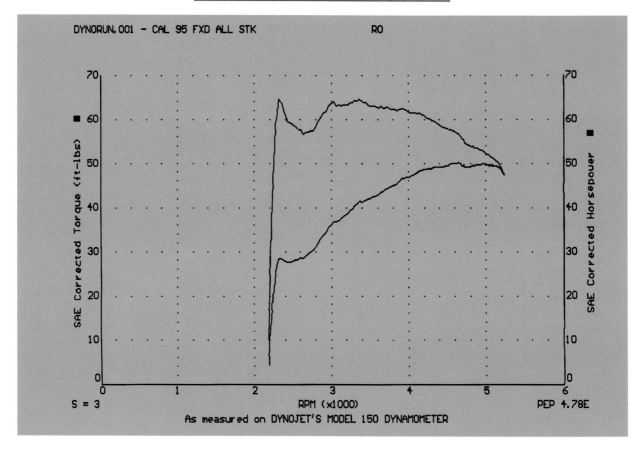

DYNORUN.001 - CAL 95 FXD ALL STK   RO

S = 3   RPM (x1000)   PEP 4.78E

As measured on DYNOJET'S MODEL 150 DYNAMOMETER

ABOVE

What you see here is a fairly representative run for a box stock late-model Big Twin. Notice the pronounced dip in the torque curve between 2,000 and 3,000 rpm? This is EPA jetting at work. This is also where most of us spend a lot of our throttle time—cruising speed.

RIGHT ABOVE

Things pick up after installing Screamin' Eagle off-road mufflers and a K&N filter inside the stock air cleaner. Unfortunately, the mufflers scavenge well enough that they steal a few horses from the middle rpm range and give them back only at high rpm. In fact, this setup makes the leanness even more pronounced.

RIGHT

The addition of a Screamin' Eagle air cleaner assembly and the Yost CV40 Master Kit virtually eliminates the lean mid-range problem. Better yet, it puts out a full 60 horsepower. That's 10 horses that can be had with three inexpensive items—mufflers, air cleaner, and Yost kit. Here's something else to ponder: the mid-range torque has jumped up 10 foot-pounds, and the bike revs nearly half a second quicker to 5,000 rpm.

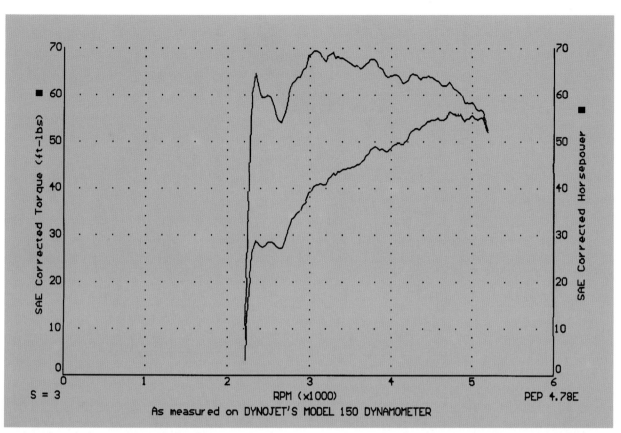

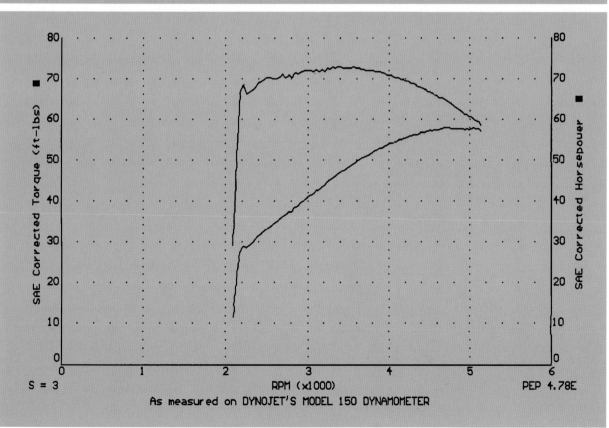

FUEL AND EXHAUST

PROJECT 16 • SWAPPING CARBS

Time: 2 to 4 hours

Tools: Depends on the carb, but it wouldn't hurt to have all your standard stuff handy

Talent: ▮▮▮

Tab: $$$-$$$$

Tinware: Intake seals and gaskets, carb-to-manifold gasket, carb-to-air-cleaner gasket; if throttle cables aren't supplied, you're very likely to need new ones, most often for pre-CV applications, which is no big deal if you didn't have a CV carb in the first place (stock or Barnett cables for 1984–1989 Big Twins and 1986–1988 Sportsters will work on late models unless you've got high bars or a non-stock throttle twist-grip design)

Tip: Buy extra brass ferrules (#56508-76) if you change cables because these are easy to lose

PERFORMANCE GAIN: Surprisingly, not all that much below 4,500 rpm, unless you are replacing one of the butterfly Keihin carbs fitted stock from 1984 to 1989 on Big Twins and from 1986 to 1987 on Sportsters. These simply aren't up to speed as a performance carb no matter what you do at any rpm. Most aftermarket carbs carry their payoff in the high-rpm range

COMPLEMENTARY MODIFICATION: A high-performance intake manifold (if the carb doesn't come with one) and an air cleaner (a hot carb will do you no good with a stock air cleaner)

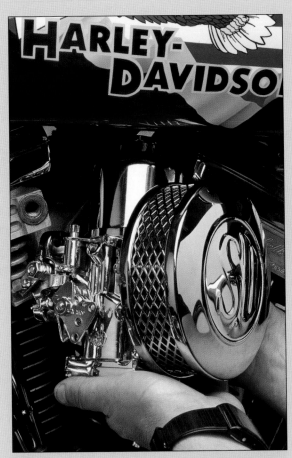

1 For fans of CV carbs that want to try the original CV, namely the S.U. (Skinner's Union), carburetor and air cleaner kits, they are available from Rivera Engineering. These carbs are still considered a hot item by Shovelhead riders, but their popularity as an effective option on Evos has waned. They do offer the superior looks so important to many of us, and once dialed in, the S.U. works as well as any and better than most. Still, it offers no clear advantage over the stock unit.

There's nothing new under the sun. Every basic type of carburetor available for Harleys is of the jet-discharge style that was first used in the nineteenth century. Over the ensuing 100 years, many design changes, extra circuitry, and sophisticated pieces have been added to the equation, but the basic principle remains: a series of "jets" and orifices combining fuel and air into an atomized mixture. If it's done right, the engine then turns this mixture into horsepower. It's surprising, after this long a time and this much familiarity, how often it is done wrong. The most basic fact is that there's no secret weapon in carbs these days, more like variations of the same theme, meaning you're not going to bolt on a mixer that magically makes your bike fly. Sure, some carbs are better choices than others under certain circumstances, but the differences are subtle, not quantum, and often it comes down to just liking one better than another—no objective criteria required. The three types of carburetors used on Harleys—CV (constant velocity), butterfly, and slide types—all do the job.

CV CARBURETORS

The CV carburetor is a hybrid carb using both a round, pivoting (butterfly) throttle plate and a vacuum-operated slide. Harley has used Keihin CV as stock since 1988 on the Sportster and since 1990 on Big Twins. The CV's trick is using a vacuum to raise the slide to establish venturi size based on engine demand. Open the throttle and the vacuum increases in the carburetor's throat

2 QwikSilver carbs, offered by Edelbrock, are the direct descendant of a long line of flat slide, metering rod based carbs, notably the Lectron made popular by Kenny Roberts and others in the 1970s. The beauty of this carb lies in its simple, yet sophisticated, metering via a rod with a precisely machined "flat" on one side. Simply moving the rod with a micrometer-type built-in adjuster "tunes" the unit to various requirements. It works well as a performance carb, compensates for altitude like the stock CV, and is available in "street legal" (smog legal) form. The flat slide design makes for crisp throttle response and good turbulence and velocity through the venturi as well.

3 Mikuni's HSR42 is an updated version of the 40-millimeter carb that has been so popular for the last decade. As with all Mikunis, it is infinitely tunable, offering not only swappable fuel jets, but air jets as well, for each circuit. Ironically, that may be its biggest downfall for Harley riders. It's "too complicated," they think. Well relax, 99 percent of the time, these carbs require no special tuning to work exquisitely well.

behind the butterfly, sucking the slide up. The higher the slide rises, the more the vacuum in the carb's throat decreases. The slide stops moving when throat vacuum is equal to the vacuum in the chamber. The CV is just the ticket for emission control, but its big drawback is that air must flow around two obstacles—the bottom of the air slide and the throttle plate—to get into the intake manifold, so throttle response isn't always crisp.

SLIDE CARBURETORS

Slide carburetors can produce the most power and have the smoothest transition from idle to full throttle. There's no butterfly in the way, and since the slide itself controls venturi size, air speed across the jet is sometimes 10 times as fast as in a butterfly carb of the same size. That translates into fantastic part-throttle smoothness and excellent low-speed throttle response—if you can get fuel to react fast enough to keep up. Fuel is more dense than air, so it just doesn't accelerate as fast as air. To compensate, slide carbs are fitted with a bewildering number of circuits, with jets for both air and fuel in many cases. You get 'em jetted right, and nothing's better. Get 'em wrong—you'll hate it. For example, the needle sizes and height increments in the slide are offered in a seemingly endless number of combinations. With all this choice, adjustments must be done in a certain order. You start by dialing in the high-speed circuit, then move to the mid-range, and finally low-speed/idle. That can amount to hundreds of settings and as many hours to get them just right. Tuners

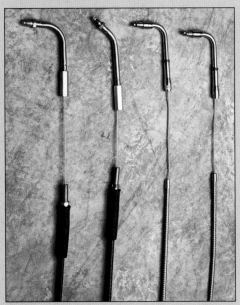

4 The ever popular S&S "Shorty." Available in 1 7/8-inch (Super E) or 2 1/16-inch (Super G) variations, these simple, elegant mixers have been the five-to-one "fave" for hot-rod Harley owners for decades. They look superb and make top end power as well or better than anything. Adjustments are comprehensible to normal humans, and they have maybe 10 percent as many components as the Mikuni. What the S&S is not so great at is trolling around. This carb is for folks who want to go. And even though it may look slick in the photo, the velocity stack is a drag race only option. Forget it for street use.

5 Most aftermarket carbs require a throttle and idle cable change. Some, like the Mikuni, come with what you need (if not always exactly what you want). Others, like the S&S, mandate a swap to the early-style factory cables (1984 to 1989). Why? Because the free-length, which is the distance from the bitter end of the wire to the sheathing, is shorter on those early cables. Most of the carbs were developed prior to 1990 (and the CV carb), hence the cable change. The three basic groups of factory cable designs are 1984–1989 (1988 for XLs) with the shorter free-length, 1990–1995 (1989 for XLs) for CV and CV-sized throttle wheels, and lastly, 1996–on, which have no threads on the ends that screw into the twist grip housing. Something to think about before you try to stick an S&S on a brand-new Evo is finding a cable with the right free-length that fits the new throttle.

love 'em. Mechanics often don't. The most popular slide carburetors are those from Mikuni and QwikSilver.

Ninety-five percent of the time, these carbs are a bolt-it-on-and-forget-it proposition, as delivered in the kit. Still, the other 5 percent need some fiddling to work with your combination of pipe, cam, and compression—95 percent of that fiddling coming down to improper pipe choice. Harleys are so systems sensitive that a carb that puts plenty of mixture into the equation isn't going to get along with a pipe that won't get it out—so no drag pipes!

BUTTERFLY CARBURETORS

The S&S, RevTech, and Zenith carburetors are butterfly types, which use a pivoting throttle plate to control the airflow through the carb's throat. Their hallmark is simplicity, and manufacturers have labored many, many hours subtly honing their designs to perfection. For good high-rpm throttle response and sheer top-end power, they're tough to beat. Lately, S&S and RevTech have added some secondary circuits and an accelerator pump to smooth out the carburetor's overall response. The lesson is clear—it's easiest to overcarburet with a butterfly carb. Getting top-end rush can lead to low-speed mush all too easily. It boils down to intended use then, doesn't it? Bonneville burning or Autobahn blasting favors these carbs. Trolling the mean streets and putting around at idle tends to show up their shortcomings.

INSTALLATION

Swapping carbs is usually a bolt-on operation, once you have all the ancillary goodies to go with it. Usually. If you've got a new one, it'll come with instructions. If you've bought a used one, beg, borrow, steal, or photocopy a set of those same instructions. Believe it or not, you can call the manufacturer for a set and for detailed answers to questions that come up as you are installing it. Take your time and lay out the stuff that comes off the bike in logical groupings on the bench. Sticking the new stuff back on is best done in a sort of "layered" fashion. That is, intake manifold first, cables second, carb third, air cleaner last.

One fly in the ointment that should be addressed up front is the so-called compliance fittings. These rubber boots were fitted on Harley Big Twins from 1984 to 1989, and they suck—literally. If you still have them (and there are a dozen reasons why you may not by now), trash 'em. Get the Screamin' Eagle intake kit #20946-88A and install that first, then worry about hot-rod carbs. Likewise in 1988, the factory got stupid on Sportster intake manifolds. They're rubbery plastic, and they rot. If your Sporty is so afflicted, use manifold #27004-88A, which is aluminum.

Time: 1 to 2 hours

 Tools: An open mind

 Talent: 👤👤

 Tab: $-$$$$

 Tinware: Catalogs and your telephone

 Tip: Choose wisely if performance is what you're after

 PERFORMANCE GAIN: Huge if you get it right, perhaps a couple of horsepower higher in the range if you don't

COMPLEMENTARY MODIFICATION: A low-restriction air cleaner, a carb rejet (or replacement), ignition upgrades, a good cam, and a bit more compression

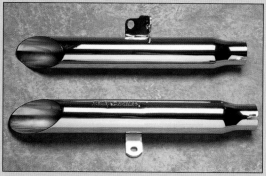

1 The ubiquitous slip-on muffler is the value-for-your-money champ. For the price, you simply cannot beat the proven performance increase these mufflers offer.

2 The next level is essentially the same mufflers physically attached to the headers. These are hugely popular for their inherent simplicity and good looks, and when combined with a so-called anti-reversion device incorporated into the head pipe design, they work very well.

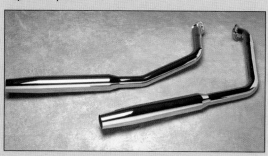

Being down considerably on power is a situation Harley riders seem to be locked into. But it's a prison of our own making. The key, the way to escape that particular prison, is to trash convention when it comes down to the pipe. Everybody that becomes disenchanted with the ordinary urge of an Evo dives right into the drill: so-called high-performance air cleaners, jet kits, cams, carbs, and ignitions. But *high performance* is a relative term isn't it? Never mind that you can't possibly match newer engine designs in terms of total power potential. Concentrate on this notion: You have all you need—if you're willing to use it. Believe it or not, it's not the motor's potential that's ultimately holding you back. It's your own attitude about style gettin' in the way of the substance. You don't need more potential, just a bigger chunk of what you haven't powered up yet.

The problem? It's that ridiculous staggered dual exhaust that's been part and parcel of most H-Ds for so long; they look downright un-American without them. Too bad. Because, without reservation, damn near anything that was designed to exhaust properly (as opposed to look and sound good) would be better.

The guy who blew the whistle on this pig-ignorant pipe game was Erik Buell, the ugly-muffler king. Who cares? You should. If you haven't ridden one, it's you who can't possibly understand Buell's work. The extra steam a Buell generates cannot be matched by a Sportster with equivalent equipment elsewhere only because you can't hang that type of pipe on one. Cam, carb, and ignite your knickers off, and you just wasted your time and money, unless you throw away everything you thought you knew about Harley pipes. If you want that dog to hunt, think big. Real big! But let's start small to give you time to get used to the idea.

Use tried and true off-road mufflers as a base line:

One, they are smaller in diameter than the stock stuffed-up units.

Two, they'd work a damn sight better than they already do if they were the same diameter as the stockers.

Three, Harley's not entirely in the dark. They've now got a line of big-bore, street-legal mufflers that promise to be less blatant and just as potent as the older, smaller, noisier ones. These aren't as loud as traditional off-road slip-on mufflers yet make as much power and most likely more torque in the mid-range. And Harley's got them available for their full range of models.

These systems and mufflers are more like it, good, in fact, but are not near enough for true high performance. Now, if H-D (or anybody else, as far as that's concerned) would get on with the task of designing an exhaust system that employs stepped-diameter, equal-tuned-length headers, a collector of the proper dimensions and placement, and finally, but foremost, a howitzer-sized muffler, they'd have it whipped. What are the odds?

If it comes to it and a serious pipe can't be bought, you may have to build it.

As shown in the dyno chart in this section, a typical built 80-inch Evo with a Screamin' Eagle bolt-in cam, big Mikuni carb, milled heads, hot-rod ignition, and off-road mufflers makes about 68 horsepower and not quite 80 foot-pounds of torque. That's the proverbial bottom line. Not bad.

The big line in the chart shows what that motor is capable of. Guess what's different? The pipe alone. Mild motor turned monster. Buell-think on a Big Twin. Ugly? You betcha! But can you say "inner beauty"? Put another way, if you don't like it, you can look at the scenery instead, but chances are this bike will run so far in front, you'll barely get a glimpse anyway. Want to really get nuts? A guy could hang the howitzer underneath the frame and point the exhaust tips on either side of the tire. You could even spend a fortune and build a two-muffler version with the things stuffed under or alongside the re-engineered rear fender—à la Ducati 916.

Truth is, it may actually be cost-effective to go to these exhaustive lengths because you'd spend more to match this kind of power using "conventional" hop-up techniques. Geez, come to ponder it, could be you just can't beat that torque on any 80-incher any other way no matter how much you spend. Can you imagine what a full-house 96-inch (or bigger) engine could do with this pipe? If so, more power to ya.

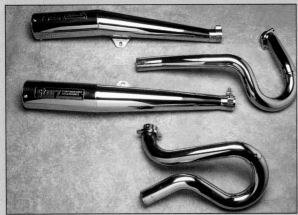

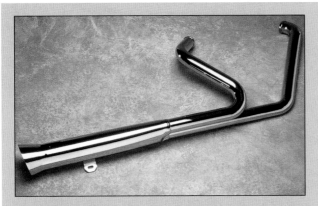

3 There's really not much out there that beats a good two-into-one design, largely because of the length of the head pipe, the diameter of the collector, and the nonrestrictive nature of large mufflers. Not all two-into-ones are a high-performance certainty, but the percentages are with you.

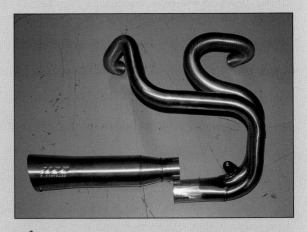

4 The XR-style flat-track systems are not for everyone, but they are a powerful pipe design. They usually sport something close to "tuned length" headers and large nonrestrictive megaphone mufflers. The biggest obstacle to happiness with these pipes is the added weight high on the right side of the bike, reduced legroom, and the difficulty of mounting saddlebags.

5 The top of the heap so far is the Buell Pro Race pipe. Its 38-inch equal-length headers, 2.5-inch collector, and no-restriction muffler give it the best power of all the available pipes. You may think it's a loser in terms of appearance, but you can't beat it for power. It has more poop than you can stand, everywhere in the powerband.

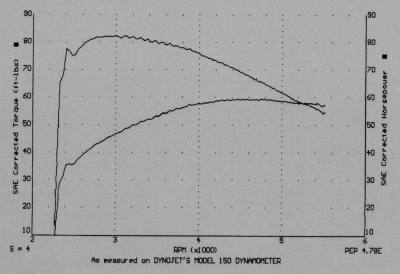

DYNORUN.002   65.8 °F   29.82-0.30 in.Hg.   0 ft.   CF=0.98   RPM/MPH=49
ANDREWS EV 27 CAM HS40 MIK BUB EX W/BAFFELS JACOBS IGN W/MULI FIRE

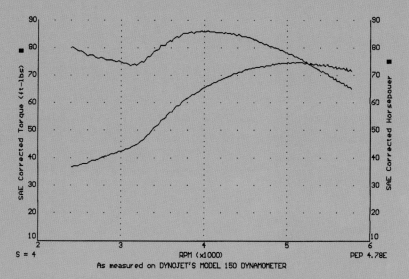

DYNORUN.004   71.1 °F   29.62-0.41 in.Hg.   0 ft.   CF=0.99   RPM/MPH=49
ANDREWS EV 27 CAM HS40 MIK CCI EX W/BAFFELS JACOBS IGN W/MULI FIRE .050
milled heads/.015 milled cylinders.

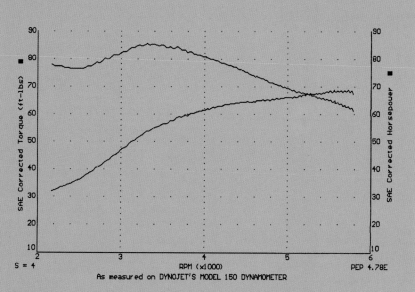

DYNORUN.009   72.0 °F   29.72-0.34 in.Hg.   0 ft.   CF=0.99   RPM/MPH=49

Choosing Power Spreads

One of the keys to picking a pipe is where you want to make power. Dyno charts are perhaps the best way to see just that. These three charts show three different pipes on an 80-cubic-inch Evo with bolt-in cam (Andrews EV27), HS40 Mikuni carb, 0.050 inch milled off the heads, police ignition module, and Screamin' Eagle coil and plug wires. As you can see, each of the pipes gives a slightly different curve. For day-to-day riding, a smooth, solid curve with plenty of juice in the 2,000–4,000 rpm range is the hot ticket. You can get bigger gains by sacrificing some low end, and you'll bounce through the gears with more authority, but your buddies stocker may pull you in top gear roll-on.

6 You may have noticed that many hard-working exhausts use the Supertrapp disc system. Once the discs are dialed for best power (preferably with a dyno), you can continue to play with the sound using this little gizmo from White Brothers.

7 Whatever pipe you choose, certain details of installation remain the same, such as getting at the exhaust nuts in the head. It helps a lot to have a deep socket on a wobbler extension if you have to remove or replace those nuts very often.

10 Tight rubber-mount models, especially 1991 to 1994 Dynas, love to shake the exhaust loose. If you own one of these models, make it a religion to tighten the various clamps and mounts before or after every long ride. Since the mufflers are bracketed together but not tied to the motorcycle's chassis, it's not an unknown event to have a pair of mufflers blow off neatly into the street.

8 Big Twins up to 1994 used one design of muffler bracket, and from 1995–on they used another. The mufflers are updatable or back-datable from any year to another, if you have the right bracket. You can get chrome or black brackets for any year from the aftermarket, usually for a lot less money than H-D wants.

9 If you're just using mufflers on stock head pipes, do yourself a favor and put some sealant inside the joint. This keeps exhaust leaks to a minimum and helps keep the muffler tight.

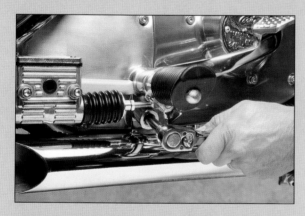

11 Save time on Sportsters by removing the nut under the right footpeg and backing off the rear master cylinder Allen bolts. Don't attempt to disassemble the clevis and pedal; just get it out of the way for pipe mounting.

12 Looks tough; sounds rough! When it's all said and done, you do it for the sound.

FUEL AND EXHAUST
PROJECT 18 • REPLACING VACUUM-OPERATED PETCOCKS

 Time: 1 hour

 Tools: Wrench for the petcock, clamps for the fuel line, and possibly a funnel

 Talent:

 Tab: S

 Tinware: A drain container for the fuel, a new fuel filter (now's the time), and new 5/16-inch hose clamps

 Tip: Make sure the gas cap is venting properly or the fuel won't drop—a vapor lock sort of thing

PERFORMANCE GAIN: Harder pull at high rpm

COMPLEMENTARY MODIFICATION: External fuel filter or Fuel Stat

1 For decades, Harley riders have had to train themselves to turn off their manual petcock (the one on the left). Then, in 1994, Harley decided it was time to relieve us of that chore by fitting an automatic petcock, only to have this nifty convenience cause more trouble that it was worth because the rubber parts couldn't stand up to the new reformulated gasahols that were mandated in some cities. The problem has been solved with stouter rubber internals on new machines and by a recall on the older automatic petcocks.

Harley-Davidson introduced vacuum-operated petcocks (fuel valve) on its 1995 models. Harley thought they were doing us a favor because most of us forget to turn the manual petcocks off, which can turn into a puddle of gas leaking from your carb. The company figured this fool-proof, fail-safe design that prevents fuel from leaking past the carburetor's needle seat when the bike's motor is not running was safer and smarter. Then reformulated MTBE gasoline hit the tanks in the summer of 1995. A tank or two of that stuff and riders were "running out of gas" on full tanks even though the lever on the vacuum petcock hadn't been touched. To correct this problem, Harley introduced a revised vacuum petcock with a different rubber compound on the internal diaphragm and a new filter screen. It's identified by the letter "M" stamped on the right side. The new filter screen can be identified by its orange color.

Another problem the redesign may or may not have fixed is the fuel diaphragm unsnapping itself from the vacuum diaphragm inside of the petcock, which immediately stops gas flow. Amusingly, this problem seems to happen mostly to the old timers, who were used to manual fuel valves. They turn the gas off at the lever and then forget to turn it on again before they start the engine. The tremendous initial suction from the engine firing with the lever in the off position just rips up the diaphragm. This is absolutely no problem if you leave the petcock on.

The simplest fix for this is to convert to a manual petcock. You have the option of three styles of Harley-Davidson manual petcocks or aftermarket petcocks such as those from Pingel, Accel, RevTech, and generic styles sold by others. What you need to pay attention to when buying a petcock for a 1995 and later Harley is which direction the outlet nipple faces and that the mounting thread on the petcock body is 22 millimeters. Pingel valves and some others require an adapter nut to hook up to your stock tank; don't forget to get it when you buy the valve. You will also need a vacuum-line cap to plug the unused nipple extending from the carburetor to the petcock. As for the direction the outlet nipple faces, that depends on the fuel tank you have. Some tanks need to have the nipple facing the front of the machine, some the rear, and others straight down. Make sure the replacement valve faces the same way as the original, or find one that has a rotating nipple.

The most important fringe benefit of switching petcocks is increased fuel flow, in some instances three times as much as any OEM petcock, which is sometimes necessary for high-performance Harleys. Usually, aftermarket petcocks look better than the pot-metal stockers. That's good because if it's a looker, maybe you'll look often so as to remember to shut it off when not in use and turn it back on when it's time to go.

Changing a fuel valve is simple enough, as long as you try to remember to do it with a tank that's more empty than full. Drain the fuel, remove the fuel line, unscrew the nut holding the petcock to the tank, and let everything quit dripping. Use some teflon tape or TSP in a tube (they are pretty much the same thing) on the threads of the petcock nut and screw it on the valve. Once it's hand tight, snug it up a bit with a wrench; as long as it doesn't leak and can't be moved by hand, you're good to go.

2 For those afflicted prior to the recall, the only fix was to swap petcocks. Most opted to return to the good old manual version. Others, knowing that the stocker only passes about one-third the fuel volume of some high-performance aftermarket petcocks, opted to upgrade to a high-flow unit like this Pingel. Not that all problems go away with the change. You still need to remember to manually shut off the valve, and most hot-rod petcocks have very little reserve capacity. The average Pingel gives you about 0.2 gallon (5 to 10 miles) of reserve fuel, so you'll need to learn to run off of the top half of your fuel supply or never get too far from a gas station.

FUEL AND EXHAUST
PROJECT 19 • INSTALLING A FUEL STAT

 Time: 15 minutes

 Tools: Knife or razor blade and a screwdriver

 Talent: 👤

 Tab: $$

 Tinware: A couple of mini-hose clamps

 Tip: Annual smog inspection for motorcycles is bound to become a reality in the near future; this is one way to avoid the grief and aggravation of reinstalling stock parts to comply with the regulations

 PERFORMANCE GAIN: Minor, in and of itself, but it "cleans up" the performance you've gotten from other mods and, therefore, will help you comply with the EPA

COMPLEMENTARY MODIFICATION: Consider Nology spark plug wires and possibly "low-restriction" catalytic mufflers

1 This unassuming gadget may hold some of the answers to the conflicting requirements of clean air and high performance, if the government will retain a shred of common sense and make the inevitable smog checks for motorcycles a simple pass/fail standard—regardless of equipment or hardware on the machine. A straightforward "sniff" test that says you burn clean or you don't will bring devices like the Fuel Stat (and other clean burn aftermarket goodies) into their own. The Fuel Stat deionizes the fuel and literally allows a performance engine to run better than ever and still cuts emissions to below most proposed legal levels.

For nearly 20 years motorcycles have escaped the net of annual emissions checks. Sure, the manufacturers, including Harley-Davidson, have built the bikes to comply with smog laws all over the world, but once they wind up in the hands of the consumer, the violations to the letter, if not the spirit of the law, are rampant. And why not? Motorcycles are not a major contributor to pollution, probably less than 0.1 percent. Doesn't matter! Sooner or later this little loophole, the one that lets motorcycle owners (if not H-D) mess around with performance modifications, will turn into a noose around our necks. Most likely it will happen right after we spend a fortune on hot-rod parts.

The only hope is that when the day comes, the inspection will make some kind of sense. It shouldn't be about leaving the motorcycle absolutely stone stock. Any emissions compliance should be determined, literally, by what emits from the tailpipe—no more no less. It's the only measurement that should count. If you can comply with the clean-air standards in your particular region, however you manage to do so, that should be good enough.

The Specialty Equipment Manufacturers Association (SEMA) is doing its best to make sure

that's the way is happens, when it finally happens. The aftermarket and specialty equipment companies can and do make hot-rod parts that don't dirty the air. These parts should be legal, simple as that. To go one more step, some of the same companies are working on equipment that will actually clean up emissions. The Fuel Stat, made by Throttle Up, Incorporated, is one of them. It looks and installs just like a fuel filter, but it does a lot more than that.

In essence, a Fuel Stat does to incoming fuel what a catalytic converter does to outgoing exhaust fumes. While a "cat" burns off the bad stuff on the way out the tailpipe, a "Stat" deionizes fuel on the way in, much like a water softener. It removes "static cling" in the gas, releasing more energy for the job at hand. The details are patented; the results are for real.

The tests listed in this section were conducted on a Fuel Stat-equipped, big-inch hot-rod Softail using a DynoJet dynamometer 150 and an EGA to reach the conclusions shown. Suffice it to say, the Fuel Stat does some pretty amazing things.

Looking at the test data, it's clear that the Fuel Stat makes power and enables the engine to run cooler. What's implied is that it also makes the engine more fuel efficient. Doing more with less. So far so good. The Fuel Stat will probably succeed on that much alone.

But there's more, and in the end, it's this "more" that gives the Fuel Stat its true impact on the Harley world, indeed on the motorcycling world at large. You don't see the results of the EGA test here, but you probably wouldn't believe them if you did because the Fuel Stat reduced emissions to something like half the levels this high-performance engine produced without it. This is not just impressive; it's revolutionary. It implies that in the face of ever-tightening regulations, we can have our cake and eat it too, at least as far as high-performance Harley-Davidsons are concerned.

PROJECT 20 • TROUBLE-SHOOTING FUEL INJECTION

Time: 1/2 hour (with a Scanalyzer)

Tools: Scanalyzer

Talent:

Tab: $$$ (for the tool)

Tinware: Shop manual and the chart in this project

Tip: As you can afford it, update 1995–1996 models to the later Electronic Control Module (ECM) or a Stage 2 kit (see Project 22: Fixing Clunking Wide Glide Forks)

PERFORMANCE GAIN: Instant starting, little or no warm-up required before riding, better mileage, and more torque

COMPLEMENTARY MODIFICATION: Keep the air cleaner clean and change fuel filter frequently (about twice as often as H-D recommends), especially if you live in a gasohol state

Emissions standards are tough and getting tougher. As a measure of the factory's success in this area, it should be noted that with their first shot at fuel injection, Harley undercut the latest standards by nearly half. In the process, Harley has bumped up torque by about 10 to 12 percent. Fuel efficiency is improved (by approximately 5 percent) and more consistent. Chokes and enrichers are a thing of the past, and cold starts are a snap. Plus drivability (partly due to the new base gasket improvements) is such that as soon as the bike is running, you can be riding. And you can't flood it. The idle speed adjustment is automatic, so no more erratic stumbling or racing or weirdness on excessively hot or cold days. The system will also adjust for barometric pressure, altitude, engine temperature, and intake air temperature. There's a single-fire ignition on top of all that, and if that doesn't add up to engine management with a capital M, I'll sell you my Tillotson!

The Harley EFI system is about as reliable as anything mechanical or electronic can be. However, should the unthinkable occur, the Electronic Control Module (ECM) will turn on the check-engine light. Head for the dealer, because as good as it is, if the system develops a problem, you won't fix it at home. The factory special tool kit is about $3,000 and consists of such goodies as a Scanalyzer and a breakout box for the ECM, as well as injector removers and an electronic fuel injection (EFI) harness. Relax. The odds are better you'll be hit by light-

ning than stopped by this engine management system.

While the preceding is true in general, let's go through a few things you can do, both if you can somehow gain access to the tools and if you can't.

QUICK CHECK: EFI IDLE

If the hot idle speed on EFI models falls too low, you should check for low fuel pressure, possibly from a hole in the fuel hose inside the tank. If fuel pressure turns out to be the problem, it requires removal and inspection of the fuel feed hose from the fuel pump to the filter.

If the hot idle speed fluctuates or increases while the bike is running, there may be a problem with the engine temperature circuit. Other symptoms include high idle, rough running, and black smoke coming from the exhaust pipes. You can verify this by monitoring Scanalyzer readings when the problem occurs. (Not that a Scanalyzer, #H-D 41325, is something you'd have lying around the house, unless you're a fuel-injection technician for GM. However, if you intend to do much of this yourself, you have to have access to this tool. Your dealer probably bought one for about $3,500, but you might find a better deal through an automotive source, or get to be real good friends with that dealer. The thing plugs into the ECM on the scoot through a data link port and tells you more than you ever wanted to know about the health and well-being of your system via a cartridge inserted in the main body of the Scanalyzer.) The normal Scanalyzer reading should be more than 284 degrees Fahrenheit. If readings are higher, then further diagnostics are required. Most of the time, this condition will not show up as a trouble code. You should perform a "wiggle" test on the electronic temperature sensor (ETS) circuit as described in the shop manual. Poor connections are usually the culprit. If not, then a new sensor may be necessary.

Several of the key menu readings should be as follows:
- rpm—1,000 rpm
- SC—0 Steps
- ET—less than 284 degrees
- TP—3.2 degrees
- IP—0.4 volts
- Inv PW—3.9 ms
- Advance—15 degrees
- IDLE/WOT—Yes

If the high idle condition occurs after a hot restart and the idle speed control (ISC) pintle appears to be extended, you'll need a new one.

Other causes of high idle speed are improper throttle or cruise-control cable adjustment or engine temperature circuit problems. Never forget basic troubleshooting, either. An intake leak is an intake leak, carbureted or fuel injected. The same thing applies to dirty air filters, bad electrical connections, contaminated fuel, and so on down the line. Start with common sense; finish with the Scanalyzer.

FUEL AND EXHAUST

PROJECT 21 • HOT-RODDING FUEL INJECTION

Time: 5 to 8 hours

Tools: All the stuff you'd need to do this kind of thing to a carbureted bike plus a Scanalyzer

Talent: 👷👷👷

Tab: $$-$$$$$

Tinware: Stage 1—no real extras required. Stage 2—all the stuff you'd need for a cam change on a carbureted bike (cone gasket [#25225-93B], cone seal [#83162-51], tappet gaskets [#18633-48D/18634-48C], and adjustable pushrods [#17900-87] or rocker box kit [#17042-92A] and no pushrods); (see Project 51: Installing an Aftermarket XL Camshaft)

Tip: Harley-Davidson's Stage 3 fuel injection kit is simply an ECM remap cartridge for folks who depart from the factory offerings to implement their own ideas about cams, compression ratios, and such.

PERFORMANCE GAIN: Stage 1 gets you 5 to 6 horsepower and better low-end torque; Stage 2 gets you about 70 horsepower and over 80 foot-pounds of torque; Stage 3 gets you a potential 80-plus ponies, but the torque peak moves up in the rpm range, so you may find it less useful than Stage 2

COMPLEMENTARY MODIFICATION: Aftermarket exhaust; Vance & Hines, H-D's own Screamin' Eagle, or SuperTrapp exhaust all have a proven track record as power producers

In 1995, Harley-Davidson took a leap into the future with the introduction of the 30th Anniversary fuel-injected Ultra. Although at the time, it may have seemed more a marketing ploy than a genuine advance, that first factory engine management system signaled a commitment to save the company's V-twin engine.

So far, fuel injection has proved its merit. A new fuel-injected Harley provides more torque, more horsepower, better fuel economy, vastly superior drivability, relative indifference to altitude changes and atmospheric conditions, onboard diagnostics, and the potential to be hopped up. Harley-Davidson offers three different kits for your fuelly, all designed to bump the output.

The EFI Stage 1 kit offers better than 80 foot-pounds of torque across the board and peaks at nearly 90 foot-pounds down low at 3,000 rpm, where you

1 Modifying a fuel-injected Harley-Davidson begins here with the Stage 1 kit. There's a lot more air to be had with the Screamin' Eagle filter kit. Never think, even for a minute, that after modifying the stock air box with a bunch of holes it will work as well as this does.

2 The Stage 2 kit gets more involved thanks to more potent injectors, a very nicely tailored cam, and an updated cartridge for the ECM (for 1997 or newer bikes)

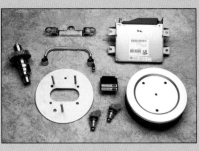

3 If your bike is a 1996 or older model, you need this version of the Stage 2 kit which includes a whole new brain (ECM) to "smarten up" performance.

can use it. The 10-percent increase in horsepower is a nifty fringe benefit. This power increase is accomplished without the benefit of a high-performance exhaust, retains virtually stock fuel mileage, and is completely smog legal.

The Stage I parts kit includes a free-breathing filter, an adapter to install it, bits of miscellaneous hardware, and a computer (well, more accurately, an ECM if you own a 1996 or older model, or a module to update the ECM you already have, if you own a 1997 or newer fuelly). The air filter everyone's seen before; it's not magic. The ECM enables both the increase in power and the clean air, which is a neat trick that would be nearly impossible to match with a carburetor.

Fuelly hot rods make sense. The Stage 2 kit may make the most sense—especially in view of the fact that, once again, there is no mention of exhaust mods required to attain this power. In addition to the same goodies provided in Stage 1, there are a pair of high-flow (41 percent more) injectors and an SE-3 cam.

If you already have the Stage 1 kit installed, you can just buy the cam and injectors to bring your bike up to Stage 2. Bear in mind that Stage 2 is approaching the limit of bolt-on power. Astute observers will note that the

4 What's the point of letting in more air if you can't get a little more fuel to go with it? The updated injector from the kit looks identical to the stocker except the body is red instead of black, and the red ones push 40 percent more fuel.

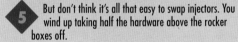

5 But don't think it's all that easy to swap injectors. You wind up taking half the hardware above the rocker boxes off.

6 Last but most, you must rethink your engine strategy, or at least get the ECM to. Late models, like this 1997 Road King, just need the magic module (which you can barely see) sticking out of the Scanalyzer. Early models (1995 and 1996) need to change their minds completely (a new ECM) before they can be persuaded to think horsepower. Either way, an updated program (fuel map) is what you're after.

power charts shown with the kits indicate that Stage 2 has the broadest, most usable power spread of the bunch.

Although Stage 3 consists only of a calibration cartridge, it requires all sorts of things to make it work: higher compression, more radical cams, high-performance intake and exhaust systems, and valvetrain upgrades are the most obvious. While this kit would work well with a bike headed for the drag strip, its value on the street is questionable. The price tag is high, and the factory-supplied numbers show only about a six horsepower gain. For racers and other hotrodders looking to build the ultimate EFI engine, this kit bears a closer look. For anyone on the street, Stage 2 is the better choice.

SECTION FOUR
SUSPENSION AND CHASSIS

It's regrettable to admit, but the area where H-Ds could stand the most improvement is right here. The factory reasons, and rightly so, that most Evo riders are cruising' through life, so they provide little more than the fundamentals when it comes to chassis and suspension. The bad news is, like a lot of other things about Evos, you're left with the feeling you just paid all that money for a machine you must finish yourself. The good news is that's exactly where the fun comes in. It is entirely likely that if and when you do notice any shortcomings in ride or handling, they can be, well, handled. Tailoring suspension to suit you personally—be it via lowering, changing spring rates, damping rates, swapping shocks, messing with steering geometry, or, in extreme instances, rethinking the basic design—is nothing new to the aftermarket. Understanding the principles on which these changes should be made and what's most likely to result from them is where this section can assist you.

SUSPENSION AND CHASSIS

PROJECT 22 • FIXING CLUNKING WIDE GLIDE FORKS

 Time: 1/2 to 1 hour

 Tools: Mity-Vac, Phillips screwdriver, fork oil, measuring container (graduated cylinder, baby bottle, or Ratio-Rite cup), and a lift or stand

 Talent:

 Tab: $

 Tinware: Screamin' Eagle fork oil (optional), new drain screws or sealing washers, and a drain pan

 Tip: Consider draining all the fork oil, then refilling instead of just adding to existing amounts

PERFORMANCE GAIN: Losing that mysterious noise without spending a fortune

COMPLEMENTARY MODIFICATION: Changing fork oil viscosity—some prefer Screamin' Eagle heavy (not extra-heavy); a fork brace such as the one from Custom Cycle Engineering

It's not unheard of to find yourself on a brand-new Softail, Dyna, or dresser model featuring H-D's famous Wide Glide fork assembly and having it go "clunk" on small, sharp bumps. The fork seems to work well otherwise, but this clunking thing has got to go. Presuming you don't already have designs on lowering the front end or upgrading the fork in some other manner, the easy way to eliminate the clunk is to add more fork oil.

Check the manual for the exact recommended quantity of fluid for your particular model and year and then add 1 ounce per leg to the recommended amount. It's that simple. While you're at it you may want to consider changing the fluid to a heavier grade if most of your riding is on smooth-ish highways and byways and if you spend most of your riding time fully loaded with passenger, luggage, and all.

Wide Glide forks tend to feel too plush during the first inch or two of travel, then too stiff the last couple. The spring rate is on the soft side as well, hence, the addition of air-assisted forks on dresser models to deal with extra payload. That trapped air operates as a true progressive spring, not affecting initial travel much but making its presence felt in a big way as you approach

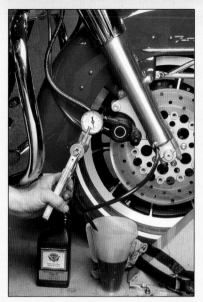

1 The easy way to reduce clunking from your Wide Glide forks is to replace the fork fluid, adding an extra ounce to the recommended amount. This trick is especially effective on Softails and Dyna Wide Glides with their longer forks. If you regularly ride with a heavy load, you might also consider using a heavier-weight oil. Changing, draining, or adding fork oil is much easier with a Mity-Vac. Virtually no disassembly of the forks is necessary this way. You set the tool to perform the function you require, pump in or suck out and go. Routine maintenance is a lot cleaner, quicker, and simpler since you needn't remove the fork caps or the cowling (on dressers). Unless you intend to take the forks apart to upgrade, repair, or lower the suspension, it's the hot tip.

the limit. So a light ATF or 5-weight oil is used as the damping medium in an attempt to control the movement of the fork, and a light spring allows such movement in the first place. It's the worst of both worlds. And they are two different worlds. Damping, dependent on the amount and viscosity of the fork fluid, determines how fast and far the wheel will move once it gets moving. The spring rate is in charge of just how much of a bumping/dipping force it will take to get the wheel moving in the first place. If the wheel bounces up radically at the slightest provocation, switching to heavier fork oil may just allow the bounce to transfer to the chassis. If the fork acts like it doesn't have spring in it, but once the wheel finally moves it doesn't throw the front end towards the sky, the spring's probably just too stiff (consult the Race Tech fork spring chart for some guidelines on this). Back to the clunk.

First, prop the bike up solidly on a lift or stand so the front wheel's off the ground and the fork's unloaded and at full travel. Loosen the fork drain screws but don't remove them just yet. If you're going to change the fork oil, get the Mity-Vac set to vacuum, with the drilled end of a Bic pen cap stuffed in the end of the hose. Quickly remove the drain screw on one side and "screw" in the Bic cap. Once it's securely in place, suck the fork oil out with the Mity-Vac. Reset the tool to pressure, fill the reservoir with the correct quantity of fresh oil (plus that extra ounce) and pump it in. The trick is to get the hose out of the drain screw hole without leaking fork oil back out. Usually a quick thumb or finger will do the trick, but keeping very light pressure on the fitting as you remove it helps. Quickly replace the drain screw and repeat the same thing on the other side. If you lose a drop or two in process, don't panic, the fork won't know the difference. Once the bike is on deck again, straddle it and work the front end up and down a bit to purge air. Then test ride for real. The clunk should be history.

PROJECT 23 • INSTALLING A CARTRIDGE-FORK EMULATOR VALVE

Time: 4 to 6 hours

Tools: Torque wrench, flat file, 0 to 25-millimeter micrometer, drill, 5/16-inch drill bit, air impact wrench and air supply (optional), 6-inch-deep 6-millimeter Allen socket, soft-jawed vise, solvent, soft brush, clean rags, sockets for fork pinch bolts, wrenches and Allens to remove fender, funnel, Ratio-Rite or graduated baby bottle, lift or stand, and tiedowns

Talent:

Tab: $$$

Tinware: Race Tech emulators and fork springs, new fork seals, possibly fork bushings, fork oil (Race Tech), snap-ring retainers, possibly drain screws with sealing washers, damper rod Allen screws, and blue #242 Loctite

Tip: Heavy cruisers and dressers benefit from this upgrade as much or more than the lighter bikes

PERFORMANCE GAIN: Quantum leap in ride quality and handling

COMPLEMENTARY MODIFICATION: Upgraded brakes and quality rear shocks

Good suspension and Harley-Davidson are terms rarely used in the same sentence. Prior to the introduction of the cartridge-forked Sportster 1200S and the Buell line, Harley front suspension was all of the older damper-rod design and at least a generation behind current top-shelf suspension design. Sure it works adequately for most, but if you really ride a Harley hard, that design's inadequate damping and soft springs leave your bike bobbing and weaving like a drunken sailor.

The traditional ways to improve these forks were to add heavier fork oil or stiffer springs. Often all that really did was turn the front end into a pogo stick or a jack hammer. The best solution was to swap for a fork of a better design, which is way too expensive for most of us. There is another way, however: Convert your existing fork to a cartridge design, or at least an emulation of one.

Race Tech's Gold Valve Emulator is a variable-pressure valve that, when installed, basically replaces one

1 The closest thing cartridge fork, i terms of function if expense, is a pair of these little devils. Race Tech's Go Valve emulators transform stock H-D fork's ability to its job. Coupled with a set proper springs, it makes so much difference you'll hav hard time believing it's yo old front end.

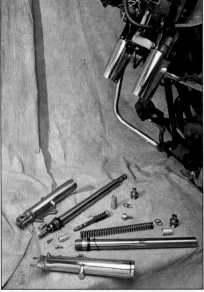

2 Don't think it's a in proposition, however. While th installation isn't rock science, it's not for the mechanically challenged e If you're going to tear dow the forks to swap for chro lower legs (like this dresse to lower it (or for any oth reason), you may as well install the Emulators. Just follow the excellent instru that come with the fork ki be prepared to scatter fro end parts all over.

3 Because the sto front forks are made in Japan, yo need at least one metric to long 6-millimeter Allen bit. American tool you'll need is the air gun that bit's attached to. Without these partners in crime, fork disassembly is nearly impossible. With them, ne simple.

function the damper rod has and makes your fork work much like the more modern cartridge-type forks.

The emulator takes care of compression damping, a task covered by the damping rod on the stock fork. Rebound damping, which is a more constant function since it deals with returning the mass of the front end to its original location, can be dealt with by the rod.

Compression damping is the one that has to cope with most of the road's surprises. It has to be more flexible in its abilities. That's where the Gold Valve Emulator comes into its own. Using an adjustable shim stack to tailor the day-to-day compression damping, it also provides a "safety valve" of sorts for the chuck holes in life. The stack is spring-loaded and will get the hell out of the way of all that fork oil rushing away from nasty jolts.

The result is a much smoother, more controlled ride. The superior damping allows the addition of stiffer springs, which eliminate the mushy feel of the stocker. The neat thing is they make Emulators for all Evo H-D forks: 39-millimeter, 41-millimeter, and even the old-style 35-millimeter forks.

To install a set of Emulators, you will need a bike lift (or a couple of jack stands) to get the front wheel off the ground, a shop manual, and the instructions that come with the kit. Remove the front wheel, speedo drive, brakes, and everything else until the fork tubes are out of the triple clamps. If you have an impact gun, use it to remove the Allen bolts out of the lower legs. If you don't have an air impact, remove the fork tube caps (be careful, they are spring loaded) and have a friend jam a broom handle, or its equivalent, down on the spring as hard as possible and then remove the Allen bolts.

When you have finished taking your fork apart, you will have a workbench covered. Look the parts over carefully because there's no future in reusing damaged or worn-out pieces. Another important thing to do is check the fork tubes for stone-chip damage. Take a clean, soft cloth and slowly wipe the fork as you search for burrs that snag the cloth. If you find any, use a very fine grade of emery paper and carefully buff the nick smooth. If you don't do this, you've wasted your time installing new fork seals; they'll end up getting torn up by the fork tubes and will then allow fluid to leak out. During the course of the inspection you'll often find the Teflon coating on the fork bushings worn away. If any brass shows on the bushings, they must be replaced.

A look at the Emulator from the bottom gives away all the secrets. When the fork compresses, the fluid is forced through the three orifices in the valve. These orifices are pressurized by a spring-loaded shim that creates more pressure than the damper rod can, slowing the compression up in proportion to the size of the bump. When the fork rebounds, the valve does the same thing in reverse. A really neat idea.

For the next step in the installation, you'll need a drill, a 5/16-inch bit, and a de-burring tool. Drill out the larger (compression) holes in the damper rods and be sure to de-burr all of the surfaces because one loose metal sliver could damage your fork internally. Once you are done drilling, begin to reassemble your fork, but before you install the spring, place the Emulator on top of the damper rod with the adjuster facing up. For most bikes you should set the adjuster at four complete turns.

Generally, stock H-D spring rates are too soft by as much as 50 percent. Since the wheel travel is now under control, it's not only possible but advisable to increase spring rates up to the range of 1.87–2.10 pounds per inch, or perhaps more on heavier bikes. (When in doubt about which spring to choose, contact the boys at Race Tech.) No "band-aid" progressive rates required here either. When damping works, so can the spring. If you install heavier-rate springs, you get back some of the travel that the soft springs cost you, the bike doesn't nose-dive so much under braking, and it flat out feels better. Make sure you set preload via the provided spacers. Cut them to allow about 1 1/4 inches of suspension sag when you hold the bike upright and sit on it. This may take some experimenting and trial assembly. Be patient. Once you've got it, your fork will work much better than if you don't.

Pull the springs and add some fluid. Bleed each leg by gently cycling the tube up and down in the slider a few times. Then set the correct fluid level with the leg compressed and the spring still out.

Gently replace the springs and reassemble the fork as per the shop manual. Pay particular attention to torque figures for the pinch bolts and axle and do it in the proper sequence—from the bottom up. The Race Tech kit instructions include information on how to fine-tune compression damping with the gold valve and rebound with fork oil viscosity. In the end that's the neat thing about this setup: It's totally tunable to your riding requirements.

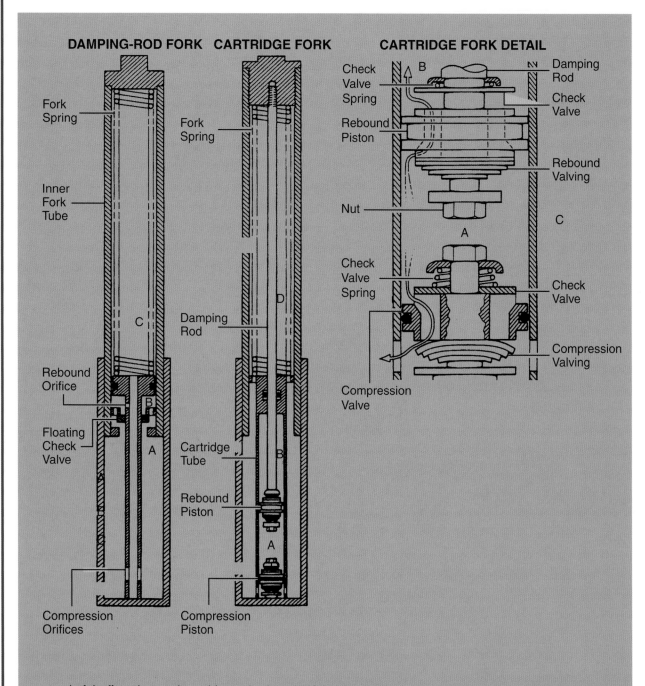

DAMPING-ROD FORK

Fork Spring

Inner Fork Tube

Rebound Orifice

Floating Check Valve

Compression Orifices

CARTRIDGE FORK

Fork Spring

Damping Rod

Cartridge Tube

Rebound Piston

Compression Piston

CARTRIDGE FORK DETAIL

Check Valve Spring

Rebound Piston

Nut

Check Valve Spring

Compression Valve

Damping Rod

Check Valve

Rebound Valving

Check Valve

Compression Valving

Cartridge forks offer much more sophisticated damping than damping rod forks. Two separate stacks of metal and rubber shims control rebound and compression damping seperately, providing highly tunable, controlled action.

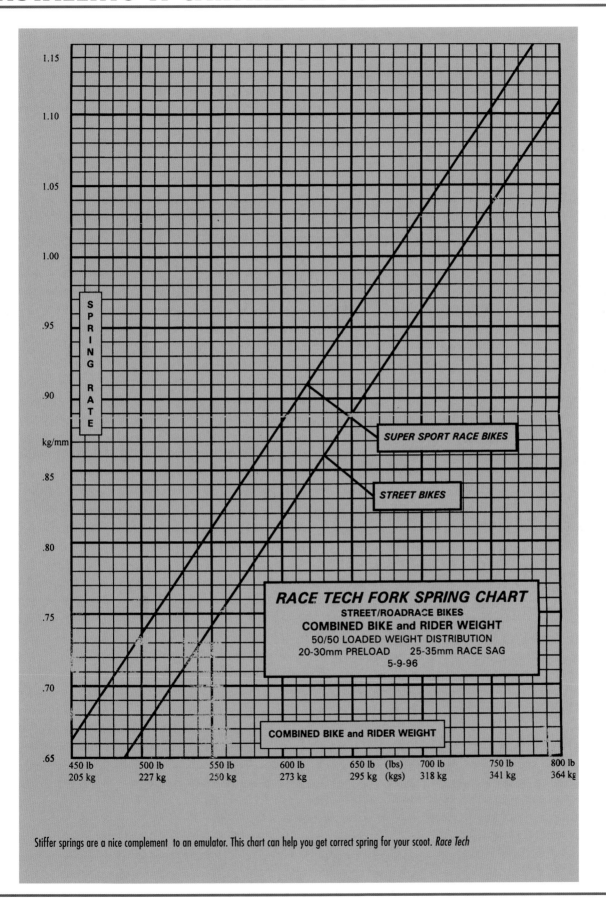

SPRING RATE

SUPER SPORT RACE BIKES

STREET BIKES

RACE TECH FORK SPRING CHART
STREET/ROADRACE BIKES
COMBINED BIKE and RIDER WEIGHT
50/50 LOADED WEIGHT DISTRIBUTION
20-30mm PRELOAD   25-35mm RACE SAG
5-9-96

COMBINED BIKE and RIDER WEIGHT

| 450 lb | 500 lb | 550 lb | 600 lb | 650 lb (lbs) | 700 lb | 750 lb | 800 lb |
| 205 kg | 227 kg | 250 kg | 273 kg | 295 kg (kgs) | 318 kg | 341 kg | 364 kg |

Stiffer springs are a nice complement to an emulator. This chart can help you get correct spring for your scoot. *Race Tech*

PROJECT 24 • RETROFITTING 1200S CARTRIDGE FORKS AND SHOCKS

 Time: 4 to 6 hours

 Tools: Lift or stand, tiedowns, torque wrench, flat file, 0 to 25-millimeter micrometer, drill, 5/16-inch drill bit, air impact wrench and air supply (optional), 6-inch-deep 6-millimeter Allen socket, soft-jawed vise, solvent, soft brush, clean rags, sockets for fork pinch bolts, wrenches and Allens to remove fender, funnel, and Ratio-Rite or graduated baby bottle

 Talent:

 Tab: $$$-$$$$$ (fork only) or $$$$ (rear shocks)

 Tinware: Fork dust shields, 1200S fork legs (and triple clamps if you have a 1987 or older model), 1200S shocks (optional, and for XL and FXR models only)

 Tip: You can have even these fine suspenders upgraded by Race Tech

PERFORMANCE GAIN: On smooth highways, a vastly superior ride, and on rough roads when you're in a hurry, an immeasurable improvement

COMPLEMENTARY MODIFICATION: Brake upgrades

1 This ordinary rear shock is less than wonderful when the going gets tough. The damping, marginal when new, generally goes away completely in less than 20,000 miles.

All Harley forks (except those in the new 1200S Sportster) are a damper-rod design. Damper rods control the rate of acceleration as the wheel moves up and down by means of a fixed series of holes drilled in the rod in strategic locations and to specific sizes through which the fork oil is forced. Both compression damping and rebound damping are controlled in this manner. It's simple and can be very effective but is often limiting. On most Harley forks, the damper-rod holes are of a certain size and in a certain location and consequently have little or no adaptability. What you get is what you're stuck with—good, bad, or ugly.

The 1200S Sportster got a fork of the cartridge design. As used on the 1200S, this is an inherently superior setup (compared to older Harley forks) for several reasons. It allows independent adjustment of rebound and compression damping, offers more oil capacity for fine-tuning the damping characteristics, and employs lighter, stronger springs. They work better, and they're adjustable.

The 1988 and later "narrow-glide" models (having a conventional Showa front fork as opposed to the Wide Glide 41-millimeter), both Sportster and Big Twin, come stock with the 39-millimeter fork, and it's a snap to swap the leg assemblies alone for a fork conversion to the 1200S cartridge fork. These Evo models from 1984 to 1987 have 35-millimeter tubes and can be retrofitted with the cartridge fork with a bolt-on change of triple trees and leg assemblies.

The 1200S rear shocks offer benefits similar to those of the cartridge fork plus the unique value of the reservoir (bottle). The bottle does for the shocks pretty much what an oil cooler does for an engine—prevent overheating. Carry a passenger, run at high speed, find a real bumpy road—any or all of the above—and the shocks will not fade, pogo, or lose their damping.

These superb shocks are pretty much an FXR and Sportster exclusive, however, as they won't work on Dynas or dressers, and Softails continue to go their own way with extendo-shocks under the frame. Mounting

2 A better initial spring rate and superior damping that's adjustable for both rebound and compression make the bottle (remote reservoir) shocks from the 1200S the best performing units in Harley history. Their versatility and polished road behavior give aftermarket shocks a run for their money. Adjustments are simple as well, requiring no tools and less than a minute to tailor to your riding requirement.

3 There are an abundance of things you want to get right in any swap involving fork legs or triple trees. Not the least of these is that the tubes are exactly the same height as they protrude from the top tree. WD-40 cuts a lot of friction and gives a little protection to the new legs as you slide them home. Once that part is set, you must go through a particular torque sequence to button it all down. Start at the bottom with the axle, then torque the axle caps and lower tree pinch bolts, top tree bolts, and fender. Check for binding after you tighten each assembly. If the triple clamp swings freely, move on to the next. If not, loosen and retorque.

these bottle shocks on Sportsters back to 1982 is a basic no-brainer but is not necessarily so on FXRs. It's also worth noting that the shock's mounted angle has a great effect on ride quality and perceived "stiffness." This means that on early (pre-1987) FXRs and 1981 and older XL models you may notice a considerably firmer ride because the shocks sit more straight-up.

Here's a brief list of components needed for the basic conversion:

For 1988 and later models, you need one each of the following—#45943-96 right leg assembly, # 45944-96 left leg assembly, #54552-96 right shock, #54542-96 left shock, and maybe a few more parts like the ones listed below.

For 1987 and earlier models, you need the parts listed above plus the following: #4029A pinch bolt, #6701 washer, #7038 lock washer, #7783 nut, #43895-87A axle, #6590HW washer, #7068 lock washer, #7845

axle nut, #45563-87 lower stem (triple clamp), #45739-87 top triple clamp, #4460 bolt (or #4453 bolt, tapped for chrome cover #45668-90), #6655 washer, two # 4351 pinch bolts, and two #4047 upper pinch bolts.

Needless to say, don't even try this without a shop manual. Also, here's some precautionary advice. Prop the motorcycle up securely on a stand that allows both wheels to be dangled in the air. Work slowly, methodically, and be careful!

You must modify the 1200S shock bushings to fit the U-channel lower shock mounts on early FXR frames. Press out the shock bushings slowly so they don't fly across the room when freed. Measure the bottom bushing carefully to get a snug fit on the lower mount.

Now cut them. The bottom bushing must be cut on both sides, the top on the outside only. A hacksaw will work, but be sure to avoid damaging either the rubber or the spacer portion of the bushing. When

4 After a fork swap (or anything else) that involves replacing the triple trees, the neck (steering head) bearing tension will need to be set. Called *fall away* in Hog Speak, it literally amounts to setting tension on the bearing adjuster so that once the front wheel is nudged an inch from dead ahead straight, it will fall away to either side equally. This is critical to steering performance, so take plenty of time and be precise with the adjustment. Then check it again after a few hundred miles. The procedure is described in detail in the shop manual—make sure it gets the attention it deserves.

5 The object of the exercise manifests itself here. Rebound damping is the function that gets the tire back on track, literally! No tarmac no traction. Take the time to feel out the most secure settings for your riding style, and two months later when you try to ride your buddy's standard suspension Hog as hard as you can now ride your own, you'll wonder how you ever got by without these forks.

6 Where you normally find a drain screw, you now discover the joys of "dial-a-ride." Call 1-900-Boogie, and a couple of clicks away (in both senses of the word), you'll realize that forks don't have to bounce over, mush through, or jackhammer to death. Simply put, if rebound damping helps put the wheel back on the road, the right compression damping keeps the wheel there in the first place. And fixed damping rates simply can't cover as many contingencies as the adjustable type.

you push the modified bushing back into the eye of the shock, remember that the thick part of the top bushing must be next to the frame. In order to clear the larger diameter of the bottle shock top, it may also be necessary to cut out a portion of the lower part of the rear fender rails (struts).

After blocking up the front end, strip the old fork as per the service manual. Calipers, front wheel, and fender come off regardless, but don't get carried away. If you haven't already, now is the time to disconnect the battery, protect the gas tank with a blanket or thick towel, and find some short bungee cords to tie off subassemblies as they are removed. The secret here is to remove subassemblies, big chunks if

you will, with as little disassembly as possible. Brake calipers are two bolts each, the headlamp assembly is two bolts, the handlebar and instrument cluster is two nuts, and so on. You do not have to take every nut off of every bolt or undo every cable and wire to get most components off. It may not be pretty, but it's efficient. Work from bottom to top. When the subassemblies are safely out of the way, loosen all pinch bolts on both triple trees, loosen the center stem bolt, remove the fork tube caps, and remove the fork legs.

If you have to change the triple clamps (older models) and the old top clamp has wiring running through the center hole and you want to avoid spending your life rewiring, simply cut the top triple clamp with a saw or rotary cutter to free the wires. (Use a screwdriver to protect the wires from damage, and use eye protection to protect yourself.) You can "Wiz-Wheel" around your wiring problem in about 2 minutes flat.

Older models lack a fork stop that's compatible with the new lower triple clamp. After some test fitting and measuring of the new clamp, weld on a fork stop of round stock, cut, bent, and painted to match the frame.

There's also a fork-lock tab on the frame that needs to be either bent out of the way or cut off. If you bend the tab carefully, you can still use it for locking but test-fit the upper and lower triple clamps to ensure that you have adequate clearance and absolutely no obstruction to smooth side-to-side movement. Leave the center stem bolt only finger tight. Remount the handlebar and instrument cluster and the headlight subassembly.

This is also an opportunity to cleanly reroute wires and double-check the ground wires that screw onto the triple clamps. Likewise, if you need to service or replace steering neck bearings or do any other "spring cleaning" chores you've been saving up for this much-neglected area of the machine, here's your chance.

Fit the new legs into the clamps using a little WD-40 or light oil to ease the task and to help prevent scratches on brand-new parts.

Once the legs are fitted, torque the top pinch bolts only to 30–35 foot-pounds and make sure that the distance from the top of the fork leg to the top of the upper triple clamp measures 1.735 to 1.745 inches. Remember to reuse the original right-side spacer and fit a new foam dust seal on the speedo drive. Then mount the wheel. The new axle should be a snug push fit by hand, without pounding. Torque the front axle nut to 50–55 foot-pounds. Install the pinch bolt in the right lower leg and torque to 21–27 foot-pounds. Install the front fender and torque each fastener to 9–13 foot-pounds. Do it in this order.

Install the front brake line to the underside of the lower clamp, then mount the calipers, and torque the caliper bolts to 25–30 foot-pounds. Before you proceed, take a minute to check all your work and make sure you haven't missed tightening anything.

With the front end still blocked up, put a strip of masking tape on the fender and fabricate a pointer mounted dead ahead of the bike on the floor. If the steering head bearings are properly adjusted, they should literally "fall- away" an inch, either way, from straight ahead, if the fork is gently nudged. If it moves more, tighten the stem bolt; if it moves less, loosen it. Once fall-away is on the mark, tighten the Allen bolt in the top triple clamp to 30–35 foot-pounds to trap the stem bolt. Now, torque the lower stem bolts to 30–35 foot-pounds. Re-check the fall-away. Can you tell this is crucial?

With the bike on deck again and you sitting on it, check the fork action. It should be smooth and linear. If not, loosen all the fasteners in the fender, triple trees, and the axle, then re-torque from the bottom up, testing as you go, until you find the bind. (Ninety percent of the time, if there's a problem, it turns out to be improper axle torque procedure or a tweaked front fender, but fork braces are known offenders as well.) Then set the spring preload (not to be confused with damping, okay?) so that the fork settles about 1 1/2 inches with a rider onboard and the shocks drop not quite an inch. The fork preload adjuster is the bolt on top of each fork cap. The shock preload adjuster is a collar below the spring.

Find the adjuster on the lower fork legs. They adjust compression (bump) damping. Turn the adjusters clockwise until they stop (firmest setting) and then back off eight clicks. This is your base-line setting. Do both legs exactly the same.

The top fork adjusters control rebound (bounce-back) damping. They sit on top of the spring preload bolts that are above the fork caps. Adjust these clockwise to full-stiff as well and then back off 13 clicks. Again, both legs need to be adjusted to identical settings.

The top shock adjusters are for rebound. In other words, the location of rebound adjustments for the shocks is opposite that of the fork. The adjustment procedure is the same, however: Turn them clockwise to full-stiff and then back off, in this case, six clicks.

Compression damping adjustment for the rear shocks is done by means of a little thumb wheel at the base of each shock body below the five-position spring preload adjuster. From full-stiff (all the way clockwise), back off eight clicks. *All settings must match on both shocks.*

You can alter these settings as you see fit for your particular style or riding conditions, but do it in small increments of one or two clicks at a time. Rotating clockwise stiffens damping on all adjusters, and rotating counterclockwise softens it. No two riders seem to agree on specific settings for "perfect" suspension, but generally the idea is to keep the tire in contact with the ground. Compression damping should be supple enough to soak up a bump without jarring the rider, and rebound should be firm enough to force the wheel back to the ground as soon as possible, without it bouncing back.

(One tip on setting spring rates for FXRs: Leave the rear shock spring preload on its softest setting and crank the fork spring up as stiff as it will go. The fact is FXRs and Dynas are nose heavy, and heavier outright, than Sportsters. That's why the stiff fork. The different angle of the rear shock is why you want the rear springs softer, or with less preload, on FXR models.)

The transformation is complete, and this should be one comfortable, agile, 600-pound gorilla.

SUSPENSION AND CHASSIS

PROJECT 25 • LOWERING FORKS

One of the signature style points of Harleys is their long, low stature. Since Big Twins in particular have a center of gravity somewhere between your ankles, the result is an overwhelmingly attractive sensation during a ride. If low is good, lower may be even better, huh?—especially, if you're "inseam impaired" and need the lowest ride possible to feel in control.

The factory addressed this when they introduced the Low Rider as an official model decades ago. More recent confirmation came when they introduced the Hugger version of the Sportster. You think that bike was intended for basketball players to ride?

Bear in mind that there's a limit below which you should not stoop. For instance, to try to lower a Hugger already lowered by the factory is to court disaster. Ride quality can disappear and leave you thinking you're aboard a rigid-framed antique. Ground clearance goes away to the point that

1 Both ends of your Harley can be lowered. In most cases, both should be, preferably at the same time. Instead of just slapping shorter shocks on the rear, lower the front too. One of the most popular options for doing so is the White Brothers kit. It flat-out gets the job done in either of two possible increments, 1 1/4-inch drop or 2-inch drop. Don't be tempted to go all the way to 2 inches without giving it serious thought. Dropping the front end that much is a radical move. Since the White Brothers kit allows for later changes, if you simply must slam the bike to the deck, start off sensibly. Notice two black triangular metal brackets shown right below the two bottles of fork oil. These brackets are the cheapest way to lower the rear end of every Harley model except Softails.

some parts of the primary and footpegs drag on every turn. Big Twins can be even worse. Some have been dropped to the point that they are virtually unrideable as regular motorcycles. Instead they take a city block to make a U-turn and use matchbooks for kickstands. Any curve in a road becomes an object of fear and loathing and requires way-in-advance-planning. That was never the point. All lowering should do is enhance the qualities of a well-ridden Harley.

FORK LOWERING USING A KIT

When you get ready to install a fork lowering kit, such as ones from White Brothers or Progressive Suspension, be careful. Remember that when the front wheel is removed, the balance of the bike changes, so be sure everything's secure. Once it's safe, do the following:

Use a simple scissors jack to raise the front end 4 to 6 inches off the deck.

With the motorcycle raised and secured, remove the front wheel, brakes, and fender.

Drain the fork oil into a container.

Remove the fork-tube caps. Fork-tube caps can be hard to remove, but don't clamp them in a vise. Instead, use the bottom triple clamp to hold the

2 This photo gives you some idea of what the assembled innards of the lowering kit for the forks looks like. All White Brothers suspension kits come with good, thorough instructions, and since there are many variations depending on your personal desires, detailed information is difficult to offer in this short overview. Suffice it to say, good suspension depends on good installation. Any time you modify forks and shocks, the steering and ride quality of your Harley will change, sometimes to an extreme. There's a reason a bike that's been lowered is often referred to as "slammed."

3 Look closely at these two different treatments of Sportster forks. The set on the left is clearly lower than the forks on the right. The actual measurement is only 2 inches of difference, although it looks like more. The headlight on the left, for instance, is hanging from the bottom tree, enhancing the illusion of low. The chrome encased tall risers are hard to miss as well, making it look like there's a lot of space between the top of the forks and the bottom of the low bars. If you want to lower the bike for look more than function, these types of tricks will serve you well.

tube while you loosen the fork-tube cap with a wrench. Then drop the fork tube out and carefully remove the top cap. Those caps are under pressure, so be ready in case it springs out at you.

Use an air-powered impact gun to remove the bolt holding the damping-rod assembly to the lower slider. (If you don't have an air impact wrench, you'll fight the thing all day. The only alternative is to stuff a broom handle or length of electrical conduit down the leg and attempt to hold the damper rod while the screw—if you're lucky—comes out.) Incidentally, the damper retainer is a metric Allen screw that requires a longer bit to reach inside the fork slider.

Once the bolt is removed, the damper rod will slide out of the top of the fork leg, complete with some oil left clinging to the springs.

To lower the front end 1-inch, first slide the steel collar that comes in the kit onto the damper rod and then slide the short spring from the kit on the damper tube. The steel collar is drilled and tapped and comes with a set screw that tightens the collar to the damper tube to prevent movement. You want 2 inches? Then, you'll need to use the spring supplied with the kit and the stock spring instead of the steel collar.

Kits usually come with a piece of plastic PVC pipe that you cut to length in two equal pieces for the main-fork-spring preload. It's best to cut the pipe in a lathe or with a power saw, but if you can be neat with the cut, a hacksaw will do. Typically, you'll want a 1-inch preload on the fork spring. To determine how long the spacer needs to be, clamp the fork leg back in the lower triple clamp and tighten the pinch bolt. Next, place the flat washer from the kit on top of the spring; this is the time to add the fork oil. Measure from the flat washer to the top of the fork tube and subtract the length of the fork-tube cap that threads into the tube. Add 1 inch (the suggested preload) to this measurement for the correct length of the spacer.

Reassemble and repeat for the other fork leg.

When everything's put together, double-check all torque, especially the lower triple clamp and pump the fork a couple of times to check for binding. Remember, tighten axle first, then slider pinch bolt, and so on, as specified in the shop manual for your model.

FORK LOWERING WITH A DIFFERENCE

Race Tech has come up with a lowering kit with a difference. The difference? It includes the company's excellent cartridge-fork Emulators. (The

Emulator is a tunable valve to control compression damping, eliminating that function from the damping rod; see Project 23: Installing a Cartridge-Fork Emulator Valve.) The result is that you get improved damping along with the lowering. Emulators are not just for sportbike riders. The difference between a 500-mile day on good suspension or on bad suspension is the difference between wanting to go do it again the next day or not.

The kit is ingenious, yet simple. Your fork-leg length or extension is governed by how far the tube can come out of the leg. Stock top-out springs are 1 inch long, so the leg is restricted 1 inch. The Race Tech kit provides you with additional top-out springs (1 or 2 inches) to restrict how far out your tube can go, lowering your fork 1 or 2 inches. The kit goes on to improve your suspension by supplying Emulators for each leg. A set of supplied fork springs and a preload spacer do the rest.

To install the kit, grab the shop manual, disassemble the forks by the book, then proceed as follows:

While things are apart, check the Teflon-coated fork bushings; if you see any brass, replace them.

You will need to remove the 6-millimeter Allen bolt at the bottom of the fork leg assembly to get the damping rod and bottom spring out.

On 41-millimeter Wide Glide forks (dressers, Softails, and Dyna Wide Glide models) you will need to use an included spacer on top of each damping rod before installing the Emulator.

The stock top-out spring is 1 inch long. Each additional spring added will lower the bike 1 more inch. If you use both included springs, you will lower the bike 2 inches.

Use a fork-seal installation tool to fit the new fork seals. These tools are pretty expensive, but a decent substitute can be made from 2-inch diameter PVC pipe. Sandwich the old seal between the new one and the pipe to prevent damage as you install.

Install the Race Tech fork spring in place of the stock H-D spring. Don't be fooled by the appearance; the stocker is softer and sags much more than the new unit.

Measure for the length of the preload spacer. Be sure to lift the fork tube up to its maximum height and then measure the distance from the top of the spring to the top of the tube. Now measure the length of the fork cap, subtract it from the first figure you recorded, and add 38 millimeters (1.496 inches) for the proper preload.

Cut the included spacer material to length (with a pipe cutter if possible). Verify your measurements and be sure that there is proper 1 to 1 1/2-inch preload before you proceed. Remove the spring again.

Add fluid (usually 5 weight or Race Tech's own) until you reach the proper level in the fork tube.

Carefully pull the leg and then collapse it again a few times to bleed the air bubbles out.

Install the fork springs, spacer and fork cap, and the fork leg is ready to go back on your bike.

Repeat for the other leg.

Install both legs, making sure to tighten everything according to the sequence in the shop manual for your machine and to the specified torque.

Put the assembled bike back on the ground and double-check suspension sag when you're sitting upright on it. If you have 1 1/2 inches or less, you're set.

PROJECT 26 • LOWERING THE SOFTAIL REAR

Time: 2 1/2 hours

Tools: Torque wrench, flat file, 0 to 25-millimeter micrometer, drill, 5/16-inch drill bit, air impact wrench and air supply (optional), 6-inch-deep 6-millimeter Allen socket, soft-jawed vise, solvent, soft brush, clean rags, sockets for fork pinch bolts, wrenches and Allens to remove fender, funnel, and Ratio-Rite or graduated baby bottle, lift or stand, and tiedowns—plus a small torch or heat gun

Talent:

Tab: $$$$

Tinware: Anti-sieze, Locktite, lowering kit

Tip: No matter how tempted you are, *don't* drop a full 2 inches right off the bat; try the lowered bike at 1 1/4 inches or so first to get used to the differences (and compromises) involved

PERFORMANCE GAIN: Stylish, easier to touch the ground for smaller riders

COMPLEMENTARY MODIFICATION: Lowering the forks

1 Softails need a longer shock for a lower look. Many companies, including Harley-Davidson, offer these shock assemblies. But once again for those who either aren't sure how low they want to go or don't want to throw away perfectly good shocks, White Brothers has a different solution. They sell what amounts to a replacement shaft section, both in fixed lengths and in adjustable length varieties. Removing the stock shaft to replace it with, for instance, the adjustable shaft, is about a 2-hour job involving removal of the stock shock, applying heat to the shaft, and unscrewing it from the shock body. Once you've gotten that far, it's a simple matter of screwing the shaft back into the stock shock and fitting it back on the scoot.

The simplest way to lower the rear of a Softail is to change to shorter rear shocks, but you can get it done by modifying the stock shocks with an "eyebolt" lowering kit. There's one little glitch in both of these approaches, however, and that is getting the stock shocks off. A regular socket doesn't fit the hidden nuts, and using an end wrench requires Hulk-sized arms. Fortunately, Snap On makes adapters (part No. SRES 24) that allow you to use a socket-wrench-type breaker bar for leverage but fit like a box wrench. With the proper tools in hand and access to a heat gun, begin, but first support the bike in a stable fashion; you'll be jacking the rear end up and down so make sure it's not "tipsy."

For the example in this section, we'll use the White Brothers Adjust-A-Ride kit. This kit uses threaded eyebolts that let you change the length of the shock, thus controlling the bike's height. The end of the eyebolt that mounts to the swingarm incorporates a Heim joint for added durability. The shock mounting

bolt is threaded into a boss on the frame, so you don't need to worry about getting to any hidden nuts. Once you get the original shocks out of the frame, proceed as follows:

Remove the shafts from the shock bodies, one at a time. A vise and some heat are a major help in getting the things unscrewed from the shock bodies.

Install the new adjustable shafts. Back off the jam nuts on the Adjust-a-Ride adjusters and set them to approximately 3/4 inch longer than the stock shafts were, if they weren't set already at their "as delivered" length.

Slip the rear of the shock in first, passing its eyebolt through the hole in the frame cross-member.

Raise the rear wheel up until the eyebolt holes on the front at the shocks line up with the mounting bolt boss on the frame.

Insert the eyebolts and torque all four mounting bolts to 120 foot-pounds.

Lower the bike to the ground; reset ride height (only if needed) after a brief test ride.

SUSPENSION AND CHASSIS

PROJECT 27 • LOWERING TWIN-SHOCK REAR ENDS

 Time: 1 1/2 hours

 Tools: Torque wrench, flat file, 0 to 25-millimeter micrometer, drill, 5/16-inch drill bit, air impact wrench and air supply (optional), 6-inch-deep 6-millimeter Allen socket, soft-jawed vise, solvent, soft brush, clean rags, sockets for fork pinch bolts, wrenches and Allens to remove fender, funnel, and Ratio-Rite or graduated baby bottle, lift or stand, and tiedowns—plus a small torch or heat gun

 Talent: ▮▮▮

 Tab: $–$$$$

 Tinware: Shorter shocks, anti-sieze, Loctite

 Tip: Use a jack to lift the rear end

 PERFORMANCE GAIN: Stylish, loss of handling clearance

COMPLEMENTARY MODIFICATION: Lower the forks

Lowering the rear of a twin-shock model is much easier than on a Softail, with the possible exception of the Dyna models. You've got to watch out for the belt guard slamming into the rear fender on those. Otherwise, with the bike secured and jacked up in the rear, do the following:

Remove the axle and spacers and let the tire and wheel sit on the deck; there's no reason to remove them completely.

Remove the shock bolts and the shocks, one side at a time.

Install each new shock.

Once both shocks and any additional mounts are in place and snugged up, stand back and "eye-ball" the shocks, making sure they are straight and not binding or hitting.

If everything looks good, go back and tighten everything using Loctite and a torque wrench to make sure they stay that way.

1 The preferred way to lower rear shocks is with shorter ones. This would seem to be as obvious as the photo, but some inseam impaired types want even more than short shocks will give. Swapping from 13.5- to 12-inch units, as shown here, makes about an inch difference at the saddle. A narrower, lower saddle can often make the difference between a flat-footed stance and tip-toes for some. Don't resort to those bolt-on "shock back" brackets. Once you've shortened the shocks, adding a set of shock back brackets alters the chassis geometry beyond reasonable limits. This can create handling problems, a buckboard ride, and plain old tank slapping instability. Low is cool, but don't be a fool.

2 The set of rear-end lowering brackets shown is for dresser models, but White Brothers makes them for almost all applications. While they are cheap and effective, they are not the preferred method, mainly because they affect rear geometry. Doing that can affect both the esoteric qualities of handling and pragmatic issues such as fitting saddlebags. Nevertheless, if you simply can't find shorter shocks that fit your budget and riding style or there's some reasonable reason that eliminates any other option, these are a good last resort.

SUSPENSION AND CHASSIS

PROJECT 28 • INSTALLING A TORSION-BAR SUSPENSION ON A SOFTAIL

 Time: 4 to 6 hours

 Tools: Torque wrench; lift or stand; small scissors jack; 1/2-, 3/4-, and 1 1/8-inch sockets; 7/16-inch swivel socket; 3/32-, 3/16-, and 3/8-inch Allens; anti-seize; and blue #242 Loctite

 Talent:

 Tab: $$$$ to $$$$$+

 Tinware: Sofspension or Sofspension II kit

 Tip: Pay particular attention to getting the spring rate of the torsion bar absolutely right for your riding habits and payload before you select a kit

PERFORMANCE GAIN: Smoother, more comfortable ride

COMPLEMENTARY MODIFICATION: Fork upgrade

Although Softails have cosmetic appeal, they punish their riders a bit due to the suspension's limited shock travel, poor damping calibration, and sluggish rebound reaction time. A Softail may react adequately to a single bump in the road, but multiple bumps and ripples or full-blown chuck holes overwhelm the suspension so badly that you could be on your head before you recover. That 1940s look gives 1950s results.

Here's a much better idea: a torsion-bar suspension system to fit the Softail chassis, such as the Sofspension kits from K.T. Components.

Torsion bars are simple springs that function just like coil springs. A torsion bar twists about its axis when a load is applied. The rate or stiffness is determined by the effective length and diameter of the bar. Torsion bars are linear springs. The rate does not change per unit of deflection. Longer bars are softer in rate, whereas shorter bars are stiffer. Similarly, larger diameter bars are stiffer in rate, whereas smaller bars are softer. A linear spring rate coupled with a re-

1 Probably the best favor you can do your Softail and yourself is to install the KT Components Sofspension, either in its original adjustable-ride-height form, as shown here, or the less expensive but equally well made nonadjustable version. This kit is as near as you're likely to get to a total fix of the designed-in defects present in the standard rear suspension. The key is the torsion bar spring, but the re-valved single shock included in this well-engineered solution also helps make a night-and-day difference in a Softail's ability to make things soft on your tail.

valved (for 50/50 damping rates) shock transform the ride quality as well as the suspension's capability.

As with any suspension system, you begin by determining the most workable spring rate for your application. Use the following as a guideline. A single rider up to 300 pounds just cruising on an un-lowered Softail Custom probably needs a "soft" torsion-bar. A single rider at 150 pounds on a high-performance, lowered Softail Custom should consider the "firm" bar. A two-up rider sport (primary rider at 185 pounds, passenger at 135 pounds) riding on a slightly lowered Softail Custom should consider a "medium" bar.

The chart presented with this project shows combinations of torsion-bar springs and levers that are frequently used in suspensions. The deflection and the angles 1 and 2 are measured from a reference line that is perpendicular to the applied load and passes through the center of the torsion bar. They are counted as "positive" when their relationship to the reference line is as shown in the diagram.

There are two flavors of Sofspension, the adjustable and the nonadjustable. The beauty of the adjustable setup is its ability to allow easy alterations to the ride height of the motorcycle. Even if you think

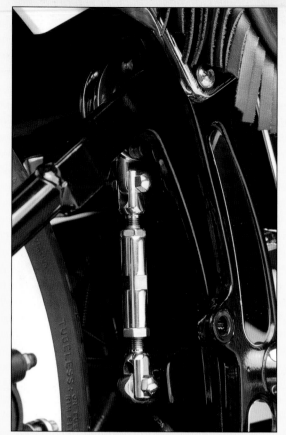

2 The chrome shock in the kit is just that, a proper shock absorber. It has a differently valved damper that, unlike the factory shocks, does not have springs inside and features more travel than the stocker as well.

3 The torsion bar, which lives under the rear fender and in front of the tire, is invisible when installed. If you opt for the adjustable version, the adjuster takes the form of a chromed turnbuckle linkage, unobtrusively located just inside the right frame member.

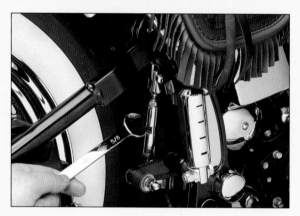

4 To set the ride height, you simply loosen the jam nut, crank the adjuster a few turns, lock it down again, and go. It couldn't be much simpler to get the benefit of vastly improved suspension performance—and the ability to raise or lower the bike at will.

you'll never want yours any different than it is right now, consider that the slammed sled you love is so low you can't carry a passenger without bottoming out on bottle caps. Or maybe you find yourself going 6 miles out of your way to avoid "speed bumps." Well, with the original Sofspension and a couple of minutes with a wrench, you can have it both ways—up for go, down for show. Think about it!

If you never had any intention of lowering your Softail in the first place because it's a Heritage and the wife would kill you or maybe since you refuse to sacrifice ground clearance for looks, you can get by with Sofspension II (nonadjustable) and save a few bucks in the bargain.

Replacing the progressively wound coil springs that support the rear suspension of all Softail models may be the best favor you ever did yourself. The big difference between the two styles of springs is that if it takes 200 pounds of pressure to compress a progressively wound coil 1 inch, then it might take another 400 pounds of pressure to compress it the next inch, and even *600* for the last fraction

of an inch (Softails don't have that much travel, sorry!). What that means is that as your bike begins to use the suspension travel that was designed into the chassis at the factory, it becomes increasingly harder and harder to compress until it's so hard to compress you'll think it really is a rigid frame as you get smacked in your tailbone. The torsion bar has a constant rate of compression; that is, its spring rate doesn't increase as it goes through its deflection, making it easier for your bike to use all of its rear wheel travel.

Typically, the torsion bar for a Springer or Softail Custom has an 0.880-inch diameter. Heavier relatives like the Fat Boy or Heritage get a 0.920-inch bar.

K.T. Components will be happy to advise you on spring rate, if you're still in doubt, and their enclosed instructions make installation of the Sofspension kit a no-brainer.

And while changing the springing medium to something sensible is a good move in and of itself, fixing the damping via an upgraded shock absorber allows the kit to really show its stuff.

SUSPENSION AND CHASSIS

PROJECT 29 • TAMING VIBRATION—SERVICING RUBBER ENGINE MOUNTS

 Time: 2 to 3 hours

 Tools: 1/2-, 9/16-, and 5/8-inch wrenches, the same size sockets, ratchet with a short extension, torque wrench, lift or stand, small scissors jack, WD-40, and chain lube, Tri-Flon, or equivalent

 Talent: ▮▮

 Tab: $$

 Tinware: Real high-milers may need new swingarm bushings (#47556-81), and no matter what, it's a good idea to have new nylon spacers (#47513-80) when you do the swingarm rubber mounts

 Tip: As long as you're in the neighborhood, it couldn't hurt to lube the adjustable stabilizer links at the Heim-joint with chain lube or Tri-Flon Teflon spray

 PERFORMANCE GAIN: A ride as smooth as a Dyna's (or at least as smooth as when the bike was new)

COMPLEMENTARY MODIFICATION: The rubber mounts on the oil tank (a mysterious source of vibration) are easily replaced, and you'd be surprised at the difference it makes

The very thing that makes FLT- and FXR-model Harleys so special is the rubber mounting system that isolates the engine and tranny from the chassis. As trouble-free and clever as these rubber mounts are, they don't last forever. If your once smooth-as-glass "Rubber-Glide" is beginning to feel like a paint shaker, it's time to think about swapping the old rubber mounts for new ones. If you've gone more than 50,000 to 60,000 miles on your rubber mounts, it's almost a certainty they'll need replacing.

The quickest way, aside from vibes, to tell if the time has come is to pop off the little chrome plugs in the diamond-shaped swingarm pivot covers and see how close to dead in the middle the ends of the pivot shaft are. If they're sagging and clearly off-center by more than about 5/16 inch, it's a clue. Some insist on ignoring this clue until the next comes knocking—literally. The mount, once it sags badly, is prone to shearing in two. You can't really blame it too much

1 If you feel a sharp, but not intense, "jackhammer" effect in a certain narrow rpm band, typically when you snap the throttle shut after a hard pull, you probably need to replace your bike's rubber mounts. Everybody seems to pay sufficient attention to the rubber mount you can see, the front "donut" on FLTs and FXRs. The two that are out of sight and out of mind need just as much checking, and they aren't all that much more difficult to service. Once you've pulled the chrome inspection cap/dust shield, you want to see the end of the pivot shaft sitting high and mighty, nearly centered in the hole. If it's not centered, especially if it's sagging toward the top, chances are you need to replace the mount.

2 After you've secured and jacked the bike up and unloaded the pivot, strip the diamond-shaped end caps off the bike and remove the mount. Often you'll find that the old mount turns out to be torn or shows bare metal from contact with the frame.

3 The pivot shaft itself has been through a few iterations. The early three-piece type, in the foreground, has a few ugly tendencies such as seizing, slipping, and snapping that make replacing it with the newest version, in the background, a smart move. Once you've accomplished all this servicing and updating, you're likely to find yourself amazed at the difference it makes in smoothness and handling.

because all that throttle whipping you've been doing, the on-and-off-the-gas transitions, the burn-outs, and even the foot-stompin' heavy panic stops, they hammer hard at the two pivot-mounted rubber biscuits.

Since they are basically constructed of a pair of heavy-duty metal washers sandwiching a thick vulcanized rubber donut, brutal treatment as well as time and tide, simply overwhelm one of the washers and rip it right off the rest of the assembly. You typically realize things have gotten to this stage when, as you roll off the throttle sharply, the broken piece judders and buzzes against the pivot shaft itself. Sometimes it's more noticeable when you get on the throttle sharply. Either way, the mount is torn and useless. The remaining pivot mount and the front isolator try to soldier on without their partner (two out of three ain't bad, right?), but it's not much use. And you may as well budget to replace all three musketeers, since if one is gone, the others are ready to retire as well.

Note: Early Evo FXRs and FLTs (1984 to 1986) have a three-piece pivot shaft that occasionally breaks while you're trying to replace rubber isolators. Budget for an updated version if yours is original and it's time for new rubbers. You can always take it back if you don't use it. The first FLTs (Shovel or Evo-engined to about midyear 1985), using the first version of the front "donut" isolator, would sometimes collapse the donut after high mileage, under heavy loads, or when flogged mercilessly. You knew when this happened because the bracket would rattle loudly when it contacted the frame. New mounts from the factory don't seem to have this problem. They wear out, sure enough, but they don't collapse. Don't let the difference fool you. It helps sell a lot of high-dollar aftermarket donuts.

DYNAS

As good as the rubber mount system is on the FLT and FXR machines, the one on the Dynas is even better. It uses a different set of rubber mounts entirely. These are real automotive-looking and appear to have a service life far in excess of the FXR and FLT setup. That said, they can shear, and hints that this has happened include bottoming out and banging the lower rear mount when the bike rolls over a sharp-edged bump—the edge of a chuck hole, for instance. If your Dyna suddenly develops a vibration after a close encounter of that kind, that's the first thing to check. And on Dyna's it's easy. Simply crawl under the bike and look at the rear mount located centrally behind the engine and directly in front of the back tire. If it's damaged or sheared, it's due to be renewed.

BUELLS

The "Isoplaner" system used on Buells is a sophisticated version of the FXR and FLT design, differing principally in that instead of the engine sitting on the front mount, it hangs from it. The loads on that front mount and the zeal with which Buells are often ridden foretell a need for frequent replacement. Also, Buells have a casting that attaches to the front head as part of the system. It says "Do Not Remove." Don't unless you have to. The factory torque sequence/process is touchy, and you wouldn't want the bolts to come loose or snap off at an inopportune time—it drops the engine instantly.

Time: 1 to 2 hours

Tools: 7/16-, 1/2-, 9/16-, 5/8-inch wrenches, 3/16-inch Allen, Torx wrenches, screwdrivers, drain pan

Talent: 👤👤

Tab: $$$

Tinware: The arm/brace and a tranny gasket (#36801-87B)

Tip: You shouldn't need to remove the clutch cable, but it may help to give it some slack at the adjuster

PERFORMANCE GAIN: Improved stability during full-throttle acceleration and hard cornering

COMPLEMENTARY MODIFICATION: Double-check wheel alignment and lube the stabilizer links

1 The extra stiffness offered by the Carlini Torque Arm or the H-D Race Brace helps keep the engine and transmission inline and takes the Dyna to a whole new level of handling prowess. For early Dynas without the ribbed primary and for virtually any 90-plus-horsepower Big Twin, this type of add-on brace is a must. There's actually a bit more to it than simply installing the shiny arm itself, however. To completely address the issue, you need to substitute some grade 5 crank case bolts with grade 8 fasteners and other details. Once dealt with, the payoff is commensurate with the elbow grease and dollars involved.

2 Tying the cone to the tranny effectively makes a stiff box out of the open-ended gearbox, inner primary, and crankcase. The increased stiffness can be felt in the handling department. It also prevents cracks in the inner primary, and it looks good as well.

3 Installation of the Torque Arm or Race Brace is pretty straightforward. Be sure to carefully route the ignition wires into the provided groove, and realize that certain exhaust systems and foot controls don't get along with the thing very well. Rest assured, though—H-D has done as much as they can, offering 8 different versions of the kit, as well as 3 exhaust bracket adaptors and 12 transmission offset kits.

Unlike "short primary" FXRs and FLTs where the tranny bolts to the engine and the rubber mounts form a three-point triangle, the Dyna Glide H-Ds employ rubber mounts in line along the center of the drivetrain.

Consequently, under load, the engine and tranny want to flex in their mounts. On Dynas, the problem is compounded because the transmission is not directly connected to the engine. Essentially, the design amounts to a box with only three sides, and even at stock power levels the primary has its work cut out for it in keeping the other two in line. Add lots of load in the form of additional torque or horsepower, and it's no surprise that the inner primary case can become the weak link in the drivetrain, turning a nice smooth machine into a real squirrel under pressure.

Fact is, on 1991 to 1994 Dynas the inner primary case has been known to crack at the bosses where the case attaches to the motor. One of the reasons that 1995 and newer Dynas incorporate all that dandy ribbing in the inner primary case is to beef up the inherent weakness of the stock "three-sided box."

Just the same, if you ride a Harley-Davidson Dyna Glide and have any intentions of installing more power,

you should also consider installing the Torque Arm/Race Brace. This arm connects the bike's motor and transmission together opposite the primary case, forming a far more rigid box consisting of the motor as the front side, the primary as one side, the tranny as the back side, and the torque arm as the last side. The extra reinforcement relieves the stress transferred to the inner primary case by the rubber-mounted Dyna's motor and transmission during hard acceleration and cornering.

Don't forget, to install this mod, you will need a transmission end cover gasket and gear oil in addition to the hardware included in the Torque Arm kit. Look before you leap on the exhaust pipe issue as well because some won't work with the Torque Arm. Oil pump covers won't work with it either, and be sure to note that the kits are different for bikes with forward controls than for those with regular controls.

Once you've got the right one, whether from Carlini as Torque Arm or Harley as Race Brace, this rose, by any name, comes with very thorough instructions, making the installation a matter of time, not gray matter.

SECTION FIVE
TIRES, WHEELS, AND BRAKES

This is the deep end of the pool in more ways than one. While there's not much doubt that cutting-edge tires and brakes are one of the best upgrades you can lust after, A) they don't come cheap, and B) they frequently involve rethinking the wheels they're attached to. Add the trend to wide rubber and rims, and you've got the makings of a major re-engineering project on your hands. Sometimes this "wide drive" mania, applied to modifying a stock, factory Evo gets all the way into moving the engine and trans over to the right side of the chassis by as much as 1/4 inch. Look good it may; steer well, it may not. It's beyond the scope of this book to cover all these "engineered" variations of wheel, tire, and brake combos. Beyond certain tried and true options, you are sailing in dangerous waters. This section, then, is about some of those tried and true options.

TIRES, WHEELS, AND BRAKES

PROJECT 31 • INSTALLING WIDE TIRES AND THIN BELTS

Time: 3 to 5 hours

Tools: 7/16-, 1/2-, 9/16-, 11/16-, 3/4-, 13/16-inch wrenches, rubber mallet, Allen wrenches, Torx wrenches, torque wrench, screwdrivers, clutch puller (Jim's #1004A), compensator socket wrench, air gun, 1 1/4-inch socket, 1 7/8-inch countershaft sprocket nut socket (#94660-37A), lift or stand, floor jack, tiedowns, and the usual assortment of hand tools

Talent: 👷👷👷

Tab: $$$ to $$$$$

Tinware: The H-D or Dalton kit, all the gaskets and seals for inner primary removal, and blue #242 Loctite

Tip: Any time you're into the inner primary, check the condition of the front pulley; there should be no leaks, no squeaks, and no free-play—it should feel like it's welded in place

PERFORMANCE GAIN: Stylish, better straight-line stability, and improved ride quality; drawback is slower handling

COMPLEMENTARY MODIFICATION: A chrome pulley cover (with H-D kit); change the size of the front pulley to alter overall gearing

There was a time when Harleys had the fattest tires in motorcycling. Nowadays, that trend seems to have reversed itself. Even commuter scooters, it seems, have more rubber on deck than an 800-pound Hog. Almost everybody wants wide rubber on the back of their H-D. The dream is to step up from the stock 130, to a 150-series tire on the stock rear rim, or even better, an extra-wide rim with a 180- or 200-series tire.

The difficulty is that most of us don't want to give up our belt drives to get it, so until recently, the only way to have your cake and eat it too, was to get involved in expensive and complicated conversions of one kind or another. You could install one of those offset kits that, fundamentally, move the whole driveline to the right about 1/4 inch. Unfortunately, that requires tearing apart half the motorcycle and can make the bike "left heavy" when you're done. The only other option is to buy a whole new wide-drive chassis. All that takes is complete disassembly of your bike, a couple weeks' time, and a few thousand dollars, which is an awful lot of hassle just to pop on a big meat.

1 Since the only financially sensible way to run wider rubber on Softails in the past was to convert to chain drive, this wide drive belt kit solves a lot of problems. Though neither factory nor aftermarket kits allow for a tire as wide as the 180-section tire on this wide drive chassis, they both allow up to 160 widths with no further modifications.

2 Harley's wide tire kit gets you a 150-16 K591 Dunlop tire, the narrowed pulley and belt, and both belt guards in chrome, as well as all necessary gaskets. Harley says the kit is for 1997 and newer models. Even so, you can fit it to any year or model of Softail, providing that you don't object to a change in overall gearing. The kit gives a 3.15:1 ratio, the same as stock from 1994–on but taller than the 3.37:1 ratio used on 1986 to 1992 models and shorter than the 2.94:1 ratio used in 1993. Don't worry about the front pulley. As long as the wheel is aligned properly, the belt will run quite happily on the left two-thirds of the stocker. If you don't care for the rather bland stock look, there are no less than six styles available from Fine Line for Softail models from 1984 to present. Kits for FXRs and Dynas may be offered in the future.

Jim Dalton struggled with this pain-in-the-rear rear-tire issue for quite a while. Finally, he'd had enough. So he drew the line—Fine Line. That's the name of his new 1-inch Kevlar belt and billet pulley kits for Softails. What Dalton Design has come up with is *the* answer to those who want to run contemporary rubber out back.

But simple doesn't mean easy. It took a lot of work to engineer the thin, Kevlar-reinforced Dayco belt so that it would be stronger than the 1 1/2-inch factory unit. It took more work to create not just one but *six* different styles of billet rear pulleys.

Was all that work worth it? You bet! As the brochure says: "Installation is virtually as simple as changing your original belt and rear pulley." Again, simple, if not necessarily easy, as this means removing and reinstalling the inner and outer primary and rear wheel. But on the bright side, the job should only take 3 to 5 hours, and you'd have to pull the rear wheel to change the back tire anyway.

The instructions that come with the H-D kit are very complete, including which tools you'll need. The Dalton kit instructions are not so good, but since installation techniques are virtually identical to stock, the shop manual has all the information you need.

PROJECT 32 • BUILDING AND MAINTAINING WIRE WHEELS

Time: 4 to 6 hours

Tools: Spoke wrench, truing stand, dial indicator, and wheel removal and installation tools

Talent: ▮▮▮

Tab: $$$ to $$$$$

Tinware: New hubs (seals, bearings, center spacer, and so on, usually come with the hubs), correct external wheel spacers (usually two of #43654-86A), plus a left-side spacer and duct tape or a rubber ring to cover the inside of the rim center

Tip: If you're building a wide wheel, check clearance before spending a lot of time lacing and truing; be sure and measure the tire—widths vary between brands

PERFORMANCE GAIN: Wider wheels and tires improve braking and acceleration but slow steering a bit; lighter wheels improve handling

COMPLEMENTARY MODIFICATION: Tires wider than a 150 or 160 series require some kind of modification to provide clearance (thin belt kit like H-D's 43684-98 or the Dalton kit or conversion to chain drive via an offset sprocket kit); see Project 31: Installing Wide Tires and Thin Belts for the best recommendation on accomodating wide wheels

1 The building blocks—rim, spokes and hub—of your new wire wheels. Building blocks aren't the same as built wheels, so be sure the combination you've chosen is a workable one. The sheer variety of rim designs, materials, and sizes has mushroomed in the last few years, so the options can be bewildering. Hubs, too, have changed lately, with many choices available. On top of that, what used to be the simplest decision, spokes, is no longer limited to chrome or stainless steel in some form or another. Now, you can run anywhere from the standard 40- to 120-spoke wheels! That many spokes makes for a wheel so heavy it's not likely to respond well to bumps in the road, and you could have nightmares about truing such a monster, but wire wheels have never been about anything logical—they are art.

Despite all the simplicity, strength, and minimal maintenance requirements of one-piece mag wheels, spoke wheels survive and thrive on Harleys. Why? Tradition and style are most likely the main reasons people use spoked wheels, although there is one significant advantage: you can make a wire wheel to suit you. They remain, after all these years, the ultimate custom wheel. You can widen the rim, add spokes, use custom hubs—the options go on and on.

Whether it's repairing a stock wheel or building a custom wheel from scratch, the first order of business is coming up with the correct spokes for the job, from Buchanan's, Wheel Works, Custom Chrome, or one of many, many other suppliers. Or if you can't find what you want ready-made, you can always begin with long spokes and cut them down to the exact length with a small shear.

Then there's the hub. Stock hubs remain popular (as long as they're chrome, it seems), but there are plenty of alternatives, some capable of using as many as 80 (or more) spokes.

Last, but usually most, we have the rim. Chrome steel, alloy, even titanium (or unobtainium, whatever), in different widths and diameters, from 15 inches to 21 inches and from WM1 to WM7. That said, the trend is toward 17-inch-diameter, 6-inch-wide rims that allow use of the new ultra-wide rubber available and look like a million bucks.

Once all the choices have been made and the measurements taken (you'd better make sure everything's going to fit the motorcycle, hadn't you?), you begin the assembly into the finished wheel. Here's how:

Lay a soft towel out on the work space, hub spokes and rim upon it, and make sure everything, including your hands, is clean. By now, you should already have determined if your spoke pattern is going to be to a "cross-three," "cross-four," or another pattern. Once you've got this planned, you execute.

Starting at one point on the wheel, the spokes are placed into the holes in the rim, and the nipples are loosely screwed into place as you work your way around the wheel. Once all the right-hand spokes are in on one side of the wheel, lace the left-hand spokes in loosely on top of the right-handers. Turn the wheel over gently and repeat the performance on the other side.

Once all the spokes and nipples are in place, run the nipples down snug but not tight into the rim with a screwdriver.

Mount the wheel on a truing stand to see how much work needs to be done to get the wheel perfectly straight and concentric to the hub. Before any of the spokes are tightened down any further, check the offset of the rim in relation to the hub to ensure the rim is where you want it to be (especially important on wide rims and Wide Glide front wheels).

With a dial indicator in place, or some equivalent means of checking your work, progressively snug up the spokes, spinning the wheel at intervals to see where you're at. If you warp the rim by overtightening spokes on one side, back them off before you tighten the other side, and check constantly for true. When run out (up and down) and deflection (side to side) of the rim is less than 1/32 inch, it's true enough.

Next, pack the wheel bearings with grease and install them, making sure you install the center spacer in the hub first.

With the bearings and spacer in place, install the axle and torque to 60-65 foot-pounds rear or 50-55 foot-pounds front so bearing endplay can be checked, as per shop manual spec for your year and model.

Now you get to mount the tire. Wrap the center of the rim with a couple layers of duct tape to keep the nipples from puncturing the tube. Rubber strips work too, but there is a chance they will move around inside the wheel when the tire is being mounted. While you've got the tape out, use it on any parts of the new wheel you don't want the tire machine to scratch. Go at it gently on the tire machine while you're mounting and use lots of lube and protection on the tire tools.

Mount the rotors from the old wheels and the drive-belt pulley.

The last move is to spin balance the entire assembly.

As hinted at earlier, wire wheels need attention, especially newly laced ones. Inspect the wheels for loose spokes or other problems every 200 miles or so. Obvious problems should cause concern—dented rims, broken or loose spokes, stuff like that. If a set of spokes is really loose, they will make a dull thud when tapped with a metal object like a wrench, or if you grab a bunch of spokes and they move when you squeeze them, then they need immediate attention. Tighten up any loose ones with a spoke wrench. Every time the tires are replaced, look them over more thoroughly and even check to see whether they are still true. Most spokes break where the head meets the hub, so you should spend a couple extra minutes cleaning and inspecting that area of your bike during every wash. It may be the only warning you'll get.

TIRES, WHEELS, AND BRAKES

PROJECT 33 • SERVICING YOUR BRAKES

Time: 1 to 2 hours

Tools: Mity-Vac, some clear tubing, an old-fashioned oil can, sockets and Allens, screwdriver, a jar to catch brake fluid

Talent: 👤

Tab: 0 to $

Tinware: New pads, brake fluid, brake banjo washers, and master cylinder gasket or diaphragm

Tip: Gently snug (rather than heavily tighten) the bleeder screw

PERFORMANCE GAIN: Maximizes brake performance

COMPLEMENTARY MODIFICATION: Stainless brake lines

1 Get too deep into brake service, as you easily may if you swap to chromed calipers for example, and you'll need everything you see here, in addition banjo washers for the brake lines.

The most neglected system on the motorcycle is the one you bet your life on every ride—the brakes. Don't procrastinate on this project; a thorough brake service only takes a couple of hours.

REPLACING BRAKE PADS

All 1984 to 1998 Harleys use single-piston sliding calipers that each squeeze a rotor just like a hydraulic C-clamp. The design principle of the front and rear brake calipers is the same, but the way they are mounted and their respective pads are different.

To install new brake pads, you'll need a 3/16-inch Allen wrench and a 5/16-inch socket wrench, along with new pads and a tube of anti-seize. Here's how to do the fronts:

Unbolt the front caliper from the lower fork leg and slide the caliper up and off the rotor.

Insert a large flat-bladed screwdriver between the pads in the caliper and use it as a lever against the outer pad to push the caliper piston back into the caliper body.

Remove the outer pad carrier from the caliper body and remove the inner pad. It's rigidly mounted to the rear of the caliper body via a small bolt. The other pad is probably already on the floor, so removing that one is a no brainer.

Inspect the caliper and replace anything that's damaged or worn beyond service limits. (Check the shop manual.)

Reassemble the calipers with the new pads. When reassembling the caliper, make sure that the rivet head is inserted into the cutout in the sliding nut. The retaining spring keeps the pad from vibrating.

Slide the caliper onto the rotor and insert the mounting bolts. When reinstalling the caliper mounting bolts, give them a light coating of anti-seize lubricant which will allow the caliper mounting bolts and outer pad carrier to move freely and align properly with the disc. And use a torque wrench to properly tighten.

If your bike has twin front brakes, repeat the process for the other brake.

The procedure for the rear is nearly identical to that used in replacing front brake pads. The major difference is that a #45 Torx bit driver is needed for removing the rear caliper bolts on most models (although some early rears used Allen fasteners).

BLEEDING THE SYSTEM

Even though the hydraulic brake system on your Harley is sealed, its fluid can get contaminated and lose efficiency. The main source of contamination is water that mixes with the brake fluid due to condensation within the brake system. All Evo Harley brake systems are designed to use DOT 5 brake fluid, and DOT 5 has a lot of advantages, so you should stick with it. DOT 5

2 Many a chromed caliper needs to have its bore honed slightly to get rid of the crud that's deposited inside during the chroming process. The caliper piston must be a light, sliding fit, but without any noticeable side-to-side slop once it's pushed home.

3 You may find it to your advantage to run a well-oiled tap down the threaded holes in the caliper as well. This may be the only way to ensure no-problem installations on chrome pieces (not just brake pieces either). Once you've gone this far, it only follows that you should check that the internal passages are clear, and then meticulously clean the thing.

4 Over-polishing, and chrome flash can inhibit a good retention of the dust seal and piston O-ring. Make sure both parts fit properly and stay put before you proceed. Use DOT 5 brake fluid to lubricate these rubber parts when you install them.

5 Chromed master cylinders take a moment or two of contemplation and preparation, just like the calipers. Clear and clean the bore and any threaded areas. Then install the plunger assembly, as shown.

6 Light sanding of the hole where the fluid level sight glass fits and lubing the rubber with DOT 5 brake fluid will help in sealing it.

7 If the chrome stuff kicks up brake fluid Geysers like this stock one, once bled, you have good braking.

fluid is a synthetic fluid made of silicone. It has a higher boiling point, absorbs less water, and lasts longer than the alcohol-based DOT 3 or 4 fluids. Finally, unlike DOT 3 or 4, DOT 5 won't harm the paint if you happen to spill some on your bike's tank. The only disadvantages of DOT 5 are that it is more expensive and that it is slightly more compressible than DOT 3 or 4. Even so, the small extra expense and slight amount of extra "sponginess" you'll feel at the brake lever are minor compared to all the advantages of DOT 5.

The brake fluid should be replaced every two years. The easy way to change the brake fluid without getting air in the system is to bleed it clean, which you can do in an hour or so, or even less if you use the right method. Be careful of two things: keeping dirt out of the master cylinder reservoir and using the correct brake fluid. Clean the cap of the master cylinder before you remove it to keep dirt out and use only DOT 5 fluid, for the reasons already stated.

Three different techniques can be used to do the actual bleeding. No matter which you choose, a few basics are the same. First adjust the handlebars so that the master cylinder sits flat, then clean and remove its cover. Fill the master cylinder to about 3/8 inch from the top; this gives the cover gasket-bladder some room. Then bleed the brake fluid down to about 1 inch from the bottom of the reservoir before filling its cylinder with new fluid. Continue to bleed the fluid until it comes out clean at the caliper. Then refill the reservoir and bleed the other caliper, if there's another connected. When all done, top up the reservoir and replace the cap.

The cheapest bleeding method is to use a 60-cent piece of clear tubing and an old plastic soda bottle. The main drawbacks with this method are that it's a two-person job and that it takes what seems like forever (maybe an hour), unless you get lucky. Use a clear bottle so you can see the fluid. Connect the tubing to the caliper's bleed nipple and stick the other end in the bottle. With this setup, one person squeezes the brake handle and holds it back while another person opens the bleeder fitting at the caliper. When the flow stops, the second person closes the bleeder nipple. Repeat until the fluid flows clear, and then repeat for each caliper. Don't forget to keep filling the master cylinder.

The next easiest (but more expensive) bleeding method is to use a Lisle "One Man" bleeder kit. The kit comes with a special cup, two pieces of tubing, and three special bleeder-fitting adapters that allow you to bleed your brakes without assistance. Attach the long hose to the outside of the lid of the special cup and the short piece to the inside of the lid. Attach the other end of the long hose to the caliper's bleeder nipple using the correct adapter. Then pour a small amount of brake fluid into the special cup so that when the lid is installed, the end of the short piece of tubing is immersed in the brake fluid. Open the bleeder fitting about three-quarters of a turn and slowly squeeze the brake lever. You don't need to close the bleeder screw before you release the lever because by having the short piece of tubing sitting in brake fluid in the bottom of the cup, air will not be drawn up into the system when the master-cylinder piston rebounds. Keep an eye on the reservoir. Don't let it run dry. When the brake fluid comes out clean, close the bleeder fitting, disconnect the bleeder, refill the master cylinder, and repeat for the other calipers. Refill the reservoirs and replace the covers when done.

The most expensive, easiest, fastest, and most fool-proof method is to use a Mity-Vac bleeder. Attach one end of the hose from the Mity-Vac catch bottle to the caliper's bleeder fitting, pump the Mity-Vac handle twice, and open the bleeder fitting about three-quarters of a turn. The vacuum will suck out the brake fluid without anyone touching the brake lever. Pump the handle a couple more times and more fluid will come out. Again, make sure to add new fluid to the master-cylinder reservoir before it runs dry to prevent air from being drawn into the system. After the brake fluid comes out clean, close the bleeder fitting, disconnect the Mity-Vac, refill the master cylinder, and repeat for the other calipers. Refill the reservoirs and replace the covers when done. It'll take about 10 minutes—honest!

PROJECT 34 • UPGRADING BRAKE DISCS

 Time: 1 hour per disc, basically

 Tools: Heat gun or small torch; impact driver or air gun; Allen, Torx, or socket for disc fasteners (all three types have been used over the years); 1/2-, 9/16-, and 5/8-inch wrenches; screwdriver; and rubber mat

 Talent:

 Tab: $$ to $$$$

 Tinware: New disc fasteners (just in case) and blue #242 Loctite

 Tip: Heat and leverage win the day here; you will not remove disc fasteners with a 6-inch tool and good intentions

PERFORMANCE GAIN: A 10-percent decrease in stopping distances when you install a factory floating rotor

COMPLEMENTARY MODIFICATION: Dual-action calipers or upgraded pads for stock calipers; a dual disc conversion is ideal for models fitted with narrow glide forks

Years ago Harley used dual 10-inch discs on some models (like Wide Glides). They stop better than drum front brakes, but that's about all you can say for them. Even the single disc on Evos works a lot better than the dual 10-inchers did, but is that enough?

All Evos use 11.5-inch brake discs, but that doesn't mean all Evo rotors are created equal or that they are state of the art in the 1990s any more than the dual 10s were in the 1970s. For instance, dressers have used a bewildering assortment of designs for their rear brake, most of which cannot be replaced by upgraded aftermarket discs. The rest of Harley's stock brake rotors come in two flavors—solid and floating. The solid variety is what most are familiar with and is most likely to be on the job since it's been around for 15 years. The design may be the same, but the metallurgy has been mucked with a few times over the years. The original "-84" number is trouble-free if not inspiring. The -84A part was made of a modified alloy and was less successful. Used in 1990 and 1991 for the most part, these were developed to work with a new brake pad compound developed at the same time. The problem was these discs could and did

1 Anyone who remembers the rather dismal performance of the older 10-inch disc (on the right) used by the factory in the 1970s will attest to the improvements that the bigger discs make to the stopping ability of the newer Harleys. A single new 11.5-inch brake on an Evo will out-brake a pair of the old 10-inchers, hands down. To build an even better binder, try using the factory's new floater rotor (on the left), so-called because of its two-piece carrier and button-mounted disc. This design allows more and better contact with the pads. The result? Quicker, shorter, surer stops, under any and all conditions.

2 Better yet, jump all the way to a 13-inch (300-millimeter) disc such as this one from Braking Systems. The kit includes an adapter bracket (on the right), to allow use of the factory caliper, and their own brake pads, compounded to work best with this disc and the stock caliper. Don't let the rectangular pads in the photo confuse you; those are for dual-piston calipers. What you need to know now is that with no further upgrades, larger discs alone will improve brake performance because the contact surface is increased, improving cooling and fade resistance. Need more? Add a disc or upgrade the caliper.

crack. Nothing catastrophic, mind you, but definite hairline cracks, generally radiating outwards from the little cooling holes drilled in the disc. In 1992, the alloy compound was changed again; the part number also changed to, surprise, -92, and there were no more nasty cracks.

The next move by the factory came in 1995 with the introduction of so-called floating rotors. Made up of a carrier that bolts to the wheel itself, the disc, and a series of pins that connect the two, this design allows a defined amount of movement in the disc, which means it will run flat between the brake pads, giving more and better contact. It also means slightly better heat dissipation and altogether superior stopping power. The most logical recipient of the new stoppers, considering its intended image, was the 1200S (Sport) Sportster. The most ironic recipient was the Bad Boy, with its springer fork. The bikes that should have gotten them are the dresser models and the Heritage and Fat Boy versions of the Softail. Fortunately you can add what the factory forgot and, in fact, go it one better.

The current state-of-the-art in brake rotors are indeed the floating design, but bigger ones than the Harley discs. You need look no further than the Buell to see these in action. A Buell is a 450-pound high-performance machine with a feature other sportbike designers thought was nuts at the time—a single front brake. The joke was on them. That single front brake was, in fact, composed of a 13.4-inch floating disc and a massive six-piston caliper. It will stop as well as anything on the market. All Heritage and Fat Boy owners should take note: The closer you can come to matching that setup the better your odds of avoiding the rear end of a bus someday.

Aftermarket companies such as Performance Machine and Braking Systems market both large-diameter floating discs and killer calipers to go with them. Call it brake aid. Or better yet, call them, and bring this underbraked insanity to a screeching halt.

Needless to say, if you find your machine lacking anchors, you can upgrade via a step process, as your budget allows:

One, the budget deal is to upgrade to factory floating discs. They run about $125 a pop but help you stop, so they're worth it. Stock pads work fine, but don't be shy about experimenting with different pad materials and brands to find the characteristics that suit your stopping style.

Two, install larger 13-inch discs or use dual-action calipers along with the factory floating discs. These alternatives are approximately equivalent in terms of stopping power improvement and cost. You need to plan your approach carefully because if you pop for calipers, you want to ensure they will transfer over to 13-inch discs if you want to go that route later on. There's not much point in buying zoot calipers if they wind up obsolete for use with larger discs.

Three, throw away all the factory stuff and go with 13-inch discs and dual-action (preferably four- or six-piston) calipers. This is expensive as all get out but offers the ultimate in stopping power. It makes more sense to go this route if you only have one front brake but makes almost no sense for the rear brake, since that one is all too easy to lock up, even when bone stock (see Project 36: Upgrading Softail Brakes).

Installation of H-D's floating discs is virtually identical to that of stock discs:

Prop the bike securely with the front wheel off the ground about 6 inches.

Remove the axle and speedo drive box (if you have one) and drop the wheel out.

Lay a rubber mat or other padding on your bench and place the wheel (disc side up) on it. Apply a little heat to the disc retaining fasteners, and use your impact tool or air gun to remove them. If one or two just won't come out (it happens), drill or cut the heads off, leaving a stub so you can get Vise Grips clamped on to extract what's left. Remove the old rotor, install the new floater, and using new fasteners (preferred), torque the floater in place in a cross pattern. If you reuse the old screws, apply some blue Loctite to the threads before you install them.

Replace the wheel, axle, and speedo drive (with new dust seal), and torque properly. Test spin the wheel and check the brakes before you drop the bike back on deck. Unless, of course, while it's up there, you convert to dual discs. This is not so easy on Softails due to the embarrassing lack of an afforadable kit; it's a relative snap for narrow glide forks. Harley has a kit (#44090-96) for models with the 1996 and later master cylinder and another (#44090-92) for everyone else. Or if you choose not to use factory discs and calipers, here's a breakdown of the individual components:

*PART NUMBER	DESCRIPTION	QUANTITY REQUIRED
852	Bolt	1
855A	Bolt, Caliper Mounting	1
3655	Bolt, Rotor Mounting	5
6019	Washer, Caliper Mounting	1
41731-88	Brake Line Gaskets	6
41747-82A	Banjo Bolts	2
44023-83	Caliper Assembly	1
44136-84A	Brake Rotor	1
45013-85A	Brake Master Cylinder Assembly	1 (to 1995)
45013-96	Brake Master Cylinder Assembly	1 (1996—on)
45140-87	Brake Hose	1
45405-75A	Bolt and Washer, Fork Leg	1
45922-87	Fork Leg	1

* You may find different specific things, like brake hose length, mean different specific part numbers for your bike, so use this only as a guide.

PROJECT 35 • INSTALLING MULTI-PISTON BRAKE CALIPERS

Time: 1 to 2 hours

Tools: Varies a bit according to your choice of caliper design, but you'll need Allens and Torx bits, the "three wise men" of wrench and socket sizes (1/2-, 9/16-, and 5/8-inch), and a proper size wrench for the brake bleeder

Talent: 👬

Tab: $$ to $$$$$

Tinware: Brake fluid, banjo gaskets, anti-seize, and Loctite

Tip: Unless you are going racing, go with dual discs up front with four-piston calipers or a single disc with a six-piston caliper

PERFORMANCE GAIN: Two- or even one-finger braking with outstanding control

COMPLEMENTARY MODIFICATION: Stainless brake lines

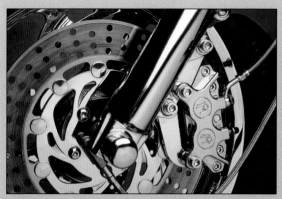

1 For those lucky enough to have dual discs, a swap to two dual-action four-piston aftermarket calipers, in conjunction with a pair of H-D's 11.5-inch floating discs, should be more than enough to do the job. Even heavy bikes like dressers can have tire squealing, fade-free, single-finger front brakes with a setup like this. The most popular four-piston calipers are from Performance Machine (PM), as shown, but CCI (RevTech), GMA, Wilwood, and several others are available.

Technological trickle-down of high-tech solutions that offer split-second advantages on the race track translate into second chances at intersections of the mean streets upon which most of us ride. One of these tech-trickles is the differential-bore brake caliper, which requires a little translation of its own.

Basic Harley calipers offer only one live piston and one active (moving) brake pad to do the job of pinching the brake disc and converting all that kinetic energy into heat. The dead pad just sits there. A more sophisticated approach is the dual-piston design, which grasps the disc from both sides, thus exerting twice the pressure. Better stops and more consistent performance are the benefits.

Jump to the mid-1990s, and this kind of arrangement has multiplied. Now there are brake calipers with four or even six pistons forcing the brake to stick to the task at hand. All this is marvelous, but when the poor brake pads are rubbing on a disc, it generates staggering heat. So much so that the air, moisture, road grit, and brake lining trapped in there are literally vaporized. And, as we all know, hot gases expand. So this gas tries desperately to blow the pistons back

into the caliper. Multiply this effect by the many little pistons involved, and there are potentially uneven forces at each piston, reducing the effectiveness of the whole caliper, especially considering that temperatures are not the same at the front and rear of the caliper. It all adds up to uneven wear and less than 100 percent consistency in the stop storehouse.

Enter the differential bore. The notion being if pressure and heat are going to play these games, the way to outsmart them is to make the pistons (and their bores, naturally) different sizes to deal with the particular problem in their immediate vicinity. The lead piston (farthest rearward on the caliper) lucks out because the disc has had nearly a complete spin around the block to cool off, so that piston needn't be so large to deal with the conditions it encounters at this point. The next one up the line must be bigger, and the next one bigger yet, to balance the braking force. In the case of a six-piston differential bore caliper, you'll note how each piston set is slightly larger in diameter than the one that precedes it. Now you know why.

For better stopping power you need more leverage. No, not longer handles on your master cylinder, but more hydraulic leverage. To get it, you need to boost the quantity or quality of the pistons in the brake caliper. The stock 1984-to-present Harley front caliper has a single piston that boasts just over 2 square inches in contact area. A high-performance four-piston caliper sporting four l-inch diameter pistons gives over two times more area and, therefore, more braking capability for any given amount of pressure at the brake lever than the stock caliper. Plus the disc gets an equal squeeze from both sides of a four-piston setup since it's a dual-action design. A really nasty six-piston caliper takes it right to the current limit of brake technology and available tire traction as well.

FRONT CALIPERS

High-performance front calipers come in many sizes and styles. The four-piston calipers are the most popular; these are available as direct bolt-ons or as models that use special brackets to attach to the fork leg. Along with the calipers, use high-performance braided-steel brake lines. The standard rubber brake hose can flex (if it is old and weather checked) under the hydraulic loads when the brakes are applied; this flexing absorbs the braking power. Choose components carefully. You can get style along with "brick wall" stopping and one finger control.

Performance Machine (PM) is the company most recognized for quality brake components, but GMA, Wilwood, and Braking are major players as well, offering brakes a quantum leap ahead of O.E.M. stoppers. Speaking of leaps, look before you do where stainless brake lines are concerned. There's nothing inherently wrong with them, but as a breed, stainless hoses have been marketed as a panacea for braking deficiencies,

usually on stock systems. They are frosting on a good brake cake—no more. Should you choose to use them, bear in mind that they can be abrasive to paint and aluminum, if carelessly routed (and they aren't clear plastic-coated), and most of the perceived improvements in brake feel and stopping ability would show up just as well with new rubber hoses and a good brake bleeding.

REAR CALIPERS

Harley's rear caliper operates on the same principle as the front, but the company mounts the pads in a large casting that attaches to the rear axle and swingarm. The pads have grooves at each end that fit over two bosses cast in the mount. The caliper fits down over the pads and is held in place by a pair of Torx bolts that have dowel pins extending from their ends. This way the caliper can slide side to side on the dowel pins, centering itself for full contact as it clamps the pads to the rotor. This system works fine as a rear brake, primarily because leg power beats hand power for applying pressure to the control and because with a Harley's long wheelbase, rear brakes are less likely to lock up uncontrollably than on most other motorcycles. The result is that the need for caliper upgrades for the rear isn't as acute as for the front. Unless you really have to have the latest billet caliper on the rear, spend your money elsewhere.

PROJECT 36 • UPGRADING SOFTAIL BRAKES

Time: 1 to 2 hours

Tools: Torx bits, Allen bits, heat gun, torque wrench, Mity-Vac, stand or lift, tiedowns, small jack

Talent:

Tab: $$$$$+

Tinware: Besides the caliper and rotor of choice—Dot 5 brake fluid, new banjo washers, TSP (teflon seal or tape), and new disc fasteners

Tip: 13-inch rotors and four- or six-piston calipers make sense on Softails because the swept area increases to something like (or over) the amount offered by dual stock brakes

PERFORMANCE GAIN: What this does to braking is equivalent to what a cam, carb, pipe, and ignition does for the engine—wakes it right up

COMPLEMENTARY MODIFICATION: Sticky tires

1 Here's a stock setup that's taken a step in the wrong direction. Chroming the caliper will trap heat. This poor overworked stocker could easily fade in the heat of repeated heavy braking. Since there's only one to count on up there, this is a case of style that is very likely to overcome substance.

2 A better plan would involve the use of a Harley 11.5-inch floating disc and an aftermarket four-piston caliper. A 13-inch disc and four-piston caliper (shown) should be considered the next step. It follows, therefore, that the ultimate setup for a single disc front end is a six-piston caliper working on a 13-inch floating disc. But it is possible to swap to a double-disc front end like the one the FLT/dresser family gets. Unfortunately, the original front fender won't fit, and the tops of the sliders will be exposed and ugly. After applying a little ingenuity in addressing those two issues or coughing up the really big bucks for Arlen Ness' dual-brake forks for Softails, you can stop as well as the best of 'em.

Does this make sense to you? The heaviest non-touring bikes that Harley builds, the Softail Heritage and Fat Boy models, get a single front brake. The fact is 80 percent of the stopping capability of any motorcycle comes from the front brake. Big H-D cruisers are no different.

Sure, it's possible that this fear of overbraking in front comes from the fact that the Softail Custom, which begat the Softail Heritage and the Fat Boy, comes with a skinny 21-inch tire. With rubber that narrow, loaded to the gills with nearly 800 pounds of bike and rider in a panic stop, the bike could skid. But even 21-inch rubber has come a long way in terms of traction in the last few years, so that "thin" logic is flawed. Besides, the fat 16-inch footprint that the Softail Heritage and Fat Boy possess provides plenty of area and more than enough traction for any brake.

Whether you have fat or thin rubber up front, the big Softails don't have enough "whoa" to match their go. By comparison, the 1200S Sportster, even though it weighs several hundred pounds less, gets two of the factory's new floating discs up front and dual calipers to match. Even the Bad Boy gets a floater, and it runs a skinny 21-incher, so what gives?

The most economical way to upgrade your single-disc front end is to use a multi-piston caliper and a 13-inch floating disc (see Projects 34 and 35). The ultimate upgrade is to add a second front disc and caliper. There are two options for doing this. You can use the lower fork legs (sliders) and an extra disc, hose, and caliper from one of the dresser (FLT) models or buy a dual-disc kit such as the one from Arlen Ness. However, if you choose the former method, the original front fender won't fit, and the tops of the sliders (which are hidden under fork tins on dressers) are exposed and ugly. With a little ingenuity, you can make them look okay, and you'll really love the additional stopping power.

Changing to FLT lower legs (sliders) is a straightforward shop manual-type swap, except for the fender just mentioned. But about all you can do to clean up the gap between the fork sliders and the tins is find or make some tins about 2 inches over stock length and install them at the same time. That this isn't as easy as it sounds is probably the major reason this dual-disc swap isn't done more often. The sole alternative, the Arlen Ness kit, is a fantastic-looking bolt-on solution, but you pay big bucks for that convenience.

SECTION SIX
ENGINE

Harley-Davidson's identity revolves around their V-twin engine. The Evolution represents years of pragmatic engineering philosophy that dates back to the dawn of the sport. Large V-twin engines powered bikes at the early part of the century, and they will undoubtedly continue to do so into the next.

A large unstressed engine makes a lot of sense for nearly any application. These types of engines move their respective masses across great distances reliably, economically, and without apparent effort. Ample torque at low revs, anvil-like durability, and a sense that there's always more to be had if you need it, make tap dancing on the shifter of a high-strung multi-cylinder seem more trouble than it's worth. Harley-Davidson power is accessible, non-threatening, easy to use, and, best of all, useful.

What you need to know is how to capitalize on the inherent strengths of the H-D powerplant. The Evolution engine is designed to work for a living. It's the difference between an big ox and a quarter horse, an ax and a fencing foil. If you understand that, the surprise might be that it can be so versatile. It can work at many things, including letting you play. That's what this section is for.

The Evo is amenable to modification and has vast power potential. If you know where you want to go, this engine can get you there.

ENGINE

PROJECT 37 • FINDING YOUR BUILD DATE

Time: About 5 minutes

Tools: Flashlight and some aerosol engine cleaner

Talent:

Tab: 0

Tinware: None—unless you want to make a tracing which takes thin paper and a number two pencil or black crayon

Tip: A good way to double-check the legality of the machine— the VIN number, engine number, and the crankcase numbers should all agree

PERFORMANCE GAIN:

COMPLEMENTARY MODIFICATION: Scribe these numbers in hidden spots all over the motorcycle to protect yourself in case of theft

1 These sometimes hard-to-find stamps are actually very informative, if you take the time to find and read them. Not to be confused with VIN numbers, the code in case numbers explains many of the details of displacement, build date, and even the state or nation the machine was originally destined for.

Ever wonder when your engine was built? No, not just the model year, but literally the birthday of your red-blooded Yankee V-twin—day, month, everything. Well, you can figure it out fairly easily as long as you can translate the day of the year (numbered 1 through 365) into a month and date of the month. Here's how it works:

First, locate the crankcase number. Not the same thing, by the way, as the VIN. On Big Twins this identification number is located on the left engine case in front of and slightly below the nose of the primary case. It may be a trifle hard to locate if you have forward controls, as these sit right on top of the numbers. Even so, persist, and they can be spotted. Sportster identification numbers tended to migrate a little from year to year, but most are stamped on the right crankcase just in front of the oil pump. Sportster numbers are very difficult to read even after you've found them because the oil hoses run right in front of the numbers. If you can't find the external location of the identification stamping and you're anal retentive enough to persist, the numbers can be found inside the crankcases as well. The internal stamp on Big

Twins is inside the cam cover (cone), and Sportster's are inside the primary cover. Nifty symmetry, huh? Outside stamping on one side of the case, inside stamping on the other.

The 10-digit series will begin with a 15 on 49-state Big Twins and a 20 on California Big Twins. On Sportsters, the list of prefix numbers is a bit more involved. A 24 is an 883, 25 a 1200, 26 a California 883, 27 a California 1200, 29 a Swiss 883, 30 a Swiss 1200, 31 an International 883, and last but not least, 32 is an International 1200.

The next two numbers in the series will be the model year—simple as that.

With the next three numbers the plot thickens. These numbers represent the day the engine was built, but it requires just a little decoding, a calculator, and maybe even a calendar to turn it into something you can relate to. For instance, say your bike is a 1997 model, and the three numbers are 090. Well, it's like this. January has 31 days, February has 28 (29 during a leap year) and March has 31 days also. All three add up to 90, this means the engine was built on March 31. If the number was 115, your bike's engine was born on April 25. A 119 would make it April 29, and so on. See?

There are just three more numbers in the series of 10. These three final digits represent where in the production your pride and joy's construction fell on that particular day, for example, 012. If you have that number on your engine, yours was the 12th engine built that day.

One note: The 11th digit on a Kansas City-built Sportster will be the letter 'K'. The three digits preceding the 'K' indicate how many Sportsters were built in Kansas City that day.

Anyway, now that we've broken the engine numbers down, it's time to put them back together. Check the chart, then mark your calendar. That way as you and your Hog grow old together, you can both celebrate your respective birthdays.

ENGINE

PROJECT 38 • KEEPING EXCESS OIL OUT OF YOUR AIR CLEANER

 Time: 1 to 5 hours

 Tools: Allen wrenches, screwdrivers, standard wrenches and sockets, and drill (all for drain-hole enlargement)

 Talent:

 Tab: 0 to $ (to enlarge drain holes), $$$ (for Krank Vent, Total Seal ring conversion, and spacer or oil-seal fitment on Sportsters)

 Tinware: Rocker-box gaskets

 Tip: Do one step at a time and carefully assess the problem; the simplest fix may do the trick

PERFORMANCE GAIN: A dry right leg and no more oil spray all over the motorcycle

COMPLEMENTARY MODIFICATION: If you install a high-flow air cleaner, don't plug the vent hose into it; instead, route the hose cleanly to somewhere else closer to the ground, and cap it with a small K&N filter

1 Installing the Krank Vent Plus a snap. You will need an air cleaner adapter kit similar to Harley's Screamin' Eagle version (#2931 93), which most of us already have. If b some quirk of fate, you still have a stock air cleaner, now's the time to switch to a high-performance type. Run a 3/8-inch hose from the nipple on the adapter dov to the bottom of the frame. Then plug th end of the Vent (marked C) into the hos and clamp it down good and tight. Once Krank Vent and the filter have been installed, double-check that all the conne tions and clamps are very securely faste and that there are absolutely no kinks o bends in the hose. That's all there is to it

2 To install Total Seal rings, you'll need to tear down the top end per the Harley service manual instructions for your model. Then the cylinders must be chec and specially honed. Use 280-grit stones and hone to a more oil-retentive 60-degree angle instead of the usual 45 degrees. Then finish with even finer grit to "knock the tops off" the standard, rather coarse, cross hatch. Check your end gap for t top rings. Position the end gaps of this two-piece ring 180 degrees opposite one anoth Once installed, do not oil the rings. Instead, smear a thin coat of light oil on the inside the ring compressor and the cylinder.

Due to the fact that Big Twins since 1992 and Sportsters since 1991 vent their considerable crankcase pressure through holes in the cylinder heads, these bikes can soak the air filter with oil when ridden at 70 miles per hour or so for a couple of hours or more. It's not really harmful; it's not even really an oil leak, but it is a real nuisance. This problem gets worse on modified bikes, which can soak your pant leg with oil when conditions are right.

How do you fix this? Here's how, from the simplest method to the most complex:

1) The stock arrangement has an oil-filled high-pressure zone (the rocker box) connected more or less directly to a low-pressure zone (the intake system, air cleaner, and carb), thus creating a siphon effect—like sucking through a soda straw at high rpm. Allow your "head breather" to vent to atmospheric pressure, and you minimize the problem. In other words, don't let the carburetor suck all the oil out of your top end. This isn't so easy with the stock air cleaner, but using a high-flow unit, like Screamin' Eagle, makes it feasible to simply reroute the vent hose to the atmos-

phere rather than plumb it back into the air cleaner like the instructions tell you to.

2) If that isn't a complete cure (and sometimes it isn't), you can remove the rocker boxes and slightly enlarge the oil drain down holes. Usually one drill bit size larger than the existing hole is plenty.

3) If it's still not licked, you can degree the timing of the crankcase breather (on Big Twins only) to make sure that the problem isn't simply a $6 plastic breather gear. Sportsters have asymmetrical breather timing (none at all, in short), so this trick won't work on them.

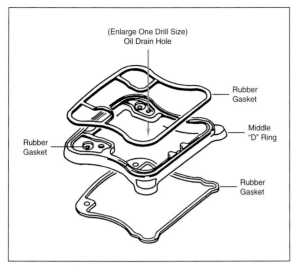

(Enlarge One Drill Size)
Oil Drain Hole

Rubber Gasket

Middle "D" Ring

Rubber Gasket

Rubber Gasket

Sometimes, all it takes to control oil build-up in the rocker box is a bigger drain hole. Enlarge yours as per this illustration. To go a step further, you can also insert a short piece of small diameter tubing into the drain hole to effectively raise (say 1/8- to 3/16-inch) the top of the drain above the level of the oil. Bear in mind that these fixes can be very effective, buit they are not a factory-approved repair. Use them carefully and with common sense.

4) What might help a Sportster, especially a 1991–1992 model, is to replace the motor sprocket spacer (# 40240-89) with one that fits tighter, and replace the left crank seal (#35151-74)—spring side in, flat side out—with the factory tool. Replace the seal with any other device than the factory tool and you are more likely to create a problem than solve one. If you're going to that much trouble, you might as well update the oil pump to a 1998 and later one while you're at it.

5) Install Total Seal piston rings and Hayden's new Krank Vent. This is probably the ultimate solution to the problem. Here's why:

At its root, this whole mess comes down to pressure control. Control in the sense that if there wasn't too much pressure in the rocker boxes at some point, there probably wouldn't be so much oil in your air box. If there wasn't too much pressure in the crankcase at some point, the excess probably wouldn't get pumped up into the heads. If there wasn't so much blow-by in the rings, case pressure would be more consistent, and oil would pump out when it should, and so on and so forth. It's a very dynamic process, trying to get oil where it needs to be, then getting it out again before it gets in the way. And the whole deal becomes more complex as rpm increases because the scavenging intervals become shorter at the same time that vacuum decreases. Oil begins to accumulate in the crankcases. This costs you power and makes a fine mess of things in more ways than one.

You must control it. That's what the Krank Vent Plus does. It helps to control oil by controlling air. Within two engine revolutions on start-up, the Krank Vent Plus begins letting air out of the engine and prevents it from coming back in. Think of it as an exhaust pipe for your cases. Actually, it does let minute amounts of air back in, but only as required to maintain a partial vacuum at all rpms, thus eliminating excess pressure in the crankcases.

The Krank Vent will work even better if you have some means of preventing combustion pressure from leaking past the piston rings directly to the bottom end. Stock Harleys with top ends in good condition still "leak-down" to the tune of 6 to 8 percent. If the rings are tired, this figure can go well over 10 percent. And what if the rings "flutter" at really high engine speeds (which they can easily do)? Under those circumstances, you may have no vacuum at all in the lower end. Instead, you might go from, say, 6 inches of vacuum to over 30 inches of pressure.

Total Seal piston rings, properly installed, cut leak-down percentages to less than 2 percent. In many cases (pun intended) it's virtually zero. Think about that for a moment. If you can keep combustion pressure out of the crankcases and above the rings where it belongs and control what's left of the air pressure generated by the pistons as they pump, you are well on your way to eliminating oil in your air cleaner and having an engine that revs quicker and makes 3 to 7 percent more power. Not having oil drag and air pressure to fight makes that much difference. Now you can take that long hard run and have nothing to show for it—at least not from your air cleaner.

Both the Krank Vent and Total Seal rings come with explicit instructions which should be followed to the letter. (For instance, details like the angle of the cylinder cross hatch for Total Seal rings is critical, and the filter on the end of a Krank Vent makes all the difference in its long term function, so deviate at your own risk.)

ENGINE

PROJECT 39 • BLUEPRINTING YOUR ENGINE

Time: 20 to 40 hours

Tools: Everyone you own and some you don't, plenty of precise measuring instruments, a gram scale, and balancing equipment

Talent: ▮▮▮▮

Tab: $$$$$+

Tinware: Overhaul gasket set, new bearings clips, retainers, and seals for the engine

Tip: If your motor has to come apart for a major overhaul (nothing lasts forever, you know), you may as well go the extra mile and blueprint the thing

PERFORMANCE GAIN: Smoother running, longer life, and more power

COMPLEMENTARY MODIFICATION: Lapping mating surfaces, increasing compression, balancing flywheels (crankshaft), cc-ing combustion chambers, decking cylinders, setting bearing preload—being absolutely precise with every part of the motorcycle

1 There's a whole lot more to the whole process of blueprinting than this photo indicates, but hopefully you'll realize attention to something this simple is just the beginning. For instance, ensuring that the cylinder bore is straight and true, as well as determining how much clearance you'll have using this piston in it, is more about the mindset that blueprinting takes than the actual measurements. Engines with improper clearances throughout cannot even approach the levels of performance and reliability that correct clearances guarantee.

An old friend of mine said it best, "A machine carefully hand built by an expert will outrun and outlast anything that rolls off the end of an assembly line." That is the essential philosophy behind blueprinting.

The process of blueprinting is to take the engine apart, make all of the reciprocating parts precisely match factory tolerances, and put it back together, again matching factory tolerances, in order to improve performance.

The primary objective is to allow, trick, or force every piece involved in the motive function to perform as well as it possibly can. The secret is combining surgically precise assembly with a highly defined and developed touch. At the high end, blueprinting is almost a Zen discipline. Riding a bike gone through by one of these wizards is a magical experience.

Blueprinting is not just for motors anymore. Case in point—a friend of mine has been known to go through 10 to 20 wheel bearings before he finds the 2 or 3 that (to him) have the perfection he requires to win coasting races. He spends hours setting perfect endplay on those bearings, balancing the wheel, experimenting with tire pressures, belt tensions, and—well, you get the idea. This fanaticism applied to the motor, to the transmission, to eliminating brake drag, and to all the myriad details involved in building the perfect motorcycle does pay off.

So what is the opposite of blueprinting? Watch how you answer the question. In fact, before you answer, think about when you had your cam installed. Sure, you probably checked the endplay and made sure that you "matched" the cam gear to the pinion gear and double-checked the valve gear for proper spacing and "coil bind." Did you check what they were before? When you put the trick heads on, what was the trapped volume in each chamber in cc? Is the compression reading between cylinders dead even? The fact is, more often than not, when we change anything on our machine, we are effectively doing just the opposite of blueprinting—even if the motorcycle runs better after the work. In short, we have a tendency to just "bolt it on and go" and call it good. It isn't!

As delivered from its plastic wrapper, a new wrist pin bushing must be reamed or honed to *exact* clearance before it can do anything, let alone give its best. If it winds up too tight, there are frictional losses, heat build-up, performance, and a short life in store for the bushing. Too loose and you get and power loss. Forget performance. What about reliability? If you don't sure it, you can't count on it.

Let me cite a real-world example. A 95-cubic-inch Softail—this thing's list of motor goodies reads like a Who's Who of the aftermarket hot-rod brand names: Mackie heads, S.T.D. crankcases, Axtell barrels, Crane cam, S&S Super G carb, to name a few. It doesn't run badly. It has no nasty habits. It works noticeably better than a stock bike. Yet it's fair to say that this engine should be capable of something like 1 horsepower per cubic inch, but it isn't. It makes 70. A sharp 80-incher makes as much. This is a de-blueprinted unit if there ever was one. So apart it comes, and some 40 hours and lots of measuring and fiddling and honing later, the same parts carefully assembled make 104 foot-pounds of torque and 84 horses.

Forget horsepower; it could be fuel mileage, oil consumption, braking ability, or outright reliability. Anyone with patience, touch, shop manual specifications, and measuring tools can find improvements—all over the machine. The saying goes like this, "Perfection is not gained by improving one thing 100 percent, but by improving 100 things by 1 percent." That's blueprinting!

ENGINE

PROJECT 40 • BREAKING IN A NEW ENGINE

 Time: Hours and hours of dedicated throttle restraint

 Tools: Your right wrist, a leak-down tester, and compression tester

 Talent: ♦♦

 Tab: 0

 Tinware: None

 Tip: Proper break-in can make all the difference in longevity, oil consumption, and performance of a fresh engine

! PERFORMANCE GAIN: Longevity

COMPLEMENTARY MODIFICATION: Oil temperature gauge and cylinder head temperature gauge

The classic definition of an air-cooled engine is, "A device used to heat surrounding air."

Air and oil as a cooling medium leave a bit to be desired. Air cooling works in two ways, radiation (when heat dissipates into the air around it) and convection. Convection is kind of a share-and-share-alike deal the parts of the engine work out among themselves. They share the heat, passing any excess back and forth between the parts. No, they don't like it much, but what the hey! It's a living, right? The point of all this is that the more uniform the friction losses are during break-in, the less work the cooling system has to do and the more power and longer life you can expect from the engine. Unfortunately, a lot of folks (including some at the factory) have spread a lot of misleading information about how to properly break-in an engine. Here's how to do it right:

• Don't treat the break-in suggestions in your owner's manual as "holy writ." Use full choke only to start the motorcycle. Back off the choke to a partial setting (as near off) as possible, as soon as the engine will take throttle cleanly.

• Warm the engine thoroughly before driving off (preferably 'til the valve covers are warm to the touch).

1 Even with its high-tech Teflon-esque coating, this piston didn't survive the break-in process as successfully as you'd want. It makes no sense to ignore proper technique if it leads to this. The old adage about break 'em in fast, they'll run fast is B.S., pure and simple. Not only did this piston die young from that philosophy, but more to the point, the top piston ring shows evidence of being completely worn out, while the second ring isn't even scrubbed in! The scuffs on the piston skirt are the most prominent giveaway. This slug has been in an engine that has been overheated and over-revved. The piston goes oval, squeezed by excessive expansion against the cylinder wall, and the rings haven't got a hope of sealing properly under those circumstances. Once searing heat gets past the rings to the cylinder wall, the rings, pistons, and standard cylinder bore are scrap. The bike couldn't have run well this way, and the owner just bought himself a needless bore job, thus losing 50,000 miles of cylinder life in the process. That dark ring around the wrist pin is more testimony of heat and abuse that prematurely ended this poor engine's life.

At the same time, avoid prolonged warm-up. If you can cook your breakfast on the motor, you've overdone it.

• Drive in a normal manner, avoiding both over-revving and under-revving. Lugging the engine can do as much damage as over-revving. Keep it under load and vary the rpm as much as possible without over-revving.

• Try to use "cool-down" cycles of progressively longer intervals as mileage accumulates. In other words, get the engine to operating temperature (ride 15 to 20 miles at least), and then let it cool off for approximately 10 to 15 minutes minimum. On the next trip, try 25 to 50 miles and 15 to 20 minutes of cool down, then 50 to 90 miles and 30 to 40 minutes, and so on. This bit is for the benefit of those fresh rings and cylinders more than anything, and after 300 to 500 miles, they're pretty much handled. You can revert to normal usage right at that accumulated mileage.

• Check oil level and condition at every fill-up. Regardless of mileage between oil changes, if the oil turns dark or smells burnt, change it.

• As mileage increases, you will probably notice how much more freely the engine will rev and how much more responsive it will feel. Harley-Davidson motors take a long time to get really loosened up (as much as 5,000 miles or more), so don't worry; if you break it in properly, the motor will probably outlive us all.

ENGINE

PROJECT 41 • SETTING CAM AND IGNITION TIMING

Time: 2 to 3 hours

Tools: Crane cam installation tool (Drag Specialties #DS199098); Allen wrenches; Torx wrenches; screwdrivers; 3/8-, 7/16-, 1/2-, 9/16-, 5/8-, 11/16-, 3/4-, 13/16-inch wrenches and sockets; rubber bands; paper clips; rubber mallet; degree wheel; micrometer; strip feeler gauges; assembly lube; anti-seize; and Loctite, a degree wheel and possibly a dial indicator or TDC tool (the radicals among us, especially Sportster owners, who want to do this right, may need to cut and weld cams as well)

Talent:

Tab: 0 to $$$

Tinware: Cone gasket #25225-70B to 1992 or #25225-93 for 1993–on and cone seal (#83162-51)

Tip: If you pressed a different cam gear (like the factory original, for example) on the cam you've chosen, make sure you pressed it on exactly where it belongs, or cam timing will be off

PERFORMANCE GAIN: Major if you find out that the cam timing or ignition timing are not in harmony

COMPLEMENTARY MODIFICATION: Upgraded ignition and cams

Proper cam and ignition timing are more important than you'd think because if the marks are off by even one tooth, the bike will not run at its best. You will not get the performance you paid for from that new cam.

Cam timing and ignition timing are not the same thing. They are, however, closely related. In fact, they work in the same "office" in the cam case. Sportster cam timing marks on the four one-lobe cams are there to ensure precise opening and closing times for the valves as the gears run against one another. Big Twins do the same thing but have different marks because their one cam has four lobes, and the cam gear only runs against one pinion gear. Ignition timing marks are there to create combustion at precisely the right point in the travel of the pistons and valves.

The different marks are particularly obvious in the case (pun intended) of the quadruple-underhead-cam XL engine, since the timing hole and the cams are on the same side of the engine. With the timing plug removed and the cam cover off (cams still in place), you

1 Here's a five-speed XL with its cam timing marks lined up correctly. Lined up might be too strong an expression. The fact is you simply want the dots on the cam gears and the dash on the pinion to be as close as you can get 'em.

set the cam timing marks in alignment. Then slowly rotate the flywheels, until the timing mark comes up, centered in the timing hole. Now look at the marks on the cams. See? They're no longer aligned. Move the flywheels a little further, and the cam marks line up again, though the timing mark has disappeared.

To check cam and ignition timing on a Sportster, do the following:

Sportsters should have the cam cover pulled off, cams in place in case, and a series of marks on the cam gears should line up, after a fashion. Of course, clear illustrations of correct cam timing marks are in your service manual, but there are illustrations here as well to help guide you.

After the cam timing has been verified, reinstall the cam cover and the ignition components. Then it's time to set the ignition timing with a timing light. That procedure is presented in "Timing Your Engine," but it doesn't hurt to reiterate here that 1996 and newer models reference two side-by-side dots on the flywheel (usually referred to as a "lazy 8") to set timing, whereas 1995 and earlier models use a single dot. The line, also marked on the flywheels, indicates top dead center (TDC) only.

To check cam timing on Big Twins, again, double-check your shop manual, but as a guide look at the accompanying illustration:

It may not seem possible, but accurate ignition timing, on top of accurate cam timing, is even more crucial on Big Twins than Sportsters because of the difference in stroke between the two. A degree or two on Sportster timing represents less distance traveled by the piston than the same degree or two in a Big Twin. Either way, the bottom line is that both types of timing are important to the engine's output.

Lining up the provided marks isn't even accurate enough for some people. Legends abound regarding the painstaking lengths the racers would go to, including cutting and welding cam lobes, just to get that last tenth of a degree of perfection in the cam timing. Once you've gone to that much trouble, it makes no sense not to back it with a dead nuts shot on the ignition timing, does it?

ENGINE
PROJECT 42 • INCREASING COMPRESSION RATIO

 Time: 6 to 10 hours

 Tools: Torque wrench, Allen for the intake manifold, 12-point socket for the head bolts, and the rest of the toolbox

 Talent: 👷👷👷

 Tab: $$

 Tinware: Top-end gaskets

 Tip: If you mill 0.50 to 0.60 inch off the surface, you will need to recut the counterbores to prevent leaks

 PERFORMANCE GAIN: Crisper throttle response, more snap at low rpm, and better pull right through the rpm range

COMPLEMENTARY MODIFICATION: Port or extrude-hone the heads

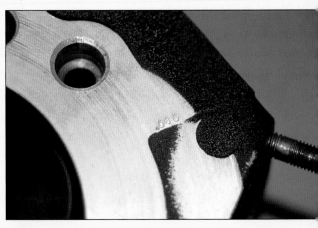

1. There are two things you should spot on a properly milled head. In this shot you see both: how much it's been shaved, 0.60 inch (stamped clearly on the machined surface) and the re-counterbored holes for the locating dowels.

The question for those who want to build Hyper Hogs is what compression changes will do for them (and to them) at any given increase in ratio. Like anything else, compression is best looked at, not in isolation, but in terms of how it serves the power producing "system." You need to understand how any alteration relates to everything from reliability to fuel choice to cam selection. There are lots of details to be concerned with. For instance, if you take 0.050 inch off the head, you need to machine the intake manifold to suit. Like the man said, "Nothing's ever simple."

While a figure like 10:1 makes for easy mental images of spatial "values" in the cylinder, it doesn't necessarily indicate (and was never really meant to) the true relationship that pressure has to power, let alone durability, in an engine. A better way to measure this pressure is to take an actual reading, in pounds per square inch (psi), of the engine in question. Commonly called a compression test, this reading—along with its partner the leak-down test—can supply valuable indicators of the engine's general health and help determine power output.

This is how it works. Suppose you have a burning desire to increase the power output on your Big Twin. The thing already has 50,000 miles on it, a bolt-in cam, and an efficient air cleaner and exhaust; it runs fine and doesn't burn any oil to speak of, but you can see puffs of smoke coming out of the exhaust once in awhile. A buddy has told you that bumping compression to around 10:1 will make it run a lot sharper. Hmmmm? Now what? No, you don't jerk the heads off, mill them 0.060 inch, and boogie. Instead you do compression and leak-down tests.

Suppose also that the compression test reveals that you have 145 psi in the rear cylinder and 120 in the front. Those numbers should be higher, with no more than a 10-percent difference between them. Okay, on to the leak-down test. Ah ha! Leak-down says the rear is fine, but the front has 34 percent leakage (any more than 8 to 9 percent is no good), and it's leaking out the exhaust pipe. Translation? The front exhaust valve is not sealing, you need a valve job, and you might need to hone and re-ring the cylinder, or bore out the cylinder.

Let's see now, the head has to come off anyway, and you're thinking you might as well do both heads and raise the compression while you freshen up the top end. Good plan, but how much? At this point you can't be sure if taking 0.050 to 0.060 inch off will get you 10:1, 42:1, or a trip to Disneyland. Meanwhile, your buddy has faded into the background and is keeping very quiet. You decide to

▶w To Determine How Much to Mill Your Head

Old Compression Ratio: 8.5:1
New Compression Ratio: 10.0:1
Stroke: 4.25 inches

$$\left[\frac{(\text{New CR} - 1) - (\text{Old CR} - 1)}{(\text{New CR} - 1) \times (\text{Old CR} - 1)} \right] \times \text{Stroke}$$

$$\left[\frac{(10.0 - 1) - (8.5 - 1)}{(10.0 - 1) \times (8.5 - 1)} \right] \times 4.25$$

$$\left[\frac{(9.0) - (7.5)}{(9.0) \times (7.5)} \right] \times 4.25$$

$$\left[\frac{1.5}{67.5} \right] \times 4.25$$

$$[0.022] \times 4.25$$

Amount to Mill the Head = 0.094 inches

▪nical compression ratio is greatly affected by cam timing. A more reliable measure is ▪ng pressure. Most street-driven Hogs benefit from an "optimum" cranking pressure of ▪ 175 psi.

▶alculating Mechanical Compression Ration

$$\left[\frac{\text{Cylinder displacement} + \text{net combustion chamber volume}}{\text{net combustion chamber volume}} \right]$$

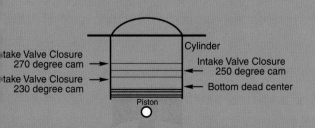

Cylinder

Intake Valve Closure
270 degree cam

Intake Valve Closure
250 degree cam

▶take Valve Closure
230 degree cam

Bottom dead center

Piston

▪stration shows how valve overlap effects compression. As duration increases, the piston ▪ up in the bore when the intake valve closes, effectively raising the compression ratio.

study up on things a little before you make your move. Good decision!

The easiest method of increasing the "squeeze" in the chamber is to have the heads milled down. The formula for figuring out how much to mill is shown with this project. All you need to know is your current compression ratio, the bore of your engine (stock 80-inchers use a 4.25-inch bore), and the compression ratio you desire. Plug the numbers into the formula, whip out a pocket calculator, and you come up with how much material you need to shave off of the head to get the desired compression ratio.

For Big Twins with stock heads, you can get an approximate number by figuring that every 0.30 inches you remove increases compression half a point. The formula doesn't work for Sportster and Buell owners, because those bikes have six different head designs. Don't forget that the thickness of the head gasket you choose to use makes a difference too.

Once you've determined how much you'll have them milled, follow these basic steps:

Strip the heads off the motorcycle.

Decide if you're going to port them.

If you aren't going to port them, send them to a reputable machine shop and ask to have whatever amount you've decided on milled off the gasket surface (and have the dowel holes counterbored).

If you are going to port them, remove valves, retainers, guides, and springs and ship the heads off to the "porter" of your choice. Then stuff rags in the cylinders (if the cylinders and rings are okay) and wait a few days. Otherwise, freshen up the bore while you wait.

If your bike was built prior to March 22, 1994, think about updating the cylinder studs and base gaskets to the newest production versions introduced after that date. These are vastly superior designs (see Project 43: Fixing Base Gasket Leaks).

When the heads are ready, reinstall them. Make sure you torque the heads absolutely by the book if you're using stock gaskets. (Ask your dealer about Service Bulletin #M-1043 if you need further details.) If you choose to use aftermarket base or head gaskets, torque them to the manufacturer's specs.

When done, fire up the engine and let it warm, but don't rev it up. Once it's at operating temperature, shut it off. Go in the house and relax until the motor's cooled off again.

ENGINE

PROJECT 43 • FIXING BASE GASKET LEAKS

Time: 5 to 7 hours

Tools: Factory shop manual, Trock cylinder resurfacing tool, cylinder torque plates, torque wrench, cylinder hone, and a full set of standard tools (at this stage you'd better have a lot of tools)

Talent: ŤŤŤ

Tab: $$$

Tinware: Top-end gasket set, Hayden Oil Fix dowel kit, James silicone/metal base gaskets, cylinder studs (1994 and earlier models), and possibly new piston rings if your bike has over 5,000 miles on the old ones (see Project 44: Checking Cylinders)

Tip: Disassemble as little as possible to get at the cylinder base; removing the heads, intake system, and exhaust as a unit can save hours

PERFORMANCE GAIN: A reliable, durable, leak-free joint between the cylinders and the crankcases

COMPLEMENTARY MODIFICATION: Add updated cylinder studs to the budget if you have a 1994 or older model

1 If you really want to permanently prevent oil leaks at the base gasket, install the Hayden Oil Fix dowel kit and James metal and silicone base gaskets. The dowel kit "sleeves" the oil passages from the cylinders to the crankcase. Oil traveling down the passage travels through the dowel, never even coming in contact with the base gasket. It cannot leak! The reason for using James base gaskets is primarily because of their durable metal construction. They are far less likely to "scrub" themselves to death during the repeated abuse of expansion and contraction of the cylinders and cases than are fiber gaskets.

Harleys occasionally blow cylinder base gaskets. Harley-Davidson combats the problem with ever-improving gaskets and revised cylinder studs. Their hard work has made quite a difference, which doesn't change the fact that Harleys will still blow the occasional base gasket.

The latest version of the base gasket incorporates a silicon bead on one side of the gasket material (Harley-Davidson calls it a "print-o-seal" type) that is much like they've used on primary gaskets for quite some time now. Likewise, they redesigned the cylinder studs for possibly the fourth time in midyear 1994. The new studs look like the earlier studs but need to be installed "upside down" to work. This is major progress, as the incidence of base-gasket leaks since this midyear 1994 upgrade has dropped dramatically. Still, after more than a dozen years and several so-called solutions to this persistent problem, do you suppose the leaks are history?

One of the simplest ways to avoid blown base gaskets is to warm your bike up thoroughly before thundering off. When you first fire up a Harley-Davidson, the thing applies 80 to 100 pounds of oil pressure (instead of the 15 to 20 at normal operating temps) to a cold joint, so you're asking for it unless you warm-up your bike at least 3 to 4 minutes. The bike is ready to roll when the valve covers are warm to the touch and not before.

That said, there's still room for vast improvement in the fundamental design flaw that makes for leaking base gaskets. Look hard at the area where the cylinder meets the crankcase; there's nothing between the bottom of the cylinder and the top of the case to prevent oil from escaping the joint except that thin, fibrous gasket. Plus, in the 4-cubic-inch area around the left rear cylinder stud (the most likely spot for a leak), there's a bolt holding the case halves together,

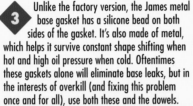

2 The Oil Fix dowel in place. Much like the larger dowel on top of the cylinder helps locate the head and prevent oil leaks at that joint, the dowel at the cylinder base ensures returning oil has no place to go but where it should.

3 Unlike the factory version, the James metal base gasket has a silicone bead on both sides of the gasket. It's also made of metal, which helps it survive constant shape shifting when hot and high oil pressure when cold. Oftentimes these gaskets alone will eliminate base leaks, but in the interests of overkill (and fixing this problem once and for all), use both these and the dowels.

4 The Harley-Davidson flat-rate manual quotes less time allowance to replace cylinder base gaskets than to remove the heads—by several hours! How can that be? Well, one reason is that most flat-rate mechanics will pull both heads, the pipes, and carb as a subassembly, if none of those components need service or repair of their own. This is a good thing to know if you're in a hurry.

a stud, and an oil drain-down hole in addition to the seam in the case joint itself. What's more, it's one of the hottest spots in the cases. As a result, this area is almost constantly changing shape and distorting during ordinary everyday use. Even the bottom of the cylinder itself is occasionally pulled out of shape and distorted by the stresses. A warpage depression of as much as 6 to 8 thousandths of an inch can develop along the mating surface of the cylinder where it bolts to the case. That much gap just makes the 0.020-inch-thick base gasket's job that much harder.

When you can see pieces of either stock gasket emerging slowly but surely from under the cylinders, even if there's no evident leakage at this stage, you can be sure the gasket will start to leak soon. If there is obvious leakage, try letting the bike warm up longer before you ride it. If that doesn't reduce the leaking, it's time to replace the gasket. And if you're going to replace the

base gaskets, replace them with the excellent metal gaskets from James. Here's the basic procedure:

First remove the top end heads. Unless you suspect a problem with the cylinder heads, carb, or pipes, you'll save a lot of time in disassembly if you remove both cylinder heads as a unit with the carb and exhaust pipes intact.

Once you have the top end stripped off, per the factory shop manual, the first move is to stuff some rags into the case, surrounding the connecting rods. You don't want any small but critical pieces, like the Hayden dowels, to fall in.

With the cylinders on the bench, install one dowel in each base oil hole, using Three Bond #4 or Hylomar to glue it in place.

If you don't already have the updated crankcase studs, now's the time to update. These studs (H-D #16832-86C for Sportster models and #16837-85C for

Big Twins) were introduced into production on March 22, 1994. Install them with the shoulder down, towards the crankcase. Simply screw them in and torque to 10 foot-pounds. They already have thread-lock cement on them, so there's no need to do anything more.

Check the base-gasket surfaces on both the cylinder and the crankcase with a straight edge. If there's daylight showing, even a bit, you need to reface the surface until it's totally flat. Use the Trock tool for this job. A little valve grinding compound applied between tool and surface, a couple of minutes twisting back and forth, and you're set.

Check the condition of the cylinder bores and the piston rings. Scratches in the bore mandate ball honing before reassembly. Likewise, if the rings are shiny bright all the way down the outside edge, they need replacing. New rings are a dull gray color on the outside, and Harley says they are still good to go, regardless of mileage, as long as the shiny bright on used ones doesn't go more than halfway down the outer edge. Generally, if the top end has more than 5,000 miles on it, it's cheap insurance to hone and re-ring, no matter what. Sure, you can do this yourself, but you need to use torque plates on

Evo cylinders to fool them into thinking they are in service on the engine to hone or bore them. You'll also need a 3.5-inch ball hone. Neither are cheap. For a one-time deal, it's best and often cheapest to let a pro do the honing.

If you insist on doing it yourself, you must have the torque plates, use the old gaskets along with them, and follow the procedure in the shop manual *precisely*. Believe it or not, this is one of the least talked about yet most screwed up processes you can perform on an Evo, so extra effort here pays off. Once the barrels are prepped, install them along with the Oil Fix dowels and James gaskets. Place the heads back in position.

Next torque the heads, using the procedure and torque settings that James recommends in their instructions. The James metal base gaskets can handle more torque, and the James process is simpler.

Once the top end is put back together, double-check everything and then start the engine. Let it get all the way up to operating temperature. Then shut it off and let it cool off completely. If new rings are involved, remember to break-in the motor as if it were new.

PROJECT 44 • CHECKING CYLINDERS

Time: 1/2 hour

Tools: Dial bore gauge

Talent: ▮▮

Tab: 0 to $$$ (the latter if you need cylinders)

Tinware: Torque plates, surface plate, or plate glass

Tip: Take measurements at room temperature

PERFORMANCE GAIN: Better performance and much longer mileage between top-end rebuilds

COMPLEMENTARY MODIFICATION: Bump up the compression (see Project 42: Increasing Compression Ratio)

1 Unlike the rest of the cylinder measurements, which involve precise dial bore gauges and the like, a bad liner can often be determined just by looking at it. The easiest to recognize symptom of failure is a steel liner that protrudes above the level of the alloy at the top of the cylinder. You can flip the barrel upside down on a surface plate and see if it rocks back and forth, or run your fingernail inwards from the gasket surface to the liner (if there's a lip, you'll feel it). Even if you can't tell for sure any other way, you can certainly manage to prove things, one way or the other, with a simple feeler gauge. This unit has a 0.005-inch gap!

When you see visible smoke exiting the exhaust pipes on an otherwise properly tuned Evo, traditionally, there are two main sources—something in the valvetrain has failed, or the rings aren't sealing in the cylinder anymore. Even fresh engines can stumble onto this pain in the ah . . . er . . . exhaust, and, in fact, if it's a low mileage engine, 9 times out of 10 it is the cylinder causing the grief. Oil consumption problems? Smoke out the pipe or no, that problem is most often traceable to the barrels as well. Call it the smoking gun theory, and what smoking gun doesn't have a barrel? It's curious, then, in view of this rather predictable program that one of the few unchanged parts in a 1998 Evo Big Twin engine (compared to the 1984 Evo engine) is, of all things, the piston. That's right, in an Evolution engine in which virtually every piece has been changed or modified since its 1984 debut, the piston has the exact same part number it started with. (In Harley-speak, the last digits in a part number indicate the year the part was designed.) Thus, the piston, sporting an -83 suffix, is now a teenager at 15 years of age. In tech terms, that's more like Methuselah, but so far there's been no need to redesign it. The cylinder, by number, has only been changed once in all that time as well. It's an -83A, which is to say it's been revised only

one time since 1983, unless it's a black cylinder. The black wrinkle bit showed up in 1986, so the painted powder-coated barrel gets an -86A. Otherwise it's identical. Obviously, The Motor Company has not found fault with the basic layout of these two partners in crime. Still that doesn't mean Harley owners will not on rare occasions.

There are a few things that can go wrong even with brand-new off-the-shelf cylinders. Mainly it boils down to—the hole isn't really round or straight!

An egg-shaped bore makes life hell for pistons and rings, especially rings. Uneven wear on the rings might mean that your bore is no longer perfectly round. When Harley (made by Hastings) rings are brand new, the outside edge should be a dull grayish silver. Broken-in properly, the ring's outside edges begin to look like bright shiny chrome about halfway down from the top. The bottom still looks dull silver.

If the outside edge of the ring is shiny from top to bottom, it's worn out. Rings that are shiny in only a part of the circumference, or look new in parts and completely worn out in others, are clues that your bore is out-of-round. Most of the time, there are more or less corresponding scrubbings on the piston. Either way, if you see uneven wear on the rings, you should check to see that the cylinder measures to specs. If don't have the necessary micrometers and such, take the cylinder in to someone who does.

If it's possible to have an oval hole in the barrel, it's downright probable that the bore may not be straight. Harley-Davidson takes great pains to avoid that pitfall, and you can look no further than the recommended method of clamping the cylinders in "torque plates" for re-boring for proof. Fact is, almost all the barrel's resistance to shape-shifting comes from this clamping. You can take a fresh cylinder assembly, which comes with its own matched piston, set it upside down on a bench or table, lightly oil the bore, stick the ringless piston in halfway, squeeze the cylinder flange with your hand, and watch the piston drop. Your squeezing efforts have changed the shape of the unclamped barrel. In service, clamped under a properly torqued head and into the crankcase, this doesn't happen. Nor does it happen if you use torque plates to bore a new oversize hole. The plates or engine studs pre-load and pre-stress the cylinder so it will grow and contract concentrically as it runs. The likelihood of a crooked hole is directly tied to the effort expended in the proper torquing or pre-loading of the cylinder, not to mention the boring process.

If your barrel liner is warped, the rings will be all scraped up, dinged, tweaked, twisted, and bent. Take a magnifying class to the rings, and you'll be able to see whether the rings are relatively smooth or all torn up. If they are, a new set of rings and a cylinder might save you. If the barrel or the rings are visibly chewed up, you may have to replace the cylinder.

The last problem is the steel liner pulling away from the alloy shell, which seems to occur most often in the Sun Belt. Those who live and ride in areas where it's possible to do both year round put on more miles in more heat in less time than the snowbound. So it follows that folks stuck in traffic on a 110-degree day in Vegas are more likely to suffer from this problem than a rider moving down a back road on a brisk day.

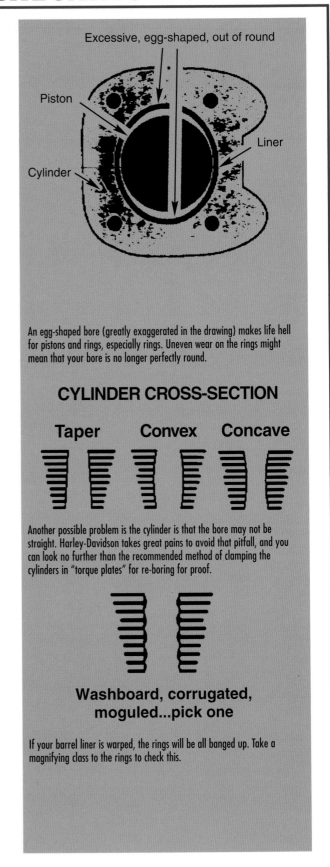

An egg-shaped bore (greatly exaggerated in the drawing) makes life hell for pistons and rings, especially rings. Uneven wear on the rings might mean that your bore is no longer perfectly round.

CYLINDER CROSS-SECTION

Taper **Convex** **Concave**

Another possible problem is the cylinder is that the bore may not be straight. Harley-Davidson takes great pains to avoid that pitfall, and you can look no further than the recommended method of clamping the cylinders in "torque plates" for re-boring for proof.

Washboard, corrugated, moguled...pick one

If your barrel liner is warped, the rings will be all banged up. Take a magnifying class to the rings to check this.

ENGINE

PROJECT 45 • CHOOSING HIGH-PERFORMANCE HEADS FOR YOUR SPORTSTER

 Time: 4 to 6 hours

 Tools: 3/16-inch Allen wrench, 7/16-inch wrench/socket, 1/2-inch wrench/socket, 12-point 1/2-inch socket, gasket scraper, and all the stuff needed to pull the gas tank, exhaust, and carburetor

 Talent: ♙♙♙

 Tab: $$$$$+

 Tinware: Top-end gasket kit and possibly new piston rings. Older models (pre-1994) may need updated cylinder studs and upgraded base gaskets

 Tip: Although this information is aimed at owners of 1200 Sportsters and Buells, porting 883 heads, especially 1986 883 heads, can bring tremendous results

PERFORMANCE GAIN: More power

COMPLEMENTARY MODIFICATION: High-flow air cleaner, high-performance exhaust, bolt-in cams (Screamin' Eagle/Buell or Andrews N4s), and ignition upgrades

1 If you notice any resemblance of a Screamin' Eagle/Buell 1200 head to that of its junior cousin, the 883 head, you're onto something. These two have much in common with each other, yet very little in common with a standard open-chambered 1200 Sportster head. Why should this be? One of the reasons is volumetric efficiency, which has always been higher per unit of displacement on 883s.

2 In between the 883 and the Screamin' Eagle/Buell heads you'll see what looks suspiciously like a so-called bathtub-chambered head. Well, it is a bathtub head. It arrived from the factory bolted onto the first big-bore Evo sporty, the 1986 1100. It was an interesting idea, using bathtub chambers and big 1340-sized valves, but it only lasted for the 1986 model year. The introduction of the 1200 saw a re-think of combustion chamber shapes and a shrinkage of valve sizes. From 1988 to 1998, The Motor Company has been faithful to what would appear to be (but isn't) a less effective head.

When the Evo Sportster engine appeared in the summer of 1985 as a 1986 model, its displacement was 883 cc. Rather than mimic the D-shaped combustion chamber of its big brother, it took a different path to efficiency. Blessed with a shorter stroke and a bore 1/2 inch smaller than the 1,340-cc Big Twin engine, the Sportster engine had different needs. As the engine has grown and its performance potential increased, the heads have changed as well. While this can lead to some confusion about optimal heads for your Sporty, or Buell, for that matter, don't get anal about it. There are virtually no bad stock heads on "X" motors, but which is best depends entirely on what you want from the finished machine. In the torquey, low compression, non-fuel fussy category, stock 883 and 1200 heads are perfectly suitable. Those who want Buell power levels on XLs need to consider the higher compression S1/Screamin' Eagle heads. Those for whom nothing but Max Pressure (in both senses of the word) will do—Thunderstorm/White Lightning Buell heads and

pistons are the latest word. But the further up the combustion chamber food chain you travel with head swaps, the further up the rpm band the payoff hides. In rigid mounted XLs, this can too often lead to the horsepower coming in at such high revs that you and the engine are too shaken to use it. That's one reason that the 1986 XL1100 "bathtub" heads only lasted one model year. They made plenty of top end but shook like mad when you got there. Better to have a broad usable powerband if you'd rather enjoy the ride than brag about peak dyno numbers. To beat this point to death, it so happens that many an 883 to 1200 conversion, using stock reworked, small valve 883 heads, will beat a "born" 1200 with it's bigger valves in a (pardon the expression) head-to-head roll-on from, say, 40 miles per hour to nearly 95 to 100. Got that through your head?

Although all Evolution Big Twin Harley engines are fitted with the same cylinder head design, Evolution Sportster engines have six variations:

1) The original head design for 883s used a

3 A look at the valves themselves offers an insight into corporate thinking. Left to right are 1100, 1200, and 883 valves. What did H-D hope to accomplish by opening the chambers and reducing the valve sizes? The 1100 had no reported power production problem, but it was noted for fuel fussiness and vibration. Also, most owners don't rev a Sportster hard enough to realize they've got all that top-end power. So the factory's decision to go from one extreme to another may have been nothing more than an attempt to reduce vibes and spread the powerband and move its bulges down to a rev-range that would be more useful. They succeeded in every objective, except, perhaps, the fuel fussiness. By de-tuning the big Sportster motor, Harley may have made it slightly less efficient but a lot more effective.

4 When Buell came on the scene, interest in sheer "Sporty" horsepower was revived. First lesson: The 883 chamber was good—just add a squish band to control pinging, put valves in sized to increase velocity not just volume, and pay attention to port shapes, and you get a 10-horsepower bolt-on. That was state of the art as of 1996. A scant few years later, there came yet another variation, the Thunderstorm head. A refined version of the 883 cum Screamin' Eagle/Buell pattern, the Thunderstorm was designed to be similar to the 1100 head in concept, if not in execution. Bigger valves (again and even more sophistication in port design have made these heads the performance choice. Just remember, to get all you pay for with these heads, you have to visit the redline frequently.

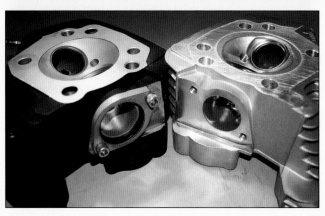

5 Don't discount the potential of the stock open-chambered 1200 head, on the left, just because it doesn't offer the squish band of its Buell relative, on the right. There's a reason that the stock head is the head "for the rest of us." With valve sizes identical to the Screamin' Eagle/Buell variety and port shapes that are clones as well, flow numbers should be in the same ball park. What the standard 1200 heads don't like is compression. Most of us riders don't either. In a way, it comes down to whether you want a slogger or a slugger—you don't build the same motor to pull a load up a hill as you do to pull low ET at the drag strip.

relatively small, tight chamber with a squish band incorporated in the layout to prevent detonation and increase "swirl." Despite smaller valves and a chamber shape that, for lack of a better term, was "semi-hemi," the 883 engine turned out roughly 80 percent as much power as its bigger brother, while being only 60 percent the size. Pretty impressive! Not long after its introduction somewhere in the 1987 model run, the 883 got a different head casting with subtle changes to chamber and ports. Most folks agree that it slowed them down too. The 1986-model 883s are considered the best runners of the bunch.

2) Could be that part of the reason for the casting change in mid-stride was that the 883s had a new

sibling forthcoming in the form of the 1100 Sportster—same stroke, bigger bore (but not a full 3 1/2 inches yet), and completely different combustion chambers. If you didn't know better, you'd swear that the factory had had Jerry Branch design these critters. There were the "bathtub" chambers so near and dear to Branch's heart and Big Twin-sized valves. Yes, the intake and exhaust valves were identical in head diameter to those used on the Big Twin motor, and the notion was that with a tight chamber and big valves, the 1100 would be a rocket ship. It didn't do too badly, but for some reason or other Harley-Davidson wasn't satisfied. After a short production run, the big Sportster was given a 3 1/2-inch bore and yet another set of heads. It became the 1200.

3) Nineteen eighty-eight and later 1200 Sportster heads are damn near hemispherical. The factory took a totally different direction with this design, using smaller valves and a very open chamber. One suspects that The Motor Company took a page from Ford here. Ford had tried a head much like the 1100's in the 1986 Mustang 5.0 V-8—for that one model year only—and the 5.0 cognoscente ruled it a low-powered, albeit clean-burning, mistake. The very next year, and from then on, Ford was back to open-chamber heads. Could it be that Harley discovered the same situation existed with its own 1100 heads? Whatever the motivation, the open-chambered 1200 heads are still with us on base 1200 Sportsters.

4) The Buells, however (with the exception of the S2), do not have these open-chambered 1200 heads. As soon as Buell had access to Harley-Davidson's deep pockets, out popped the S1 Lightning head. Surprisingly, these heads hearken back to the 883's basic chamber shapes, which tightened up the chamber for increased mechanical compression and featured an extended squish band to accommodate the larger bore thus keeping detonation out of the picture. As anyone who's ever ridden a Lightning will attest, it helped a bunch. The Lightning heads are largely responsible for putting the "sport" back in Sportsters.

5) Introduced in 1997, the XL1200S was The Motor Company's response to Buells. Though a far more traditional machine than the Buells, the 1200S at least let hard-core Harley buyers know that the factory still had a trick or two up its sleeve where the granddaddy of Superbikes was concerned. It was good when it appeared and got better this year. In 1998 we saw yet another iteration of the Sport 1200, this time utilizing S1-style heads with a twist—an extra spark plug hole. While extra plugs are often used to increase performance, Harley used them here primarily as a means of getting a cleaner burn with the 1998 1200S's hot new cams.

6) Meanwhile, the boys at Buell weren't done developing heads either. Content with pursuing their secondary roll as "Skunk Works" for Harley-Davidson performance (as well as motorcycle manufacturer), they've developed yet another set of heads, the Thunderstorm and White Lightning version. It's right here that we find a departure in concept from all the other incarnations of Sportster heads.

White Lightning of the distilled variety is generally kept in a jar, or at least a container it won't eat through. Mechanical White Lightning needs a container of its own. The head provides the lid, the cylinder forms walls, and the piston the base, and basis, of this new power bottle. Unlike the other heads, to work as designed, Thunderstorm heads need domed pistons. Not massively domed but noticeably more proud than the flat tops of yore.

The system works like this: The heads bring bigger valves, recontoured ports, and unshrouded guides to the party. The pistons make back the losses of trapped volume in the combustion chamber that accompany the improved head configuration. At 10:1 mechanical compression, it's a zero-sum game relative to regular S1 heads. However, the Thunderstorm heads are a quantum improvement over S1 heads when it comes to performance. Make no mistake, the Thunderstorm beats the Lightning like the Lightning beats the Thunderbolt.

A simple horsepower solution for owners of older Evo Sportsters is to swap the existing heads for a later, better-breathing variety. Happily, for about $700, you have your choice of two flavors of better breathers: Screamin' Eagle/S1 heads only or Thunderstorm/White Lightning heads and the pistons you must use with them. This is cost-effective power at its finest. Unfortunately, the few aftermarket cylinder head choices for "X" motors are all much more expensive, and none work any better—at least for 1200-cc street engines. At the risk of oversimplifying, the best way to build a 1200 Sportster is to duplicate a Buell as nearly as possible, though the differences in exhaust keep you about 10 horsepower under the Buell, all else equal. The best way to build a Buell is to use the Thunderstorm top end and add the factory's Pro-Race kit.

ENGINE

PROJECT 46 • CHOOSING HIGH-PERFORMANCE HEADS FOR YOUR BIG TWIN

 Time: 4 to 6 hours

 Tools: Same as for base gaskets, including 3/16-inch Allen wrench, 7/16-inch socket, 1/2-inch 12-point socket, and torque wrench

 Talent:

 Tab: S x 10 or 15, depending on the heads

 Tinware: Top end gasket kit, Hylomar 3-bond #4

 Tip: Billet heads look great, but they don't offer any more steam on the street

PERFORMANCE GAIN: 20 to 30 percent more power

COMPLEMENTARY MODIFICATION: The sky's the limit, but remember that increasing airflow is the key to more power

If what you're after is real neck-snapping performance, then you're going to have to do something with the cylinder heads. This can be as simple as milling the gasket surface to bump compression, or it can involve taking the stock heads to a qualified flow expert for any of a number of porting stages. A third alternative is to simply buy and fit a set of new heads from one of more than half a dozen aftermarket vendors of high-performance Big Twin cylinder heads.

These aftermarket designs go beyond the limits of the stock cylinder-head castings, incorporating the latest thinking and execution of port shape, combustion-chamber design, and manufacturing techniques. Plus they often feature technology proven on big-inch race cars, like Edelbrock's heads, which have automotive-style square-port intakes. These ports don't have the "dead air" in the center as round ports do. And both the Custom Chrome Inc. (CCI)/RevTech and the S.T.D. heads come pre-drilled and tapped for dual-plugs, so you may easily upgrade your ignition, which

1 The traditional D-shaped combustion chambers, a hallmark of Big Twin Evos for 15 years, have far more going for them than you may think. This design's fundamental shortcomings are the limits of flow at the exhaust port, restriction of the intake charge by the close proximity of the straight edge of the "D," and the large, round port shapes. Since the stock compression ratio is conservative, extra power can be easily gained by milling these stockers 0.50 to 0.60 inch. As a point of reference, California Highway Patrol FXRPs came from the factory with 0.050 inch off the heads and 0.015 inch shaved from the cylinders, which actually improved octane tolerance without compromising reliability. Considering the abuse a motor officer can dish out (in this case, mechanical), this says a lot about the Evolution Big Twin's ability to take it.

is a good thing for huge bores where flame travel may be too slow otherwise.

Each manufacturer tends to have its own tested and preferred cam, carb, and pipe combinations, or at least strong recommendations for those items. It helps to bear that in mind, referencing your existing setup, when comparing options. It will do you no good to drop a fortune on hot-rod heads and lose the benefit by running a bad combination of critical components. In fact, you can screw up a $2,000 investment by doing something as innocent as using the wrong exhaust gaskets. So pay attention to the details and what the builder says. If you want to know what you're up against, ask. For example, an S&S head conversion may also require the use of special pistons, and all this can get pretty involved. Swapping those pistons requires special tools, procedures, a bit more expertise, and, under certain conditions, the services of a machine shop.

Heads from S&S, CCI/RevTech, Edelbrock, Patrick Racing, Pro-One, and S.T.D. have lots in common and several important differences. The Patrick Racing and Pro-One heads are machined from billet stock, whereas the CCI/RevTech, Edelbrock, and S.T.D. heads are all machined from castings. While the structural advantages of a billet design (handling extreme tensile and thermal stress better) are negligible on a street bike, for

2 Harley's new Screamin' Eagle heads for the 80-incher incorporate the design lessons learned in the last decade. Probably the most significant of these is the switch to so-called anti-reversion, D-shaped ports. The notion behind the port shape is that it can stop exhaust pulses from reversing direction in the pipe and thus "stuffing" the incoming charge.

3 The intake port benefits from a low-rise "fin" placed at the base of the valve guide in the middle of the port. It creates two small nasty vortexes instead of one big lazy one, mixing fuel and air rapidly and more completely on its way into the chamber. The exhaust port gets its own fin on the chamber side of the anti-reversion dam, as well. These seemingly subtle alterations from the regular Big Twin ports result in more turbulence and more volume of flow in a faster moving mixture—neatly creating a fair increase in top end power and a great increase in low- to mid-range power.

4 For years now, it's been common knowledge that true high-performance Harley heads incorporate what have come to be called a "bathtub" combustion chamber shape. What's not so commonly known is that one of its primary benefits is the increased "squish" area the shape provides. Fuel-air mixture is supposed to burn controllably, not explode. A flat shelf in the combustion chamber squishes the mixture to such a degree that it's nearly impossible to get it to explode (detonation), regardless of compression ratio. Since most all increases in power also involve increases in compression, this comes in very handy. "Bathtubbing" amounts to squeezing more mixture, under greater pressure, into a smaller area, with less risk.

drag racing they may be central. And simple aesthetic and financial differences can be enormous. Needless to say, fit and finish are important considerations at this level of dollar involvement.

Another issue is intake manifolds: All but the Edelbrocks are compatible with the stock mounting system, but each manufacturer supplies or recommends a particular intake manifold. Are they going to be compatible with your current setup, or will you need to budget for a new carb, air cleaner, and manifold? Possibly the single biggest advantage to these aftermarket heads, aside from the flow potential, is that they are set up to accept high-lift cams, which means basically unlimited cam choice.

As nice as it is having plenty of choice, it's certainly no guarantee. None of these choices will give their best without proper tuning and dial-in, so save some money for dyno time. Take the time to get it right, and most combinations will provide all the good, usable torque and horsepower you'll ever need.

As it turns out, perhaps the safest bet overall is the new H-D Screamin' Eagle heads. These heads incorporate all that's been learned over the years (anti-reversion, high velocity porting, and bathtub chambers with oversized valves, to name the notorious) and offer it at

a truly competitive price of $800 to $900 assembled. And they are clever in that their 72-cc chamber volume gives a sensible 9.5:1 compression ratio with stock pistons, while offering a more radical 10.5 option if you use the new Screamin' Eagle pop-up pistons.

Screamin' Eagle offers a number of different heads, including Silver #16851-98 for $800 or Black #16854-98 for $900. They will handle .600-inch lift cams, through 1.90-inch intakes and 1.62-inch exhausts. More importantly, these heads flow a factory rated 153 cubic feet per minute going in (20 percent better than stock) and 115 cubic feet per minute headed out (a whopping 30-percent improvement), with valve springs and retainers that allow blasts up to 6, 500 rpm safely. Kids, there's plenty o' power in them there heads. If you would like to raise the compression, you'll have to bore the engine 0.005-inch over to run the 10.5:1 pistons (#22766-98). There is no standard bore version, however, because this way, you're forced to set clearances properly. If you need even more oversized units, they can be had in 0.010 inch (#22767-98) and 0.030 inch (#22768-98) for $280—in any size

If you need replacement parts or separate components for the heads or pistons, don't guess; see your dealer.

PROJECT 47 • SEALING YOUR ROCKER BOXES

Time: 1 to 3 hours

Tools: Modified 3/16-inch Allen and the usual hand tools, including torque wrench, extension, 3/16-inch Allen deep socket, gasket scraper, surface plate or plate glass

Talent:

Tab: $ for gaskets, $$$$ for aftermarket rocker boxes

Tinware: Rocker gasket kit, Hylomar or Three Bond #4 sealer, and aftermarket rocker boxes

Tip: Find a piece of plate glass or surface plate and lay the cover or D-ring on top of it; if either rocks at all, replace the part

PERFORMANCE GAIN: A neat and tidy appearance after a hard run

COMPLEMENTARY MODIFICATION: Chrome boxes to replace polished ones

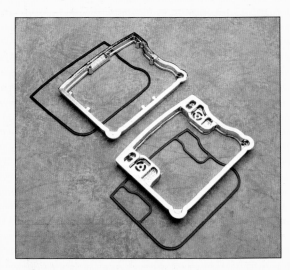

1 All 1984 to 1991 Big Twin models use the D-rings shown at left and either cork or rubber gaskets. All 1992 and later Big Twin models use the head-breather type on the right and more intricate rubbers. Enlarging the oil drain holes slightly or inserting a small hollow dowel to raise the level of the drain holes can help keep oil from blowing into the air cleaner on head-breathers.

One of the signature features of Evolution Big Twins and Sportsters is the distinctive stacked or sandwich-type rocker-cover assemblies. These covers are probably the main reason the Evo's nickname is "Blockhead." Unfortunately, these rocker covers are often a source of headaches in the form of leaks.

There are at least four incarnations of lower rocker covers and four or five versions of the middle cover, or D-ring, as it's often called (aside from the obvious difference between a chromed one and a polished one). The earliest type (1984–1987) has smooth lower mating surfaces (designed for use with cork rocker-box gaskets). The first redesign was made of a zinc alloy (chromed versions which virtually guaranteed warpage and in 1989 was responsible for many a leak). These l'il buggers were introduced, best guess, midyear 1988, but H-D kept trying to use them up until 1990 on first year Fat Boys. In 1990 (unless you bought a Fat Boy), the design was changed to an aluminum type with the herringbone pattern bottom mating surface. Finally, they were changed again for 1991 Sportsters and 1992 Big Twins. And these later "head-breather" rocker boxes are most definitely not interchangeable with the early ones.

One of the main motivators for all the changes on early models was the factory's desire to replace the cork gasket material with rubber. It was a good idea, but if you happen to own one of the earlier Blockheads that require the corks, you best not try to sneak by with the new factory rubbers—they will not work. Scan Harley-Davidson service bulletin #M 984 before you attempt to reassemble leaking rocker boxes on 1984–1991 models.

The head-breather rocker boxes on the later models was intended to clean up, cosmetically, the oil pump area on Big Twins, the cam cover oiling on XLs, and to provide better EPA-defined oil control. It entailed redesigning the internals of the rocker boxes and the associated gaskets to allow the crankcase to vent up to the boxes instead of out to the air, theoretically, to "re-breath" the gases scavenged from the crankcase. As it turns out, it wasn't a total success, as oil can accumulate in the rocker boxes to the point that it blows into the air cleaner. This happens most often during long, hard high-speed rides.

Nevertheless, when rocker boxes leak, it's usually because over- tightening or overheating has warped

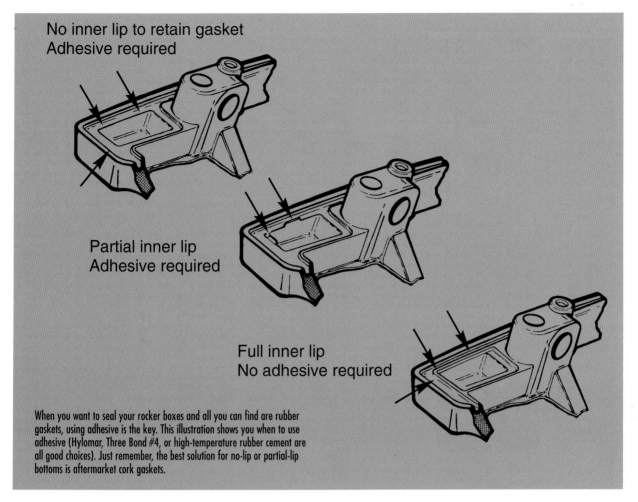

No inner lip to retain gasket
Adhesive required

Partial inner lip
Adhesive required

Full inner lip
No adhesive required

When you want to seal your rocker boxes and all you can find are rubber gaskets, using adhesive is the key. This illustration shows you when to use adhesive (Hylomar, Three Bond #4, or high-temperature rubber cement are all good choices). Just remember, the best solution for no-lip or partial-lip bottoms is aftermarket cork gaskets.

them, or the cork or rubber gaskets have been pinched or split, or both. Sometimes the D-ring moves out of alignment when hot. This happens when the herringbone pattern of ridges on the bottom of the D-ring isn't able to hold the thing in place. The fiber gaskets between the rocker boxes and the cylinder head leak about 1 percent as often as the rubbers, and then only if the gasket is pinched or the metal surfaces are gouged. Leaking rubbers can happen; leaking fibers shouldn't.

Since you cannot get genuine H-D corks for early models anymore, you have three choices if your bike has the 1984–1986 1/2 rocker boxes designed for corks: Buy aftermarket corks (James Gaskets, for example), "glue and screw" for hours to attain dry rocker boxes using late-model rubbers that aren't really compatible, or buy updated factory parts or aftermarket rocker boxes from Arlen Ness, Rick Doss, Pro-One, or any one of a host of others. Most are a fancier, or simply more fanciful, alternative to the factory item. Some are a two-piece design with one less seam to potentially leak. All are expensive. If you simply must have 'em, examine the mating surfaces for precision sealing and intelligent (preferably stock)

gasket retention design. No matter how cool they look in the catalog, they will not look too hot if they leak oil all over your bike.

Just like the shop manual says, removing rocker boxes is a straightforward operation, except for the tight access clearances on some models, such as Softails. Late-model Softails have an access hole in the frame above the Allen fastener that's hard to reach. However, lots of folks still grind the short leg of a standard Allen down to about one-third normal length so they can get the tool in to loosen that fastener. Removing gas tanks isn't always necessary but is always a good idea, if for no other reason than to keep from scratching them and, of course, improving access. A good upgrade for early models is to budget for the late-style stock Allens. These late-model screws (H-D # 882) have a trapped washer that seals the threads better than separate washers.

Reassembly isn't rocket science. Tighten the fasteners in a cross pattern to 10–12 foot-pounds of torque, and don't over do it. Remember, you don't want to split or pinch the brand-new rubbers or warp the D-ring.

PROJECT 48 • INSTALLING ROLLER ROCKER ARMS AND ADJUSTABLE PUSHRODS

 Time: 5 to 8 hours

 Tools: Allen wrenches; brass drift; hammer; 7/16-, 1/2-, 9/16-, and 5/8-inch wrenches or sockets; and a torque wrench

 Talent: ▮▮▮

 Tab: $$$$$

 Tinware: Roller rockers, adjustable pushrods, and a rocker-box gasket kit

 Tip: If your bike has 50,000 to 60,000 miles on it and it's never had the top end off, you may be a good candidate for this conversion because your stock rocker arms are probably showing signs of wear anyway

 PERFORMANCE GAIN: Valvetrain components live a lot longer, especially with radical-lift cams

COMPLEMENTARY MODIFICATION: Fancy rocker boxes

1 The secret's in the tip, and the tip's the secret for high lift cams. The roller bearings cut friction and reduce side loads on the valve stems. Why slide when you can roll? Strip the rocker boxes off, remove the pushrods, and dri out the rocker shafts. Check the condition of the rocker shafts and valve tips. If the damage or excessive wear, you need to replace those parts to get the best from yo new roller rockers.

2 High lift cams and roller rockers beg for chrome-moly adjustable pushrods. Optional for bolt-in cams, they become a near necessity for aggressive cams with more than 0.550-inch lift that will be used at 5,500 rpm or better. Why? Because stock aluminum pushrods have four times as much flex in 'em at high rpm. So stiffer moly rods will accurately follow the most aggressive cam profiles.

Stock H-D rocker arms and pushrods work fine in stock motors, but they will wear quickly and can be extremely noisy on engines with high-lift aftermarket cams or milled heads because the rocker arm, especially on Big Twins, gets hit by this pushrod at a less than a perfect angle, due to the valvetrain geometry of the Big Twin motor. The result is a certain amount of loud side-swiping amongst rocker arm tips, pushrod tips, and, most importantly, the valve stem tips.

The best way to cut valvetrain wear and noise to a minimum is to use roller rockers in conjunction with adjustable pushrods. Roller rockers have a roller on their valve arm that cuts friction between the rocker and the valve stem by as much as 200 percent, thus using up less engine power. While the roller rockers are not all that much quieter themselves, they prevent a lot of expensive noises down the road. The adjustable pushrods are typically stiffer than stock and allow easier changing of cams and other components because they can be collapsed out of the way.

If and when you contemplate a switch to high-lift (over 0.500-inch) cams, especially those with aggressive ramping, you really need roller rockers. Typically since these cams require valve-spring upgrades as well as special collars and keepers anyway, removing the heads is a given. While the heads are off, it's a simple matter to install roller rockers and adjustable pushrods. The increased longevity of your valvetrain, along with the improved performance and reliability, make this upgrade a smart move.

To install the rockers and adjustable pushrods, follow the instructions in your shop manual to remove the gas tank and expose the rocker boxes. Then do the following:

Remove the rocker-box lids and the center sections (D-rings) and undo the pushrod tubes to access the pushrods. You can hold the tubes out of the way with clothes pins, rubber bands, paper clips, or with any other method that keeps them from interfering with the next task.

With a bolt cutter cut the stock pushrods until they can be removed. Remove the pieces.

Remove the rocker-shaft retaining bolts.

Drive the rocker shafts out with a soft drift and

3 Roller rockers in place, complete with an upgraded valve spring kit. This is a great combination to tame a radical cam. All that remains is to re-seal the rocker boxes and adjust the pushrods. (Note: Some roller rockers, in addition to rollers on the tips, have needle rollers on the rocker-shaft bearings. This may not be a good setup for the street because the hardened needles have been known to cut through the surface hardening of the shafts, destroying them relatively quickly.)

light taps with a hammer and remove the stock rocker arms.

While everything is stripped out of the rocker box, check the parts for wear and damage. For instance, replace any rocker-shaft retaining bolts that have a notch worn into them. Make sure that the tip of the valve stem is virtually as good as new. There is no sense installing new roller rockers on damaged or worn tips.

Fit the new roller rocker arms in place and gently tap the rocker shaft back into place. Do not use excessive force because the shafts and arms are a snug sliding fit—better to keep it that way.

Make sure the notches for the shaft retaining bolts are positioned to allow the bolts to drop into place easily. Drop them in place and then tighten them.

Install and adjust the pushrods according to the manufacturer's instructions.

Fit the pushrod tubes in place using new pushrod-tube O-rings.

Reinstall the air cleaner cover and gas tank.

Start the bike and check for leaks.

ENGINE

PROJECT 49 • CONVERTING SPORTSTER 883S TO 1200S

Time: 8 to 12 hours

Tools: 3/16-inch Allen; 7/16-, 1/2-, 9/16-inch wrenches and sockets, wobbler extension, 12-point 1/2-inch socket, gasket scraper, screwdrivers, rubber mallet; and be sure to keep the rest of your hand tools close by. You may also need a burret for measuring combustion chamber volume, a dremel-like grinder (and factory template) for modifying 883 heads, perhaps even a boring bar and bead blaster

Talent: 👷👷👷

Tab: $$$$$+

Tinware: Depends slightly on which method you choose to get from 883 to 1200, but for sure a top-end gasket set

Tip: Justify this financially by realizing the conversion pays for itself in two to three years if you don't tell your insurance agent it's a 1200

PERFORMANCE GAIN: 30 horsepower and 30 percent more torque

COMPLEMENTARY MODIFICATION: Ignition module, cam, carb, pipe, and taller gearing

Easily the best way to get the most out of an 883 is to make it a 1200, either after you've already put all the hot-rod goodies you can stand on the ol' 55-incher, or first, before you do any of the rest.

The process, stripping the top end off, is the same no matter which path you choose to arrive at increased displacement. For that matter, it's the same as replacing base gaskets or pulling the thing apart for a regular overbore. It's the same thing your service manual tells you it is in terms of wrenching it apart and back together again. It's just that there are lots of decisions to made in between at lots of different prices and levels of completion.

OVERBORING

The most common method is to bore the cylinders, install factory flat-top 1200 pistons, and machine the 883 heads to suit. Pros: reuses all the original stuff except pistons and gaskets. Cons: getting a good deal on boring (not everybody can

1 The 883 cylinder (right) is nothing more than an under-bored 1200 unit (left). Due to this, the 1200 cylinder 5 pounds lighter. The factory 1200 pistons, however, give a little of that weight back because they are heavier than 883 slugs. You can convert your 883 to a 1200 by simply bolting the 1200 cylinders (left) on to your bike. Using factory pistons and cylinders like these will work, but you'll need to do some cylinder head work and crankshaft rebalancing to make it all work right.

2 Another option for an 883-to-1200 conversion is to use the 883's heads and light, stock-883-weight aftermarket pistons, like these Wisecos. Because of their cutout crowns and trimmed skirts, engines fitted with them require no crankshaft rebalancing and no head cutting. There's a fringe benefit to using stock 883 heads that's often overlooked as well; the smaller valves make for amazing midrange punch. As a result, 883s converted to 1200s often out-run factory 1200s in freeway roll-on contests, clear to 90 miles per hour! Who needs trick heads?

3 Factory pistons have a flat top, so using them in a 1200 conversion means whittling extra room into the combustion chamber of an 883 head. This is expensive, tedious, and not totally effective. A better plan is to use the Wiseco piston with factory piston rings. The Wiseco's dished-out crown eliminates the need for head work. With factory piston rings, the pair weighs about what the standard 883 slug does, so no re-balancing of the crank is required, and vibration levels remain consistent. The Wiseco's partial skirts cut friction and help rev-abilty, and the silicon content of Wiseco's means serious strength and very little shape-shifting.

cut the holes a 1/2 inch larger cheaply), and machining the heads is a pain. Unless you can do the machining yourself or have a good friend who can help, it can cost close to the price of new Thunderstorm Buell head assemblies. Since you have to buy pistons anyway, using the Thunderstorm domed pistons makes sense (see "Buell Pistons, Heads, and Aftermarket Cylinders" below). Should you choose to bore existing barrels rather than simply swapping for Harley 1200 barrels, it should be because, A) you believe that a "cured" cylinder (one with plenty of miles on it) will not change shape and will maintain a straight bore better than a new "green" cylinder, or B) you get a deal on boring or can't afford $230 worth of new barrels. Here's a breakdown of the costs:

    1200 piston kit: $135
    Boring cylinders: $150–250
    Machining 883 heads for conversion: $200–400
    Top-end gasket kit: $70

INSTALLING STOCK 1200 CYLINDERS

The next most expensive method is to swap to black wrinkle stock 1200 cylinder assemblies, complete with pistons. Here's a breakdown of the costs:

    1200 painted cylinder assemblies: $475 a pair
    Machining 883 heads for conversion: $200–400
    Top-end gasket kit: $70

AFTERMARKET CYLINDERS

The next method (and probably the cheapest) is to replace cylinders with unpainted "conversion" barrels and use aftermarket "dished" pistons so you don't have to machine the stock heads. This method costs about $200 to 300 less than method one, but you can't use these pistons if you change heads later. See how this works? Here's a breakdown of the costs:

    Conversion (unpainted) cylinders: $260 a pair
    Dished pistons: $190–210 a pair
    Honing (required for use of dished pistons) $30–40
    Top-end gasket kit: $70

BUELL HEADS AND 1200 CYLINDERS

Method three uses Lightning (Buell S1) cylinder heads and the regular 1200 cylinder assemblies with flat-top pistons. Here's a breakdown of the costs:

    Lightning or Screamin' Eagle heads: $700–750 a pair
    1200 painted cylinder assemblies: $475 a pair
    Machining 883 heads for conversion: $200–400
    Top-end gasket kit: $70

BUELL PISTONS, HEADS, AND AFTERMARKET CYLINDERS

This method uses Buell Thunderstorm pistons (or aftermarket equivalents with 10 to 10.5:1 compression), Thunderstorm heads, and conversion barrels to give the most power of any of the options. This method actually costs about $100 less than method three and produces more power. A breakdown of the costs follows:

    Thunderstorm heads: $500 a pair
    Thunderstorm pistons: $130 a pair
    Conversion barrels: $260 a pair
    Top-end gasket kit: $70

OTHER OPTIONS

You can of course do a combination of the above. Bear in mind that dished pistons only work with stock 883 heads. Standard 1200 heads, modified 883 heads, and Lightning heads use flat-top factory 1200 pistons. Thunderstorm heads need domed pistons with 10:1 compression. Now, if you don't want to or can't afford to buy heads, don't panic. Just be aware that the necessary head machining for a 1200 conversion, using factory pistons, can cost close to half the price of a set of Thunderstorm heads, and if you need a valve job while the heads are off—be aware.

The other way to go, if you can't afford heads, is with Wiseco pistons. They make conversion pistons with machined depressions in the crowns that eliminate the need for reworking stock 883 heads. They cost $200 a pair, give or take 10 bucks, which is a bit more than the factory pistons. Also, Wiseco has a cagey way of making you set clearance the way they want it by making the pistons about 0.005 inch oversized, so you must hone the cylinders to proper clearance. Thus, there's additional work and expense, and it's not quite the bolt-on proposition the stock parts are. Lastly, Wiseco offers two different ring-groove widths. You want the thicker one that will take stock H-D (Hastings) replacement rings.

One more thing: Factory 1200 pistons are heavier than 883 pistons. Wiseco pistons are nearly as light as 883 pistons, and there are other aftermarket piston choices that run the gamut. If you don't go nuts with compression and ensure that the pair of pistons you choose weigh the same, you should not have to worry about excessive vibration. Crankshaft rebalancing is, or should be, a non-issue.

MAKING THE CONVERSION

Whichever method for conversion you choose, the basic steps to fitting the parts is the same:

Remove the gas tank, ignition switch, and motor-mount bracket to give yourself more room in which to work. Be sure to keep the bolts you remove organized right from the beginning. Part the rocker boxes. If you have never done this before, it is best to read the section in your service manual, and take a look at Project 47: Sealing Your Rocker Boxes before you start.

Remove the pushrods, number them, and be sure to return them in the proper order.

Remove the heads. The preferred method to save time (if head work isn't on the agenda) is to remove them as a pair. Take apart only what you must to get the heads off leaving the carb and exhaust on to tie the two heads together.

Lift the cylinders off the pistons and immediately block the case openings with clean rags. This will prevent anything from falling into the bottom end, like piston pin clips or snap rings. These crafty little devils have a way of flying across the shop, bouncing off the walls and ending up in your eye, or engine.

Should you choose to bore existing barrels, make sure the barrel is set into torque plates, torqued to specifications, and rough-cut on a lathe first. A lathe is used to speed things up because a nearly quarter-inch cut is required before the final boring is done, and it can take all day at 0.010 inch a pass (remember, you are going from a 3-inch to a 3.5-inch bore). In some shops, all this can be done on an exchange basis, and with advance notice barrels can be made up for you, making this truly a one-day swap. The final cut is made with a boring bar. In this step a few cuts are made to remove the final 0.040 inch. This is the most crucial of the steps, since the bore must be straight and true, so be sure this is done by a reputable shop. The last of it is honing to a final fit and finish, generally to just few thousandths of an inch, with a "cross-hatch" of about 45 degrees to retain oil on the walls. If you want to test the shop you use to bore, ask them what the clearances should be for both factory pistons and the pistons you're using—after you've read it for yourself. See if their answer matches and makes sense.

If you have your heads machined, anybody with the equipment can mill the surface, but a "litmus test" of the shop's Harley knowledge is whether or not they automatically counterbore the dowel holes in the head to keep the sealing O-rings from being pinched or cut on assembly. And the pro-touch is stamping the amount milled, in thousandths, into the head, so you don't have to remember, or the next guy who tears 'em down won't have to guess.

When installing any brand of piston, pre-check the ring fit in the barrels and on the pistons. Install the ring square in the barrel and check for proper ring end-gap. Ensure that the ring is set evenly by measuring it with a vernier caliper or by using a piston to square the ring in the bore. Too little clearance requires a different ring or a little filing of the ring ends. Too much, and you need new rings.

If you choose to paint the cylinders and heads, carefully prepare to apply a coat of wrinkle black to the fins. The barrel should be stuffed with clean shop rags to keep paint residue out. Heads should be masked off with tape in crucial (normally "closed to the public") areas. After the paint dries, take a scouring pad and rub off the fin edges. Do the same for the heads. And do yourself a favor, bring a tube of elbow grease to the party—this is work!

Mount the rings on the pistons and the pistons on the connecting rods. Use new circlips. And whether you use the trick factory tool or a pair of needle-nosed pliers, double-check that they are safely, solidly in the groove.

Once ready, a ring compressor is used to guide the piston and rings into the freshly bored, lightly oiled barrel. This step can be done without a ring compressor (if you're very talented and have money to replace the rings you might break).

Install the heads step by step by the manual. The only deviation from the shop manual will be installation procedures for non-stock heads or base gaskets. If you installed those, use the manufacturer's specs for torque.

Double-check ignition timing when you're finished just to make sure it's correct. The 1200s aren't nearly as tolerant of sloppy ignition timing as 883s and will ping like mad if you are very far off.

PROJECT 50 • CHOOSING AFTERMARKET CAMSHAFTS

 Time: 1 hour and up

 Tools: Catalogs, specifications, and perhaps a telephone

 Talent:

 Tab: $$ to $$$

 Tinware: Nothing

 Tip: Refer to the charts on pages 243-248

PERFORMANCE GAIN: Power gains from 20 percent or so over stock to much, much more

COMPLEMENTARY MODIFICATION: Free-flow air cleaner, carb, good pipes, and an ignition upgrade; on 1992 and newer Big Twin models, upgrade the cam bearing

1 Unique among modern engines is the Sportster's use of four single-lobe, cams. This arrangement allows better geometry in the valvetrain and, consequently, tolerance for high rpm and cam specs that would have a Big Twin shaking in its boots (or yours). Also, a cam for each valve allows for some seriously detailed tuning tricks.

2 Big Twins have one stick with four bumps, which is maybe not as effective as the Sportster's four, but whole lot simpler. Except even simplicity can be pretty sophisticated, as these three brands of Big Twin cams amply illustrate. For now, ignore the lumps and look closely, left to right, at construction: Andrews, Sifton, and Crane. All have slightly different details in their interpretation of Big Twin camshafts. Most obvious is the machining of the cam gear, but the gear's shoulder on the shaft and the lip on the shim side, not to mention the diameter of the shaft itself, are subtly different also.

If you talk to 10 people about camshafts, you'll get 10 opinions. There is very little agreement when it comes to the best cam (or cams, on Sportsters) for a Harley. This leads directly to major confusion. The manufacturers of said camshafts do precious little to help sort the wheat from the chaff (for obvious reasons); they all sell the "best" Harley cams, right?

Practically the only thing that's easy to get a majority opinion on is the worst cam available. Any California riders out there want to take a wild guess on which one it is? Not that the "California cam" doesn't have its virtues; it's easy on the valvetrain; it makes pretty good low-rpm torque, and the gas mileage isn't all bad. Performance, however, is poor.

Let's start from one basic premise: An engine is first and foremost a pump. It moves fuel and air in as a combustible mixture, burns it, and moves it out. The better it is able to do this the more torque it can make. The more often it can do this the more horsepower it can make. The "pump" knows naught about the number of valves, where or how big they are, what carb is used, the size or noise level of the exhaust, or anything else we riders tend to our devote gray matter and income to. All it knows is whether or not it's getting enough to pump. If you think of the cylinders and heads of an engine as the heart of this pump, then begin to imagine the cams as the lungs. If stock cams in Sportsters are only a little asthmatic, stock Big twins (especially California models up to 1994) have a bad case of emphysema. Don't panic. There is a cure, several, in fact.

Evolution Harley-Davidson pumps have two fundamental limits to their "breathing." First, they don't like 8,000 rpm. Second, the exhaust port limits the efficiency of the "heart" in the lower rpm ranges. (Having the cylinder heads "flowed" can almost be considered a transplant that can increase flow dramatically, but that is the limit.) Within those limits, a couple of general rules are known. In static terms, lift on the cam (which determines how far the valves open) isn't nearly as important as cam timing (when it opens and closes the valve in question) and its partner duration (how long it keeps that valve open). One little technique that helps to visualize statically (what's really a dynamic process) is to draw two large circles, one for intake and one for exhaust, and mark them off in degrees from the top. Then by "shading in" the area of the circle that represents the timing of each cam respectively, you get a graphic picture of what's going on (or in and out).

CAMSHAFT BASICS

There's more involved in determining the proper cam than three values. You've got to learn to speak the language if you're going to communicate effectively.

Cam (or lobe) lift is the maximum height or distance that the lifter or follower is raised off the cam. The distance is measured from the outer diameter of the base circle (the part of the cam lobe without the bumps) to the highest point on the cam. More lift generally means better top-end power, but you'll sacrifice bottom-end response. In addition, cams with high lift typically put more wear and tear on the valvetrain.

For street bikes, lift figures are best kept at or below 0.500 inch, simply because, with the right cam, you can still get all the power you can use, but you won't be needing a new valvetrain every 20,000 miles. Sure, with the right cylinder head/piston combination, lifts in the mid-0.500-inch range, even perhaps encroaching on 0.600 inch can work, but pushrods flex, geometry goes AWOL, and the extra benefits of the lift are quashed by the limits of flow through the ports (particularly the exhaust port), so why bother? Mega-lift is more valuable to drag racers who re-engineer the whole plot anyway.

Duration generally ranges from 225 degrees for a torquey bottom-end cam all the way to 295 degrees of "top end rush," typically measured at 0.053-inch lift. Lift is a pretty straightforward measurement, but duration is not. It's tricky because it's often measured at different points by different makers. Instead of the 0.053-inch specifications, some grinders measure duration starting at 0.004 lift. Others? Who knows? Just be sure when you look at advertised numbers between two contenders that they both measure the same way for the duration, which is generally at 0.053 lift (except Lienweber for some inexplicable reason). And though keeping the valve open longer may seem like the right answer, a pay-off in power higher in the rpm band costs big in terms of low-end torque.

Overlap amounts to the time the intake and the exhaust valves are both open. When you get it right, overlap helps draw in the intake charge, but excessive amounts actually reduce power by letting intake charge escape out the open exhaust valve. Lots of overlap virtually guarantees a cam won't work well at low rpm,

regardless of how strong it is wide open. In contrast, the stock Harley-Davidson Big Twin cam actually has a negative intake opening specification since it occurs after top dead center. Pretty strong on the bottom, this cam is an asthmatic wheezer by about 4,500 rpm.

Lobe separation is the angle between the center bump of the intake lobe and its counterpart on the exhaust lobe. Think of it like the two points on a pair of scissors relative to the hinge in the middle. If the scissors are nearly closed, you can cut well as long as what you are cutting is thin. To cut thick stuff, you open wider but have less leverage, so it can be harder to get the job done. The same principle applies with separation on cam lobes. Typically lobe separation for street cams runs between 97 and 118 (camshaft) degrees. The relationship between intake and exhaust is ground into the cam and can't be altered by advancing or retarding the overall cam timing. As a guideline, if the rest of the numbers are comparable, a cam with a lobe that is less separate (for example, 98 to 104 degrees) will offer a broader spread of power, while wide lobes make for a more "cammy" cam, coming on harder and later in the game.

The manufacturers' catalogs are full of performance cams and related components, Make sure to read the tips and technical information, as these can help you to choose the proper cam for your high-performance Harley.

When it's time for a cam change, don't forget the rest of the valvetrain. Chances are that the performance cam you decide on will require new springs, retainers, and keepers, Most companies offer cam kits specifically tailored to meet the needs of the new cam.

The adjustment in the Harley-Davidson valvetrain comes via the pushrods. Crane's needle-bearing, roller tip rockers are the hot setup for Harleys. Available for Shovelheads, Evos, and Sportsters (883–1200 motors), the rockers improve horsepower by reducing friction and providing a dead accurate rocker ratio to provide maximum valve lift, raising the valve farther off the seat. A number of things, however, can restrict this potential airflow, such as the cylinder head's ability to flow at a given lift value.

Let's take a stock, late-model Harley-Davidson Evo head, for instance. The head, even in most big-valve ported forms, flows to about 0.500 lift. If you were to build a wild street or strip motor and wanted to use a 0.550-lift (or better) cam, these heads would not be the ideal choice. Actually the cam would be improper for the engine combination. The message here, once again, is that the combination must work together. The other potential problem with increasing the cam lift is that there is only so much clearance between the piston and the valve. It's always a good idea to clay the piston top to determine piston/valve clearance when building a motor or installing a new cam. Increasing the lift limits this clearance, so if you're going to use a high-lift cam, make sure that the heads will flow at those lift levels and that the motor is able to utilize that much airflow.

The other problem associated with elevated lift numbers is spring fatigue. The greater the lift the farther the spring will have to expand and contract during each rotation of the cam. Cams with more lift are much harder on springs, causing a reduction in spring life. Check to make sure there is sufficient travel for the cam lift you plan to use.

Certainly there are exceptions to this general rule, as the proper cam choice for a particular application may call for increasing the duration, which may have indeed added power down low, but for the most part, stepping up in duration changes the powerband of the motor.

Camshaft recommendation for a street, V-Twin motor is a difficult, as a number of variables can greatly affect which cam works best. Motor displacement, compression, carburetion, and even intended use will all affect which cam will work best for a particular application. A low-compression 883 doesn't need nearly as much cam as a high-compression 1,340-cc Big Twin. As a general rule, lower-duration cams in the neighborhood of 210 to 220 degrees at 0.053 work best for stock-type replacement cams. The Competition Cams Evo 2000 fits into this category. Stepping past 220 degrees of duration (at 0.053) places the cam into the bolt-on, mid-range-style category. These cams work well with the stock compression, carb, and exhaust. Cams with 240-plus degrees of duration or more are beginning to step into the performance arena and generally work better with other induction, compression, and exhaust modifications. The next step up in duration above 260 degrees brings the cam to the edge of streetability, depending on displacement. Cams with this kind of duration will make power to 7,000 rpm. It is important to ask yourself two questions here: Is the rest of the motor set up to run that kind of rpm? And how much time do you spend at this level on the street? The answer is not very much, at least not on the street. These high-duration cams are good for race motors but will not make torque in the levels most often encountered on the street. Unless you live for maximum power and minimum streetability, leave these cams for the track.

It is important to remember here that the duration values given are to be used as a general rule and that increasing the duration will have an effect on the idle characteristics and overall drivability. Excessive duration kills the vacuum signal to the carburetor (or map sensor, in the case of fuel injection), which has a negative effect on idle quality. One way to increase the signal is to increase the displacement of the motor. A cam that is a bit large (excessive duration) for an 883 might be perfect for a 1,200-cc motor. The larger displacement increases the signal to the carb, thereby having the effect of taming the cam down. Note on the cam spec charts that the so-called bigger cams, recognized by more lift and duration, are recommended with larger-displacement motors. A stroker motor will be able to use more cam (and make more power), provided the heads, intake, and exhaust are optimized for the cam choice. There is really no replacement for displacement.

While this information may seem a bit much to digest, the truth is that cam manufacturers have already done most of your homework for you. Companies like Crane, S&S, Comp Cams, and Sifton offer not only a vast number of cam choices for your particular application but also the technical support to assist you in properly choosing the cam that best suits your needs. Cam selection software, cam help lines, and detailed catalogs offer a surprising amount of information on cams and related valvetrain components for everything from stockers to full-on race bikes. Rather than listening to your buddy whose bike idles as if it's got a plug wire missing, talk to the tech personnel at any of the cam companies. Your cam choice could make or break your performance motor, so take the time to do it right.

SPORTSTER CAMS

Did you know that all the factory's Screamin' Eagle cam grinds were actually designed for the 1200? Not that it matters much because they do just fine in 883s as well. But it's curious. The Vance & Hines pipe is for 883s but works on 1200s, and the cams are for 1200s but work on 883s.

This smacks heavily of marketing jargon more than anything else, an X engine is an X engine, at least at this level of involvement. So which cam should you run in your Sporty? Well, that would be one cam for five speeds (H-D #25648-91) and another if you have a four speed (H-D #25628-89). Looking at the dyno charts, it is very difficult to do any better job overall than this grind does. That said, there's not much to choose between the Harley cams and, say, #4 or #8 Andrews or #230 or #231 Siftons. Most any other grind moves too far away from the notion of broad powerbands. The Harley SE cam is standard issue in Buells (except the M2) and has seen 85 to 90 horses at the back tire on a dyno more than once. I'd have to say if it's good enough for Buell, it's probably good enough for you.

PROJECT 51 • INSTALLING AN AFTERMARKET CAMSHAFT

Time: 3 to 5 hours

Tools: Crane cam installation tool (Drag Specialties #DS199098); Allen wrenches; Torx wrenches; screwdrivers; 3/8-, 7/16-, 1/2-, 9/16-, 5/8-, 11/16-, 3/4-, 13/16-inch wrenches and sockets; rubber bands; paper clips; rubber mallet; degree wheel; micrometer; strip feeler gauges; assembly lube; anti-seize; and Loctite

Talent: 👨‍🔧👨‍🔧👨‍🔧

Tab: $$$

Tinware: Cone gasket, cone seal, pushrod tube O-rings, tappet block gaskets, rocker box gasket kit, and cam shims

Tip: Cardboard toilet paper or paper towel tube slipped over the new cam's lobe areas can protect and ease installation as you snake the cam in past the tappets

PERFORMANCE GAIN: This can go wherever you want, but 90 percent of us really need more overall power, not peak horsepower; a bolt-in cam like H-D SE-3, Andrews EV-27, Sifton 143, or Crane 316/286 will often give 15 to 20 percent more power

COMPLEMENTARY MODIFICATION: Cam bearing updated roller rockers (1992 and later models); Chrome-Moly adjustable pushrods; upgraded valve springs, keepers, and collars; increased mechanical compression; high-flow air cleaner, ported heads, free-flow exhaust, and upgraded ignition with a higher rev limit

1 The first order of business in your cam change is removing the pushrods, which isn't always easy. Stock 5-speed Sportsters/Buells without collapsible pushrod tubes require that you pull the rocker boxes and move the rocker arms and shafts out of the way in order to remove the pushrods. If you want to reuse the stock pushrods, you have to get 'em back in the same spot, which is not to tough since they are color-coded from the factory. Be sure and note which pushrod comes from where; you won't know what the color codes mean if you don't write it down somewhere. Sifton makes a neat alloy set of adjustable pushrods and replacement collapsible tubes, which are a good upgrade.

A cam change isn't rocket science, but as with anything else, there's a wrong way and a right way. The trickiest concept is that even the right way has two or three variations. As long as you keep your trusty service manual handy and consult any specific instructions peculiar to your cam choice, you're safe with a so-called bolt-in cam. The nastier grinds usually require different valve springs and retainers and occasionally some clearance grinding. Your cam of choice determines the amount of skill (and tools) needed to do the job. Take the hotter jobs to a pro, if only so they can double-check your efforts.

First and foremost, as with a job involving machinery and flammable liquids, think about safety. Always disconnect the negative side of the battery cable to prevent accidental starter engagement. Then you must raise the bike on a secure and stable stand, and often it's wise to strap it down so there'll be no unintended movement—especially toward the floor.

Big Twins are a more likely candidate for a cam swap than XL models, primarily because the stock grinds (there have been four so far) for an 80-incher range from adequate to pitiful, whereas the Sportster engine has been blessed with good cams from the get-go, and Buell variations come with the truly excellent Screamin' Eagle cams fitted as standard equipment. That's just as well because for some reason most of us find changing one cam with four lobes less intimidating than changing four cams with one lobe, although there's really not much difference in terms of time and labor.

Big Twins offer two choices of basic procedure, and the choice of procedure depends largely on whether you intend to change the pushrods. If you use the stockers, which is fine for anything less than 5,500-rpm usage, you need to pull the rocker boxes off to remove the pushrods from the top of the motor. In doing so, you'll spend roughly an extra hour of your time, and you'll need new rocker-box gaskets. The other way is to simply cut the stock pushrods out with

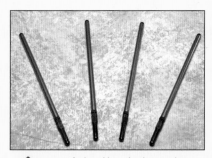

3 A set of adjustable pushrods, something like these chrome-moly units for a Big Twin, are four times stiffer than the stock aluminum types. The added stiffness is a major advantage if you intend to rev the nuts off your motor, since the flex in stock pushrods is one reason the factory rev limits are set so low. If you don't really care about what happens over 5,500 rpm or so, aftermarket alloy pushrods still have the adjustabilty advantage.

4 Once you've dealt with the pushrods, the next item for your attention should be pulling and inspecting the tappets and tappet blocks. The roller on one of these, has seen better days; it's scored and worn pretty badly after 65,000 hard miles. Find anything similar on yours, and it's a safe bet you're cam is screwed up as well. By the way, the 'text book' technique, says you should always run a new cam on new rollers. You don't have to live with that, as long as your tappets are like new, perfect surfaces on the roller, with no excessive up-and-down freeplay on the roller axles. Tappet blocks bores, (or case holes, where 5-speed XL's are concerned) should be near perfect as well.

2 If you'd rather not spend the extra hour removing the rocker boxes to pull the pushrods, you can cut the pushrods. Remove the clip on the pushrod tubes, hold them up out of your way with clothes pins (or paper clips and rubber bands for that matter), and whack 'em out with bolt-cutters. This time-saving method has a price; you'll have to buy a set of adjustable pushrods.

5 Once you get into this inspection mode, keep it going as you check the cam cavity in the cone. (Of course, you'll mark the ignition timing before you pull the cone.) After it's off, pay particular attention to the oil pump shaft and the black plastic breather gear. Any wear on the pump shaft, or evidence that the key has sheared should stop you long enough to deal with it. The breather gear shouldn't be scuffed much, and it's cavity shouldn't look like there's a bunch of shrapnel in it either. Don't let that funky white plastic breather shim get away!

6 If need be, now's the time to change the cam bearing (see Project 52: Replacing 1992 and Later Big Twin Cam Bearings). Not necessary on Sportster's or Buells, it's easy enough to do with special tools, virtually impossible with out them, and while vital on 1992 and newer Big Twin's, not a bad idea on any hard-ridden, high-mileage Hog.

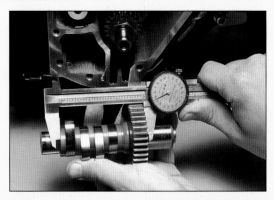

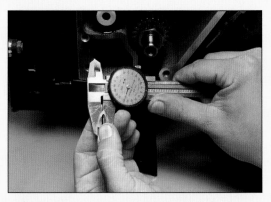

7 A word about endplay. 1990 and later Big Twins and Evo Sportsters) have endplay specs that are much looser than earlier Hogs (at least with stock cams). The only aftermarket Big Twin cam that follows this same philosophy is Sifton. The rest make Big Twin cams that most definitely need shimming to get endplay down to 0.006–0.016 inch. One way to get there is measure the new cam, then the old one, and buy a Shovelhead or early Evo cam shim to get the clearance (usually, a 0.50- or 0.55-inch shim for 1990 and later Big Twins).

8 Never trust that the shim is the right size, or the size you need, until you measure it with a micrometer or vernier caliper. The shims are available in 0.005-inch increments, from 0.045 to 0.095 inch. If it comes down to it, run it slightly loose rather than tight. All that surrounding metal in the motor expands as it heats up, after all, which is what the factory was thinking when they went to shimless cams in the first place.

bolt cutters. Then you need not mess with the rocker boxes, but obviously you will need to mess with new adjustable pushrods. If you go with adjustables, you again have two options—aluminum or chrome-moly. Aluminum flexes far more at high rpm (5,500 on up) than moly but is more acoustically dead and, therefore, much quieter in operation. Also, if you own a Big Twin built after January 1992, there's more work involved because you'll need to upgrade the cam bearing. Okay, basic choices made, appropriate parts and tools in hand, you're ready to tear in there.

BIG TWINS

With the gas tanks drained or removed, remove the spark plugs and roll the engine over using the rear wheel (with the tranny in fourth gear). Rotate until the pushrods spin free under finger pressure and the tappets are on the base circle of the cam. Then start with the heavy work, as follows:

If you're installing new pushrods, collapse the pushrod tubes, and cut the old rods out.

Otherwise remove the rocker boxes to allow removal of the pushrods. Remove each pushrod and its tube, and if you're going to reuse them, do some sort of labeling so you remember which one goes with each valve.

Remove each lifter-block assembly, complete with tappets. Inspect all the parts for fit and wear. Clean and inspect the tappet rollers for pitting and sideplay. If necessary, replace them as shown in the manual.

Remove the cam cover as shown in the service manual. Watch out for the little plastic washer on the end of the breather gear; it likes to fall in the oil drain pan and get lost.

Decide whether and how you intend to shim the new cam. The 1993 and newer models don't use a cam shim, and Sifton, at least, makes cams to conform with that fact. Most of the other aftermarket makers recommend shimming. There are at least two ways to do the measuring for shims. One is to slap a vernier caliper on the new cam; the other is to park the cam back in its hole and use "strip" feeler gauges inserted down through the tappet block hole to measure from there.

If the cam needs shimming, install the shim (start with 0.50 inch but have both thicker and thinner shims handy), the cam, and the old gasket onto the engine case. Assemble the cam cover with at least three screws and torque to 90 *inch*-pounds. (It doesn't matter at this point whether or not all of the timing marks are lined up.) You should end up with 0.004 to 0.0010 inch of endplay. A little more won't hurt as much as too little will.

Cams that require head modifications may also require removal of a small amount of material in the cam cover because of interference. As long as you're at it, measure the cam and the pinion-shaft bushings for tolerance, as indicated in the manual.

Take everything back out because it's time to make another important decision—about noise. In a cam train noise is usually from the cam gear's relationship to its pinion gear—and nothing else. So decide whether you care and, if you do, what you're prepared

9 If you're going to run something really nasty in here, make sure there's room for it! High-lift (read non-bolt-in) cams need to be checked very carefully for lobe clearance in this area, between cam bearing and pinion shaft. You may need to grind some aluminum out of that semi-circle with the drop of oil laying in it, before the cam does it for you the expensive way.

10 Stuff the cam in and bolt the cone cover back on temporarily with at least three screws torqued to 90 inch-pounds, using the old gasket. Double-check the endplay with a strip feeler gauge, as shown. If it measures to suit, pull it all back off.

to do about it. The best option is to simply press the original cam gear onto the new cam. If that's not workable for you because you don't have or can't find a press or if you're worried about cam-to-gear alignment (which, when screwed up, affects cam timing), then you may need to swap pinion gears. Most new aftermarket cams come with a "red" clearance on the cam gear. If the pinion on your bike is also red, no problem. Otherwise it requires a measurement. And the measurement technique varies from year to year, depending on the pinion-gear design. Check the manual or with your dealer to make sure you get it right.

Install your new cam. Align the timing marks as described in your service manual. Remember that all of the gears must align to two sets of timing marks.

Check the breather gear endplay. With the gasket in place, use a straight edge and feeler gauges. You should end up with 0.005 to 0.015 inch endplay. Shims are available at any Harley shop. You must subtract 0.006 inch from your final measurement for gasket squish before you finish the installation with the new gasket (unless you check it with the old gasket).

Once all is checked and set, reinstall the cam cover and, if necessary, replace the timing cover seal. Then torque the screws properly, by the book.

Reinstall the lifter-block assemblies as shown in the manual. Use a lifter-block alignment tool and torque to 90 *inch*-pounds.

With fresh pushrod-tube seals and steel washers in place, reinstall the pushrod-tube assembly. It may save time and make it easier for you (whether using new pushrods or old) to put the rod in its respective tube and then install it on the engine.

Reinstall the rocker arm, lube the shafts with oil, install in the appropriate location, and retorque the cinch bolts.

Reinstall the rocker boxes using new seals and gaskets. Torque the fasteners to spec. (Easier said than done when you're forced to use a cut down Allen wrench, but you get the idea.)

If you used them, adjust the pushrods per the manufacturer's recommendations (almost never more than four turns though). Take your time and let each pushrod bleed down before you go on to the next one.

Once everything's buttoned up, reinstall the carburetor, ignition, and exhaust system.

It's time to check ignition timing. See Project 9: Timing Your Engine.

Start the engine and make sure you've got good return of oil into the oil tank and no spastic noises or leaks.

That's really all there is to it. Yet it's just the beginning in many ways. No cam, no matter how well chosen, will overcome bad choices made elsewhere (most notably, exhaust), so if you get what you were after with your cam, thank the cam and your good installation. If you don't, if you find new flat spots in the powerband or incredibly poor mileage yet you're sure the cam was installed correctly, blame something else. And remember, horsepower looks good on paper, but torque works good on the road.

11 Now, replace the tappet block assemblies, carefully wiggling the cam in there. If you didn't remove the rocker boxes, feed the pushrods—already inside their respective tubes, set as short as they will go—back into the tappet blocks and heads, and you're near ready to button up the job. If you did pull the rocker boxes, drop the pushrods back in place, and screw all that back together. Once done, via either method, you may have to wait for the hydraulic lifters to bleed down before you're able to adjust or fire up.

12 Here's the new cam with the timing marks lined up correctly (see Project 41: Setting Cam and Ignition Timing, and get it right). Note that the tappet block assemblies have been removed in the photo; don't you forget 'em when you get ready to bolt the cone back on. If there's any confusion, take five, and check your shop manual.

SPORTSTERS AND BUELLS

A Sportster cam change is no more complicated than on its 80-inch counterpart—just different. By definition, bolt-in cams are designed to work with stock valvetrain components and settings and don't require additional parts replacement or adjustments other than shim spacing. The only quadruple underhead cam engine in the world has its own quirks when it comes to cam-swapping. Here's how to take advantage of those quirks:

Remove the gas tank, air cleaner, and carburetor to make your job easier.

Disconnect the battery and drain the engine oil. Some models require removal of the rear brake pedal and linkage as well as the right-side footpeg mount.

On four-speed Sportsters, remove the rocker boxes unless you have adjustable pushrods already fitted. Remove the pushrod-tube retainers and loosen the pushrods. Remove the pushrods and tubes, keeping track of where each one came from. They must be reinstalled in the same order. Remove the tappet blocks and tappets, marking each with its respective position.

On five-speed Sportsters, pull the rocker boxes (with one-piece pushrod tubes, there's no second option here, at least the first time). If you want, you can get collapsible tube assemblies from the aftermarket, notably Sifton.

Remove all the gear-cover screws. You'll know if you got them all because if you didn't, the cover won't come off. Along with a sharp pop or two with a rubber mallet, it should come off—easily.

Check the cam-cover bushings for wear or galling. If your motor has more than 20,000 miles on it, check the bushings with a micrometer to make sure

they're in spec. If you don't have a micrometer, you can take the cover to a local machine shop for measuring. If replacement is necessary, you will have to have it done professionally.

Cam gears are numbered one through four, starting from the rear of the motor. Pull gears two and four, then one and three. Make sure the shims don't fall off, and keep them with their respective gears.

On four-speed models only, remove the dog-bone thrust washers, but mark them for reinstallation in the same position. These thrust washers have a bevel on the inner diameter that must be placed in the same position upon reassembly (the bevel towards the cam).

Clean and inspect all the cam-gear needle bearings for wear and free movement. Check the pinion gear and the oil-pump drive gears for chipped, cracked, or worn teeth. Check old cam gears against new ones to make sure the lobe position and the timing marks are the same.

Next (also only for four-speeds), measure and shim for cam-gear endplay. To do this, it is necessary to install the cams and the gear cover. Use original shims for initial measurements because if they're within factory specifications, shimming is done. Install new cam gears one and three, then two and four, using those original shims and thrust washers in their original positions. Timing-mark alignment is not important for this step, but make sure the gears move freely without binding. Cam gear two should have the shims installed on the motor side journals, and gears one, three, and four may have them on either side, preferably the cam-gear-cover side. Fit a new, dry gear-cover gasket, and tighten down the cover snugly but not enough

13 If you need to kill time while the lifters bleed down, take a few minutes to replace the cone seal. Even if it's not leaking, replacement at this point is a form of cheap insurance to prevent future leaks. Drill a small hole in the metal lip of the old seal, then insert a sheet metal screw, as shown.

14 To remove the seal, grab onto the head of the screw with Vise Grips, and pop or rock it out. A thin block of wood, or thick rag helps keep from marking the chrome, if it takes more than a simple pull to get the thing to come free.

15 Once the seal is out, lightly oil the new seals' outside lip, and start it back in the cone by hand. Then use a socket and rubber mallet to gently pound the seal into place. If you're a bit paranoid about bending the metal on the new seal, lay the old one on top of the new, then proceed, rapping at twelve o'clock, then six, then three then nine, until the sound goes "dead' and the seal sits flush in it's bore. Install the ignition components, and double-check your work on the assembled engine.

16 If the lifters are finally bled down, adjust the pushrods (if/as required, generally 3-4 turns), fire up the engine, listen for any weird noises, check for leaks, and get ready to ride.

17 Some of us don't like the idea of inaccessible, nonadjustable pushrods on five-speed Sportsters. The option in this arena comes courtesy of Sifton. Their kit offers telescoping alloy pushrod covers and adjustable rods. A nice touch is the fact that the Sifton pushrods can be removed from the machine without disturbing any other area. Cam change time drops from over 2 1/2 hours to about 1 hour.

to fully crush the gasket. Use a flat feeler gauge to measure side-to-side gear movement. A small flashlight might help getting a good look inside the gear cavity. Make notations of each gear's measurements. After doing all four gears, remove the gear cover and the gasket. Compare your measurements with factory specifications, and add or subtract shims as needed. After all the shim dimensions are calculated, reassemble the cam gears with appropriate shims in place and reinstall the cam cover.

Cams on five-speed models do not need shimming.

Apply assembly lube to all gear contact surfaces, including gear teeth, bearing journals, and lobe faces. A thin coating is all that's needed, and a little dab on the cam-cover bushings won't hurt either.

Reinstall all the gears and align the timing marks. Be careful not to drop any (four-speed) shims. Install the cam cover using a new gasket, and then tighten the cover screws in a crisscross pattern. Later models with Allen screws should be torqued to specifications.

On four-speed models, remove and replace the tappet-block O-rings. (Since five speeds don't have separate tappet blocks, this is a no-brainer, right?) Then reinstall the tappet-block assemblies in the same positions from which they were removed. It's best to press them in as far as you can by hand, then tap them in the rest of the way with a soft mallet. Torque the hold-down bolts to spec.

On all models, replace pushrod-tube O-rings.

Reinstall the pushrods and the tube assemblies in their respective positions.

Reassemble the rocker boxes.

If you have adjustable pushrods, now's the time to adjust them. Starting with the rear exhaust, rotate the engine so that the tappet is at its lowest point in the tappet block. Adjust the pushrod so that it can barely be turned, then tighten the jam nuts. Repeat this procedure for the remaining pushrods, then reinstall the spring keepers. Your cam swap is now complete—except for the potential waiting time for the hydraulic part of the tappet (sometimes called the lifter) to fill with oil. There's really no way to rush this or do it by hand, so go have some coffee and check back from time to time until they are ready.

Refill engine oil and install the new filter.

Reconnect the brake linkage and install the spark plugs.

Start your bike and then warm it up thoroughly.

It may be necessary to rejet the carb, so check the spark plug color after approximately 50 miles.

PROJECT 52 • REPLACING 1992 AND LATER BIG TWIN CAM BEARINGS

Time: 3 1/2 hours

Tools: Everything for a cam change plus the bearing removal tool (Jim's 95760-TB) or equivalent and installer (Jim's 97272-60 and handle 33416-80)

Talent:

Tab: $

Tinware: The usual cam-change goodies plus a Torrington cam bearing

Tip: This bearing has been known to fail in totally stock bikes

PERFORMANCE GAIN: Reliability

COMPLEMENTARY MODIFICATION: A high-performance cam

If you install a high-performance camshaft in a Big Twin that was built after January 1992, you need to replace the cam bearing at the same time. Likewise, if you own a 1987 to 1990 model that had a bad case insert, the new factory crankcases that The Motor Company so graciously donated to your cause need the same treatment. Here's the scoop.

For 20-some years, the factory used a Torrington-type cam bearing. Then they decided in late 1991 to change over to an INA-type bearing. The motive was pure. They honestly thought the life and high-speed durability of this critical part would be better than ever because of the switch. You can read their side of the story in service bulletin #M-973. What's not said, or even implied, in the bulletin is what happens when the cam train deviates from stock. The INA bearing, you see, has about half the number of rollers as the older Torrington. Radical lift cams, stiffer pushrods, and stouter valve springs do not get along with this new bearing.

1 It's easy to spot the preferred Torrington-type cam bearing; it's the one with the most needle rollers—and the most bearing area. Harley switched to the caged INA-style bearing in all Big Twin production since January 1992. The reasoning was that the INA cage keeps the needle rollers in alignment and prevents them from climbing on top of each other at high rpm. In practice, it hasn't quite worked out that way. Always switch to the Torrington bearing when you switch to a high-performance cam, just like the manufacturers of those cams tell you to in their installation instructions.

2 To swap cam bearings, you'll need either the Kent-Moore (official Harley) tool, which amounts to a split collet and slide hammer, or if that's a bit too brutal, the Jim's tool. The Jim's tool (shown) extracts the old bearing by "unscrewing" it out of the case, rather than popping it out.

3 Installation (regardless of tool choice) is a matter of sticking the new bearing on the shouldered end of the tool (as shown).

4 The last step is to drive the new bearing home with a hammer.

Whether or not you have a high-lift cam, the INA bearings tend to go south eventually. The result can be anything from a roached bearing to a ruined cam to trashed crankcases. The solution is simple. Change the bearing to the good 'ol Torrington.

The aftermarket cam companies are wise to this. Instruction sheets included with Andrews, Sifton, and Crane cams from 1998 and later spell it out pretty clearly. If you installed an aftermarket cam sometime before that, the instructions wouldn't have said anything about Torrington bearings. So, if you or someone you know are running around with a nice cam and a nasty bearing, even if it's been in there trouble-free for several years, you have just been warned. Changing the cam bearing today will likely save you some very expensive hassles later.

For specific how to instructions on changing the bearing, refer to your shop manual.

PROJECT 53 • BALANCING YOUR ENGINE

Time: 4 to 6 hours (on top of standard rebuild)

Tools: Gram scale and a balancing jig.

Talent: ▮▮▮

Tab: $$

Tinware: Full overhaul gasket set, seals, O-rings, new main bearings and rode bearings, and fresh pistons and rings

Tip: The best time to do this is when you have the engine apart for a major overhaul. If you don't need one, try installing a fluid balancer (see Project 72: Installing Fluid Balance Masters).

PERFORMANCE GAIN: *Smooth* performance and better long-term reliability

COMPLEMENTARY MODIFICATION: Blueprinting

The design of the Evolution engine incorporates a certain amount of shake and shudder. So no matter what you do, there's going to be some vibration. You can minimize the problems by balancing the reciprocating masses in the engine. This is commonly referred to as crankshaft balancing.

Bear in mind that crank balancing requires complete disassembly of the engine, so most of us won't do much about it until the engine has to be overhauled anyway. It's also important to mention that anything in the motor that moves up and down cannot be balanced, only counterweighted. The only things that can be balanced are parts or systems that revolve (like flywheels).

When someone talks about having a crank balanced, they mean some poor devil has the unenviable task of adding or subtracting weight in the flywheels to adequately offset the mass rotating in your engine. To do this, you must determine the exact weight of each reciprocating part. This is a job for experts, but we'll go through the basics so you'll understand what has to be done to balance your crank.

First we need to discuss the balance factor to use, and it's one of the hottest debates around. Balance factor is how much the flywheels are counterweighted to offset the weight of the reciprocating parts (pistons, pins, rods, and rings) to minimize vibration. The balance factor is referred to as a percentage. As a

general, but not absolute, rule of thumb, a high percentage smoothes the motor out at high rpm. What constitutes the perfect balance factor for our beloved imbalanced Milwaukee vibrators? The answer to that depends on what you're going to use it for.

For Harleys, the range of counterweighted balancing can be anywhere from 35 to 85 percent. A drag racer using a light chassis (more on that later) and a 140-cubic-inch motor that lives at 8,000 rpm for 8 to 10 seconds at a time may need to balance to the extreme 85-percent end of the scale to keep that big motor from tearing itself and that lightweight chassis apart. A Shriner carrying a half-ton of bagger at an idle for hours at a time might go the other way, going as low as a 35-percent balance factor. Frankly, current, prevalent thought calls for from 60 percent to 66 percent on production-based street motors.

As with most things in life (and in engine design), this is a compromise that, for most, accomplishes the two main objectives of engine balancing. First, it keeps the main bearings and crankcases alive and well, and second, it means humans can "sit" the vibration for a few hours of riding. Oddly, the frame has more to do with it than you might think, and it's not all that unusual for a formerly smooth engine with "stock" balance to shake badly when stuffed into a chopper frame. The shakes and quakes that were absorbed by the original chassis suddenly find themselves free to turn the new one into a tuning fork playin' E-flat!

Despite what you might hear on the street, if you ride a rubber-mounted Harley (ELT, FXR, or Dyna), you still can benefit from a balanced motor. The "Rubber Glide" chassis isolates some of the vibration, but you'll still be smoother, and the engine will be longer-lived with balancing.

Once you have decided on the percentage factor for your professed application, the next step is to weight the flywheels appropriately. The weight must be added in the same plane (vertical or horizontal) in which the assembly reaches its maximum value. This is not easy to do, and it is one of the main reasons the job should be left to the experienced pro. If you place the weight in the wrong plane, the resulting imbalance will try to hammer things, in one plane or the other at some given rpm, somewhere between the cylinder axis and the 90-degree position of the crank. The center of effort for a smooth and healthy bottom end needs to be revolving smoothly along the crank's axis (not wobbling around it like a spinning top that's about to fall over or that's jack-hammering to get out of the crankcases) and evenly distributed through the bearings into the crankcases. A skilled balancing technician can get it right the first time.

And when the balancer gets it right, you'll have a much smoother engine, and the smoothness will help get you 100,000-mile reliability.

ENGINE
PROJECT 54 • CRANK ASSEMBLY REPAIR

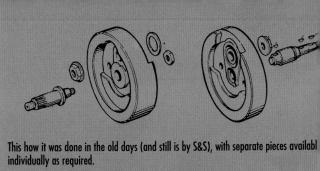

This how it was done in the old days (and still is by S&S), with separate pieces availabl individually as required.

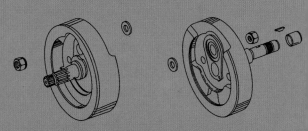

Both sides are now one solid chunk, and neither of them can be had separately. If you want one, you buy a pair attached to a new set of rods; the whole thing is commonly called a crankshaft assembly. This can get expensive.

 Time: 2 to 3 hours (trued and semi-balanced)

 Tools: Brass hammer, truing stand, flywheel nut wrenches, and crankpin nut wrenches

 Talent: ♟♟♟

 Tab: $$$ to $$$$$+

 Tinware: Depends on whether you stick with a factory crank or go aftermarket, but you'll need a full overhaul gasket set, seals, bearings, snap rings, and all other parts necessary for a complete overhaul

 Tip: Worn pinion shafts are, as often as not, also damaged in the keyway area; check them carefully

 PERFORMANCE GAIN: Increased stiffness

COMPLEMENTARY MODIFICATION: Upgraded connecting rods and perhaps mild 89-inch stroker flywheels, which are a reasonable financial alternative to a stock rebuild

If you're riding along minding your own business and suddenly hear an ominous growl coming from deep inside the engine, it could be that the pinion shaft on the ride side of the crankshaft (more commonly, the right flywheel in Harley-speak) has lost its surface hardening and will need to be repaired or replaced. It's not a pleasant thought because it means a complete engine teardown. The thing is, you can do that in a weekend, if you plan it right.

So if that is the problem (pull the cam cover—if you find excessive up-and-down or side-to-side play on the end of the shaft, the pinion shaft is the problem), you need to know a couple of things before you scatter the motor all over the workbench.

From about 1909 to 1986, H-D crankshafts were actually an assembly of separate, individual parts. These pieces consisted of connecting rods, big end bearings and cages, left and right flywheels, a sprocket shaft, a pinion shaft, and various washers and fasteners. In 1987, H-D integrated the two shafts (sprocket and pinion) with their respective flywheels, making each half one piece. This is a good because it

makes for a tougher, less flexible assembly. If you damage this assembly, however, it'll cost you $600 or more to replace the whole thing.

A more economical solution can be found with aftermarket suppliers. A number of companies will be glad to help with any specific component you need to get back on the road. The only thing is, all they can supply are pieces for Shovelhead and early Evo-type assemblies. Even then, it can get expensive to replace a pinion shaft and a flywheel with aftermarket parts when the only thing you really need is the stock shaft.

If the only damage is to the pinion shaft itself and you take your maimed wheel to your friendly local H-D dealer and ask real nice, the dealer might, just might, tell you about Department 621. Department 621 is really a guy named John Parker and a few of his cohorts. The factory created Department 621 with the idea in mind of repairing damaged pinion shafts under warranty. In fact, technically, all John and the boys in 621 do is warranty work.

Department 621 can repair a damaged pinion shaft for a reasonable cost. There are limits, though. They can't repair extensively damaged shafts, and they won't take on simple tasks that a local machine shop can do. More importantly, you can't go directly to Department 621 for help. Only the dealer can do that, and you have to convince them to do so.

If the pinion shaft is repairable and if the dealer can persuade John to do the job, the turnaround time is usually two or three weeks, and costs will vary, but $100 to $150 is usually in the ballpark. Just remember that Department 621 is a last resort, not a first choice.

ENGINE

PROJECT 55 • REPLACING DEFECTIVE CRANKCASES

Time: 12 to 16 hours

Tools: A low-pressure air supply (10 to 15 psi), assorted compensating sprocket spacers, a spray bottle of S100 cleaner (or soapy water), a 3/8-inch hose nipple (#63792-77), a few feet of 3/8-inch oil line or hose, blue #242 Loctite, a small propane torch, and a tube of 3M #800 sealant (H-D #99650-81)

Talent: ♟♟♟♟

Tab: $$$$$+

Tinware: If you pass the test, most everything removed to take the test can be reused. If you fail the test, you'll need, at minimum, the items listed in the text

Tip: Baby powder is a great leak locator, and not just for bad inserts in crankcases

PERFORMANCE GAIN: You can take a 500-mile ride without oil leaking out of your engine and into your primary case

COMPLEMENTARY MODIFICATION: As long as you have to take the whole rig apart, you may as well consider a little more displacement or other hot rod mods

From the dawn of the Knucklehead age in 1936 to the Year of Our Hog 1990, factory Big Twin cases sported a steel insert to support the left main bearing. This time-honored arrangement began to malfunction in a rather large way in the middle 1980s. Harley found themselves replacing a high percentage of these cases due to the insert's inability to stay put in its aluminum workplace. The cure was to eliminate the culprit entirely, as you can see in the 1991 and later case on the right. While the simple expedient of losing the steel insert did solve the riddle of oil transfer, it created a whole new set of questions—many yet to be answered satisfactorily. Can stock cases handle super-stock levels of power and the increased torque of a big stroker? Fortunately, the aftermarket offers cases with superior strength for a competitive price.

Let's say that you own a 1986 to 1990 Big Twin, and it appears that the oil level is dropping in the oil tank every time you check it. You may think it's burning oil, but no smoke is visible out the exhaust, and it runs fine. If the primary seems to be filling up on its own, however, you may have a bad insert in the left crankcase.

Factory crankcases from this era were made by casting the aluminum of the case around the steel insert that provided support for the left main bearing. This was a time-honored practice, and no one seems to know for dead certain why it quit working as designed, but it would appear that the likely reason is because of the stiffer, one-piece flywheel halves, implemented at roughly the same time. Or it may be that quality control was just a little slack. Perhaps no one foresaw what this combination of less flex in the crank and questionable flex in the bearing retainer would lead to.

No matter what the cause, once the crankcase insert fails, you have a big problem. Replacing the cases with new factory versions (1991 or newer) that no longer incorporate the steel insert is one option.

Aftermarket cases are another. Repairing, or attempting to repair, the original left case is also possible, if not particularly promising. No matter what you choose, if your engine is afflicted, it must come apart to be cured.

First and foremost, test your crankcases to make sure this is the problem. If you recently purchased a used 1986 to 1990 model, don't be shy about calling the factory to see if yours is one of the thousands that got new-style replacement cases under warranty. Otherwise this testing involves removing the primary cover and stripping out the alternator, per the shop manual, to get a visual inspection of the oil seal in the left case. In some cases, the problem isn't the insert, it's the oil seal. If the seal is leaking, replace it first, using the factory tool. Don't cheap out here. Using this tool is the only way to install a seal and be certain it won't leak. Then test the insert.

You have some options in testing. Prior to teardown, you can add phosphorescent dye, available at most auto parts stores, to the engine oil, heat the case with a heat lamp or heat gun, and check for leakage between the steel insert and the aluminum case with a black (ultraviolet) light. Or once you've stripped the primary, heat the case and apply baby powder to the insert area. Any oil that bleeds through the insert will then show up as a black stain in the white powder.

Sometimes severe cases won't even need this much diagnosis because the insert will be loose to the touch, actually moving in the aluminum. Up-and-down play at the sprocket shaft of the crank is a dead giveaway.

If the visual inspection isn't conclusive, here's how to perform the definitive test:

Remove the primary cover, and then remove the compensating sprocket, primary chain, clutch, and chain adjuster as an assembly, just like the shop manual says.

Remove the alternator rotor and stator, but stick the screws back in the holes. (On pre-1989 rigid-mount engines, you must remove the inner primary before the alternator can be removed—sorry!) Make a note of the sprocket spacers thicknesses because they must be installed in their original location to align the primary chain sprockets after the test is over with (or the repairs completed).

Measure the thickness of the alternator rotor at its bore and pick a sprocket spacer about the same thickness. Install the spacers (the sprocket spacer you just selected and the original factory ones).

Then replace the extension shaft, cover assembly, and nut but no more.

Tighten the compensating sprocket nut to 80–100 foot-pounds of torque. This simulates the normal preload.

Next remove the oil tank vent hose from the right crankcase and the to-oil-filter hose at the oil pump. Leave the feed line alone. Unplug the crankcase breather hose from the air cleaner backplate (if it's there in the first place), and then connect the oil tank vent fitting to the to-oil-filter fitting on the oil pump with a piece of the 3/8-inch hose to seal the tank vent temporarily.

Set your air supply for 10 to 15 psi (or the motor will turn over) and connect it to the crankcase breather hose using a 3/8-inch hose nipple (splicer fitting).

Pressurize the cases and then spray the left crankcase with soap solution from a squirt bottle. Watch for bubbles anywhere in the area, especially between the steel insert and the aluminum case material. If you see bubbles, you've found the leak.

If there's no leak, use a propane torch to heat the stator mounting surface for 3 minutes. Don't use a gas welder or anything more potent because you'll wreck the case, if not melt it. Pressurize the case. If there's still no leak, you wasted your time but answered an important question.

Just to be extra safe, check the spacer for burrs and buggers; replace the thing if it's messed up and install a new crank seal. Coat the outside diameter

(OD) of the new seal with a very thin application of 3M 800 sealer (you don't want it squishing into the bearing) and install. You must use the special tool #39361-39 if you expect it to seal. Pounding it in there with a big socket won't get it, okay? Recheck for leaks.

If there's a leak because the case is defective, you need to replace the case. Aftermarket or factory, it's up to you. Harley factory cases from late 1990–on no longer have that pesky steel insert, so replace the case with the later model if you decide to stick with Harley cases.

Replacing defective cases obviously necessitates a complete teardown of the engine. It also raises some questions and requires some decisions. In most states, motorcycles must have engine numbers that correspond to the frame numbers. The only place to get new cases with matching numbers is from the factory. Factory cases are only available to you if you turn your originals back into the factory in exchange, which sometimes entails a two- to four-week wait.

Installing aftermarket cases, which don't have matching numbers, requires a trip to the DMV for a so-called blue tag, meaning a whole new registration.

You'll have to make that decision. If you can wait for the factory replacements, it'll save you the registration hassle. If you can't wait and are willing to wade through the paperwork, the afterwork offers some gorgeous pieces that will solve your problem in style.

Once you know the cases are the crux of your problem, you'll need to remove the engine and pull the whole thing apart (see your shop manual for details).

Parts Required for Crankcase Replacement

Parts Required	Quantity	Part Number
Pinion bearing, white	1	24626-87
Pinion bearing, green	1	24628-87
Pinion bearing, red	1	24641-87
Pinion bearing, blue	1	24643-87
Cylinder studs	8	16837-85A
Engine gasket kit	1	17035-83B
Oil pump circlip	1	11002
Pinion bearing circlip	1	11177
Primary O-ring	1	11147
Primary gasket	1	varies w/ model
Stator screws	4	varies w/ model
Timing cover rivets	2	8699
Hose clamps/fuel	varies w/ model	10014
Hose clamps/oil	varies w/ model	10080

*These are the just the basics, and you obviously won't really need all the different pinion bearings.

ENGINE

PROJECT 56 • AFTERMARKET XL CRANKCASES

Time: 12 to 16 hours

Tools: All of 'em

Talent: ▮▮▮▮

Tab: $$$$$+

Tinware: Overhaul gaskets, seals, O-rings, and possibly much more, if you build a monster motor

Tip: The strongest factory cases are the ones from 1995 and newer models. They have much wider mating flanges between the halves

PERFORMANCE GAIN: Cases as such don't make horsepower, unless you count the reduced drag on the flywheels due to the built-in scraper, but they will withstand huge power levels reliably

COMPLEMENTARY MODIFICATION: The works. This makes the most sense for big-bore, high-performance engines

1 Punching a 4-inch hole in stock cases isn't a good idea. There'd be nothing left to tie the case halves together between the holes but the bolt, and even that would probably need to be shaved. No such problem with these STD cases. There's plenty of beef left, including the area around the hole to support the cylinder spigot. These cases are purpose-built to accommodate such big-bore shenanigans. As such, they cost a bit more, but they're worth so much more.

Historically, Sportster cases have shown an interesting assortment of weaknesses. The first motors dating from the late 1950s were notorious for chunking out the drive side of the case at the sprocket. In fact, the aftermarket offered a repair section to weld in a repair. The cases were beefed up a bit at time over the next two decades, but Iron XLs tended to spread the tranny shafts when the hammer went down on a really potent Sporty motor.

In the end, circa 1984 1/2, the alternator and the Torrington tranny ouput shaft bearing appeared, along with a myriad of more subtle changes. Believe it or not, there are seven OEM part numbers for Sportster cases spanning the 1982 to 1984 era. H-D may have finally solved most of the problem with the new five-speed cases, which are proving to be very solid units.

That being the case, why worry about better-than-factory alternatives? Style is one reason. Handling serious horsepower, however, is the main reason to make the switch. You can put about 90 horsepower into a 1,200-cc Sportster motor and have it hang together pretty reliability. If you want more

than that, you'll need to go to aftermarket cases. Displacement is also a major issue; if you want to go bigger than 96 inches, dump the factory cases.

Outfits like S&S and STD, on the other hand, have charted more than their fair share of large displacement, unlimited power turf. Both build cases based on what they've learned through that effort. If a 120- to 160-horsepower XL engine is something you've just got to have, the aftermarket can deliver.

Simply swapping the stock crankcases for aftermarket replacements is a major chore but not beyond the capabilities of the average person who is willing to use the shop manual, has the proper tools, a large tube of elbow grease, and a free weekend. Scratch building a monster motor with something like S&S Superstock cases as the basis is considerably more complicated—and not found in books. That said, if you know what you want and are willing to seek professional advice from S&S and other reputable engine builders, farming out any machine work or assembly you just aren't able to manage on your own, you can create a fantastic one-off powerhouse.

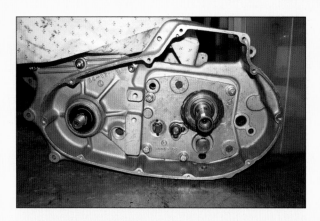

2 Just to give you a rough idea of how much beefier aftermarket cases can be, here's a shot of stock cases from a 3-inch-bore iron XL, circa 1971. Though you may not be able to see them well in this picture, there are cracks in this case that you can see (all too well) with the naked eye. Employing a mere four bolts and a couple of locating dowels, the tranny "trap door" on the old factory cases can be a weak point in high-powered applications. It's thin and flat and allows too much spread.

3 Aside from the structural differences, there's a materials upgrade in aftermarket cases. Both S&S and STD use 356T6 alloy with a hot strength far superior to the 319T4 or T6 material in stock cases. In short, these won't stretch, fade, peel, crack, warp, or stink in hot weather—compared to stockers. There are six major fasteners here, holding a much stouter door in place. Look closely, and the thicker casting around the primary becomes apparent also.

PROJECT 57 • REPLACING NOISY PINION GEARS ON BIG TWINS

Time: 2 to 3 hours

Tools: The measuring pins, all the tools to pull the cam and cover, Crane cam installation tool (Drag Specialties #DS199098), Allen wrenches, Torx wrenches, screwdrivers, set of combination wrenches and sockets, rubber bands, paper clips, rubber mallet, degree wheel, micrometer, strip feeler gauges, assembly lube, anti-seize, Loctite, and possibly a hydraulic press

Talent:

Tab: S

Tip: Possibly a pinion gear and a new cam-cover gasket

Tinware: Even factory fresh, stock machines occasionally have noisy pinion gears

PERFORMANCE GAIN: Makes life easier for your cam train and your nerves

COMPLEMENTARY MODIFICATION: As long as you're in there, check the cam, the cam bearing, the rollers on the tappets, and the condition of the breather gear

1 The 1977 1/2 to 1990 gear is on the left; its most recognizable feature is the keyway slot. The gear on the far right is the 1991 to 1992 unit, which has no keyway, and (though hard to tell unless side by side) is also shorter than its older brother. Since 1993, Big Twins have used the no-keyway, no-recess style in the middle. Not only are there 3 different designs as shown above, but there are 7 color-coded sizes of each different version. If you change cams, you have to be sure that you have the correct version, and that the color codes match up to the cam gears.

2 The flip side of the same three gears shows the 1977 1/2 to 1990 version standing tall among its peers. The slender shorty in the middle is the 1993–on design, leaving the one on the right as the 1991 and 1992 gear. Note that the 1990 to 1992 design has a recess, unlike the 1993 which has a flat surface. The latest design has been beefed up a little with a flat back design, and it incorporates the spacer that was once a separate part. The 1993 and later version is the best of the three, but it is not an interchangeable part.

Evolution Big Twin engines use matched pinion and cam gears to reduce noise emissions. The parts are built in seven different matched sets, all indicated by color-coding. Simple enough, right?

Not quite.

Three different sets of these color-coded gears have been used on Evolutions. The first set was used on 1977 1/2 Shovelheads through 1990 Evos. The second set was used on 1991 and 1992 Big Twins, while the rest of the Evos (1993 and later) used a different set. The color codes are the same, but the actual design and the clearances from group to group are not. The different versions are not interchangeable largely as a result of redesigns of the pinion shaft.

Where you run into trouble with the matched gears is when the fit isn't right. Improper fit between the cam gear and the pinion gear can lead to anything from excessive noise to excessive wear. Too loose a clearance results in a clicking sound as the cam lobes pass maximum lift and the loads on the pinion change direction. It's annoying but won't really hurt anything.

A more significant problem with slack in the cam gear train is the resultant inaccurate cam timing. Inadequate clearance creates a whine that's very noticeable and in extreme cases can destroy the gear teeth and the bearings. Worse, all the metal particles and debris from this action can circulate through the oil system and—Bang!

Bear in mind that clearance is rarely an issue with stock cams. If you change cams (or are thinking about it), then you need to worry.

THE CURE

First, grab the shop manual for your particular year and model, pull the cam cover apart, and make sure you have the same color code on the both the cam gear and the pinion. (Most aftermarket cams come with a red code, which is in the middle of the range.) If the codes do not match, you can press the original cam gear off your stock cam and press it on the new cam. Then use the procedures shown in the shop manual to check the sizes and mesh clearance of both pinion and cam gears.

Basically, the procedure is as follows. On 1990 and later engines you measure by laying two 0.108-inch-diameter pins (H-D #38361 from Kent-Moore Tools or the aftermarket equivalent) on the gear's teeth exactly 180 degrees from one another. Then measure their outside diameter with a micrometer.

Measure both the cam gear and the pinion gear. Check these measurements taken on the new gears against the measurements of the originals.

Subtract the new cam gear size from the original size.

If the new gear is smaller, you add the difference to the size of the pinion, meaning you'll need a bigger pinion gear.

If the new cam gear is larger than the original, subtract the difference in size to figure how much smaller the new pinion gear must be.

That measurement will allow you to select the proper color-coded pinion gear from the selection listed in the manual.

Note that the process for 1989 and earlier engines is the same, except you use 0.105-inch-diameter pins (H-D #95632-79 from Kent-Moore Tools or the aftermarket equivalent).

Only a small number of engines are fitted with the large size original cam gears. These are coded green or black. If you happen to get one of these rarities in your motor, you are pretty much stuck with a pinion gear change. If, on the other hand, you have the more common red or blue code cam, you most likely will not need to change pinions. The truth is, if you're not a total perfectionist, a pinion that's within a couple of colors of a perfect match will be okay. For example, a red cam gear is compatible with an orange pinion, maybe even a yellow one. A white code pinion with a red code cam, however, is not likely to be a good way to go.

CAM/PINION GEAR COLOR CODE CHART (1993 AND NEWER)

		PINION GEAR			CAM GEAR	
Color Code	Part no.	Size (in.)	Size (mm)		Size (in.)	Size (mm)
ORANGE	24040-93	1.4853/1.4850	37.727/37.719	NOTE:	2.7472/2.7476	69.779/69.789
WHITE	24041-93	1.4849/1.4846	37.716/37.709	Check parts	2.7477/2.7481	69.792/69.802
YELLOW	24042-93	1.4845/1.4842	37.706/37.699	catalog for	2.7482/2.7486	69.804/69.814
RED	24043-93	1.4841/1.4838	37.696/37.689	cam and	2.7487/2.7491	69.817/69.827
BLUE	24044-93	1.4837/1.4834	37.686/37.678	pinion sets	2.7492/2.7496	69.830/69.840
GREEN	24045-93	1.4833/1.4830	37.676/37.668	part numbers	2.7497/2.7501	69.842/69.853
BLACK	24046-93	1.4829/1.4826	37.666/37.658		2.7502/2.7506	69.855/69.865

NOTE
- Use 0.108 in. (2.74 mm) pins to measure.
- Cam gears have two grooves on face.

ENGINE

PROJECT 58 • REPLACING THE TIMER COVER

 Time: 15 minutes

 Tools: Drill, 1/8-inch drill bit, flat-blade screwdriver, Phillips screwdriver, possibly a small Allen wrench (usually comes with the new timer cover that uses it), and a rivet gun

 Talent:

 Tab: $

 Tinware: The timer cover and your choice of 8-32x5/8 inch fasteners (Allens, buttonheads, regular screws, even bolts) or rivets (#8699)

 Tip: If you have switched to points, you'd better have a gasket or never ride in the rain; if you're electronically ignited, you probably don't need to worry (the factory doesn't)

PERFORMANCE GAIN: Improved access to the ignition and a handsome personal touch

COMPLEMENTARY MODIFICATION: Check ignition timing or add an aftermarket ignition system

Big Twins since 1970 and Sportsters since 1971 have employed a round metal cap about the diameter of a soda can to cover the mysterious inner workings of the ignition. Decades later, the modern version of this timer cover possesses a little mystery of its own for new owners. Replacing it, either for the look or for easier access to the ignition system, is not nearly as simple as it should be.

From the factory, these "tamper-proof" timer covers have rivets holding them in place. Trivia hounds take note: the rivets on a Big Twin cover are at the 12 o'clock and 6 o'clock positions, while the Sportster's are at 3 and 9, respectively. I'm not sure anybody really knows why, so never mind.

Suppose you want to change the cover or just remove it to check the timing? The first thing is to replace those pesky rivets.

The soft aluminum rivets can be removed in a number of ways. Drive them out with a center punch and a hammer or drill them out with a bit that's the same diameter (about 1/8 inch) as the rivet body.

1 It seems a simple thing, but you'd be surprised at how much confusion resides under these two little rivets. In order to remove this cover, you'll need to drill the heads off the rivets.

2 This is the inner cover you encounter once the rivets have been drilled out. You can tap the holes where the rivets used to live to enable the use of most any timer cover you want. If you switch to points ignition, discard this inner cover and use longer pillar bolts and a gasket. Speaking of which, deciding on which length and style of pillar bolt to use for your timer project involves some choices. Bolt #32608-70, used from 1970 to 1978 1/2, with a long shoulder and short threads, is the expensive, well-machined one. Bolt #32606-82 is the short one, used from 1982 to present. Bolt #32601-78 is the longest and was used from 1978 1/2 until 1982. Don't use the short one (or put a washer behind the shoulder) if you need more clearance between the cover and whatever's inside.

Once the cover is removed, you'll see a second inner cover. This cover is retained by two small Phillips screws. No problem here, just remove the screws and pull off the inner cover.

Oops! Now what? There's all kinds of weird stuff inside the timer cavity. Just pay attention to the two pillar bolts used to "stand off" the inner cover—you know, the ones you just took the screws out of. These two bolts are the key to your future plans for buttoning up this hole.

Once upon a time, there used to be a heavy gray paper gasket in the timer hole too. This gasket was to

3 What time is it for your timer cover? The one with mounting holes at 12 o'clock and 6 o'clock is actually for Sportsters. The one with holes at 3 o'clock and 9 o'clock is the same design for Big Twins. The plain chrome unit will obviously work on either one. However, if the design you prefer isn't available for your application, you can make any of them work on any model by using screws instead of rivets to mount it. If the design has side-to-side holes, just take a couple of 8/32x5/8-inch screws and screw the thing onto the pillar bolts. If it's a top-to-bottom hole pattern, tap 8/32-inch threads in the inner cover and mount to those holes.

4 Even with holes tapped in the inner cover, you can always revert back to stock mounting, as long as you have a rivet gun and a couple #8699 special rivets.

keep water and dirt out of the points, when Harleys had points. Since they haven't had points for over a decade now, no more gasket. Electronic ignitions are waterproof, see? The pillar bolts that are stock with electronic ignition are shorter in length than the ones the factory used when it used a gasket. Yes, the difference in length can make a difference. If you switch to points, use the longer pillar bolts.

Okay, what if you have a Sportster but the custom timer cover you've just got to have on your bike is only available in the Big Twin bolt pattern, or vice versa? No problem.

With the right pillar bolts and the timer cover of choice you can:

1) Eliminate the inner cover and just screw the new timer cover on, at 3 o'clock and 9 o'clock, with two 8-32x5/8-inch screws. (Remember, always use either blue Loctite or star-type lockwashers if you want the screws to stay in. That's the other reason the factory uses rivets.)

2) Reuse the inner cover and two rivets (H-D #8699) to install the cover at the 12 o'clock and 6 o'clock positions.

3) Tap threads into the holes that hold the rivets to the inner cover. Then use any timer cover you want in any position you like, either with or without the inner cover.

One or the other of these methods should help you "timer" it just right.

PROJECT 59 • DYNO TUNING YOUR ENGINE

 Time: 1 to 2 hours

 Tools: Tiedowns, handlebar protectors, earplugs, and eye protection

 Talent: 👤 (if you work with a good dyno operator)

 Tab: $ to $$

 Tinware: Fresh spark plugs and a tire inflation gauge

 Tip: Make sure the bike is in A-1 condition before you strap it onto the dyno

 PERFORMANCE GAIN: Subtle improvements that can turn into big gains

COMPLEMENTARY MODIFICATION: This project is a complement to any performance upgrade

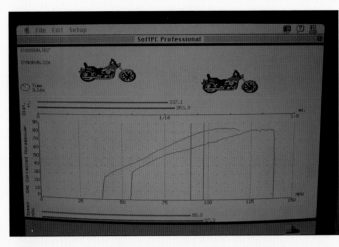

1 There are two basic types of dyno runs, a roll-on, usually in fourth gear, and an all-gear run, which, just like it sounds, amounts to a rolling-start drag race from first gear clear through top gear. There are things to be learned from both types after a good run is logged into the computer. Here, for instance, using the dyno's simulated racing program, are two Big Twins that seem to make similar peak power "racing" one another. The lesson is that the red bike makes its power quicker and earlier in the rev range and pulls ahead in the roll-on every time. Which one of the two do you suppose feels stronger on the street?

You don't guess about your health; you go to the doctor. Don't guess about the health of your H-D's engine either. Go to a dyno. Nothing else makes as much sense when it comes to perfecting the package, let alone keeping it healthy. Think of a chassis dyno as a treadmill for your Hog. Frequent workouts and evaluations will keep that V-twin heart pumping longer and harder, and you'll know it's gonna stay healthy.

A dyno (technically, dynamometer) is used to measure the force that is commonly called "horsepower." Horsepower can be measured about 40 different ways, from gross, net, SAE, or DIN, but the bottom line is you need a reliable way to measure this motive force.

Over the years, many tools have been developed to measure this old expression of force. Using water or electric motors generating resistance, early dynos would measure torque, which was then converted to horsepower using calculations done in long hand. These machines were time-consuming and sometimes inaccurate. Then came computers.

Attaching a computer to a heavy roller for measuring horsepower against the resistance of a rolling drum of fixed weight and mass meant accuracy and speed of measurement were dramatically improved.

Known as a chassis dyno (as opposed to the time-honored "brake" dyno, which loads an engine at a fixed rpm and generally measures output at the crank), this device takes its readings from the bike's rear wheel, which sits on the heavy roller and rotates it as the motorcycle engine develops power. Power is measured where it counts—at the back tire.

A simplified description of the dyno's workings is that a sensor attached to the rig informs the computer how fast the heavy roller is rotating. As the roller is rotated faster and faster by the motorcycle's rear wheel, the computer times it, like in a race. In short, it's an accelerometer. A motorcycle that can accelerate the heavy roller from, say, 1,000 rpm to 6,000 rpm in 5 seconds puts out more horsepower than one that does it in 8 seconds. The computer compares the amount of time taken to a preset program and pops up the amount of horsepower that was generated at the motorcycle's rear wheel.

Because the dyno uses electronics to measure the time needed to rotate the heavy roller, it is very accurate in its readings; a run takes very little time, and the run is non-abusive to the motorcycle. All you must do is control a few variables. That is the key. The first is friction at the rear-tire-to-roller junction, in the wheel bearings, and in the clutch and transmission. The added friction of a mis-inflated rear tire can cost several horsepower, for example.

CALCULATING HORSEPOWER

The math works like this: The rotating force of the crankshaft (torque) is measured in foot-pounds and multiplied by the engine's rpm at the moment the measurement is taken. That multiplication is then divided by the constant number of 5,252. The result is how many so-called horsepower the engine is generating at that given rpm.

Just make sure tire pressures are on the firm side of the specs, clutches are adjusted properly, and the brakes aren't dragging.

Next we have ambient air temperature, humidity, and barometric pressure. All of these can affect the horsepower measurement. A 3-degree rise in air temperature will measurably reduce a bike's output. There's not much you can do about these things other than to strive for consistency. The dyno will correct (hence "corrected" horsepower) for atmospheric conditions, within limits, but a run on the hottest day of the year and a run during a blizzard aren't likely to be comparable.

A well set up, professional dyno shop will usually have a dyno "cell." The cell is nothing more than a purpose-built room with sound deadening and airflow and climate control systems that help control many of the environmental variables that affect power measurements. With a cell, dyno runs can be conducted all day long and good comparisons can be made.

This is the real value of dyno testing. The mere reading of horsepower and torque is almost meaningless (aside from occasional "bragging" rights) in and of itself. But when you want to diagnose a little misfire, see if the engine is running lean in the mid-range, or verify that a cam change actually helped the powerband, you can't beat a dyno. Used by someone who knows how, it cuts out 80 to 90 percent of the guesswork. Tuning issues that used to take days or even weeks to resolve can be isolated and dealt with in minutes using a dyno. The solution can most often be checked out and verified just as quickly. There is simply no other way to do these things as efficiently and quickly.

The seat of your pants is dead. Long live the dyno!

ENGINE

PROJECT 60 • USING DESK TOP DYNOS

Time: You'll spend hours!

Tools: A PC (or a Mac with PC emulation software), the program of your choice, and a printer

Talent:

Tab: $ to $$

Tinware: A personal spec sheet for your specific machine (cam, compression, and so on) to establish a base line

Tip: Accurate information on your bike is the key to good results; actual power increases are usually slightly over what the software predicts

PERFORMANCE GAIN: Saves money; especially helpful for choosing cams and compression

COMPLEMENTARY MODIFICATION: A second software program

You've got questions about cams, carbs, pipes, headwork, compression, and a dozen other things. You want to know what to expect before you lay down your dollars and build your high-performance engine. Until recently the only way to get a clue was to ask around. If you listen to the right people and make some good guesses, you may have something going. But what if you aren't that lucky?

There is a better way.

Enter "predictive" engine building software. This is good stuff, folks! And, although there are doubtless more than the two choices I've sampled, these both are accurate enough for the task at hand.

First, a program called Desk Top Dyno. While this is not Harley-specific software, you can "build" almost any motor with it, at least on the computer screen. Desk Top Dyno allows you to input information about everything from bore and stroke to head flow and cam timing, and then it spits out reasonably accurate information about expected power levels using the combination of figures you input. If you don't like the first answer, you change a couple of parameters, say, compression and exhaust specs and run it again until you get it right for you. Once that's figured, it's safe to spend your dollars on the hardware that the software says will do the job. The $40 program is worth every cent for its ease of use, support,

1 You'd be surprised how much insight there is to be gained by testing your choice of cam, compression, exhaust flow, head flow, and a host of other variables in advance on an engine-building program. Not quite as accurate as a real dyno, it's still an excellent way to predict how a given engine configuration will work before you make any expensive mistakes. Need to know how camshaft option A will affect the amount and characteristics of power? You can check it against option B or even the cam you already have in there. The other little known electronic secret to staying on top of the technical side of Hog ownership is the availability of factory parts and service bulletins on CD. While not as much fun as building virtual engines, these bulletins can be just as valuable to the long-term health and enjoyment of your Harley.

and accuracy—with one limitation. That limitation is that it's perhaps too generic for hard-core Harley work. You make certain allowances for that by selecting, in automotive terms, things like "single plane manifold" or "open headers" from the menu choices available. If you can live with these minor "work-arounds" you'll find that Desk Top Dyno is up to the task.

On the other hand, if you've simply got to have the Harley-specific software of choice, perhaps the best alternative is the Accelerator Pro software. It boasts several useful features, including its ability to "build" a simulated engine with data entered by the user and then predict the horsepower and torque potentials of that engine. While a few unsuspecting computer jockeys have experienced severe cases of "dyno shock" when comparing a simulation to the real thing, the program has earned a reputation for uncanny accuracy if given correct data.

Installation can be a bit tricky on this DOS-based software. It is designed to be "pirate proof." Therefore, you only get one shot at installation, on one computer only. So pay attention to the installation instructions or you'll be sorry. Once the program's properly installed, the first step is to select one of the pull-down menus and enter data. You'll be prompted to enter all kinds of information on your dream engine, from bore and stroke to cam choices—you can even design your own cam!

Once you've built the engine of your dreams, Accelerator Pro prints a chart of its horsepower and torque potentials at different rpm levels and then stores all data for future reference. This last feature is especially handy for folks wanting to track their purchases and a guide for future upgrades.

One last note of caution: Remember that a desktop dyno or engine-build software has limits. First, realize that it's not foolproof but can take things from the "wild guess" stage to the educated-opinion stage better than any other method, short of a real dyno. Second, be honest and accurate with what you tell the program, and you'll be pleasantly surprised at how honest and accurate it will be for you.

SECTION SEVEN
LUBRICATION

Oiliness is next to godliness! And since Harley's don't leak it out anymore, what you put in is more important than ever where care and feeding of Evos is concerned. Unfortunately it's one of the least understood aspects of these air-cooled behemoths, let alone the machine's various sub-systems—like transmissions, clutches, control cables, and even front forks. It seems we all get on the "frequent oil change" band wagon quickly enough, but generally that's as far as it goes. What this section hopes to help you with is comprehending the radical changes in motor oil itself over the last decade and how they should affect your decisions on vital lubricants. There's news about fluids for use in the gearbox and primary chain case as well. Once you've "absorbed" the multi-grade info, you'll learn about brake fluids, fork oil, and even the sort of stuff to use on your clutch and throttle cables.

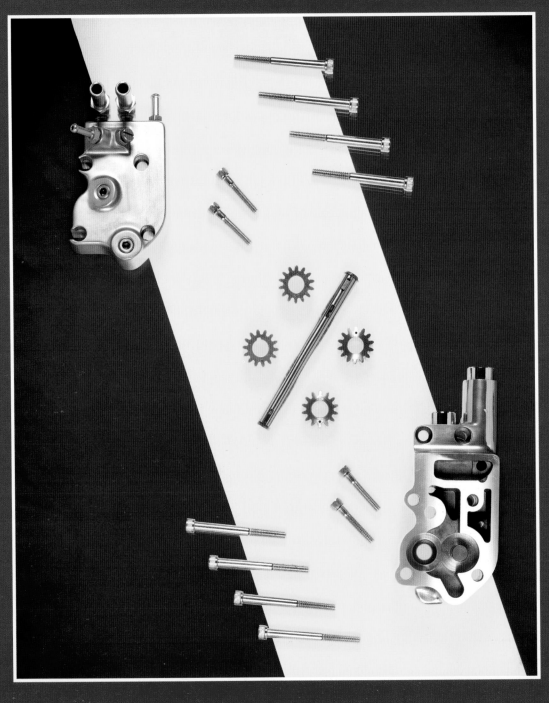

LUBRICATION
PROJECT 61 • INSTALLING AN OIL COOLER

 Time: 1/2 to 1 hour

 Tools: Screwdriver

 Talent: ▮

 Tab: $ to $$$

 Tinware: Zip-ties and fancy clamps and guides to clean up and route the oil hoses (some coolers don't affect hoses)

 Tip: If you use a cooler, use a thermostat

! PERFORMANCE GAIN: A properly designed and installed oil cooler will add to engine life by maintaining stock operating temperatures, even on seriously hot-rodded (especially high-compression) engines, which generate vast amounts of heat

COMPLEMENTARY MODIFICATION: Accurate oil temperature gauge and cylinder head temperature gauge

If you have a 80-horsepower or more engine capable of generating, say, 100 percent more power than a standard one or if you frequently ride hard on long trips of 100 miles or more, you should probably consider an oil cooler. If you are aboard a stocker for no more than 20 minutes at a time, you might still consider a cooler—at least in the hot months of the riding season.

If you choose to install a cooler, you'd better get one with a thermostat. That way it won't bring the cooler on-line during short hops, allowing the oil to get up to operating temperature. And if you actually

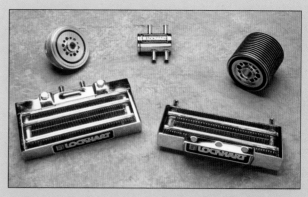

1 Stock Harleys really don't need coolers under ordinary circumstances, but the next best thing to water-cooling is to use an oil cooler to take the heat off. Two things to bear in mind: If you use a cooler, don't use high-viscosity oils. Secondly, unless the cooler is the easily removed screw-on type that goes behind the filter, use a thermostat to open and close the cooler. The screw-on units should be considered a seasonal or conditional add-on for hot summer rides or extra-hard usage. For short hops, like back and forth to work in the winter, they can do more harm than good.

read the owner's manual and live in the latter part of the twentieth century, you'll realize that a cooler combined with a multi-viscosity 10/50 or 20/50 motor oil makes a lot more sense for the majority of riding environments than any heavy, molasses-like 50- or 60-weight straight grade oil. In fact, the quickest way to wear out a top end is to use straight-weight oils in cool conditions for short rides. It's that simple. The second quickest way is to use a thin multi-grade oil on days when it's too hot, you have too far to go and way too much power to get you there, and you're stuck in traffic, smelling hot metal and cooked lubricant.

Nothing can cover you for all riding conditions, but using 20/50 Harley oil, or a good synthetic, and a quality oil cooler with a thermostat covers more of the bases than anything else.

Select a kit from one of the reputable manufacturers and follow their instructions for installation. It's a relatively simple addition that can save a lot of wear and tear on your engine. Lockhart, Jagg, and Billetcool all offer quality coolers that will do the job well.

LUBRICATION
PROJECT 62 • FIXING YOUR SPORTSTER'S OIL TANK

Time: 3 to 5 hours

Tools: 7/16-, 1/2-, 9/16-, and 5/8-inch wrenches and sockets; 6-inch extension and ratchet; pliers; WD-40; 12-millimeter socket; torque wrench; screwdrivers; and hose-clamp pinch tool; keep all your tools handy though (like the Mity-Vac)

Talent: 👤👤👤

Tab: $$$

Tinware: Correct oil tank kit, screw-type hose clamps (if you don't want to use the pinch-type factory units), engine oil, exhaust gaskets, DOT 4 brake fluid, and brake banjo washers

Tip: Avoid used tanks

PERFORMANCE GAIN: No more worries that you'll have the life blood of the motor leaking all over the rear of the bike as you ride

COMPLEMENTARY MODIFICATION: If you've got an old battery, now's the time to install a new one (preferably sealed type #66672-96)

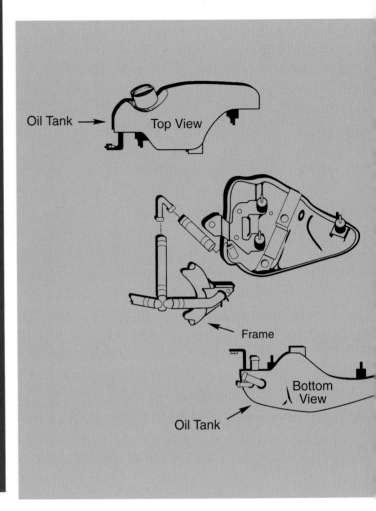

Oil Tank → Top View

Frame

Bottom View

Oil Tank

For over 10 years the design of the oil tank on Sportsters was pretty much the same. That's good in that it means there are plenty of good used ones out there, just in case you need one. Why would you need one? The 1982 to 1993 oil tanks are prone to cracking. If you own a Sporty that suffers from this malady, your options are as follows:

1) Remove the culprit and try to repair it by welding the cracks. Your expense should be in the vicinity of $30 to $50. Odds against a permanent cure are about 70 percent. Usually, once cracked, it will re-crack after you repair it.

2) Replace the tank with one of those thousands of used ones we just talked about. Expense is whatever the traffic will bear in the used XL oil tank market, usually $75 to $125. Odds for a permanent cure depend on the age and condition of the used tank. Bear in mind that the tank may last at least as long as your original did, or it could crack two days later.

3) Bite the bullet and install one of the factory's "retrofit" Sportster oil tank kits. These little devils are far more expensive than they ought to be, and a complete pain to install, but it is the only permanent cure. The kit essentially includes everything required (and that's a lot) to turn the battery box, rear brake hose, and the oil tank itself into the setup they are using on the 1994 and newer models. The kit for 1982 to early 1987 models is H-D #62482-93 and will set you back around $208, not counting sales tax or labor. The one for late 1987 to 1993 models is #62472-93 and costs $228.

If you decide to pay someone at a shop to do the dirty work for you (not a bad idea, frankly), figure on many additional dollars to get that handled! Generally it's a four-hour job, so you're looking at approximately $200 extra. You can do it yourself, though, and here's how:

DISASSEMBLY

Remove the exhaust system.

On 1982 models you also get to take off the front chain guard. (Are we having fun yet?)

Drain the oil tank.

Take the seat off, unhook the battery, unplug the

starter relay, and pull all the hose clamps and lines off the oil tank.

Unbolt the oil tank, unscrew and remove the starter relay, and then take the tank out and off.

Remove the little clamp thingy (that's the technical description) that holds the brake pipe to the sprocket cover.

Remove the rear brake hose—every clamp, screw, and Allen bolt. Make sure you don't forget to unplug the rear brake switch.

Take the sprocket cover off. The oil feed line under the cover needs to be unclipped and temporarily moved to below the motor. There's a nut on the rear motor mount you'll have to loosen up to remove the battery ground cable. Go ahead and do it.

Remove the positive battery cable from the starter motor.

Take the triangular cover off the ignition module and pull the rubber stud mount that holds the battery tray off of the frame. Incidentally, there's a couple different rubber stud mounts in the oil tank kit. Don't get 'em mixed up with the ones off the bike, okay? Believe it or not, you're finally ready to install the kit.

INSTALLING THE KIT

It's a good idea to start by taking the rubber stud mounts in the kit and screwing them into the new oil tank.

While you're at it, you might as well clamp the 3-inch length of oil hose onto the big nipple that comes out the back of the tank.

Top the hose with the 90-degree elbow fitting and then put the starter relay back on.

Take the three protective moldings in the kit and tap them onto the inside curved edges, both top and bottom, of the tank with a rubber hammer.

This next part is a little tricky. You need to "subassemble" the rest of the oil lines and tee fittings and such, as shown in the drawing.

Find the new "siamese" battery cables from the kit, and then attach the bottom of the negative to the rear motor mount. Not sure what terminal goes where? You'll spot an indicator mark on the connection you want to start with. You've got it right when the indicator faces rearward after it's bolted on. Now

torque the rear motor mount to 65–80 *inch*-pounds. Install the positive end on the starter and torque that to the same spec.

Put the new battery-tray rubber stud mount (that's the odd one) onto the frame. Make sure at this point to pull the oil lines over to the right side of the bike so you can get them reinstalled without playing "go fish."

Ready? Set? Bolt on the new oil tank! Just don't get berserk. Torque on the rubber stud mounts is only 3 to 5 foot-pounds.

By now you're far enough into this you'll want to get finished quickly. Don't! This is where you want to hook up the subassembled oil lines, and it's worth going slowly to prevent mistakes, leaks, and subsequent insanity. (Common sense goes a long way in these situations; certain years, such as 1982 to 1984 1/2, may need to have the hoses trimmed or otherwise adjusted slightly.)

Once you're comfortable with the oil-line routing and everything's clamped up good and proper, put the sprocket cover back on. Torque the three Allens to 90–110 *inch*-pounds.

On 1990 through 1993 models, when you go to put the brake hose on, remove the T-bushing from the frame tab and put on the new clip nut from the kit.

Finish installing the brake lines using new banjo washers. By the way, over the years the factory has used two different types of banjo washers on the brake lines. One of them is zinc-coated copper. Tighten that type to 30–35 foot-pounds. The other type is steel with a built-in O-ring. Tighten these to 17–22 foot-pounds. And please don't mix and match. Stay with the original banjo washer (your friendly H-D parts dealer can help out if you're not sure what was original on your bike).

Using the shiny new hardware in the kit, install the new battery tray. From here on out, you'll have to finish putting the bike back together. It's just little things like the module cover, the battery, the seat, the exhaust pipes, and, oh yeah, oil in the new tank.

Check for leaks, good oil return to the new tank, and, after you bleed the rear brake, hook up the brake light switch.

If all went as planned, you just cured a nasty problem in a slick fashion.

LUBRICATION
PROJECT 63 • UPGRADING YOUR SPORTSTER'S OIL PUMP

 Time: 1 hour

 Tools: Screwdriver, 3/16-inch Allen socket, ratchet, small side cutter, and 3/8-inch bolt

 Talent: ▮

 Tab: $$

 Tinware: 1998 oil pump, oil-pump-to-crankcase gasket, two Allen screws, hose clamps

 Tip: You shouldn't have to remove the exhaust; five-speed Sportsters and Buells allow easy access to the oil pump, and it can be removed with the engine in the frame

 PERFORMANCE GAIN: More consistent oil pressure—useful on stock engines and vital on hopped-up mills

COMPLEMENTARY MODIFICATION: Stainless oil lines

1 On Sportsters built from 1986 to 1997, the stock pump measures 1.4575 inch at the body. The 1998 and later pump at 1.640 inches is holding scavenge gears that are 0.200 inch taller and do 40 percent more work. Notice the "trou cut into the conical part of the pump from gear to body? That's what allows the oil to d right, straight into the pump, instead of hanging around in the cam cover. The 1998 ar later pump has a cavity cut into the body as well. Measuring nearly an inch long and about 3/8 inch wide, the cavity, along with these other design changes, cures many of major oil control problems of previous years and might even offer up an extra horse o two at full throttle.

Harley's proven high-volume, low-pressure oiling system complements the rather unique ball-bearing engine construction, so much so that overly high pressure in the system can be detrimental (think about that before blindly bouncing your oil pressure readings as high as you can get 'em). The arena for true improvement is in fine-tuning the amounts of oil trapped in the bottom end or cam cover. Get the oil to the critical spot at the right time and then out of the way before it slows down, stops, or pools up, and blows out.

You don't need a cup full of the stuff lagging in the cases, dragging on flywheels. You don't need pools of the stuff backing up into the rocker boxes and puking into the air filter. You really don't need an extra few ounces backed up in the cam cover waiting to drain back into the pump. You especially don't need widely varied powerful pulses of negative, then positive, pressure screwing around with the oil's direction of flow every nanosecond.

Since it was given its fifth gear in 1991, the XL engine, whether Sportster or Buell versions, has suffered from oil-scavenging problems. All sorts of fixes have been tried, including drilling oversized rocker-box drain holes, flipping the motor seal 180 degrees, and tightening up tolerances on the sprocket-shaft spacer, all to minimum benefit.

The problem persisted until 1998 and the long awaited re-think of the oil pump. And guess what? It scavenges better and bolts right on older five-speed models. This is one of the best and most effective mods you can make for $180 and an hour or so of your time.

LUBRICATION
PROJECT 64 • UPGRADING YOUR BIG TWIN'S OIL PUMP

 Time: 3 to 4 hours

 Tools: Snap-ring pliers, drill, Allens, 7/16-inch wrench, oil dump pan, and rags

 Talent:

 Tab: $$$

 Tinware: Oil pump gaskets, cam cover gasket, hose clamps, and possibly a drilling fixture

 Tip: On Evo Big Twins through 1991, there's just no margin for error when installing the pump-to-case gasket, and it's difficult to avoid leaks. A *very* small dab of sealant (Hylomar or 3-bond #4) around the stud holes and not the oil passages might help. Nineteen ninety-two and later models have studs that aren't so close to the oil passages and are much easier to seal up

PERFORMANCE GAIN: Better oil control, mostly at high rpm, which can result in extra power because less oil accumulates in the bottom of the engine cases, so there's less oil drag on the fly-wheels at speed

COMPLEMENTARY MODIFICATION: Oil cooler, pressure gauge, temperature gauge, and stainless oil lines

Factory Big Twin oil pumps have been essentially the same since 1968, with minor updates since, including a functional improvement in 1981 and a major cosmetic redesign in 1992. Their double-gear design is up to the task for the majority of us, regardless of any hype you may have heard to the contrary. Oiling related failures are the least of your worries for moderately modified motors used in the real world.

If your Big Twin is putting out serious horsepower, however, the stock pump is less than optimal. The reasons are a little obscure, mostly because folks fail to understand the true nature of the lubrication needs of a Harley V-twin.

The key here is not necessarily increased pressure but maintaining a consistent volume of oil in the motor and then getting it all back out again. A Harley's ball-type main bearings simply don't need fire-hose levels of pressure, as plain bearings need. Instead, the trick is to "splash" oil in precise amounts

1 The venerable, gear-driven Big Twin oil pump has been updated and tweaked enough in its lengthy career to provide essentially trouble-free operation, even on today's Evos. The aftermarket has gone perhaps a touch further in developing the potential of this basic design for true high-performance applications, as this high-capacity (and gorgeous) show-polished unit will be glad to prove—given the chance.

2 The stocker's slim and trim body contains two sets of gears—one set to feed the motor its fluids and the other to scavenge the stuff back out once it's done its duty. The dimensions of these gears and the condition of the surfaces they run so close to in the aluminum body are the determining factors in the pump's ability to pump.

3 The drillings in the body and how they mate to the drillings in the crankcase determine just where and how much oil gets to what and when. Over the years, this arrangement has changed, and in fact, from 1992–on even the mounting-stud holes have been moved. As similar as the pumps may look from year to year, they are not freely interchangeable.

4 If you ever suffer an oil pump problem, it can usually be traced to one of three basic malfunctions: the oil seal (shown) in the pump body has ceased to seal, the small woodruff key used to retain the scavenge gear has sheared off, or something hard and usually metallic has managed to evade all the filters and screens and died jammed in between the pump's gear teeth, taking the pump with it in some weird murder-suicide pact.

to precise areas and suck it back out before it gets in the way of power production.

A Harley is a dry-sump motor, so oil feeds into the motor from a separate tank and circulates back out, re-cycled to lubricate again and again. The oil pump's job begins with drawing oil from the tank and directing it to the tappets and lifters. As pressure builds, oil travels up through the pushrods and feeds the top end. At a mere 5 to 7 psi the pressure regulator in the oil pump allows oil flow to the bottom end. Once oil makes it to the crankpin and does its lubricating there, it's flung out, via centrifugal force, through small drillings in the pin and collects at the bottom of the crankcases. The theory goes that any surplus is picked up by the flywheels, flung toward the cast-in "scraper" pick-up, then sucked into the breather galley, which is controlled by a timed rotating breather gear, back to the pump, into the filter, and back to the oil tank.

This system is simple enough and effective up to a point. That point tends to be the point at which an air-cooled engine gets too hot. When you add power, you add heat. Heat thins oil, and there's no radiator to stabilize or augment the limits. Building the necessary pressure when your motor is hot gets harder. On a hot day, the reading on that oil pressure gauge you installed commonly drops to zero. That doesn't necessarily mean your bottom end is getting no oil, just that it's living on the stuff that's already in there, being flung about by the rotating crank. At times like these your first instinct is to put a stiffer springs in your oil pump to raise the pressure. This probably isn't necessary or even advisable. As long as you get a reading of a few psi once you get moving, things are okay.

Where you run into problems is at the high end of the rpm scale. A common school of thought is that since the motor was hopped up to the point where it generates more heat than the system can dissipate, why not hop up the pump?

Well, installing a double-speed oil pump only solves half your problem. Again, the pressure the pump can create increases, but the ability of the gears to "grab" oil at high rpm can actually decrease because of a phenomenon known as cavitation, which is not much different than spinning the prop on an outboard motor so fast it just pumps air or vacuum, not water.

The solution to all these problems lies in the aftermarket. S&S sells a pump that's very similar in concept to the stocker but addresses the volume issue, with a clever pressure trick—allowing excess oil that may lead to either wet-sumping or cavitation at speed to "get out of the way" by returning via a shortcut in the pump itself. The S&S design also provides more consistent pressures overall, from stone-cold start-up to smokin' hot speed. It's an attractive alternative to the stock pump, as a direct replacement, let alone a high-performance modification.

The other player in pumps is Zipper's "Pro-Flow," a pump developed on a specially designed oil pump "dyno." It's perfect for drag racers, featuring a pump body machined from 6061-T651-1 billet aluminum using state-of-the-art CNC machining, allowing near perfect tolerances to be built in. Designed with Sportster-type gerotor gears, this pump is capable of pumping 200 percent more oil volume than the stocker. As if that wasn't neat enough, the return drive gear is pressed on and has no key to shear off.

Before you get too excited, you should ponder the work involved in installing one of these pumps and some of the S&S pumps. It's considerable, and involves drilling your crankcases. S&S and Kent-Moore offer fixtures to take most of the risk out of this rather radical step, but it's pretty much a "no-turning-back" mod, so be sure you need the benefits before you take the risks. Remember also that parts and replacement assemblies (should you eventually need them) won't be as readily available as the stock parts.

LUBRICATION

PROJECT 65 • KEEPING YOUR OIL PARTICLE-FREE

Time: 1 to 2 hours

Tools: Magnets. The long thin pencil-type to drag through the oil tank. The short round refrigerator type to stick on the end of the oil filter or oil tank

Talent:

Tab: $

Tinware: 1 1/4- to 1 1/2-inch magnet, other assorted small but powerful magnets (possibly one of those purpose built magnetic "mittens" that fit on the end of the filter), and an extra quart or so of oil

Tip: This is the tip

PERFORMANCE GAIN: Helps you get 200,000 miles out of a bottom end

COMPLEMENTARY MODIFICATION: Synthetic oil, frequent filter changes, and oil cooler with a thermostat; also clean and flush the oil tank with solvent every four years or so

When's the last time you took one of those long pencil-shaped magnets and actually stuck it in the oil bag to see what came out on the end of the thing? Well, when this trick was performed on a 1985 FXR with 63,500 miles and a boat load of oil and filter changes on it, the magnet came out coated with sludge. In addition, there was a layer of particles and goo about a quarter of an inch thick all over the bottom of the tank. The bike has run like a watch for all these years but, in spite of my best efforts (and all those oil filters), metal particles were accumulating in the motor.

If you want to avoid this problem, start with the same test. Stick a pencil magnet in your tank and see what comes out. If glop has begun to accumulate, pull the oil bag and brush and flush it clean with solvent.

Next, buy lots of magnets. You probably already have magnetic drain plugs for the oil tank, the tranny, and the primary case. If not, get them, but you don't have to stop there. Most hardware stores sell small magnets in a variety of sizes and shapes. I bought a couple that look like 50-cent coins, and after I thought about it a while, I got some about the size of the eraser portion of a pencil. The 50-centers have a 4-pound pull, and I stick them to the end of the oil filter. The 1-inch eraser types I stick on various spots on the outside of the oil tank and, possibly (in smaller sections), on any metal elbow fittings for the oil lines themselves. Guess what the theory is there. This level of overkill should keep iron particles attracted to anything but the motor.

The problem is magnets won't catch nonferrous materials (aluminum, for example). For protection against nonferrous shrapnel, do a "5-quart" oil change. In other words, after you've done all the routine stuff and the tank is full (or even slightly over-full) of fresh oil, unhook the return oil line and route it into a drain pan. Then, fire up the ol' horse and let it idle. Watch the dirty oil (and gook) that flows into the drain pan, but also watch the oil level in the tank, adding fresh oil as needed until the nasty lookin' sludgy stuff is flushed out and clean, pristine multi-grade comes out of the return line. It shouldn't take long, and it shouldn't take much more than an extra quart or so of oil to flush the system. Then reattach the return line and top off the oil level in the tank.

Perform this ritual about every fourth oil change and there's no telling how long the motor will last.

SECTION EIGHT
DRIVETRAIN

The support group for the Evo motor have secrets of their own. An example: Certain clutches for certain years and models are less than optimal performers. There are methods of updating and improving the primary chain tensioner. The saga and outcomes of design and installation of the front pulley for the belt drive are worth considering. You can learn something about that masterpiece of expedient engineering, the four-speed Sportster clutch basket/alternator rotor, and how to keep it from rearing up to bite.

All in all, this is the place to discover how to get the most from your drivetrain.

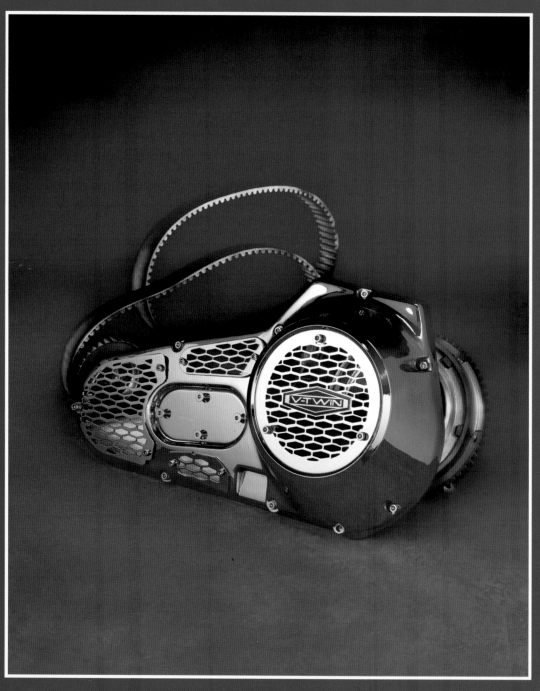

DRIVETRAIN

PROJECT 66 • UPDATING THE 1984–1989 BIG TWIN CLUTCH

Time: 2 to 3 hours

Tools: Clutch puller (H-D #95960-52C or Jim's #1004A), compensator-sprocket-nut socket (1 1/2-inch), air gun or 36-inch breaker bar, clutch-hub-nut (left-hand threads) socket (1 1/4 inch), possibly a hydraulic press to install new bearings in hub or basket, and the usual hand tools

Talent:

Tab: $$$$$+

Tinware: Primary gasket, shift-shaft O-rings (as required), and shifter sleeve (#34632-84A, if required)

Tip: Check your original clutch basket for cracks or other signs of damage or excessive wear; if you have the older all-cast clutch basket, consider updating to #37550-84A, whether the original is messed up or not

PERFORMANCE GAIN: Nicer pull at the lever, no slippage, longer life, disengages more cleanly, and it's easier to adjust correctly

COMPLEMENTARY MODIFICATION: On 1987–1989 models, update to the clutch pushrod end #37069-90 because it's got a "slinger" to keep the throwout bearing oiled more effectively

It's no big secret that the first design of the Evo Big Twin wet clutch (1984 1/2 to 1989 vintage) leaves a lot to be desired as a high-performance clutch. It certainly works well enough for stock applications, but put some serious power through it and you may find it lacking. The later version (1990–on) is a definite improvement. Having twice the friction surface doesn't hurt, but beyond that, the current clutch design is of a more durable design. It'll handle abuse.

The early clutch is also easily damaged. The four "fingers" that you screw the pressure plate onto are easily broken. Harley redesigned the fingers on newer replacements, and instead of weak aluminum, the fingers are now machined steel. That solved that problem, but it's not the only problem.

Both the early and the late versions also tend to break out the woodruff key slot machined into the inside diameter (I.D.) of the hub. This keyway, unlike its splined counterpart on the current clutch, will really only crack if the hub is installed incorrectly. If the specially T-shaped woodruff key is not perfectly placed at the point the hub is slid into place, the out-

1 There are two versions of the clutch hub for Big Twins built from 1984 1/2 to 1989 Big Twins. The factory original, on the left, has "crack me" written all over it. Most of these break "fingers" off the spline during their service life. They'll still work with missing fingers, just not well, hard, or for long. The updated hub has stronger steel fingers, along with other detail changes, making any sort of struggle with the older part more trouble than it's worth. If you intend to ride hard and a Pro Clutch is not in your plans, consider an update to the later Harley hub as mandatory.

2 Put one of these Zipper's retainer rings around the sleeve portion of the hub. There are retainers available for either version, and they're dimensionally different, but once you've got the right one in place, consider it cheap insurance. These retainers help prevent keyway damage due to an improper installation (ironically, the situation where damage is most often done), and they can save you from splitting the sleeve and destroying the hub entirely.

3 If you give up on band-aiding the original clutch on your 1984 to 1989 Big Twin and opt to pop for a 1990 and later factory clutch assembly, the only way to use it is to change the transmission mainshaft to the one-year-only 1990 version. (The 1991 and later version, on top in the photo, is machined differently and will not work with the earlier clutch parts.) Since this means a tranny teardown, it only makes sense to go this route as part of a necessary repair or upgrade in the gearbox. Otherwise, the clutch upgrade that makes the most sense is a Pro Clutch.

4 With a Pro Clutch, you get 300 percent more friction surface and you eliminate the fragile stock hub. Little bonuses include losing the factory's multi-position adjuster for diaphragm spring tension in favor of an easier to deal with and more logical setup. Just do not order any of the optional, stiffer diaphragm springs. The basic light spring, along with all that extra beef in the pack, gives you a bomb-proof, two-finger unit (see Project 68: Installing a Big Twin Pro-Clutch).

side lip of the keyway is so thin it will split—often without you realizing it. You don't discover the problem until the next time the clutch is disassembled, so you think it happened in service. Nope!

One way to improve your present clutch is to use the inexpensive "Saver" sleeve ring offered by Zipper's and CCI. The Saver slips over the outside diameter (O.D.) of the hub at the spot where the keyway is cut. This sleeve, once in place, effectively nearly triples the thickness of the hub in this crucial area, thus accomplishing two things. First, it greatly reduces the chances of cracking the keyway during installation, and second, it can save a hub that's already cracked. Two sizes of the hub saver ring are available—one for either version of the hub.

If your present clutch is damaged or badly worn, a better option might be to update to the late-model clutch. This option is fairly expensive because it requires not only the expense of the clutch parts but the installation of a newer style mainshaft (H-D #35042-90) to run them on as well. Unfortunately, the mainshaft was offered only in 1990, as that year was the last year for the mid-style main drive gear (#35029-85A) and the first year for the late-style clutch. It gets even more complicated (and expensive) if you want to update both the shaft and the main drive gear to use the late-style clutch. The reason:

Harley-Davidson has discontinued the drive gear that works with the pre-1991 shaft. Now, in order to update with factory parts, you would have to buy not just the pre-1991 shaft, but the new HCR main drive gear (#35029-94) and the mating gear (#35626-94). This adds up.

As usual, the aftermarket comes to the rescue for those who are dazed and confused by the factory's tactics. You can get any component for any version of the Big Twin five-speed tranny from Jim's or Andrew's. You can also get improved friction plates and stiffer springs, along with other goodies to improve your existing clutch setup, whatever version, from Barnett, Bandit, Rivera, Screamin' Eagle, and others. Or you can opt for a replacement clutch of a different design entirely, such as Pro-Clutch or Bandit. So if the hot-rodder in your soul (or the paranoia in the back of your mind) mandates that you keep that early Hog steamin' and screamin' as well as a new one, see the later projects in this section.

DRIVETRAIN

PROJECT 67 • UPDATING THE 1984–1986 BIG TWIN MAIN DRIVE GEAR

Time: 5 to 6 hours

Tools: All your hand tools, clutch puller (Jim's #1004A), compensator wrench/socket, countershaft sprocket nut socket (#94660-37A), main-shaft bearing race tool (#34902-84), main drive gear tool (#35316-80), optionally, a transmission stand (Jim's #1008-TS for rigid mount trans; #1008-5 for rubber mount trans), and a factory shop manual

Talent:

Tab: $$$ to $$$$$

Tinware: Primary and tranny gaskets, seals and O-rings, and new snap rings

Tip: If you're updating the main drive gear, do the pulley at the same time; Belt Drives Unlimited lightweight pulley is a good choice, weighing a scant 2.44 pounds instead of the portly 5.16 pounds of the stocker

PERFORMANCE GAIN: Reliability on high-powered bikes goes up a full order of magnitude; tranny goes from bullet-proof to bomb-proof

COMPLEMENTARY MODIFICATION: Update or upgrade front pulley and other worn gears in the box; clutch mods would be appropriate too

1 The top sides of two seemingly identical main drive gears from 1984 to 1987 Big Twins. Look closely at the one on the left. The gear is welded to the shaft portion of the assembly, and the weld is cracked. This can happen if your engine is producing 90 horsepower or more. The updated one-piece version is much less likely to fail under extreme conditions.

2 You can certainly see the two parts of the older design once it's broken. This is a rare but serious difficulty, as you might imagine, and if it should happen to you, will result in a complete transmission teardown.

3 Wear like this ruin main drive gears as well. If you find excessive play or leaks in the pulley, this is a likely culprit.

Suppose you are the proud owner of an early Evo Big Twin, one with an early five-speed tranny from, say, 1980 to 1986. Let's further suppose that you have a motor cranking out in excess of 85 to 90 horsepower. Finally, let's make the giant supposition that you didn't go to all the time, expense, and trouble to arrive at this state of affairs to go slow. Burn outs, drag racing, hard riding in general is part of your plan, right? Well, if all this is on track, you need to know one more thing.

The Harley main drive gear on 1980 to 1986 five-speed trannies is really two pieces welded into one piece at the factory, and the bitter truth is they may not stay in one piece under duress. The one you see in the photo is proof enough that, while it may be rare, they can come apart.

Sometime in 1987, when H-D went to the current-style tranny where the clutch cable routes directly into the end cover, the gear was updated. This drive gear (#35029-85A) is the only version available as a Harley replacement, and it's really one piece, so no problem. The Andrews and RevTech versions are one piece as well.

In other words, if you replace (or have already replaced) the thing with any of these options, there's nothing to worry about. If not, you shouldn't necessarily panic and rip the gearbox apart, unless you meet the criteria of a serious hot-rodder, or if one of the previous owners was. It's not as if these old-style gears are junk. They don't break unless abused. Newer and stronger designs are out there, so use 'em if ya need 'em.

It's not as though you need to drop what you're doing, and immediately tear the bike's tranny down just for this update, but it is an extensive project, so when you have other good reasons (bad splines, maybe?) that motivate you to go for it, do it exactly like the shop manual tells you to, using updated parts.

DRIVETRAIN
PROJECT 68 • INSTALLING A BIG TWIN PRO-CLUTCH

Time: 2 to 3 hours

Tools: Allens, Torx bits, screwdrivers, clutch puller (Jim's #1004A), clutch spring compressor for 1990 and later models (#38515-90), compensator wrench, 1 1/4-inch wrench, and something to lock down the clutch

Talent:

Tab: $$$$

Tinware: Primary gaskets, seals, and O-rings

Tip: Don't get anything but the standard spring with your Pro-Clutch if you have the 1984 to 1987 "arm over the tranny" release mechanism because: A) you don't need it, B) it'll tear that arm up in no time while not allowing the Pro-Clutch to release worth diddly, and C) it pulls way too hard

---

PERFORMANCE GAIN: Improved clutch grip

COMPLEMENTARY MODIFICATION: M-6 primary chain tensioner

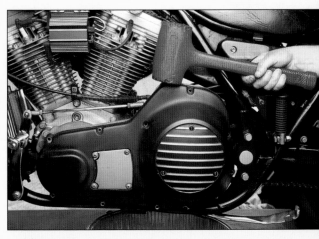

1 After disconnecting the battery and following the shop manual instructions as always, pull the outer primary cover. Loosen the primary screws (don't bother with the inspection or derby covers) and pop the cover sharply with rubber mallet if it's a little too stubborn to remove by hand. Don't go overboard with the mallet if it doesn't come loose after a shot or two; start looking for screws you forgot to remove.

We expect a lot from a clutch when you get right down to it. We want it to hook up, regardless of the power we transmit through it. Then we turn right around and want to be able to slip it mercilessly in slow traffic. We will not tolerate grabby or abrupt engagement yet want a two-finger pull at the lever. We don't want the adjustment to change when we get the poor thing smokin' hot. Nor will we tolerate even the slightest creep or drag with the lever pulled. And even under the terms of our abuse, if it doesn't last at least 60,000 to 100,000 miles, we think it's junk.

The stock Evo Big Twin diaphragm-spring wet clutches are pretty good, especially the current version, introduced on 1990 models. If you stay with stock horsepower, they all work well, and the current version is even good up to about 90 to 95 horsepower. Beyond that, you might need to upgrade.

Well, how about a Pro-Clutch? This high-performance clutch from Rivera/Primo offers the features and benefits needed along with all the performance capabilities, and they offer replacements for all the various versions:

The dry clutch that they offer for 1941 to early 1984 models comes with a diaphragm spring, thus addressing the biggest beef with that old soldier: its fiddley 10-spring adjustment process and resulting heavy clutch pull. You can get it for both chain-drive (#PC-1000C) and belt-drive (#P-1000) applications.

Their version of the 1984 1/2 to 1989 clutch (#PC-1100C) offers a whopping 325 percent more friction surface than the stocker. This goes right to the heart of the problem with the stock version, not to mention that the updated diaphragm-spring design eliminates the goofy stock adjuster plate. This should be their best seller.

Pro-Clutches for the 1990 and later version (#PC-1200C) increase surface area 100 percent. This is a good thing when power levels approach the 90- to 100-horsepower range. Also, it's important to realize the Pro-Clutch is a viable alternative to stock replacement when the time comes or excessive power shows up. The only problem is they don't offer this version of the Pro-Clutch for belt-drive Evos.

2 Start stripping the old clutch. If you don't have anything handier lying about to stop the whole thing from rotating as you wrench, you can use an old rag. Stuff it in between the chain and the clutch basket and crank. You'll ruin the rag, but you can't damage much of anything else this way.

3 Next up, you may as well remove the clutch hub nut. The position of the infamous rag is a clue as to the direction you turn this nut to loosen it. The square-shanked screwdriver wedged in the teeth of the basket is one way to lock the hub while removing it, but it's certainly not the safest, best way if you aren't very careful and intend to reuse the old parts. But if you're going to retire the factory pieces and you protect yourself from low-flying screwdrivers, it eliminates the need for a special tool. Don't slip, and even stock pieces can survive undamaged, without air tools.

4 You'll need a puller to get the hub out, whether homemade from a piece of metal strap with holes drilled in it, the Kent-Moore type of tool you see in the photo, or Jim's #1004. Once the hub's off the taper, remove the chain tensioner. If you have designs on a Hayden M6 automatic tensioner, dig it out now and stash the original. If you're going to reuse the original tensioner, check out the condition of the pad and the shoe. Any necessary renewal of these pieces should be dealt with at this point.

5 Removing the compensator is usually the toughest to deal with without air tools. Put that rag to work holding the hub in place, dig out your longest breaker bar, and lean on it with all you've got. Be forewarned: it takes tremendous effort to break this bad boy loose with hand tools.

6 There are some detailed instructions that come with the Pro Clutch, which you should have read by now. Among these is the bit about soaking the friction plates in primary oil. Optimists, who just knew they'd have no trouble removing everything from the primary, had theirs submerged from the start. Everyone else should do it right now. While the plates are soaking, contemplate how you intend to remove the original clutch hub from the basket.

7 If you have no further need for the old clutch hub, you can pound it out. Remove the snap ring retainer, support the basket on a couple of padded 2x4s, and bang the drum slowly. You'll need a new basket bearing no matter what, so count on replacing both the bearing and the new hub—without pounding. The new stuff you want to live long and prosper, so you'll have to use an arbor press to install them—gently! Press. Do not pound.

8 Once the new hub is successfully put in its place, it's time to reassemble everything. Use a new woodruff key and carefully mount the new assembly to the shaft. Take a minute here to double-check your work and make sure you have the clutch securely on the shaft and a tightly fitted woodruff key. Alternate from steel plate to friction plate in the clutch, winding up with a steel plate under the pressure plate—and don't forget the new push piece.

9 It might be a good idea to do a preliminary adjustment of the pack before you get all the primary stuff back on. Check to see that the plates are separating and that there's no excessive wobble as the assembly rotates. If you've got a clean release and the proper deflection on the spring when the clutch is engaged, proceed to put it all together again. Don't forget the copper washer on the starter jackshaft. You'd be surprised how often that happens.

10 All 1990 and later models use a different version of the Pro Clutch, the one on the right. Since the 1990 and newer stocker is a better setup to begin with, you'll get a mere 100 percent increase in surface with this upgrade. The installation process for these later bikes is virtually identical to the process for the 1984 1/2 to 1989 type

PROJECT 69 • IMPROVING THE FOUR-SPEED SPORTSTER CLUTCH

 Time: 2 to 3 hours

 Tools: Clutch puller (Jim's 1004A), clutch spring tool (#34761-84), compensator socket, clutch nut socket, and torque wrench

 Talent:

 Tab: $$$$$

 Tinware: Primary gasket, seals, O-rings, and Sport-Trans Fluid

 Tip: Do the checks and measuring and replace bearings as required—*before* the clutch basket/alternator fails

 PERFORMANCE GAIN: Your clutch will work better than ever

COMPLEMENTARY MODIFICATION: Barnett clutch plate kit

1 Once you're this far along, stripping the primary, as per the shop manual, you may as well check the splines on the clutch shaft. Potent Sportsters have been known to take these splines right off under abuse. And even the slightest wear of these fine-pitched teeth, on any portion of their length, bodes ill for long-term survival. If you can feel any play here, get it taken care of before riding. If the shaft is damaged so is the hub, which means more expense.

2 The old basket/rotor on the left has lost its magnetic charm in a big way. All six of the magnets have come adrift and rendered this pricey necessity useless. The new one is on the right, in case you wondered what they're supposed to look like, and check carefully to assure that it's not likely to repeat the performance of the junk one. Quality control on these parts is uneven. Check the part you get before you pay for it.

3 If that clutch shaft is shot or the follower in the shifting mechanism is in need of replacement, you may wind up pulling the tranny trap door and gutting the box. If your tranny fluid has been coming out metallic during changes, you may as well plan on having a look.

High-mileage four-speed XLs are occasionally victims of a noticeable charging problem, sometimes accompanied by some rather bizarre rumblings from the primary case. If you don't hear the noise, the first instinct is often to replace the battery or the regulator/rectifier (voltpack). When this sequence fails to solve the problem, there's good news: The only thing left to replace is the alternator. The bad news is the rotor portion of said alternator is the back of the clutch basket and costs an amazing $450. Sure, you might get lucky and find that the $70 stator half of the team is all that's gone south. Good for you. But either way, you're pulling the clutch apart, and while you're in there, there's a few things you should scrutinize rather carefully if you want this problem to stay fixed.

You see, all those years ago, when the bike was a brand-new, factory-fresh unit, it was manufactured with a very close air gap (0.060 inch) between the stator and rotor (the closer the magnetic lines of flux are to the stator's windings, the greater the output of the alternator). This tight gap must be maintained. Since the rotor lives in the back of the clutch basket, and the basket rides on bearings, and bearings wear out, it only makes sense that sooner or later rapidly rotating parts will contact each other. The results can be nearly instantaneous, spectacular, and brutally expensive to repair. That clutch/rotor piece alone costs about four times as much as a "normal" rotor on a Big Twin or five-speed Sportster. You'll need at least that piece and likely a whole lot more if the rotating magnets of that clutch-mounted rotor come in contact with the stationary stator windings.

It doesn't have to be that way, if you're willing to deal with the many tolerance stackups that can influence this gap. If you want to avoid this little disaster or, worse yet, a repeat performance after you thought you had it fixed, double-check the following:

Bearings: Check the condition of the large ball bearing in the access door and the two smaller bearings that support the clutch gear on the mainshaft. Don't forget the bearing that supports the clutch hub in the clutch shell. Even if they seem okay, all of these should be replaced every 40,000 miles, no matter what. And for Pete's sake, *never* reuse a bearing that's been pushed on or off or in or out with a press! That's false economy.

Splines: The power pulses from all that hot-doggin' and those banged shifts and burn outs will hammer the spline fit of the clutch gear to the clutch hub. A certain very strong, much-abused 89-inch XL goes through these things (proper repair involves the replacement of both parts) every two years. Anyway, it pays to examine these splines carefully for the slightest slop because they can leave you walking if they strip out. And they'll strip really soon with enough slop.

Primary chain adjustment: Primary chain tension is critical. Over-adjusting a primary chain into a reasonable replica of a bow-string might get the chain case to quiet down a little, but it will overload all those bearings just talked about, and every time you get on the gas, or back off real sharply, that air gap between the rotor and stator all but disappears as the sharp jerk on the chain brings these parts too close to each other for comfort. You don't want the primary chain so sloppy it bangs on the inside of the case either, but if it comes to a choice (and it does), run the primary chain a little on the loose and juicy side of the adjustment range.

All the information you need about how to check the air gap (and more importantly, how much slack you should have in that primary chain) is in the shop manual.

But one thing's not in the manual, namely that when you set slack in the chain to the specified 3/8- to 5/8-inch of up-and-down play, you should check it in more than one position. Rotate the primary drive and check the chain in at least three different places, looking for any loose or tight spots. If you've got any that vary out of the adjustment range, your chain needs to be replaced.

DRIVETRAIN

PROJECT 70 • IMPROVING THE FIVE-SPEED SPORTSTER CLUTCH

 Time: 1 to 2 hours

 Tools: Clutch spring tool (38515-90 and -91) and 1 1/4-inch wrench

 Talent:

 Tab: $$

 Tinware: Barnett Extra-Plate clutch kit, primary gasket, shift-shaft seal, Sport-Trans Fluid, and clutch cable O-ring

 Tip: Don't be tempted to go to stiffer diaphragm spring

 PERFORMANCE GAIN: Holds up to all the power you can dish out on the street

COMPLEMENTARY MODIFICATION: Add an M6 chain tensioner

1 Eight steel and nine friction plates provide something like 15 percent more hookup with the Barnett clutc The swap involves popping off the primary cover, gutting the old clutch basket, laying these plates in (in the order listed in the instructions), buttoning everything back up, and giving it a good sharp adjustment.

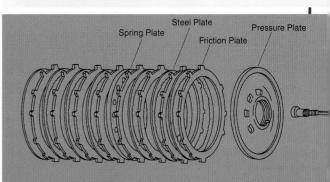

Spring Plate — Steel Plate — Friction Plate — Pressure Plate

This spring plate living in the middle of the stock clutch pack is there to keep the noise down and smooth the clutch release maneuvers. It is nice, but not necessary—especially if you're putting major pony power through it. Better to have bit more friction surface, as offered by the extra-plate Barnett setup.

Stock clutch in the five-speed XL is a very sweet, sturdy unit, one of the best ever used on a Harley. In 100-plus-horsepower Buells or 89-inch Sportsters, the stock clutch is marginal.

Well, you can increase that safety margin by at least 12 percent simply by using Barnett's Extra-Plate high-performance clutch kit (in fact, this is a good alternative to a stock clutch replacement).

What you give up, is a fairly useless oddball located right in the middle of the clutch pack. Called a "spring plate" by the factory, its main function in life is to prevent clutch rattle. Once you've installed this Extra-Plate kit, you will find it not only works superbly, but it's not noticeably noisier.

Here's how to put this kit in your Sportster:

•The first step is to soak the Barnett friction plates in a good quality primary fluid for about 1 hour before installation.

•Disconnect the negative battery terminal.

•Next, open your shop manual to the clutch section and read the part about the spring compressor tool (Jim's #38515-90 and -91 or the equivalent).

•Back all the adjustment out of your clutch cable.

•Remove the clutch inspection cover (1994 and newer models) or remove the clutch inspection plug in the primary cover if you don't have the derby, being very careful not to loose the little coil spring that sits on the adjuster lock plate.

•Turn the clutch adjusting screw clockwise to

release the ramp and coupling mechanism, and then remove the primary drain plug and drain the fluid.

•Remove the shifter using a flat blade screwdriver and a rubber mallet to spread the arm, and then slide it off the shaft. Finally, remove the primary.

•Now you're back at the snap ring that holds the adjusting screw assembly in place. Compress the clutch pack (with the tool) and remove the snap ring and spring seat from the groove in the clutch hub. Remove the clutch-plate stack. Keep track of the order—steel, fiber, steel, fiber—and which was first in line.

•Once it's out, take the time to inspect your drive (steel) plates if you plan to reuse them. They need to be flat. Warped steels will thwart your best efforts at a good clutch. If they are blued or horrendously gouged or grooved, get new ones. If they are otherwise okay, glass bead blast them or rough 'em up with fine emery paper.

Reassembling your clutch pack is the reverse of disassembly. Start by installing a friction plate and then a drive plate and continue until you get to the spring plate (between the fourth and fifth friction plates). The spring plate is two steel plates riveted together with a wave washer between them. Lose it! You've just done your clutch a favor, especially if the rivets are loose. Add the extra Barnett friction plate, thus increasing your pleasure and peace of mind by over 10 percent. Finish installing plates, apply a new primary gasket, do a little wrenching, and first thing you know, it's time to adjust your new clutch.

First adjust at the primary via the adjusting screw assembly and then at the cable to set freeplay. Set primary chain tension to 3/8 inch to 1/2 inch, (unless you add or have an M6 tensioner) and check it in several different spots by rotating things a bit, even if you have to stick it in gear and bump the wheel a bit.

PROJECT 71 • FITTING A PRIMARY CHAIN TENSIONER

Time: 1 to 2 hours

Tools: Allen wrenches; Torx wrenches; standard wrenches; 1/2-, 9/16-, 5/8-inch sockets and ratchet; a few long zip-ties; possibly a small grinder or file; and some channel-locks or Vise Grips

Talent:

Tab: $$

Tinware: Primary gasket, primary fluid, and sealing washers

Tip: Install the special sealing washers (#63859-95) on 1995 and later Softails and Dynas to prevent leaks on the cast-in posts that extend from the inspection cover area on both halves of the primary and meet in the middle

PERFORMANCE GAIN: Much crisper shifting, easier neutral-finding, and, of course, no need to adjust anything in the primary to get it

COMPLEMENTARY MODIFICATION: Balance masters (fluid-filled dynamic vibration reducers) on the clutch and compensator

It only takes a few minutes to adjust the tension on a Harley's primary chain, so what's the big deal over a device that does it automatically?

Well, the M-6 tensioner doesn't just adjust the tension automatically, it also adjusts it correctly. The stock tensioner deals with the chain as if the only time it needed tension was when underway. Sure enough, when you're rolling down the road, the stock tensioner keeps the primary chain's bottom run under control. No slack or slop allowed. But what happens when you back off the throttle? The slop and slack move instantly to the top run of the chain as the bottom run is loaded by compression braking. The factory tensioner, with its static adjustment for tension, simply can't deal with this sudden reversal of tension. The M-6, on the other hand, is spring-loaded and keeps things under control regardless of the situation.

The M-6 also offers a fringe benefit or two. Once installed, the funky clunk your tranny used to make when you shifted from neutral to first becomes a slick click. And since there are no slips and jerks left in the

1 The stock tensioner parts are on the left and the automatic M6 tensioner parts are on the right. The installation process for both Sportsters and Big Twins is the same, but the parts are slightly different.

2 First, drain the fluids and strip the outer primary off, according to the shop manual. Bend the lock tabs back, remove the bolts, and remove the stock tensioner.

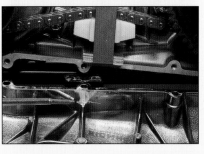

3 Some filing and trimming of the shims may be required to get the primary on properly. Once you've checked it, install the primary cover with a new gasket, add fluid to the factory recommendation, and check for leaks. The pay-off? Well, believe it or not, mostly in the crisper shifting. The lack of need for periodic adjustments is just frosting on the cake.

4 Test-fit the back half of the M-6 onto the stock stud. If necessary, trim the bottom of the M-6 so it lays flat against the serrated plate of the stock tensioner. The M-6 bottom should fit flush into the cast-in rib contour of the inner primary case. Next, grind a notch in the upper, forward left corner of the primary shims so they fit flush to the M-6 bottom. Make the notch only deep enough to ensure this. Put the smaller spring provided inside the larger one, and stick both into the bottom of the tensioner pad. Fit the pad, springs, and shims into the primary, and adjust shims for 5/8 inch of clearance in the center of the pad. Install the outer plate on the M-6 with the beveled edge (shown) facing inward. Torque the outer plate down, and check for smooth action of the pad.

primary, vibration is reduced. Since the cumulative effects of using an M-6 are all good news, we'd thought you'd like a little help with the bad news. That is, to get all these benefits, you have to install the M-6. On pre-1995 models, this is pretty straightforward. However, 1995 and later Big Twins have a bunch of ribbing and webbing cast into both the inner and outer primary cases. This makes installation a little less than a "bolt-in" proposition but still not exactly difficult, as long as you pay attention to detail.

DRIVETRAIN

PROJECT 72 • INSTALLING FLUID BALANCE MASTERS

 Time: 1 to 2 hours

 Tools: Allen wrenches, Torx bits, screwdrivers, file or small grinder, compensator wrench, 1 1/4-inch socket

 Talent:

 Tab: $

 Tinware: Primary gasket

 Tip: Double-check clearance between the balancers and the primary cover. It may take a little filing here and there on the cover (not the Balancer, thank you) to ensure there's no contact

! PERFORMANCE GAIN: A smoother ride

COMPLEMENTARY MODIFICATION: M6 Primary Chain Tensioner

There are those who believe H-D's rigid-mounted models are the last of the real motorcycles. The low speed, low frequency throbbing of a big V-twin doing its duty counts for a lot in the Harley experience. Still, a day-long ride at any out-of-town freeway speed can beat you up on a rigid mount. If you want to do something about high speed vibration, dynamic balancers can help a bunch.

Some dynamic balancers are of all metal construction, designed to hang on the end of the crankshaft assembly. They work, but they can also border on overkill, and they tend to have a pretty fair mass of their own. Sun Tech's Balance Master, on the other hand, takes a different approach. They use mercury contained in the outer rim of a simple, lightweight alloy bladder. Once attached to a spinning mass, like the flywheels themselves (if you happen to have them out of the engine), the compensator (if you don't), and the clutch (the other unbalanced mass), centrifugal force causes the mercury to move to the opposite side of any imbal-

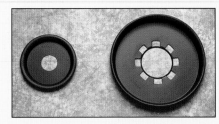

1 The little Balance Master is for the compensator and the big one's for the clutch. These liquid-filled rings (the liquid is most likely mercury), essentially fitted to the end of the crankshaft, won't make a Softail or Sportster as smooth as a Gold Wing but, man, do they knock the tops off the worst buzzes and shakes. Since the other heavy, unbalanced rotating mass you contend with is the clutch, adding the second Balance Master to the clutch helps even more. The same company also offers one that fits right to the flywheel, but adding that one requires a complete engine teardown.

2 Balance Masters added to the compensator and the clutch do a commendable job of taming vibration at far less expense than some other vibration tamers on the market, and there's no mechanical parts to wear out or stick either. They rely instead on the heavy fluid to automatically go the unbalanced area of the spinning mass it's bolted onto. It also varies the flywheel balance factor at different engine speeds, something even conventional crankshaft balancing cannot do. The clutch is never in balance in the first place. Each time you pull the lever, the plates come apart and go back together in a different position. So a Balance Master there helps solve a problem you didn't know you had. Pretty smooth operators, these Balance Masters.

ance. It works so well, because being a heavy cohesive fluid, it's free to move very quickly around the rim of its bladder to the exact spot it's needed most. It can easily keep up with rapid changes in rpm and different frequencies of vibration. Bingo! Reduced shakes.

Available for every H-D model, installation of all but the Balance Master for the flywheel takes about an hour and requires removing the outer primary, the compensator nut, and the clutch pressure plate. Detailed instructions are included, but don't sweat it—it's an easy thing to do, and it restores your "unshakable" confidence in the classic rigid-mount Harley.

PROJECT 73 • UPDATING FIVE-SPEED BIG TWIN BELTS AND PULLEYS

 Time: 3 to 8 hours

 Tools: Countershaft sprocket nut, 1 7/8-inch socket (#95660-37A), clutch puller (Jim's #1004A), 1990 and later clutch spring compressor (#38515-90), the rest of your hand tools, and the shop manual

 Talent: ††††

 Tab: $$$

  Tinware: Updated or upgraded pulley kit, primary gaskets, seals, lock tabs, possibly a new main drive gear, and all the tranny gaskets and seals, O-rings, and so on

 Tip: Always update to the latest design pulley (#40210-85D) or use a lightweight Belt Drives Unlimited pulley

PERFORMANCE GAIN: Your pulley won't fail, and you can change the number of teeth on the front pulley to alter overall gearing (see Project 76: Altering Final Gearing)

COMPLEMENTARY MODIFICATION: Pro-Clutch, an M6 Automatic Primary Chain Tensioner, Fluid Balancers, and a light-weight pulley

1 Although it may not be abundantly clear from this shot, the pulley in the upper left corner has less spline area than its updated compatriot, at upper right. That, combined with a more secure lock-plate-type fastening and a heavy duty spacer (included in the updated pulley kit [#40210-85D]) largely solves the leaky, loose pulley syndrome that's plagued too many Big Twin riders. However, the lightweight Belt Drives Unlimited pulley, in the bottom of the photo, cuts the 4-pound mass of the stocker down to a little over 1 pound, roughly the same "tonnage" as a chain sprocket. That means very little inertia and far less hammering on the drive gear's fine splines. You want to forget about the pulley and drive gear and just ride? Here's the ultimate step in that direction.

The belt-drive system on nearly all late-model, five-speed Big Twins is a clever one, offering quiet, clean, and nearly maintenance-free transmission of power from transmission to tire. In fact, the Harley belt drive has been so trouble-free over the years that its biggest problem is often sheer neglect.

As good as it is, it isn't perfect. The belt and the front rear pulleys all need a bit of attention to survive, and all three need to be up to speed to maintain the legendary reliability of this system.

BELTS

If your Big Twin suffers leakage in the primary drive area, the first thing to check is belt tension. What is proper tension? Well, using the factory tool (#H-D 35381), you do it by ensuring that there's 10 pounds of force and 5/16 to 3/8 inch of deflection in the belt.

If you don't have the factory tool or just can't figure out how to use a fish scale as a substitute, try this instead. Grasp the belt with your thumb and two fore-fingers about 1 1/2 inches back from where it exits the bottom of the primary case. Now twist the belt back and forth on its axis; you should feel serious resistance to this twisting at about a 45-degree angle from flat. If you can twist your belt close to 90 degrees with just a thumb and two fingers, it's too loose. If it feels tighter than a bow string at only 25 to 30 degrees of twist, it's too tight. This may not be the rocket science method, but it's a pretty accurate field test just the same. And believe me, the pulley can tell the difference!

A belt that's too tight can cause problems far worse than oil leaks, such as the pulley splines stripping out. Worse yet, belts don't like being bent into a radius of less than 3 inches or having their direction of rotation reversed once they've gotten used to it. If you can keep from cutting them or poking gaping holes in them with road debris, they will last for 70,000 to 90,000 miles.

Belts aren't immortal, however. These modern belts are so good, so durable, so tough, and so proven that they are virtually ignored by the majority of riders. This is a potentially dangerous thing to take for granted. And let's be honest, some of the belts out there are 10 to 12 years old or more. Do you trust oil or tires that old? Checking the belt regularly for damage and wear is a necessary part of getting the best out of them.

2 First, unfortunately, there are the many little steps involved in getting at the darn thing. You pull the outer primary per the shop book.

3 You pull the clutch, compensator, primary chain, stator, chain tensioner, and your hair.

4 Remove the inner primary and the old pulley. Examine the splines on the main drive gear very carefully. If they are worn, pitted, or cracked, you'll have to replace it.

5 If the main drive gear splines are in good shape, put the new pulley, complete with updated spacer, in place and lock it down. Now all you have to do is replace everything you took off to get this far. It'll take half a day, but at least, if you've done it right, you won't have to do it again.

In the old days, you could look at the fan belt on an automobile and easily tell at a glance if it was shot. The tell-tale signs were cracking in the rubber, frayed edges, a scrubbed kinda burnt look on the sides where they ran through the pulleys, and hey, they even squeaked! By contrast, modern automotive belts have one, and only one, remotely reliable indicator of wear. When they are new, the top edge of the belt rides proud of the flange on its pulley. When it settles to below flush on the flange, like the sun slowly sinks in the west, it's done for. To some degree it's like that with the Harley drive belt. The trouble is, it's much harder to detect or recognize, because a Harley-Davidson drive belt appears to sit down in the pulley, even when it's new. It's also covered up with belt guards.

Just the same, if you were to look at a cross section of the belt's tooth pattern, relative to it's counterpart in the pulley, you'd see that when new, the belt tooth doesn't bottom out. When broken in, it might do so slightly. When worn out, it will do it excessively. Once this stage is reached, the teeth on the belt begin to get pulled out by their root, where they attach to the cords on the outside edge of the thing.

Sometimes you can spot this early on by looking for a series of hairline cracks or wrinkles running parallel to the run of the belt on the tips of the teeth. Belts with just a few wrinkles can be considered sort of, well, middle-aged. But if the wrinkles extend from the top to the bottom of the teeth clear to the outside edge of the belt, it's all over. Keep riding on that one and you're gonna wind up toothless.

FRONT PULLEYS

The pulley is dependent on the strength of the splines and the clamp load. Both are crucial. Without enough clamping pressure, the splines alone can't take it and wear prematurely. Any noticeable wear on the splines means replacement is advisable and failure is probably not far off.

Loss of clamp load can also cue the tranny seal to leak for much the same reason. Insufficient clamp load pressure on the seal (in other words, the pulley's loose) allows oil to sneak right on through it.

To address these issues, H-D extensively redesigned their pulley in late 1993 and introduced it to the production models in 1994. The new pulley (#40210-85D) is available as a kit, including a pulley with 50 percent more spline area and a much heavier-duty spacer, along with the different oil seal required and all the related fasteners and hardware.

This design is such an improvement that it's worth doing to older, high-mileage models when the belt is replaced. In fact, immediately is none too soon for any belt-drive Big Twin with the older design pulley—especially heavy bikes, like dressers and Heritages, which have been known to chew up the pulley well before the belt wears out, some in as few as 25,000 to 30,000 miles.

The trick to perfect installation is a light smear of oil on the back (motor) side of the new retaining nut and Loctite 262 (red) to the threads. Then crank the nut on (to your left) to 50 foot-pounds of initial torque. Then, tighten an additional 30 to 40 degrees. Do not, no matter how much you'd like to, exceed 45 degrees. You can figure on 11.25 degrees of rotation per tooth on the new 32-tooth pulley, so mark the nut's initial position against the closest tooth, then "three teeth tighter" for your final position.

MAIN DRIVE GEARS

By the way, examine the main drive gear very carefully while you are in there. The condition of the splines on the main drive gear are at least as important as that of the pulley, so double-check them. Any free-play or wiggle on the fitment here is unacceptable. The pulley/drive gear should feel so tight it's like it was welded.

As long as you're scrutinizing, make sure that the oil seal that lives in the "nose" end of the main drive gear isn't trying to escape. The edge of the seal you can see in there should be recessed 0.060 inch from the outside edge of the gear.

If you're going to reuse the original main drive gear, go buy a new oil seal (#12035A), pry the old one out, check the needle bearings in the bore of the drive gear, and, if they are okay, install the new seal to a depth of 0.060 inch with Loctite 601 (green). Also, you can use the old oil seal as an installation tool for the new one, if you don't have a better way to do it.

What if you can't reuse the original gear? Well that makes things a little more complicated, in more ways than one.

Early-Style, 1979–1984

This is the chain-drive version of the main drive gear, which is basically bulletproof due to its coarse splines (and the fact that it's pulling a chain sprocket, which has much less mass and much more "cushion" than a belt, in the secondary drive). Having said that,

it is still subject to wear and tear. If it needs replacement, you still need to adhere to the techniques described.

Mid-Style, 1985–1989

The Harley main drive gear on 1984 1/2 to 1986 1/2 trannies is really two pieces welded into one piece at the factory and is supposed to stay that way. They may not stay in one piece very long if enough horsepower is applied in a "brutal and abrupt" fashion. You wouldn't want it to happen to you would you?

The first version of the five-speed (belt-drive) trans had the welded main drive gear. See Project 67: Updating the 1984–1986 Big Twin Main Drive Gear for the hot setup on replacing this with a stronger unit.

Interim Style, 1991–1994

If you own a 1991 to 1994 model that needs a new main drive gear, you should know that the original version (H-D #35029-91A) is no longer available from the factory. This is due to Harley's move to high contact ratio gears throughout the gearbox on 1995 and later production. Only the new-style gears are available from H-D, including the main drive gear (#35029-94). You must change both the main drive gear and its mating gear (#35626-94) to accomplish a repair with factory parts.

You can also resort to the aftermarket. Jim's, Andrews, and RevTech (CCI) still manufacture the 91A style main drive gear needed for 1991 to 1994 models.

New-Style, 1995 to Present

These are the high contact ratio (HCR) gears that H-D has been using in Europe for several years. There's nothing special about them beyond their ability to mesh quietly. These HCR gears were developed to meet noise standards, and rather than run two types of gears for different parts of the world, the factory decided to use them in everything. They are the only type of gear available from H-D as replacement parts for 1991 to 1994 models—meaning, at least as far as H-D is concerned, that not only the main drive gear, but any gear that needs replacement in the transmission must have its running mate replaced as well.

DRIVETRAIN

PROJECT 74 • INSTALLING A BELT PRIMARY DRIVE

Time: 2 hours

Tools: Countershaft sprocket nut, 1 7/8-inch socket (#95660-37A), clutch puller (Jim's #1004A), 1990 and later clutch spring compressor (#38515-90), 1 1/4-inch wrench/socket, and the hand tools (Allens and such) needed to remove the primary

Talent: 👤👤

Tab: $$$$$

Tinware: Belt kit

Tip: Be prepared for sharper, harsher reactions to throttle movements since there's no "cush" built into a belt drive

PERFORMANCE GAIN: Dry clutch, low/no maintenance primary drive, increased strength

COMPLEMENTARY MODIFICATION: Venting the primary with either a couple of 1/4- to 3/8-inch spacers between the case and the inspection cover or carving custom vents into the outer primary cover

1 Once you strip the primary to this stage, you're ready to install an enclosed-type primary belt. If you've read the installation instructions, you know you've got to seal off the shaft bearing first.

3 Loop the belt around the clutch basket, then slip on the motor shaft pulley, retainer flange, washer, and nut, then tighten. Air tools are a wonderful invention for situations like this.

In the 1990s, even though chain-driven primary drives are the original equipment choice of The Motor Company, belt primary drives have resurfaced as a popular choice for power-related and custom reasons alike. And low and behold, the two survivors of the aftermarket belt-drive battles of the last 25 years, Primo and Belt Drives Unlimited, have got it right. Or, rather, got *them* right? You see, there are two flavors of belt primary: exposed and enclosed.

An exposed primary belt with anywhere from 3 to 4 inches of belt width and two rapidly rotating pulleys can be a bit intimidating right next to your left foot, but it's too wide to fit under a cover. Not a good plan for the average guy who rides a lot of miles. Nevertheless, they are good for mega-horsepower machines.

The enclosed belt primary isn't as strong as the exposed type, but it is far more civilized and practical for the average rider. Since almost all Evos use a wet clutch, the other aspect of proper belt drives in the 1990s is a proper replacement clutch designed to run dry. In short, a modern kit must consist of a high-performance dry clutch, a properly engineered front pulley, and a hell-for-stout belt that is narrow enough to fit inside the primary cover. It must also be easily installable without any major (read irreversible) modifications to the stock primary. That's not as easy as it sounds—especially since the factory added all that ribbing to the primary cases on Softails and Dynas in 1994 and 1995.

It remains to be seen if belt primary designs will ever achieve the acceptance and popularity of the belt rear drive, but since most of the advantages are in common and most of the bugs are worked out, maybe a double belt drive is in your future. If so, here's how to proceed:

2 Next, install this little goodie. The Primo belt kit comes with a Pro Clutch, but it runs dry in this situation, so there is no need to soak the plates in oil. Slide the new clutch basket and hub on the shaft, and after applying the thread sealant, torque it down.

4 Once the belt is on, install the rest of the clutch, alternating steel and friction plates, just like the instructions tell you. When you think you're done and before you replace the primary cover, STOP and double-check your work. Assembly sequence, belt alignment, and torque values are critical, so you don't want to find out you forgot something during the test ride. Even the brass washer for the starter jackshaft can be forgotten, so make sure your new belt drive is set to go first, then cover it up.

First, take a moment and read through your kit's installation instructions and look through a shop manual to familiarize yourself with any potential snags and to make sure the belt drive of choice is compatible with the primary you have.

Now disconnect the negative side of the battery.

Remove the primary chain case cover bolts, and then tap the cover with a rubber hammer or plastic mallet to break the seal. Pull the cover off to expose the primary drive.

Disconnect the starter solenoid and slide it out about an inch or so to remove the starter pinion gear. Remove the attaching hardware and pop out the primary chain adjuster.

Using snap-ring pliers, remove the c-clip and the release plate on the clutch.

Stick the tranny in first gear to prevent the crank from turning, if the bike is on the ground. If it isn't, you will need to lock the wheel using the rear brake. Tie or wedge the pedal down tight, because if it slips while you're cranking hard on the primary, you'll do the "keeping my balance" dance, whilst bleeding profusely from knuckles and things.

Use an impact wrench or a 3-foot breaker bar and the special deep socket tool to remove the clutch retaining nut by turning it clockwise (it has left-hand threads).

Use an impact wrench or a 3-foot breaker bar and a 1 3/16-inch socket to remove the compensator nut.

Remove all inner primary attaching hardware and the inner primary cover. Use a hydraulic or bearing press to remove the old primary housing bearing. If you don't have a bearing press, take a minute and locate a shop that does. You've got to get this handled before you can proceed.

The new sealed bearing supplied in the kit will install a lot easier if you stick it in the freezer an hour or so, and heat the inner primary with a hair dryer around the bearing boss.

While you're fooling with the inner primary, check that it is flat and true on a plate of glass. (Units that have been chrome plated, powder coated, or polished are often warped.) If yours is warped, repair or replace it. Flat, dead flat, is critical for belt-drive alignment.

Before the inner primary is reinstalled, you'd better make sure engine/transmission alignment is correct for exactly the same reason.

Trim the forward-most thread casting to allow for some clearance between the front sprocket and the belt.

Install the inner primary cover.

Install the new clutch, primary belt, and front sprocket as a unit and tighten down the clutch nut with an impact wrench. Make positive that there is at least 1/16-inch clearance between the belt and the trimmed thread castings. If all is well, rotate the motor by hand. The belt should track slightly away from the motor but not off the front pulley.

Place the retaining cup on the front pulley, install the nut, and tighten it with an impact wrench. Really tight!

Double-check everything before you install the outer primary and new gasket.

Adjust the new clutch so the cable has at least 1/4 inch of play at the lever.

Last but not least, listen to be sure that the bendix gear engages before the starter spins.

 Attach the outside flange to the front pulley, and torque it down, preferably with an air gun.

 Slip the plates in, alternating steel and friction types.

7 Put the pressure plate in place. The diaphragm spring and retainer go on last.

 You must adjust to 0.010 inch of deflection at the diaphragm spring, as measured with a straight edge. Button up the primary, but don't forget to use a couple of spacers to "stand off" the inspection cover for extra cooling, and don't be surprised if things seem a bit abrupt when you first ride the scoot. You've no longer got a compensator or tensioner taking up slack in there, and every movement of the throttle results in an immediate action. Yahoo!

TRANSMISSION

Evos have used four gearbox designs since 1984. Some Big Twins were equipped with a four speed until 1987 and a five speed from then on. Sportsters kept their four speed for over 40 years, until "hell froze over" in 1991 and the new five speed debuted. Not to unduly irritate you, but count on this, basic design and minor engineering updates aside, both four-speed boxes are more hassle than either of their five-speed step-children. The ratios are less than great in most XL four-speeds (although you can help that), and the whole shee-bang has to survive the years of busted trap doors and flattened mainshaft rollers when you abuse 'em. Not sniping, just letting you know what you might be in for.

As for the Big Twin four-cogger—a better water trap has yet to be devised. And that, unfortunately and frequently, leads to rusted gears, bearings, and an expensive rebuild. The four-speed is a labor-intensive unit to set up correctly as well—all those shims, you see. That said, both XL and Big Twin four-speed boxes have little to apologize for. They were state of the art for decades, have a shift quality that shouts HARLEY, and properly set up and cared for, are virtually bullet proof.

The five-speed boxes are the result of late twentieth century CAD/CAM manufacturing methods—and, of course, marketing demands. (Do really think Harleys *need* five speeds?) The benefit of all this technology are two of the simplest designs you can imagine, almost no shimming, decent shifting, and the ability to be overhauled by normal humans. Still top gear is top gear, and there's no real difference between four and five in that department. Good? All of them! Perfect? None of them! As you'll see in this section, it's mainly making the most of what you've got.

TRANSMISSION

PROJECT 75 • FIXING HARD-SHIFTING SPORTSTER FOUR SPEEDS

Time: 2 to 4 hours

Tools: All your hand tools and a torque wrench, Jim's #1004 puller for clutch and tranny sprocket, and #34761-84 (Kent-Moore or Jim's) clutch-spring tool

Talent: ★★★

Tab: $ to $$$

Tinware: A new shift-cam follower, a primary gasket, and Sport-Trans Fluid

Tip: If your bike is getting more difficult to shift, don't wait until you literally can't shift; once the cam follower is broken, the odds of some piece of shrapnel damaging gears in the tranny roughly quadruples

PERFORMANCE GAIN: Improved shift quality and gearbox longevity

COMPLEMENTARY MODIFICATION: Barnett clutch, M6 tensioner, and a hard look at the clutch basket and alternator

Four-speed Evo Sportsters, especially those that have been ridden hard, typically start to shift poorly after 10,000 to 20,000 miles. Perhaps it's hard to find a gear, and lever effort gets higher every ride. Maybe neutral has just gone into hiding, not to be found without shutting the engine off, or at least notching it in while still rolling. If any of these conditions apply to your 1986 to 1990 Sporty, the odds are about 90 percent that there's a simple $6 part causing the grief.

Every time you shift up or down through the gears, you rely on a shift cam follower in the gear box that works exactly like a kid's teeter-totter. About 5 inches long, this cast alloy part has a pointed fulcrum that can go flat under abuse. Eventually, instead of rocking neatly back and forth as designed, it starts to slide around. Once that happens, aside from the difficulty in selecting neutral, the bike gets very hard to shift, or in extreme cases quits shifting into all four gears period.

When the pivot on the fulcrum goes flat on a four-speed Sportster, it's just pointless to continue beating

1 You'll notice that this follower for the shifter is broken. The reason is simple: The part should have been replaced earlier in its career, when it lost its edge. That is, the fulcrum point in the middle, was no longer pointed, so the follower doesn't rock back and forth as planned; it slides side to side. You pound the shift lever lookin' for a gear and pow—broken follower.

2 The fix is a new follower, springs, and rollers. The new follower will live longer too, because it's a harder material. As long as the old follower broke clean, the swap to the new stuff is all there is to it. If your follower ground to powder or if there's several chunks of it floating among the teeth in your gearbox, you've got about twice the work you bargained for. You see, even though the metal the follower's made of is softer than gear teeth, it can cause lots of damage if you don't get all the pieces out of there. Also, the silver powder you saw mixed with the tranny oil left deposits in the rollers of the tranny needle bearings. And it makes great grinding paste. Bottom line: Disassemble, examine, and replace, each and every part in that gearbox you even think is suspicious.

on the box. Tear it down right away. If you wait until it won't shift at all, the shift cam follower may have snapped and the resultant shrapnel could have trashed all kinds of expensive bits.

Help is, however, on the way. Here's how you tear it down and get it fixed:

Grab the shop manual, and just like it says in the book, strip off the exhaust, right footrest, brake pedal, and master cylinder until you can remove the sprocket cover.

Drain the chain case.

Bend the sprocket lock tab and pop the sprocket off. Unhook the battery.

Yank the primary cover, clutch (as an assembly), and compensator along with the primary chain.

Remove the stator screws; set every bit of that aside, and unbolt the transmission trap door.

Carefully remove the gearbox assembly. If you waited until your Sporty wouldn't shift at all to do this teardown, don't be terribly surprised to find a funky-chunky looking piece or two lying in the bottom of the cavity. That would be what broke off of the cam follower. Look closely though, because why it broke may not be all that obvious at first. It's the pivoting edge of the fulcrum that's the root of the evil here. Imagine, once the fulcrum wears out, how the follower sliding and banging around in its two little holes in the trap door could knock the ends off and crush the springs. The new one, on the other hand, has a nice sharp edge and is made of the proverbial new and improved material. It won't be near as quick to waste away.

Carefully inspect the gear cluster and shift forks for wounds from the shrapnel. Use your own judgment. If the old cam follower broke cleanly into two pieces and those pieces are accounted for, there's lit-tle likelihood of further damage to the tranny. By the same token, if the oil you drained out of the box was a gritty silver color or some "bitty" chunks of the broken follower are AWOL, you can suspected that some pieces are imbedded in the bearings; that's a clue to strip the whole box and clean it thoroughly. Check the shift forks just as thoroughly. Any galling or grooving means replacement parts are needed.

Once satisfied with all the rest, install the new cam follower.

Reassemble the transmission and slide it back into the case.

Inspect the clutch basket cum alternator rotor while reassembling the clutch and primary. The bearing in the basket can wear to the point it allows contact between the rotor magnets and the stator, and secondly, that contact doesn't do the magnets a bit of good (see Project 69: Improving the Four-Speed Sportster Clutch). You want to make sure the stator has not been damaged by the rotor and that the lead from the stator to the regulator isn't cracked, melted, or frayed. The insulation must be in perfect condition to avoid any intermittent charging problems down the road. When you reinstall the primary drive stuff, use new stator screws (#2720).

Reassemble the rest of the motorcycle. Reassembly really is the reverse of disassembly in this case. Do it by the book, and don't forget to double-check the primary chain adjustment.

TRANSMISSION
PROJECT 76 • ALTERING FINAL GEARING

 Time: 3-5 hours

 Tools: Countershaft sprocket nut, 1 7/8-inch socket (#95660-37A), clutch puller (Jim's #1004A), 1990 and later clutch spring compressor (#38515-90), 1/2- and 9/16-inch sockets/wrenches, the rest of your hand tools, and the shop manual

 Talent:

 Tab: $$$$

 Tinware: Pulleys, belts, guards, a primary gasket, seals, new lock tabs, and miscellaneous bits

 Tip: Moderate gearing changes won't require a belt change, but major ones will

PERFORMANCE GAIN: Improved acceleration, top speed, or cruising comfort, depending on the gearing ratio

COMPLEMENTARY MODIFICATION: Swapping tires, which also changes final gearing ratios

The obvious (and biggest) advantage that V-twin Harleys have is their abundant torque. As choked up and asthmatic as new "bone-stock" Big Twins and Sportsters are, they have plenty of torque. The question is how much (or how little) is right for you? You can choose to alter the parameters of your Harley's performance envelope with increased acceleration or more top speed and never touch the engine. How? By altering the gearing.

Let's say you want your Softail to go 15 miles per hour faster, have a little better fuel economy, and cut down vibration at speed a bit. In 1994, H-D did all that by reducing the size of the rear belt pulley, which lowered the overall gearing ratio, which in turn made the bike run at a lower rpm for the same speed. There's no reason you can't do the same.

Belt-Drive Big Twin Final Gearing Ratios

Model	Ratio	Comments
1985–1992 Big Twins	3.37	Quick, limited top speed
1993 Softails	2.94	Smooth, less acceleration
1993 Big Twins	3.37	Quick, limited top speed
1994–1998 Big Twins	3.15	Great overall ratio

1 Swapping the stock 27-tooth front pulley for a 29-tooth pulley is the simplest gearing option for a Sportster. While it's not a radical change, it's often enough, and unlike with rear wheel gearing changes, you don't need to swap drive belts to make it work. Almost any Sportster making 60-plus rear-wheel ponies can "pull" the 29 for longer-legged cruising, if you carry realistic payloads. Drag racer types, around-towners, heavy loaders, and bone-stock 883s are just about stuck with the 27. Not stuck, really, because one advantage Sportsters have over Big Twin's is in primary design. To change front pulleys on a Sportster is dead simple and takes about an hour. You could keep the 27 for commuting and run the 29 for that cross-country run this summer.

2 For Big Twins, the easiest gearing swap for the average rider is accomplished via the rear pulley. You have a lot of options—these fancy ones you see run from 61 to 70 teeth, with about everything in between. Front pulleys are available from 29 through 34 teeth, but the change is a guaranteed 3- to 4-hour trip into the primary side of the bike. Surprisingly, you can occasionally avoid that with the right rear pulley. If you have a Softail Custom with a stock 70-toother, for instance, you can drop to a 66-tooth rear without a belt change. You get to move the rear wheel so far back it fouls the stock license plate hanger, but it can be done. The flip side of that coin is that popping in a 29- or 34-tooth front pulley doesn't require a belt change either, so it's relatively cheap to do, providing you're willing to play in the primary half a day. The point is gearing questions on Big Twins are definitely of the multiple-choice variety.

The stock gearing on all five-speed, belt-drive, U.S.-spec Big Twins prior to 1993 was 3.37 overall. On 1993 Softails (all versions) a 2.94 ratio gearing was used. The Motor Company did it again in 1994 with a change in the primary ratio (the first since 1965) and then slapped on a 65-tooth rear pulley, resulting in a slightly more user friendly 3.15 ratio overall, using about 400 rpm less at 60 miles per hour. I'm sure Harley had their own reasons for making the ratio change on Softails only (and for not changing sooner), but the point is they have shown the way and provided the optional parts.

A stock 3.37-geared Big Twin will do about 112 to 115 miles per hour, no matter what the speedo says. The rev limiter and some simple math determine this. The 2.94 ratio gets you a much more comfortable cruising rpm but less-than-eye-popping acceleration. For stock bikes, 3.15 provides a good compromise of decent acceleration and cruising comfort.

Traditionally, the only real disadvantage of belt drive has been centered around the difficulty and expense of altering overall gearing. Considering the benefits, the lack of hassle once it's done, and the longevity of the hardware, there's more gain than pain in the long run—as long as you get it the way you want it, the first time.

If you want to make your five-speed belt-drive Big Twin accelerate harder, at the expense of higher rpm at freeway cruising speed, the following options are available:

Belt-Drive Gearing Ratios

Front Pulley	Rear Pulley			
	70 teeth	68 teeth	66 teeth	61 teeth
29 teeth	3.72	3.62	3.51	3.24
32 teeth	3.37	3.26	3.18	2.94
33 teeth	3.27	3.18	3.08	2.85
34 teeth	3.17	3.08	2.99	2.77

This shows your options with altering belt-drive Big Twin gearing. I'd recommend that you use either the 3.15 ratio or, provided you have the engine power to pull it, the tall 2.94 gives your cruiser a smoother ride and more top speed. If you're into drag racing instead of touring, something more like 3.72 overall would be the ticket, especially if you're sick of getting toasted by Sportsters in stoplight to stoplight games.

Bear in mind that motors that make more power can handle higher gear ratios. My friend John's FXR has a 1200 XL ignition module, Sifton 141 cam, 0.060 milled heads, a 40-millimeter Mikuni carb, and "gutted" stock mufflers. It pulls well enough to run a 2.80 overall ratio. Net results? The ample horsepower makes the big gaps between gears unnoticeable; he can cruise at 90 miles per hour turning only 3,500 rpm, and his gas mileage is pretty darn good to boot! Try that with a stock motor, and the bike would feel sluggish and awkward.

You probably already figured that there's nothing in life that's simple. Well, you're right—not that it's tough to change gearing; it's a 3 to 4 hour job requiring disassembly of the primary (see Project 67: Updating the 1984–1986 Big Twin Main Drive Gear) and a rear wheel pulley swap. But watch it. You'll need not just the pulleys but a different length belt and, often, different belt guards and fasteners for some. Many a time an innocent soul has slapped a 61-tooth pulley on a Softail in place of the stock 70-tooth unit only to find the bolt holding the upper belt guard gouging the crap out of that new pulley. So check everything for clearance, and if you're using factory stuff, when the instructions say you need a new guard or bolt, believe it.

TRANSMISSION
PROJECT 77 • FIXING SLOPPY SPORTSTER FIVE-SPEED SHIFTING

Time: 3 to 6 hours

Tools: Shop manual; #38515-90 and 38515-91 clutch compressor; Jim's #1004A (handy gadget); 1 1/4- and 1 1/5-inch wrenches and sockets; torque wrench; and possible access to a lathe, grinder, or machine shop

Talent: 👤👤👤

Tab: 0 to $

Tinware: Primary and tranny gaskets and seals, new clutch snap rings, and C-clips

Tip: Add a sharp clutch adjustment and cable lubing to your to-do list

PERFORMANCE GAIN: Fewer false neutrals and much improved shifting

COMPLEMENTARY MODIFICATION: Rear-sets or forward controls

The #6003 shims in a five-speed Sporty box are all .070-inch thick. A couple of them shouldn't be. If your bike shifts like a truck, measuring gear position clearances, then shaving the two shims straddling countershaft second gear can improve shifting.

One of the nicest things about newer Sportsters is their five-speed gearbox. One of the worst is the way the transmission can behave. The quality of its gear change can range from the fabled light switch to a box of rocks, and it seems no two are alike. The reason has to do with the harsh realities of modern production and manufacturing. The five-speed Sportster introduced in 1991 was designed to have its internal gear bits assembled without the need to custom-fit each gear to its shaft or stack of gears with assorted (and time-consuming) shimming, as was necessary on the good old four-speed box of years gone by. A minute saved is a minute earned on a modern assembly line. When Harley eliminated the need to shim and hand fit each part of the new Sportster transmission, production went up, but consistent shift quality went all over the map.

If yours does a passable imitation of a cement mixer every time you nail a quick shift or feels like it has an extra inch of slop between one gear and the next, a teardown might indicate a loose clearance between the shifter dogs—usually between second and third on the countershaft. When the shift drum is in the second gear position, the distance between the shifter dogs can be as much as 0.100 inch, whereas the distance between other

shifter dogs is closer to 0.050 inch. It might just work a smidge better to move the second gear on the countershaft closer to its third gear mate. To get there requires a tranny teardown, just exactly the way the shop manual tells you to. Once it's apart, things are anything but by the book. You see, what you need to fix the problem is a thinner thrust washer than the one supplied between the left side snap-ring on the countershaft (the stock thrust washer is 0.070 inch), and another needs to be put in on the gear's right side (of a thickness equal to the standard thrust washer minus the amount of the new thinner thrust washer that replaced it). There is no thrust washer at this position in the stock setup. In a nutshell, you'll need a spacer 0.030 inch thick where the stock 0.070-incher goes (right side of countershaft second gear) and one about 0.040 inch thick where there isn't one at all (left side of countershaft second gear).

But no such spacer-washers exist in the parts book. You want 'em; you make 'em. There are a couple of ways to go about it.

The hard way takes two operations and requires a lathe to modify the thrust washers, and you've got to make a mandrel. Then you need a couple of four-speed Sportster transmission washers of the appropriate thickness: one 0.030 inch and one 0.040 inch (#35343-73 and #35344-73). To make the four-speed washers work, you need to enlarge the center hole from 1 inch to 1.185 inches and cut down the outside diameter from 1.50 inches to 1.375 inches. Grind out the inside diameter on a lathe, then mount 'em on the mandrel and cut to the correct outside diameter. The job sounds complicated but only takes a few minutes on a lathe. Oh, you don't have a lathe?

The easy way is to have the standard 0.070-inch Sportster five-speed thrust washers (#6003) ground down to the thickness needed at a local machine shop that has a surface grinder with a magnetic table. Just tell them how thick you'd like the finished thrust washers to be.

Be aware that each measurement of each tranny may be slightly different, and plan to center the gear and tighten up clearances accordingly. In other words, what you take off one side, put on the opposite side. If you need a 0.030-inch thrust washer on the left side, you'll need a 0.040 inch on the right side between the second gear and the fifth gear on its right, and so on.

It's a lot of work, but if you want your Sportster to shift slicker than a hot knife through butter, it's what you need to do (or have done).

PROJECT 78 • FIXING TRANNY MAINSHAFT LEAKS ON YOUR FOUR-SPEED BIG TWIN

 Time: 5 to 6 hours

 Tools: All your standard hand tools, 1 7/8-inch nut socket (H-D or Jim's #94660-37A), clutch-hub puller tool (Jim's #1004A or equivalent), four-speed tranny main-seal tool (H-D or Jim's #95660-42), and the nerve to use them

 Talent:

 Tab: $$$$

 Tinware: Four-speed tranny overhaul gasket set, O-rings, and spacers, as listed in text

 Tip: You'll probably find more problems than anticipated when you get inside; better to do it right than do it over

 PERFORMANCE GAIN: The gearbox stays full of oil

COMPLEMENTARY MODIFICATION: Complementary Modifications: Add a kickstarter, if you always wanted one; remove it if it's just a useless nuisance to you

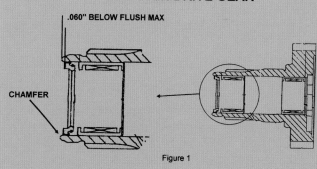

1340 MAIN DRIVE GEAR

.060" BELOW FLUSH MAX

CHAMFER

Figure 1

If you're using a main drive gear without a groove for a thick O-ring (#11166), chances are it's a midyear 1984 or older part. If it doesn't have the groove, you must use the #111144 O-ring (which will not be easy to put on—use petroleum grease and plenty of patience).

If you have a four-speed Big Twin (1984–1986) with a chronic problem of leaks at the gearbox, the oil seal probably is not the problem. The source of the problem is more likely oil that's passing between the main drive gear spacer and the main drive gear. You fix it as follows:

Remove the inner primary. (Just like it says in the shop manual.) Needless to say, this is a golden opportunity to inspect the sprocket and the main drive gear for any damage or wear.

Drain the tranny oil. (What's left of it, anyway.)

Remove the main drive gear spacer and oil seal.

Clean, clean, clean! The area of the main drive gear that mates with the spacer must be antiseptically clean.

Apply a light coat of the blue dye to the mating surface of the spacer.

Put the dye-coated spacer back on the main drive gear and rotate it. Take it off and examine the contact area. You should have even contact for a full 360 degrees. If you don't, it's time for a new spacer.

If you can reuse your original spacer, add an O-ring (#11114) as shown in the illustration. Be careful when you attempt this, or plan on buying a fistful of them. When you see this O-ring for the first time, you'll doubt that it will fit. It does, but to make it happen, you'll need to use masking tape on the splines. The early-style spacer doesn't have a groove cut in its back side, so be delicate. Apply a light coat of petroleum jelly to the inside of the spacer. This will serve as a "lead-in" lubricant for the O-ring. It needs to be in the groove directly against the shoulder of the main drive gear.

If you need a new spacer, make sure you get the correct type. Belt drives use #35070-84. Chain drives use #35079-84. These new spacers have a Teflon coating on the back side, with a groove cut into them. You assemble them just like in the previous step but use O-ring #11166 instead. Don't mix and match and don't try using any substitute parts. These are the only combinations that work.

Don't use an air tool or impact wrench to torque the main drive gear sprocket nut. The torque on this nut is critical. Use a drop of Loctite 242 (blue) on the threads of the nut only. Then lightly oil the back side of the nut and carefully torque it to 80–90 foot-pounds.

Put everything back together by the book, and don't forget to refill the tranny.

That's it. It's simple, really. Just don't confuse simple with easy—and take the time to do it right.

ELECTRICAL SYSTEMS

Meet the Machiavelli of the modern motorcycle! Forget the old "Lucas-prince of darkness" jokes, we have insolent, inviolate black boxes to deal with these days—and diodes, transistor-controlled turn signals, "lamp cord" stator plugs, reed switches in electronic speedometers, and a host of niggling wires and connectors—any one of which is capable of ruining your day. This section isn't an electronics bible, but there are bits of info in here that can keep you from tearing your hair out (and your wiring apart) for no reason. There's also some insight into the "fiery" debate over ignitions. Characteristics, advantages, deficiencies, and a more discerning attitude about what you may really need versus what you think you want can be had from close scrutiny in this department. The best use of electrical information is to apply it to your scoot and make it as trustworthy and reliable as the most treacherous technology on the machine can be made. Mission Improbable? Not really, considering that the most amazing thing about electricity is that it works at all!

ELECTRICAL SYSTEMS

PROJECT 79 • THE TRUTH ABOUT GAUGES

 Time: 1 to 2 hours (for any gauge)

 Tools: Needle-nosed pliers; pliers; wire cutter or crimper tool; soldering equipment; multimeter; and 4-, 5-, 6-, and 8-millimeter, and 3/8- and 7/16-inch wrenches

 Talent:

 Tab: $ to $$$

 Tinware: Electrical tape, shrink tubing, and conduit or sheathing

 Tip: All mechanical speedos benefit from the "horse-collar"-style rubber support #67115-91 fitted from 1991—on; they also need frequent attention paid to the mounting pins and rubbers (kit #67066-76)

⚠ **PERFORMANCE GAIN:** Avoid unsuspected breakdowns

COMPLEMENTARY MODIFICATION: Mounting bracketry that allows the gauges to be seen clearly

1 Gauge choices run the gamut from this factory Police-type tach with built-in fuel gauge (handy, albeit scarce, for those FXR owners who want a voltmeter in the tank console) to a five-in-one 1950's Boy speedo (and everything else) replacement for Softails, Dynas, and several others.

2 You can add a tach to 883s and Super Glides that don't have one. The factory offers complete kits for anybody who's not sure where that rev-limiter really kicks in or where things get dangerously exciting without a rev limiter.

3 It's impossible to keep up with all the available instrumentation for Harleys. Even where and how they are located on the machine can be a part-time occupation for the gauge compulsive among us. The oil temperature dipstick is a natural, but check out the plethora of pressure gauge options.

Until just the last few years, a speedo and possibly a high beam indicator light, a charge light, and an oil light were all that was fitted to most Harleys. Times change. Evos and generations of refinement find us with cell phones in the saddlebags, no need to carry tools, and the luxury of space for gauges.

The question is which of these manifold instrument choices are useful additions, and which are really more for entertainment. Are there any that are a complete waste? Read on.

SPEEDOMETER

You've already got one, but they are generally inaccurate by as much as 10 percent. On mechanical speedos, Loctite the little screw holding the tripmeter knobs and angle the drive box on the front wheel at about 30 degrees up from horizontal to keep the cable from snapping.

Electronic speedos can suffer from things like reed switch failures that affect the turn signal canceler, erratic readings due to electrical "cross-over" from surrounding wires and stainless spark plug wires that aren't properly grounded.

TACHOMETER

These are fun to watch, but rev limiters make 'em unnecessary. If a rev limiter is in place, you can rap an H-D to that limit with abandon. If you've built the motor, tachs become a sort of stock broker, to help you keep from losing your investment and cashing in your chips. But the bulk of us never see the redline in day-to-day riding, so who's kidding who?

The add-on tach kits that H-D sells are not difficult to install, but they are time-consuming as there's lots of wires that have to find a home in the main harness. The instructions that come with these kits are complete enough to make the task reasonably easy, but it really helps to have an electrical pin and socket tool #97362-71 (or Drag specialties #DS-310491) and a couple extra pins and sockets.

OIL PRESSURE

An oil pressure gauge is a kind of oxymoron where Harleys are concerned. They always have oil, never much pressure, and usually you can't gauge anything important—gauge or no. Check and change your oil regularly and don't bother with this one.

4 The next time you decide to clean your tappet screen is as good a time as any to install a gauge. To remove the factory tappet screen plug, you'll need a huge straight-tipped screwdriver socket that fits on a ratchet. Anything less generally destroys the slot on the plug, whether the plug comes loose or not.

5 Whatever goes back in the tappet screen hole, whether a gauge or the plug, should be treated to a dab of PST (Teflon in a tube) to keep it from leaking. PST works much better than Teflon tape—too much tape will block oil flow.

6 The tappet screen is a poor excuse for a filter that had its day before true oil filters were used on Harleys. Removing it to install an oil pressure gauge isn't a great loss. That said, if you don't run a gauge, the screen remains and should be checked and cleaned regularly.

7 Oil gauges are most simply installed in this location, but the only time you can really afford to look at it is when you're sitting still. The alternative is to remote mount the gauge more in your line of sight so it can be referred to as you ride. The extra lines and joints are another potential source for oil leaks, though.

If you've simply got to have one, the thing to realize is by adding the gauge you've also added potential leaks at every extra joint the installation requires. Use PST teflon thread seal and be extremely careful with those tiny brass ferrules and the thin plastic hose they are supposed to seal.

VOLTMETER

Fully 90 percent of all the problems that will leave you dead on the road are electrical. Arguably, the most useful gauge you can install, a voltmeter will give you clues on the condition of the battery the minute you turn on the key. As you ride, if you see the needle headed for the red, head for the house.

Consider a voltmeter an early warning system for the only system you need to be warned of, or can do much about, before it fails.

A voltmeter, or a battery charge light like the Dyna OCM-1 or DVM-1, is the most worthwhile add-on gauge there is for Harleys that don't have them. The reason they aren't more popular is it's hard to manage a clean, unobtrusive, yet visible, location. Swapping in a voltmeter or ammeter for the gas gauge would be one way to do it. You'd still have reserve and an odometer to keep track of mileage, wouldn't you?

AMMETER

See "Voltmeter" above. The ammeter differs in that it tells you more about how balanced the electrical loads are. Ideally you should have both a voltmeter and ammeter.

OTHER GAUGES

You can install (if the factory or a previous owner didn't beat you to it) a clock, compass, or altimeter, if you like. None of 'em are vital, but all three have their uses.

ELECTRICAL SYSTEMS
PROJECT 80 • CHOOSING HIGH-PERFORMANCE PLUG WIRES

 Time: 1/2 hour

 Tools: Ferrule crimpers for wires that aren't pre-cut

 Talent:

 Tab: $

 Tinware: Silicone seal or dielectric grease to "waterproof" the plug-wire-to-coil connection

 Tip: Stock plug wires are marginal when new and just get worse; if yours are more than two or three years old, this may be the best "tune-up" tip of all

PERFORMANCE GAIN: 1 to 2 horsepower

COMPLEMENTARY MODIFICATION: Replace your spark plugs

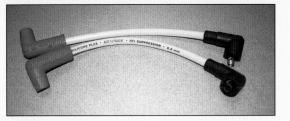

1 Accel 8.8-millimeter wires give a 1.6-horsepower increase, but they leave a hole in the mid-range. Just the same, the torque curve picks up throughout the rev-range, which is bound to make the bike feel stronger on the road.

2 These Screamin' Eagle yellow wires have to be cut to fit, just like H-D's own "universal" wire set. These probably are not the best choice for stock replacement applications, since H-D also makes pre-cut kits for all models—unless, of course, you just have to have yellow wires.

Just as a set of bum plug wires can cost horsepower, a really good set can make horsepower. If the old ones are worn out, weather-checked, frayed, or cracked, they can generate misfires and hard starting, to say nothing of their negative effect on gas mileage and spark plug life. Install new wires, and you not only restore power to previous levels, you may actually increase it.

No spark plug wire can overcome an ignition defect, such as incorrect timing or a worn-out advance unit. If a misfire or pinging problem is mechanical in its origin, fix that first before you count on any ignition upgrade to bail you out. Same story with electrical defects and deficiencies, such as a weak battery or charging system. Best keep them in tip-top condition before you worry about any benefit from trick parts.

You also need to know that a few very reputable tuners, Jerry Branch to name one, have tested plug wires and found that there's no appreciable improvement in power to be had by using "high-performance" plug wires—maybe better starting and clean firing at high rpm, better seat of the pants running, but no big bumps on the output chart. Be that as it may, it's clear that some of these plug wires make a

noticeable difference in the way your Harley runs on the street. Engine "pinging" (detonation or pre-ignition) are markedly diminished, if not eliminated. Starting improves by a full order of magnitude. Throttle response is crisper. And that, in the end, is what counts. Spark energy does affect power, and plug wires affect spark energy—period.

Stock plug wires perform in an adequate, if unspectacular, fashion, right to the 50-horsepower, 5,200-rpm limit. What they don't help is the EPA-inspired, lean-jetted dip in the power curve that shows up clearly in the 2,000 to 3,000-rpm range. Good plug wires, however, will noticeably reduce this 2,000 to 3,000-rpm hole (see dyno charts).

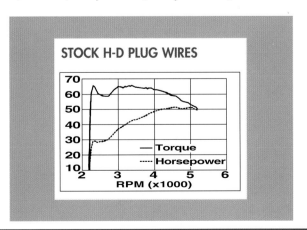

STOCK H-D PLUG WIRES

(dyno chart: Torque and Horsepower vs RPM (x1000), vertical axis 10 to 70, horizontal axis 2 to 6)

3 Braided stainless steel. The installation of these wires is a bit different in that they must be grounded to the engine with the little braided leads that sprout from the wires themselves. They look great on the bike, but beware of sloppy installations, because if they aren't well grounded, they can cause the engine to misfire or not run at all. Done right, they help the overall torque curve and flatten out the dip between 2,000 and 3,000 rpm.

4 Screamin' Eagle orange (pre-made molded) wires. These (and the optional red or black colors) are the wires H-D sells to just plug-in to your late-model stocker. You don't have to worry about fabrication, just color. These are made in one of Harley's time-honored competition colors, bright orange. With these wires installed, the infamous mid-range hole returns with a vengeance.

TAYLOR REV TECH PLUG WIRES

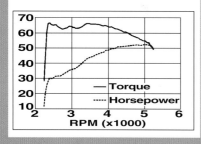

SCREAMIN' EAGLE YELLOW

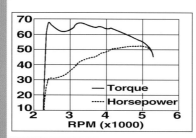

BRAIDED STAINLESS STEEL

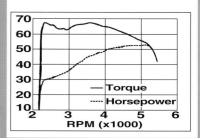

SCREAMIN' EAGLE ORANGE

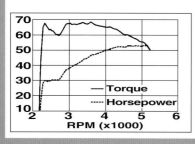

SPLITFIRE PLUG WIRES

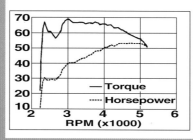

JACOBS PLUG WIRES

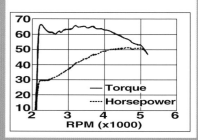

M.S.D. PLUG WIRES

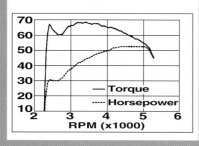

ACCEL 8.8MM PLUG WIRES

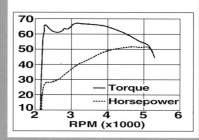

NOLOGY PLUG WIRES

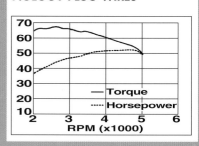

5 MSD wires. "Multiple spark discharge" is what "MSD" stands for, both the company and the technology. The MSD wires reduce the depth of the hole and improve overall power output. These blood red and dark gray wires are handsome as well. However, they too are the type you have to make up to fit.

6 Split-Fire Twin Core wires. These are designed to the same theory as their famous spark plugs—giving spark energy more than one path to get where it's going. Applied to plug wires, two cores are better than one to get the job done. The benefit is higher overall average torque and horsepower compared to stock and, most likely, very long service life.

7 Jacobs Energy Core wires. These are do-it-yourself wires that may be the finest of their kind. The kit even includes a tube of sealant that makes the completed wire set more weatherproof than many pre-molded wires. The energy core is essentially a fine wire wound around the ferrite core. More durable than metal- or fiber-core wire, it's neither as brittle as the former nor as power-robbing as the latter.

8 Nology wires. Nology has a unique approach involving special non-resistor, silver-electrode spark plugs (resistance is built into the wires instead) and externally grounded installation. As with the externally grounded braided plug wires, meticulous attention to grounding is a necessity. As if to prove the point, the dyno chart clearly shows how smooth and potent the power curves are for both torque and horsepower, with peak power the best yet at 52.3. More importantly, average power is a whopping 47.1 horsepower, compared to the stock bike's 40.9 horsepower. Another impressive statistic is the time it took the engine to reach its 5,200-rpm limit. The stocker staggered up in 5.767 seconds. The same engine, Nology equipped, did it in 4.238—an incredible 27-percent improvement! More power that can be reached more quickly means a big improvement in feel and performance on the street.

9 Nology wires (with amplifier). This shows how dyno runs can occasionally raise more questions than they answer. When adding the Nology amplifier to an existing setup, you would assume there would be another incremental improvement in power. Instead, in one example, virtually nothing was gained and, in some areas, ground was lost. Could there be other limiting factors? You bet! A stock late-model Harley has severe restrictions on its breathing capabilities. We've already seen what the lean jetting does; now we've reached another wall in the form of the stock air cleaner and mufflers. The whole purpose of any of these high-performance plug wires is to fire a proper fuel-air mixture in a less restricted engine. The fact that they can improve the performance of the standard bike as much as they did makes you wonder what would happen if they were used on more representative, well hot-rodded bikes.

ELECTRICAL SYSTEMS

PROJECT 81 • SERVICING YOUR BATTERY

 Time: 1/2 to 1 hour

 Tools: 10-millimeter wrench, multimeter, small hydrometer, dielectric grease, distilled water, and needle-nose pliers

 Talent:

 Tab: $

 Tinware: Optional sealed battery upgrade stuff from H-D, if you can't or won't deal with the maintenance of a regular wet-cell

 Tip: Don't assume that a battery can't be the problem just because it's new or you "recently" checked it

! PERFORMANCE GAIN: Reliable starting

COMPLEMENTARY MODIFICATION: Harley-sealed batteries and gel-cell aftermarket batteries; voltmeter or ammeter

1 Batteries are a tight fit and awkward to get at on most Harleys. This alone is responsible for a great many failures. People are just too lazy to wrestle with a battery once a week like the book says you should. The best alternative to regular servicing of the battery is to have a gauge (volts or amps) mounted permanently on the motorcycle. It also helps to "rig" the battery to make service a little less difficult. "Soaping" or lubing the sides makes it easier to slide the battery in or out. You can also run a small strap of polypropylene (acid-proof) rope or webbing under the battery case to "sling" it out with, if your fingers are too fat to get a grip on the little devil.

The three most important facts of battery life are that: most failures that leave you stranded are electrical, most electrical failures are traceable to the battery, and most of these battery failures are preventable.

All batteries will wear out in time, but if you take care of your battery properly from day one, you should be able to get five or six years of trouble-free starts out of it—even longer if you're lucky. Here's how to get the most out of your battery.

One of the keys to long battery life is proper initial service. A brand-new wet-cell battery needs to be filled with electrolyte (battery acid) to the proper level in each cell before it's put into service.

Once the battery's filled with fluid, it must be charged properly to ensure a long and happy life. For Harley's low-maintenance battery, you should use a variable- or tapered-rate battery charger, rated at 4, 6, 8, or 10 amps. These tapered-rate chargers might stuff anywhere between 2 and 8 amps into a new battery when you hook it up, but after an hour or so, the meter may read close to zero. At this point, the battery may make it's full voltage, but you should charge a minimum of 12 hours to "set" the plates. With a trickle charger (1 amp or less of charging current),

make that 24 hours—at least. *Never* buy a "quick-charged" battery, because even though it will work fine initially, the first time you hit the starter button and "load" the battery, you've sentenced it to an early death, and no amount of charging after that fact will make the battery live longer or work better.

It shouldn't come as a surprise that follow-up is just as important as the initial charge. They call them *wet*-cell batteries for a reason and tell you to check the fluid every month for the same reason. Batteries, like plants and humans, need watering. Use only distilled water to top up your battery—*never* use battery acid or plain tap water. The first time you look into a cell and its level is low enough to expose the plates, start budgeting for a new battery.

The hardest thing on a motorcycle battery is just letting the motorcycle sit. Inactivity of the battery causes sulfation (battery cancer), and key off or not, the chemical reactions inside the battery create a discharge of 1/2 to 1 percent per day (more in warm weather). Do the math—in 30 days you've lost 30 percent of your battery. Charge your battery at least once a month when you're not using it. Better yet, buy a Battery Tender (a sophisticated trickle charger you can buy for $40 to $60) and keep it hooked up whenever the bike is parked. That way you know your bike will start, and you'll get years of extra life out of the battery.

Short hops, stop-and-go traffic, and frequent restarts are pretty tough on battery life too. Every time you start your Harley, you should ride 20 miles, just to return to the battery all the energy you took out to start it. Added elec-

2 Late-model (1993 and newer) Softails have a much improved two-piece battery strap design. The older version was a serious wrestling match to secure, requiring a reach down into the bowels of the battery case, usually with a screwdriver or something that could draw blood when it slipped. If the two-piece strap for a wet-cell battery is an improvement, the new retrofittable sealed H-D battery is a quantum leap. These batteries provide nearly 20 percent more cranking power, last up to twice as long, and can be recharged from fully depleted dozens of times (as opposed to six or seven times with a wet-cell) and quickly at high amperage rates (as opposed to overnight like a wet-cell). They are structurally smaller than the older design, so you'll need a kit consisting of a battery pad and hold-down strap. The whole conversion can cost nearly $100, but it's worth it. Kit #66672-96 fits Sportsters, FXRs, and 1984 to 1990 Softails. Kit #66673-96 fits all the rest, except FLT models.

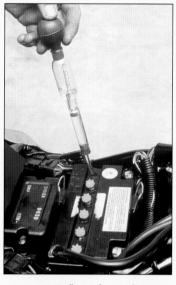

3 Hydrometers are indispensable battery tools. That said, the best are calibrated in specific gravity readings, not with little floating balls. Use what you must, but use it frequently; it's absolutely the best insurance against an on-the-road electrical failure. Be cautious whenever you get near any battery, since they have a tendency to do things like blow up, burn your skin, and wreck clothing. Rubber gloves and eye protection are intelligent, if not macho, precautions to take. Keeping fresh water and baking soda handy to apply to any spills isn't a bad plan either. You can never be too careful.

4 Perhaps the handiest electrical tool is the multitalented multimeter. You can use it on batteries to check basic voltage (with the engine off) and basic charging (with the engine on and revved up a little). The 14.4-volt reading you see here indicates that the charging system is fine on this bike. What some folks aren't ready for is that a fresh, hot battery will read 13.3 volts on its own (2.2 volts per cell times six cells). If you check regularly and one fine day find the battery has mysteriously dropped to 10 volts, you probably have a bad cell.

trical bells and whistles make matters more difficult. Bottom line: Ride farther or buy batteries more often.

Some tips to help you keep your battery in tip-top condition:

• Install a voltmeter, ammeter, indicator kit (H-D #66009-87), or some combination of these so you can monitor your charging system. It's amazing how few riders use a simple gauge to monitor the electrical system yet throw oil pressure gauges on a lubrication system that virtually never fails.

• Use star washers to mount cable ends to battery terminals.

• Keep terminals clean and dry.

• Apply a little soapy water to the battery case if it will help you slip the thing in or out of the rubber battery tray (especially Softails).

• Don't drop a battery! Even a light bounce can crack the case and make for an acid leak.

• Baking soda neutralizes battery acid. Water dilutes it. Think about it.

• Always hook up the positive cable first—after you make sure the vent pipe is clear.

• Wet-cell batteries can only be (slowly) recharged from "flat" a small number of times, perhaps 8 to 10. Gel-cell types can be charged dozens, maybe even hundreds of times—quickly.

• Harley's new "maintenance free" battery is not a gel cell, but it's quite an improvement, lasting nearly twice as long, offering at least 10 percent more power, and allowing one to forget about checking electrolyte levels. You can even mount it upside down.

In theory, a new low-maintenance H-D battery can last up to three years. The average, on the other hand, is more like 12 to 18 months. Maintenance and understanding what a battery needs is the difference.

BATTERY FAULT-FINDING GUIDE			
	Good battery	**Suspect battery**	**If suspect**
Plates	+ Chocolate color – Grey	White sulfation on plates Plates buckled	Scrap
Sediment	Little or none	Deep sediment up to plate level	Scrap
Voltage	Above 12 volts	Below 12 volts	Test charge
Electrolyte	Normal level	Low, especially if one cell is low	Fill and Test charge
Specific Gravity	Above 1.200 in all cells. No more than 0.020 difference.	Below 1.100 or wide difference between cells	Test charge
Case	Sound and leek proof	Leaking case	Scrap Wash down affected bike parts in baking soda solution

SPECIFIC GRAVITY REQUIRED	PARTS OF DISTILLED WATER TO 1 OF CONC. SULPHURIC ACID
1.25	3.4
1.26	3.2
1.27	3.0
1.28	2.8
1.29	2.7
1.30	2.6

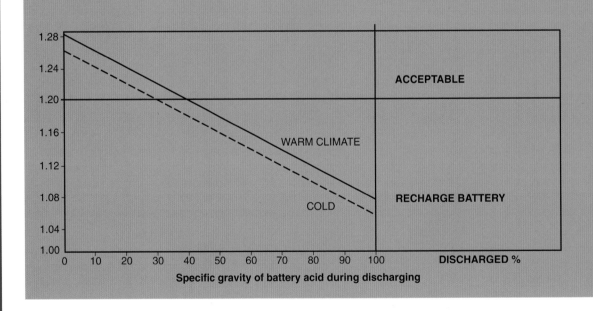

Specific gravity of battery acid during discharging

ELECTRICAL SYSTEMS
PROJECT 82 • INSTALLING A HIGH-PERFORMANCE STARTER ON BIG TWINS

 Time: 3–4 hours

 Tools: Standard sockets, 12-inch extension, wobbler, ratchet, screwdrivers, and torque wrench

 Talent: ▮▮▮

 Tab: $$$–$$$$

 Tinware: The starter, primary gasket, primary fluid, starter gasket or o-ring, or jackshaft o-ring or sealing washer and lock tab

 Tip: On Softails, loosen and partly remove the oil tank to get the starter in place

 PERFORMANCE GAIN: Far less starter "grunt" and big-inch or high-compression motors will love you for it

COMPLEMENTARY MODIFICATION: High-output battery

Any Harley-Davidson Big Twin can benefit from a starter motor with more muscle. The stock unit is frequently hard-pressed to overcome the infamous starter "grunt," that happens every so often when you want to light the bike up. When it happens, you know it, because it makes you wonder if the engine will actually be able to turn over. You hit the starter button and hear it begin it's task, then pause for what seems like forever, without completing it's mission. Often, it's easier to back off the button and hit it again than it is to wait out starter grunt.

The situation improved in 1989, when the factory introduced the so-called compound starter. These starters have been more reliable and stronger than the previous design, but since the starter clutch (Bendix) and solenoid are contained within the starter, it is more difficult to rebuild than the older set-up with it's separate, easily accessed components. On the whole, it seems The Motor Company still has not gone far enough. Starter grunt persists. In 1994 H-D took yet another step, when they redesigned the primary drive ratio, for the first time *ever*, just to address the concerns owners have about this phenomenon. It helped a little,

1 A stock starter motor for 1989 to 1993 Big Twins is on the right, and a Wag's starter motor is on the left. Look closely, and you will see a couple of subtle differences. The one that matters when you install the starter is the location of the copper stud. The stocker's stud sits at about 2 o'clock, and the one on the Wag's version is at 12 o'clock high. From the opposite side, with the Wag's starter on the left, you may notice that the mounting flange of the stock starter is cast, and the Wag's is machined from a slab of billet.

2 There are two versions of the splined starter jackshaft coupling. The shorter one is unique to 1989 models. The long one is for 1990–on. If you have any trouble getting the Wag's starter to bolt up flush without pushing the jackshaft sleeve surrounding the starter drive gear out of the inner primary case, or if the starter binds once installed, be ready to shorten this coupling or replace it with the 1989 version.

3 Once fitted, torque the fasteners to 13–20 foot-pounds. A useful technique is to go back and forth from one fastener to the other as you torque them down. Overdo it or ignore proper torque and the starter could easily bind. Tighten the cable on the copper stud, and don't forget to plug in the wire lead. Meanwhile, back over on the primary side, place your new updated O-ringed sealing washer and a new lock washer on the jackshaft retaining bolt and torque to 7–9 foot-pounds. After torquing, bend the tab over on the jackshaft bolt. Mount the primary cover over a new gasket, screw it down, and add primary fluid. Hook up the battery, double-check your work, and try out your new starter.

but still, the puny 1.3-horsepower factory starter motor has its work cut out for it, pushing two 3.5-inch inch pistons up a 4.25-inch bore, especially if the oil is thick and cold. The situation goes from barely tolerable to down right dubious when you've gone to all the time and trouble to build a high-performance engine and can't count on starting it reliably.

Basically, if you have an engine with more power, and more compression, you need a starter motor with more power too. Fortunately, the aftermarket has stepped up to help out. Several companies offer high-performance starters, among them Wag's U.C.T., who offers a 1.9 horsepower High Torque model. Available in wrinkle black finish or highly polished chrome, this super starter features a ball-bearing support for the starter drive and internal clutch, five in all, rather than the bushings used in the stocker. It also features a 4.44:1 reduction ratio, which holds the promise of providing a quicker spin of the engine, and no more grunt. The patented design has been tested on motors as large as 132 cubic inches, with a compression of 15:1.

The installation is straightforward, but not identical to bolting on a stock starter, as we are about to see.

Disconnecting and remove the battery and the primary cover.

Loosen the jackshaft bolt, taking care not to lose the washers and sealing o-ring.

Next up, loosen the bolts that fasten the oil bag. Start with the rear bolt, and it helps to have an extension and a wobbler, unless you have way too much time for this operation. Now, loosen the front bolt, right behind the rear cylinder and virtually on top of the starter. Last, loosen the bolt on the primary side. Remember, you don't have to remove the tank, just loosen it.

Remove the plug-in electrical connection from the starter, and then unbolt the heavy gauge cable from the threaded post on the starter. You may find it easier to get at the post connection on Softails by going down through the hole in the bottom of the battery tray.

Undo all the mounting bolts holding the starter to the primary. Once that's done, you can remove it. If clearance is tight, wiggle it a bit while lifting up on the oil tank.

Then, proceed as follows:

Test-fit the starter to see whether it is compatible with the jackshaft coupling on your bike. There are two versions of the splined starter jackshaft coupling. The shorter one is unique to 1989 models. The long one is for 1990-on. If you have any trouble getting the starter to bolt up flush without pushing the jackshaft sleeve surrounding the starter drive gear out of the inner primary case, or if the starter binds once installed, be ready to shorten this coupling or replace it with the 1989 version.

Fitting the Wag's starter may take an extra effort in a couple of areas. Look closely at the proximity of the copper stud and the bottom of the oil tank. Tight fit huh? The twelve o'clock position of the stud means paper thin clearance here. Rather than remove the oil tank, simply loosen a couple of the oil tank mounts a bit, and carefully lever the oil tank up, just a little higher. Then, the starter will slide past the oil tank bottom and into it's rightful place. It might help to attach the heavy cable loosely to the copper stud, before it's tucked away under the oil tank, since it's difficult to get to it after the starter is in position.

Torque the fasteners to 13–20 foot-pounds. A useful technique is go back and forth from one fastener to the other as you torque them down. Overdo it, or ignore proper torque, and the starter could easily bind.

Tighten the cable on the copper stud, and don't forget to plug in the wire lead.

Go back over to the primary side, and place your new updated o-ringed sealing washer, and a new lock washer on the jackshaft retaining bolt and torque to 7–9 foot-pounds. After torquing, bend the tab over on the jackshaft bolt.

Mount the primary cover over a new gasket, screw it down, and add primary fluid.

Hook up the battery, and check out your new starter. If you're satisfied (with 49 percent more cranking power, you should be), finish up by double-checking your work—it's time to go ride!

ELECTRICAL SYSTEMS
PROJECT 83 • UPGRADING YOUR CHARGING SYSTEM

 Time: 2 to 3 hours

 Tools: Allen wrenches, Torx wrenches, the usual suspects for ripping into a primary housing, and a torque wrench

 Talent:

 Tab: $ to $$

 Tinware: Primary gasket, primary fluid, and new stator screws

 Tip: All short primary models (FXR and FLT) allow access to the alternator assembly by merely removing the outer primary cover; early (1984 to 1988) Softails and FX models require removal of the inner primary housing, adding about twice the labor time and using more parts (look at the front portion of the primary case—if both the inner and outer halves have a round bulge where they meet, you've got a short primary)

 PERFORMANCE GAIN: A more powerful and reliable charging system

COMPLEMENTARY MODIFICATION: Secure the stator plug, install a volt/amp gauge, and secure all ground wires (especially the regulator) with star washers on clean metal

1 This is what kills most of the early stators. Look closely and see that A) the two wire leads coming from the stator body are too close together, and B) there's no insulation left on the wires where they connect to the body. Bear in mind that the inside of the primary housing, surrounded by hot oil, is a pretty hostile environment to work in, and the melted "lamp-corditis" shown is a direct result of that kind of treatment. A wire keeper, such as H-D #45095-85, keeps the rectifier/regulator plugged in tight. Although it's designed for 1984 to 1990 models, it works on newer bikes as well. Fancier versions are available, such as CCI's #19-282, -286, -287, and -288, but late models (1994 and newer) don't need them as badly.

2 Here's a new Big Twin 32-amp stator. Note the three securing ribs on the plug and the lack of these ribs on the older stator plug in the earlier photo. Note also, the thing's not dipped in rubber! The latest non-molded stators use fewer windings of a heavier gauge copper wire than did the molded or even early-style, non-molded ones. The factory also moved the two leads further apart where they join the stator yoke. It seems to work a lot better that way.

3 A late five-speed Sportster stator has a much different pigtail and plug. You feed the pigtail through a hole in the left crankcase primary cavity, over the top, and into the regulator. While tortuous to route, it's actually cleaner and less troublesome than the Big Twin arrangement (except, of course, the fuellys).

4 Late rotors have a splined center and glued magnets. Beware of losing either! This shows pretty clearly just how bad it can be. There are supposed to be six magnets spaced equidistantly around the rim. The secret is to place the two rotor washers correctly, and correct placement varies a bit from year to year and model to model. The instruction sheet that comes with the new parts will tell you what you need to know—if you read it. Don't chintz out by reusing old stator screws, and torque everything properly, as spelled out in your shop manual.

When the time comes to replace your alternator, you'll also have an opportunity to upgrade your system. The actual replacement is simple enough. It shouldn't take more than 3 hours on any Harley. Most any built in the 1990s take about 1. It's all in the shop manual.

As with most things Harley-Davidson, there's a bit of history in their alternators. This story begins way back in 1970, when Harley-Davidson decided that it was time to get rid of the generator and go to an alternating current (AC) system, even if the tradition was direct current (DC).

They chose an AC generator which is simply a magnet attached to the engine with a coil of wire right beside it (it's not quite the same thing as an alternator, although most of us can't tell the difference, and neither can the battery). Fire up the motor, and the magnet spins, producing electricity in the coil. The generator systems generate electricity, but they require some

additional pieces or the lights will be dim at idle, and high rpms will blow bulbs and melt wires.

Stuff a battery in the system, and the dim lights issue usually goes away, but there's still a couple of problems. Remember, the generator is run with alternating current, which changes direction every time the north and south poles of the magnet whip by the wire. It's not a big deal for the bulbs or the horn, but the battery just hates it. One second there's power galore being stuffed into the battery, the next it's all sucked right back out. So to keep the battery happy and working, Harley owners have to add a one-way electrical "valve" known as a diode or rectifier.

The trouble starts with a sustained high rpm ride, or worse, a lack of battery maintenance. Either one leads to electrolyte "boil off" or evaporation, and the battery starts to "disconnect" from the system. Next thing you know, you have a boiled battery, hot wires, blown bulbs—the system is out of balance.

Enter the regulator, a mechanical or solid state electronic device that senses the battery voltage and adjusts the amount of power to the rotor accordingly. The faster the rotor turns, the more electricity that comes out of the stator. Less power to the rotor = less magnetism = less stator output. Eventually the stator output drops so low the bike is running off the battery. When the voltage from the battery drops, the regulator sends more power to the rotor to get more magnetism, and so on, and so on, as the cycle repeats itself. All this good stuff applies to true alternators as well, with two major distinctions. First, *all* alternators (rotating electromagnet instead of a permanent fixed magnet) are "three phase." This means they have three coils of wire arranged sequentially at 120 degrees around the magnet. That makes 'em a bunch stronger but no bigger than an AC generator. Second, and more important to most of us, is that with an AC generator you can have a dead battery (or no battery) and as long as you can push or "bump" start the bike, it'll run. Alternators *gotta* have some juice, 'cause without it, there's no magnetism from the electromagnet, and you're walking.

Now that we know what we're dealing with, in broad strokes, we can move on to the detail differences that H-D has charged us with over the years.

1970–1975 Big Twins: From the factory, these used a 19-amp system with an unmolded stator and a plug with four male small diameter pins.

1976–1980 Big Twins: These still had 19 amps, but with a molded stator and only two small male pins in the plug.

1981–1988 Big Twins: Twenty-two amps allowed the addition of extra lights, a radio, and accessories without adding an extra battery to run them. The only obvious visible change was to the plug, which wound up with two sockets instead of two pins. The "molded" stator is coated in rubber, and it runs hot. Both H-D and the aftermarket figured out the molding wasn't protecting the stator windings from hot oil in the primary. The solution was to thin-coat the wire windings with transparent high-temp plastic-type stuff that lets heat roll off better.

1989–on Big Twins: With 32 amps available, this system is pretty much the hot setup for FX models but is still a little shy for power-hungry dresser riders. The stator still has a female plug with two sockets, but it is a larger diameter. As time rolled on, the plug body got extra ribs of improved profiles to help hold it firmly in place in the case. The newest version has three ribs and hangs in like a bear.

1995 FLT-series Big Twins: Introduced on the 90th Anniversary, this "Super High Output" 38-amp system has about the same rotor design as everything seen so far, but the stator and regulator are decidedly different. Finally, the factory moved the regulator plug outside the primary case, and the regulator that gets this new plug has a built-in LED indicator so you know if it's charging or not. You can retrofit this to any short primary model back to 1991 (FLT or FXR), as long as you use the 38-amp fuse kit (#72372-95) along with the upgrade. H-D says this system has a 50-percent higher output at idle and 30 percent more at speed than the 32-amp system.

1997–on EFI Models: The 45-amp, 1997 "Ultra High Output" package fills the needs of fuel injection, which requires additional juice. It is also retrofittable to 1995 and 1996 EFI models. The rotor is of a different design, with 12 pole magnets pinned into the shell.

1984–1990 Sportsters: These have a 32-amp system with a special plug. Replacement stators can be had either molded or not, either of which do the job just fine. The rotor is the item to watch because it's also the back of the clutch basket. If it fails, it's too pricey to think about (see the article about "Shiftless Sportsters").

1991–on Sportsters: These 32-amp units have a Big Twin-style rotor, are not molded rubber, and are no longer wedded to the clutch.

Unless you're into totally accurate restoration, there's no reason not to use an upgraded system on pre-1988 models. If your original fails, you can get either the 22-amp kit (#29982-81), which will work on any Big Twin back to 1970, or the 32-amp kit (#29985-87, shown), which will fit wet-clutch Big Twins back to 1984 1/2 (except 1984 to 1988 Softails).

ELECTRICAL SYSTEMS

PROJECT 84 • SELECTING A HIGH-PERFORMANCE FACTORY IGNITION MODULE

 Time: 1/2 to 1 hour

 Tools: None for "plug and play" swaps; you'll need a wire stripper/crimper tool to install an adapter on older four-pin harnesses

 Talent:

 Tab: $$

 Tinware: The module and an adapter harness for 1990 and older models

 Tip: Make sure the module won't let you rev the engine beyond where it will hold together; the H-D modules are the most economical option

 PERFORMANCE GAIN: Performance gains are usually related to the mechanical choices, but a good module can absolutely become the icing on that cake

COMPLEMENTARY MODIFICATION: Compression increases and a cam with more overlap

If you want to run your engine above the 5,250-rpm limit of your Big Twin or are seeking a little snappier response from that new Sportster, a new ignition module will be part of the program. The gains can be significant, but choosing the proper module for your bike can be tricky.

A wide variety of modules are available, each with a different ignition advance curve designated by a letter code (see chart). The best one for your bike depends on how many rpms your engine can survive and the level of tune.

This is a case where the aftermarket isn't always the best source. The Harley-Davidson units are priced right and do the job well.

What you really need to know, though, is that strong running Harley Big Twins and Sportsters usually need more aggressive curves than they come with stock. Bear in mind that the most aggressive may not be the right one for your motor.

The only factory modules for Big Twins that offer a different advance curve are the Shovelhead module, the so-called "HDI" module (standard since 1996), the Police module, and the Screamin' Eagle module. The

1 The eight-pin Deutsch connector on the left is used on most late models. The seven-pin Cannon connector is used on most everything else. There's no way to be positive unless you look, however, because so many folks change the module. If you have a 1990 or earlier model, you must use adapter harness (#32408-90) to go from the original, round four-pin connector to the roughly rectangular, seven-pin Cannon connector. Cannon connectors are standard on current production factory modules for Sportsters through 1993 and on Big Twins through 1998, except FLTs. From 1994 on, H-D went to eight-pin Deutsch connectors on Sportsters and FLTs. Although the factory doesn't offer an adapter harness for this type of connector, CCI offers several types. So with the proper connections, you can use any module you want on any model.

2 When you make a module change, pick the curve first and the pigtail connection style second. All Harley modules are marked in white ink, showing the curve designation by its letter code and usually the rpm limit. For instance, this Screamin' Eagle Sportster module shows rev limit on top (8,000 rpm), the factory part number upper left, the model it's supposed to work on (1200), and behind the "−" is the curve designation, "K" in this example. The gibberish on the lower right of the module is a batch designation you don't need to worry about.

3 One of the newest wrinkles in the module game is the so-called selectable curve, available from the aftermarket for awhile and H-D just recently. With its assortment of micro-switches, the initial advance can be set to any one of four built-in curves to suit your bike's needs. The pros are that this allows you to dial out pinging and sluggish low-speed response and accommodate higher compression. The cons are that it only has any effect at engine speeds below 2,500 rpm, and you must remove the module to make adjustments since the switches are on the back.

4 The conventional modules, regardless of connector type and optional adjustability, are rapidly taking a back seat to the little critter on the left. This type of self-contained module and trigger mechanism, popularized by the Crane HI-4 (among others), has it all. Like the others, H-D's version is self-contained, takes no space or clumsy wiring on the chassis, is adjustable for advance, and is even adaptable to single-fire ignition.

Shovel module's advance curve is the same as the points system, has no rev limit, does not employ a VOES (Vacuum Operated Electrical Switch) to trigger its curve, and, therefore, is not tunable in any way.

The Police module, on the other hand, uses a VOES and offers solid performance. It boasts a slightly better curve (E) and limits revs to 5,800 rpm. The Motor Company did their homework on this one and came up with a pretty good compromise. This module is less prone to ignition-related misfires and shuts the motor down just as the stock heads quit flowing and the stock valve springs start bouncing. Call it "Captain Sensible."

The last of the Big Twin altered curve modules is the Screamin' Eagle module. It has the most aggressive curve (F) and an 8,000-rpm limit (for all practical purposes, no limit)—exceeding an 80-inch (or larger) motor's mechanical limits. The newest twist on Screamin' Eagle modules is a "street legal" variation that boasts a 6,000-rpm limit.

You can run Sportster modules on your Big Twin, which might help you pick up some snap below 3,000 rpm. Bear in mind, however, that Sportsters have a different full advance timing figure than Big Twins. An 80-inch Evo runs 35 degrees and Sportsters run 40. If you run your Big Twin hard for any sustained length of time, the extra advance can cause the engine to overheat.

For Sportsters, the module that Joe Minton, Buzz Buzzelli, and other tuners prefer now is the 6,500-rpm stock (J-curve) module for the 1988 to 1990 1200 XLH. If you choose to try it on a Big Twin, it should not be used in conjunction with the VOES and definitely does not work like points.

Also, even though a "points-type" curve is the most aggressive of the bunch, that doesn't make it the best choice for your motor. The factory has had plenty of time to think about its choices (and make up new ones), yet they are still tinkering with curves. For instance, the 1996 models, (all of 'em) have gone over to the HDI modules (formerly International). The reasoning behind this is a little vague, but the presumption is that it will improve emissions and drivability. For the last few years the timing reached full advance (35 degrees on a Big Twin, 40 on a 1200 XL, and 45 on 883s) at 1,600 rpm. The HDI module gets you 20 degrees advance at 1,000 rpm, but it isn't fully advanced at 1600, indicating that the curve may be a little steeper initially but that it rolls in considerably slower than previously.

H-D IGNITION MODULES

Curve	H-D Part Number	Application	Comments
A	None, obsolete	Early Evo Big Twin	Lousy, lazy curve
B	32436-91A	Iron XL1000	Updating requires VOES
C	32399-84A	Shovel FX/FL/FLT, XR1000	No VOES, like points
D	32405-91A	1984—on Evo 1340	5,250-rpm retard
D	32426-94	1994—on FLT only	Late-style plug
E	32419-91A	Police FXRP Evo 1340	5,800-rpm limit
F	32421-85A	SE 1340	8,000-rpm limit
F	32595-96	1994—1995 FLT models	6,000 rpm, late-style plug
F	32596-96	1984—1995 SE 1340	6,000 rpm, street legal
G	32410-91A	Evo XL883/1100	Lazy curve
G	32410-94	1994—on	Late-style plug
H	32420-86A	1986—1987 SE XL	"Bath tub" heads
J	32432-91A	1988—1990 XL1200	6,500-rpm limit
K	32420-87B	SE Sportster	8,000 rpm
K	32420-94	1994—on	Late-style plug
K	32597-96	1988—1993 SE XL1200	6,800 rpm, street legal
K	32598-96	1994—1995 SE XL1200	6,800 rpm, late-style plug
M	32433-91A	1991—on XL1200	6,250-rpm limit
M	32433-94	1994—on	Late-style plug
P	32449-95A	1996—on 1340, all	5,250 rpm, late plug
P	32630-96	1996—on SE 1340	Street legal, 6,000 rpm
Q	32465-95A	1996—on XL1200	6,250 rpm
Q	32633-96	1996—on SE 1200	Street legal, 6,800 rpm
R	32466-95A	1996—on XL883	6,250 rpm
R	32632-96	1996—on SE 883	Street legal, 6,800 rpm
Adj.	32654-98	1994 and later FL/XL models, 1995 and later FX except EFI	Four selectable curves and rev limits, dual- or single-fire capable. Deutsch 8-pin connector
Adj. (same)	32655-98	1994 and earlier FX, 1993 and earlier FL/XL*	Four selectable curves and rev limits, dual- or single-fire capable. Cannon (7-pin) connector

*1990 and earlier models need #32408-90 or equivalent wiring harness adapter.

Note: For bikes with pointless ignitions, always set ignition timing to the module. The model year or the info in the shop manual may not match exactly with what's actually on the machine, so go with the module, it's the brains in the organization.

THE COMMENTS

A-Curve: Harley's first attempt at a vacuum-triggered advance curve was a bit off the mark. In fact, that's when technicians learned the VOES was adjustable.

B-Curve: If you've noticed the resemblance of this curve for Iron Sportsters and the Evo A-curve, don't worry. What didn't work for aluminum Big Twins worked very well indeed for the Iron 1000. Remember, electronic ignition on the venerable 61-inch XLs was necessary to get them through the smog screen and, courtesy of the VOES, to run decently on their relatively high compression. The bonus was unheard of intervals between ignition services. No more mechanical advance mechanism to wear out.

C-Curve: Retard the timing enough to get the thing started, then *zap*, full advance at about 2,000 rpm, and it stays there. No VOES, no hose, no nothing. Good for drag racing, but otherwise it's not the hot setup.

D-Curve: This is the stock module curve for Big Twins. The advance curve isn't bad, but if you're looking for performance that low rev limit has to go.

E-Curve: Subtle differences in the curve, but enough to prevent pinging, even in most high-compression motors. A little known bit of trivia: the 1985 California Highway Patrol police bikes were built with 0.50 thousandths milled off the heads, 0.15 off the cylinders, and no smog stuff whatsoever. This module kept them in one piece through many, many miles.

F-Curve: The Screamin' Eagle module. One thing to think about here is the seemingly minute differences all these Big Twin advance curves. It seems as though the only real difference from one to the other is the rev limit. Don't you believe it. The difference on a graph may be as little as 3 degrees, but you sure will feel it on the road!

G-Curve: The no-ping-thing for 3-inch bores. Actually, they also used this module on 1986 to 1987 XL1100 models as well. This doesn't change the fact that this one does no favors for your performance.

J-Curve: Speaking of good modules to put on a 1200 Sportster! This one is held in high esteem by many tuners, if for no other reason than its 6,500-rpm rev limit. It is nearly perfect for the mechanical limits of the stock valvetrain and legal for racing classes that require a "stock" module. Kind of like the Police module for Big Twins, this one is a great choice for street performance. It's not quite as tolerant of compression increases, however.

K-Curve: Screamin' Eagle Sportster module. It can be had with your choice of rev limit, as long as you choose either 6,800 or 8,000 rpm.

M-Curve: Current curve of choice for XL1200s. This module is stock on five-speed 1200s and is more notorious for pinging than performance. The rev limit is a bit lower too, at 6,250 rpm.

P-Curve: No graph is available for this latest module (formerly HDI). Harley's position on this is pretty clear from this statement, dated 4/16/97: "That information is considered to be confidential. Although it may have been given out in the past, we have since taken a new position of protecting that information." That said, this new module, fitted to 1996 and newer

1340 models, works better than the earlier stock module, if you don't mind the low, 5,250-rpm limiter.

Q-Curve: Another new proprietary factory curve used on 1996 and newer XL1200s and for the street legal Screamin' Eagle Sportster module. Since there is no curve available to show you, all that can be said is this one does reduce pinging significantly, as well as improve throttle response.

R-Curve: Nineteen ninety-six and later 883s get this new module to perk them up a bit. It works well enough that H-D decided to use it for their new street legal Screamin' Eagle application also.

BIG TWIN BOTTOM LINE

To 5,800 rpm with love: Use a Police ignition module (H-D #31419-91A) and you will gain a useful increase in rpm yet retain a safe rev limit.

To 6,250 rpm with care: Most tuners (well, Jerry Branch anyway) will tell you that an Evo Big Twin with stock heads hits a wall in terms of flow above about 6,250 rpm. Heads that were picking up 20 to 30 percent every 1,000 rpm up to this point get a measly 5 to 7 percent from here on up. This is also closing in on the limit of the stock valve spring's ability to control valve float.

To 6,500–7000 rpm with caution: This will require flowed heads, hot rod valve springs, beefy connecting rods, aftermarket pistons, and more expensive stuff.

To 8,000 rpm for the record: Yes, it can be done, but not often, not cheaply, and not well. Bikes with billet cases, titanium rods, specially fabricated cranks and bearing to suit, unobtainium pistons, an ultra-light-weight valvetrain, multi-valve heads, a host of other trick parts, and surgical assembly by experts can make it happen! The result is a race-only bike that needs frequent rebuilds and high-rpms to make power. Modules are the least of your worries at this point.

SPORTSTERS

To 6,500 rpm: Use the early 1200 XL module. The original H-D part number was 32410-87, but it's been superseded a couple of times (check with your dealer for the latest number). This one's a dandy because it maximizes stock performance yet keeps you out of (mechanical) trouble at the same time.

Hitting 7,000 to 7,500 rpm: With a Screamin' Eagle module and carb, pipe, and free-flowing air cleaner, the "sport" gets back into a Sportster in a big way at these rpm levels. No wonder they road race 'em!

Running 8,000 rpm: If you must play this game, be rich, get a pilot's license and a Rice Rocket hunting permit, or go drag racing!

ELECTRICAL SYSTEMS
PROJECT 85 • CHOOSING AND INSTALLING AN AFTERMARKET IGNITION

 Time: 2 to 4 hours

 Tools: Timing light, clear plastic timing hole plug, appropriate wrenches, Allens, Torx, screwdrivers, and such for the particular ignition you fancy

 Talent:

 Tab: $$ to $$$$$

 Tinware: The ignition of your choice, perhaps some extra shrink-tubing, conduit, colored electrical wire, and connectors

 Tip: Remember the object of the game

PERFORMANCE GAIN: Improved starting, crisper throttle response, and reduced vibration

COMPLEMENTARY MODIFICATION: Proper ignition module and high-output coil

1 Presuming you stay with the basic battery and coil format, avoiding magnetos and other esoteric spark makers, you may find the features of the Crane HI-4 (or others like it) very much to your liking. These fit inside the cam cover (cone) and require no real attention, being both reliable and up to the task for most applications.

4 Installation begins with a study of where to mount the computer. Jacobs recommends lashing it to the front down tubes of the frame. If you choose not to use hardware provided with the kit, go get a couple of Ness chrome frame clamps and mount the unit behind the tubes rather than in front of them.

The Harley-Davidson factory stock electronic ignition is certainly serviceable, if not necessarily a paragon of high performance. By swapping the stock dual-fire ignition for an aftermarket single-fire (or multiple-fire) ignition, you can get your bike running cleaner and smoother.

The factory ignition is a dual-fire system H-D calls V-Fire III. In standard trim, an electric signal is sent from the pick-up and reluctor (also known as the sensor plate assembly and rotor) to a single dual-lead ignition coil. This roughly 20,000-volt coil promptly passes the dual-fire down both plug leads simultaneously to both cylinders. One theoretically needing the spark at precisely that moment, the other absolutely not needing any.

Other than this wasted spark, the primary performance flaw in the stock dual fire system is insufficient spark energy. The factory ignition with its relatively impotent coil averages 4 to 6 percent misfires at idle. Upgrading to a 40,000-volt coil should be first priority. Second priority is to assure the proper spark curve and rev limit for your specific purpose, which might entail swapping ignition modules (see Project 83: Selecting a High-Performance Factory Ignition Module).

To improve the stock ignition further, your next step is to swap it out for an aftermarket single-fire setup. The biggest performance advantage to a single-fire ignition is probably not the fact that each cylinder gets its own individual spark, as much as the ability to set the timing optimally for each cylinder. Treating each cylinder individually means good spark energy, elimination of the wasted spark, and inherently smoother operation. This improves starting, offers crisper throttle response, and generates less vibration, in most cases. Whether or not there is a power increase accompanying these benefits is subject to some debate. If there is, you can bet it comes primarily from proper ignition timing. When horsepower improvements show up on a dyno, it usually

2 This variation of the Crane HI-4 got so elaborate it outgrew its little brother's ability to fit in the cone. Still, the "E" version of the HI-4 has so many capabilities—single-fire, dual-fire, VOES mode, race mode, kick start, electric start, multiple spark, single spark, adjustable rev limit, several advance curves, separate cylinder timing, and even a built-in LED timing light feature—that it's veritable smorgasbord of ignition options.

3 Possibly, the only thing more sophisticated than the Crane HI-4 is Dr. Jacobs computerized Energy Pak. Capable of working with any module, it takes igniting things a step or two further. Speed and power at the coil are state of the art, but you get away from the idea of small componentry, as this photo of an early Harley-Davidson Energy Pak clearly shows.

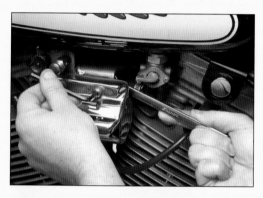

5 Once the computer is mounted securely, remove the stock coil. Wiring is next. Run the red and black stranded wires from the computer directly to the battery, but don't plug the fuse in. Now route the black lead from the computer up to the stock coil wires. Cut off excess length. The green wire connects to the negative (blue) wire from the original coil, the red wire to the positive wire. You don't have to solder these connections, but it's a good idea.

6 Now bolt up the Jacobs coil and hook up the black and white wires. It makes no difference which lead goes to which post, but you do want a good connection so use star-type lockwashers under the screws. If you route the wiring from the computer up along the frame tube and under the fuel tank, it will allow good access to the fuse. If you choose to run the wiring down under the primary and up to the battery, be aware the fuse case and the wires could be more vulnerable. Make sure those red/black wires wind up encased in a protective sheath, mainly to prevent chafing against the frame in the areas where the wire is zip-tied to the tubes. Finally, make up the spark plug wires and attach them. Since both wires connect at the front, the wires were routed behind the coil for a somewhat neater appearance. When the installation is complete, you finish off by inserting the fuse.

stems from the simple ability to alter rear cylinder timing a few degrees, which is impossible with the factory arrangement.

The next level of ignition performance is multiple spark discharge (MSD), a system that custom tailors spark requirements within the individual cylinders. Most high performance ignitions, whether dual- or single-fire, are engineered to give a serious jolt at high engine speeds, which is fine for racing but not as ideal on a street bike. At low rpms, the fuel-air mixture slows down to a relative crawl. In an H-D's 3 1/2-inch bore, the burn at lower rpms is often incomplete. If you add more bore, this problem is magnified.

Dual-plug heads ignite the mixture from two points rather than one and solve this problem reason-ably well, although they are not cheap. Unfortunately, they require an altered full advance timing to work best, and if you happen to lose one of your two plugs, you might find a hole in your piston.

No such problems with multiple-fire (MSD) setups. They address these issues correctly by using the time available at low rpm to send as many as 9 or 10 sparks into the chamber at idle, ensuring a complete burn. As rpm rises, flow speeds up, and the spark duration decreases accordingly.

Installation of virtually any choice you make is a matter of following the maker's instructions, but the pre-planning should always include checking out a bike that has the system you're considering.

ELECTRICAL SYSTEMS
PROJECT 86 • OPTIMIZING YOUR VOES

Time: 1/2 to 1 hour

Tools: Screwdrivers, multimeter, and a Mity-Vac

Talent:

Tab: $

Tinware: A new retaining nut for the VOES and silicone seal

Tip: VOES adjustment is pretty much a thing of the past and has very little value for stock Hogs. When increased compression and trick ignition advance curves need to be balanced, however, it does help liven things up.

PERFORMANCE GAIN: Improved throttle response and reduced pinging

COMPLEMENTARY MODIFICATION: Performance ignition module, compression increase, and high-octane fuel

1 This simple-looking device nesting the vee of your V-twin cylinders, the VOES, is actually a major player the ignition game. It senses the load you'r putting on your engine and tells the ignitic to "back off" before anybody gets hurt. Th is sound engineering but not without its ve own tuning potential, since sometimes the VOES backs things off more and quicker than it has to.

The Vacuum Operated Electrical Switch (VOES) is the trigger mechanism for all Evo Harleys using the factory V-Fire III solid-state ignition. The VOES takes a vacuum reading from the intake and converts that message from the engine into an electrical signal that is sent to the ignition module. That, in turn, tells the module to crank up the advance proportionately. There are two curves built into the module's microprocessor. The low-vacuum curve (hard running, wide open throttle) kicks in the retard function, and the high-vacuum curve (cruising, steady throttle) allows maximum advance. The module merely picks which curve to use based on an on-or-off signal from the VOES.

Four different VOES modules are used on Harleys, with three of the four having different switch points based on vacuum levels required to open and close them. For instance, 1984 FLTs were equipped with an A-curve module and a VOES that switched at 7 inches of mercury, a setting that was designed to cope with the heavy payloads and lower engine speeds a typical dresser has to deal with.

Well, today, the FLT uses a D-curve module, as do all Big Twins to 1995 (and a P curve from 1996–on), but still employs a VOES with a high switch point. The VOES

on FLT-series bikes switches at 5.5 inches of mercury, while all the other models have a VOES that switches at 4.0 inches. By swapping the VOES you can get the module to trigger earlier or later than it does now.

The VOES lives in the V of the cylinders (with it's black ground wire running to one of the left side head bolts), generally close behind the carb and slightly above the intake manifold. Swapping as per your shop manual instructions takes about 20 minutes but usually isn't necessary, since it's possible to adjust the VOES that's on the bike right now. That process isn't in the manual!

If you remove the VOES, you can adjust it by removing the plastic/wax plug that covers the adjusting screw. With a good vacuum gauge and an ohmmeter you can "test" incrementally greater or lesser vacuum settings to see if that helps create the responsive behavior you want. Simply put the vacuum to the VOES until the ohmmeter reads zero, check the amount of vacuum it takes to do that, and record the reading. The rule of thumb for vacuum tuning the VOES effect on the engine is "If it pings lower it! If it lags, raise it!"

The non-sanctioned test for pinging/lagging is pretty simple, if a bit brutal: with a normal payload, get the bike to operating temperature, filled with the fuel of choice in the tank, and take off from a standstill in second gear. Yes, that tends to lug the motor, but you'll know after a couple of attempts if the beast is easily able to do this or if it gives you fits when you try. This crude test and a VOES adjustment may not make a giant difference, but it can help fine-tune the ignition. Just be sure to re-seal the adjusting screw with silicone when you've got it the way you want it.

The following chart lists the major VOES types and the switch points as a reference for adjustment. Don't panic if the H-D part number for your model/year is not the same as the one on this list; the factory will change part numbers at the drop of a hat. The main concern is that it has the proper color code and that it will install correctly.

Factory Equipment VOES Specifications

Color Code	Switch Point	Models
None	7.0 inches mercury	Early Evo FLT (1984)
Red	5.5 inches mercury	Late Evo FLT
White	4.0 inches mercury	Evo FXR and XL
Blue	4.0 inches mercury	Evo Softail

ELECTRICAL SYSTEMS

PROJECT 87 • UPGRADING YOUR HORN

 Time: 1 hour

 Tools: Wrenches, Allens, drill, 9/16-inch bit, and wire cutter/crimper

 Talent:

 Tab: $

 Tinware: Rubber mounts and spacers; perhaps a 6-volt horn

 Tip: Horns are more easily heard if they are not buried somewhere out of sight on the machine

 PERFORMANCE GAIN: Whole decibels—and the extra safety that provides

COMPLEMENTARY MODIFICATION: An extra horn

1 The ineffective stock horn is why you see all those bumper stickers proclaiming that "Loud pipes save lives!" That's supposed to be the horn's job. An easy, unobtrusive upgrade that really pumps up the volume is to swap the stocker for a 6-volt unit.

2 A fancy aftermarket unit like this one often looks better than it sounds. In this case, the one saving grace is its location. Instead of being hidden away in the bowels of the bike, it's up front, where what little honk it offers can be heard clearly if not loudly.

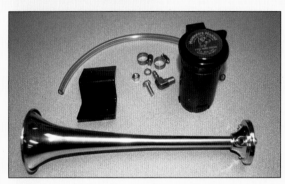

3 The high-dollar solution is to mount an air horn or two. Folks will think they just cut off a 50,000-pound diesel truck rather than a nearly invisible motorcycle. About the only thing to worry about with a horn arrangement like this is where exactly to put it all. This is no problem on dressers but is a bit of a chore on Sportsters and some FX models where space is at a premium. Still, loud horns really save lives, so take some time and find some room.

Early-model (1991 to 1993) Dyna-Glides have a terrible horn. All these models can manage is a frog-like croak. Solving the problem is easier without draping aftermarket horns all over your bike.

On Dyna models, the basic problem is that the horn isn't free to resonate. The solution is to rubber-mount it. Here's how:

Remove the battery box from the bike just way the service manual tells you.

Remove the horn. Now's a good time to test it by touching the horn connections directly to a 12-volt battery. It should bleep pretty ferociously. (If you feel the need, you can adjust the tone with the small adjusting screw in the back.)

Drill the big mounting hole out to 9/16 inch.

Install a grommet (#11458) in the hole.

Stuff a spacer (#5883) into the grommet.

Reinstall the horn but be sure to use a flat washer (#6702) under the original horn retaining nut.

When you get the whole kit and caboodle lashed back on the bike, be careful not to let anything (for instance, the battery cable or vent hose) touch the horn cover. Otherwise, you just wasted your time.

There's another trick, and this one works on all models. Use a 6-volt horn. If you're not in the habit of holding the horn on for several minutes every time you blow it, this works very well indeed. Twelve volts "pushing" a 6-volt horn is LOUD!

ELECTRICAL SYSTEMS
PROJECT 88 • TROUBLE-SHOOTING ELECTRICS

 Time: 1/2 hour to 3 hours

 Tools: Multimeter, 12-volt test light, and hydrometer

 Talent: 👷👷

 Tab: $ (fixing problems may cost more than finding them)

 Tinware: Spare connectors, electrical tape, fuses, and circuit breakers

 Tip: Starting problem are usually battery-related; light problems are most typically bulbs (check them first), grounds, or shorts

 PERFORMANCE GAIN: Once something has bitten you, don't let it happen twice; if there's anyplace on a Harley that can benefit from overkill it's electrical repair

COMPLEMENTARY MODIFICATION: Regular maintenance of all the electrics—coat bare stuff with something (finger nail polish, Battery Kote, or grease) to keep it from corrosion or rust; replace the battery every 12 to 18 months

1 You think you've got trouble? Finding an intermittent short in a mass of wiring resembling the dashboard of a loaded Cadillac can be a weekend project in and of itself. Don't panic! No matter how complex (or simple, on anything but a bagger) the wiring may seem, take your trusty test light (or multimeter), a wiring diagram, and a bucket full of common sense to the party and start looking for the cheapest, simplest things you can find. Nine out of 10 times you'll find not only the devil, but the problem, in the details. A loose connector or a chafed wire are the prime suspects in the search. A major component failure (other than an old battery) is the culprit less than 10 percent of the time.

Ninety percent of the problems that will stop your ride alongside the road are electrical. A notorious few of these are reasonably predictable and preventable.

By far the largest percentage of road failures comes down to a blown or dead battery. Nobody likes to mess with 'em, so batteries usually suffer from neglect, not to mention heat and vibration. Batteries are also known to shake a cable loose given the slightest opportunity. One of the first things to check in the event of a misfire are the battery cables. They love to work loose, so check 'em often and keep 'em clean.

The stator, rotor, and regulator/rectifier (or Voltpack, in Harley-babble) are the three major players in the charging system, and they typically quit playing without telling you the game's over. A likely suspect is the plug that connects the regulator/rectifier to the alternator, which can get unplugged, corroded, or rotted away. Run a second, or "jumper," ground from the regulator/recti-

fier to the alternator to test if the wire is conducting electricity. The best preventive measure you can take is to monitor your system with a voltmeter, ammeter, or idiot light.

The most valuable advice on this hair-tearing subject is simple: If you're ever confronted with foul play by your electrics, always start with the simplest, cheapest thing it could possibly be and don't assume a catastrophic failure of a major component has occurred. Electricity works just like water in that it takes the path of least resistance and always flows downhill to ground. Try to paint a mental picture of this process when dealing with all your volts, amps, and ohms, and with luck, some common sense, a diagram or two, and minimum tools, you can get it wired.

Time: 1 hour

Tools: Dial-back timing light and a decent timing plug

Talent: 👷👷

Tab: 0 to $

Tinware: Perhaps a different ignition module (see Project 83: Selecting a High-Performance Factory Ignition Module)

Tip: You want to know the difference between advance curves? Here's a crude way to find out

PERFORMANCE GAIN: Proper advance curves mean excellent starting, low-speed manners, and improved performance acceleration below 3,000 rpm

COMPLEMENTARY MODIFICATION: Hot coil, good plug wires, and proper spark plugs

Advance curves in electronic ignitions are key to how your bike performs below 3,000 rpm. In most cases, you can go with the ignition module recommended in project 83. Unfortunately, H-D has withheld the information on the curve of some of the latest ignition modules. If you want to know what kind of curve these babies offer, you'll have to measure it yourself.

Exactly how do you map an advance curve? Well, this method is a bit crude yet better than not knowing or being able to figure it out at all. The data collected won't be precise; if you do map your module's curve, be prepared to repeat the process until you get the same answer two or three times. Once you do, you'll have a rough idea of what goes on with electronic ignition curves.

In order to map your own advance curve, you need to:

• Find a suitable quality "dial back" timing light. These are available from Matco, Sun, and Snap-On.

• Find a reasonably decent timing plug, or a plastic rain coat! It gets damn messy with all that oil spraying over you. None of the readily available plastic plugs are all that great frankly, but unless you want to try making one out of PVC, there's not much choice. The PVC should have threads tapped onto it so you can screw it lightly into the timing hole and be about 3 inches long. You may even want to super glue some kind of clear lens on the end, say, an old flashlight lens. Once in place, nearly touching the flywheels, hook up the timing light and . . .

• Find a means to hold the throttle absolutely steady. On S2 Thunderbolts, you can install a Harley throttle lock (#56397-74C); other models can be jury rigged with pliers and a heavy rubber band. Plier jaws go around the throttle grip, handles over the brake lever, and rubber band around the handles, tight enough to hold the throttle in position.

• The timing light has a tach function, and you should go by that reading, not the one on the motorcycle. Set engine speed and shoot as per timing light instructions. Shoot to the (TDC) line on the flywheel, not the single or double (lazy 8) dot, when mapping a curve. What you're doing here is comparing curves—not shooting timing. Setting ignition timing is a process that differs from year to year. That you do by the book for the model/year you own. This is a different process (although it's a good idea to ensure the timing is spot on before you worry about anything else). Write down the results, and you have a map.

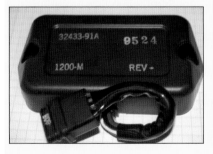

M-CURVE

rpm	advance	advance (no VOES)
1,000	21	10
1,250	24	10
1,500	34	10
1,750	34	12
2,000	34	14
2,500	39	15
3,000	40 (full advance)	17

Module: Stock 1200 five-speed, either the #32433-91A seven-pin with 6,250-rpm limit (stock on 1995 model Federal S2) or #32433-94A eight-pin with 6,250-rpm limit.

Note: The timing figures on all of these charts were shot with a dial-back timing light through a clear plastic timing plug at the line on the crankshaft. There are two timing marks on those flywheels: the line and a pair of side-by-side dots or circles commonly called a "lazy 8." Until 1995, the line was used, shot at 1,350 to 1,650 rpm. From 1996 and on, the lazy 8 was used, but at a much lower 850 to 1,050 rpm (idle speed). For your purposes, when mapping the curve and consistency, shoot to the line.

K-CURVE

rpm	advance	advance (no VOES)
1,000	28	n/a
1,250	28	n/a
1,500	32	10
1,750	35	12
2,000	37	15
2,500	40 (full advance)	15
3,000	40	18
3,500	40	18

Module: Screamin' Eagle #32420-87A or B with 8,000-rpm rev limit and seven-pin plug, #32420-94 with 8,000-rpm limit and eight-pin plug, #32597-96 with 6,800-rpm limit and seven-pin plug, or #32598-96 with 6,800-rpm limit and eight-pin plug.
Note: This module is a stand-by. It works well with open-chamber 1200 heads. Just the same, it's not the hot-tip unit for S1/Thunderstorm heads with their different chamber shapes and higher mechanical compression.

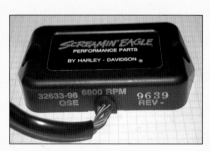

Q-CURVE

rpm	advance	advance (no VOES)
1,000	20	17
1,250	21	17
1,500	21	17
1,750	23	17
2,000	24	17
2,500	26	19
3,000	28	22
3,500	32	24
4,000	35 (full advance)	n/a

Module: Screamin' Eagle #32633-96 with 6,800-rpm limit, Buell Race Kit #32680-96Y with 6,800-rpm limit and eight-pin plug, or #32465-95A with 6,250-rpm limit and eight-pin plug (stock on 1995 California-model S2).
This is the hot item for Buells (except for S2s with stock heads), but its advance curve may be the same as for the stock unit, offering merely a higher rev limit. This is a game the factory has resorted to more and more as they fine-tune advance curves: Find one that works and then offer it with various rev limits as the only change. Late-model Harley Big Twins and Sportsters are treated this way. Why not Buells?

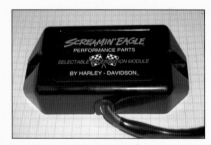

#32654-98 "SELECTABLE CURVE"

rpm	C-1	C-2	C-3	C-4
1,000	24	25	27	25
1,250	27	27	27	29
1,500	37	35	34	31
1,750	38	37	35	34
2,000	38	38	35	35
2,500	38	38	35	35
3,000	40	40	38	38

There are significant differences in the curves, but they don't necessarily give you performance gain. The module has a retard switch position, presumably for folks stuck in Mexico or somewhere where the octane of the fuel is actually worse than California's. Any other use tends to escape logic, and you can't flip the switches without removing the module. What's more, when put in that mode:
1,000 rpm = 23 degrees
1,250 rpm = 24 degrees
1,500 rpm = 29 degrees
1,750 rpm = 29 degrees, and stays there on curve one

1998 AND LATER MODULES

On 1998 and later Sportsters, Harley has done away with separate modules entirely. Current wisdom says they can do it all with the little unit that lives in the cone. Screamin' Eagle versions also fit in the cone. With two rev limits, 6,800 and 7,500, where do you want to go today? You could most likely make this piece (or an aftermarket equivalent such as the Crane HI-4) work on your Hyper-Hog with some significant rewiring.

PERSONAL TOUCHES

It's no secret that you can build an entire V-Twin motorcycle, a Harley clone, if you will, and never use a factory part. No other manufactured original has this kind of aftermarket support. The options for personalizing your machine are almost limitless, and this freedom of expression in steel and alloy is possibly Harley-Davidson's main attraction. The factory provides a basic kit, but you finish it in your own image.

For most of us, making a Hog truly personal amounts to adding small details, a little one here, a bit more there, and soon enough that Harley becomes a nice reflection of you.

"Personal Touches" provides you with a sampling of some of the things you can do to keep your bike looking sharp and make it unique. Bear in mind that the options for customization are unlimited, the variations endless. The subject is too broad and deep to do more than stick a toe into it in a few pages. This section's intent is to give you a couple of ideas that you can grow into a personal vision for your bike. After all, at the end of the day, it's up to you.

PROJECT 90 • CLEAN AND SHINE

Time: 4 to 5 hours

Tools: Bucket, rags, towels, brushes, cleaners, and waxes

Talent:

Tab: $

Tinware: Plastic bags and rubber bands to keep water out

Tip: Rather than think front to back, think top to bottom

PERFORMANCE GAIN: Many more compliments per mile

COMPLEMENTARY MODIFICATION: A soft motorcycle cover and a heated garage

1 The weekend project of choice for most proud owners is a thorough clean and shine. To do that takes as many special tools as anything mechanical. You need a variety of cleansers and polishes to go with that tube of elbow grease. Using all of them, you can have the bike sparkling from the chrome to the leather and everywhere in between in no time (okay, 6 to 8 hours; it's a labor of love isn't it?). Oh, one word about wax. Fresh virginal paint with no blemishes whatsoever can be waxed with silicone-based products. It seals the surface so well, however, that it will trap anything under the wax like a fly in amber. That's why official Harley-Davidson wax is carnauba based without silicones. Carnauba can be buffed back to clean out those little imperfections, and then a re-wax keeps the shine without keeping the dirt trapped.

You can't keep your bike new forever. Anyone that rides gets their machine dirty. But you can keep it clean, and a suitable amount of attention to basic cosmetic upkeep can make your sled look as good as new, even decades down the road.

The place to start is with a standard hand wash. Avoid coin-operated cleaning because the caustic chemicals in the detergent aren't good for most surfaces, and there's a real problem if the stuff sneaks into brakes, wheel bearings, carbs, and electrics. Don't go there! Stick with a bucket full of dish soap, some sponges and rags, and good old elbow grease.

Speaking of grease, if your bike is especially dirty or greasy, you'll need degreaser to get rid of the heavy stuff. Selecting a degreaser from the myriad of toxic spray containers can be tough. Try to find a good solvent that will not harm your paint; degreasers with bleach or reactive chemicals could cause hazing and bubbling of the paint. Be careful how and where you try these before you glop them all over the sled. Cosmoline remover dissolves just about everything and will not harm the paint. Gunk is an emulsifier that turns grease into water-soluble foam and works brilliantly, as it always has, if you can get past the smell.

If your Hog has been rolling around in the mud, try a soft bristle brush or toothbrush. Bugs are best removed with plain soap and water and gentle applications of one of those nylon sponge scrubber things you use on dishes. By the way, good carnauba wax will help prevent bugs and stuff from sticking to your bike in the first place.

If you plan on applying anti-corrosion or dressing products, do this before the final wash; it makes a mess! S-100 has a good product for anti-corrosion protection. It makes wrinkle black paint look great too. A shot of WD-40 or a good dressing like Scooter Douche or Hog Spit will make it blacker and shinier than ever. Armorall is a kind of jack-of-all-trades in this arena too. Using a small brush for the tight spots, hit the oil lines, plastic chain, belt guards, fender flaps, and any black plastic parts, and you'll get a dark, rich satiny look from these otherwise dullards.

After shampooing and scrubbing your bike, it's time for a rubdown and blow-dry. If a blow-dryer or air line isn't available, a quick spin around the block will get the job done. Dry it off with a clean, soft towel or a chamois.

Next, polish the frame. Protect All (a good spray-on polish) works well here. Be sure to let it haze over, then buff it out to avoid streaks. You can use S100 here, as well, or any spray polish you have faith in, for that matter, but frames are a bear to do with paste wax, so stick with something logical. It's the most tedious task of the bunch, but when the frame looks good, it makes everything else look better.

One reason chrome stays popular in the Harley world is that it's dead easy to keep clean. Any proprietary chrome polish, Simichrome, Majic-Mix, Mother's, or S-100 will make good chrome look great in minutes. If your chrome has started to pit, A) you waited too long to clean and seal it, B) hard rubbing with a piece of tinfoil can clean it up surprisingly well.

Polished aluminum, on the other hand, loses that factory plastic coating relatively fast, no matter what you do. Then there's a problem to solve. You either respray the part with clear top coat or you strip the rest of the plastic off the part (chemical paint stripper for big parts or fingernail polish remover for little ones) and resign yourself to a life of continuous polishing. But you should realize that one good thing about aluminum is that once it "skins" over with oxidation, it's protected for life. That's the opposite of most metals (and chrome), where the same thing signals the beginning of the end. The point being, if you can stand the (ugly) look of it, aluminum takes no care to protect, only to prettify.

For the baked-on boot bacon on your exhaust, use very fine steel wool, polishing compound, and a little cleaner wax or aluminum polish (the tinfoil thing works pretty well here too). If it's real thick, don't do anything right away. Ride the bike for a few days and see how much will burn clean off on its own. Patience pays off here, believe it or not. For what little's left, carefully try a razor blade at an acute angle, then finish with steel wool. No matter what, if it comes to this, you will not come way with unblemished chrome.

Next, move onto the paint. For heavy scratches and oxidation, use an electric buffer and very little pressure; let the tool do the work. Routine waxing by hand with carnauba is the single best thing you can do for factory paint work. Carnauba is a natural wax that can be cleaned off and stripped back to the paint without difficulty, so if you need to repair a blemish, you can get at it. Silicon-based waxes aren't so friendly. They do, in fact, shine brilliantly, but later on, after a few coats, your paint has been hermetically-sealed, blemishes, dirt, anything on the paint is buried under glass, permanently.

Finish the job using a good leather cleaner and conditioner on the seat, and properly dress the tires. There are specialty tire cleaners and dressings galore, but Armorall works quite well, as long as you don't get it on the tread. And Sno-Pruf is about the only leather dressing that compares with Harley's own #98261-91V. This stuff makes things really slippery as well, so use your head.

Finally, presume you'd do this more often if you didn't have to get on your hands and knees. Consider getting a lift to make the whole job easier. Try to find a lift that's compatible with your machine, your needs, and your situation. The simplest is the "over-center" single-bar lift, or "quik-stand." They are cheap, versatile, and handy—if you're good at finding a fair center of gravity one-handed. The castor-wheeled, bottle-jack-operated double-rail lifts, like "Hog-lift," while more stable, mobile, and easy to "single hand," can still be tricky. Make sure you're not trying to lift from under your pipes, and watch out for kickstands in funky places. Once you're comfortable with that, get comfortable yourself on a rolling stool that sits you about midway up the scooter's side and go for it.

PERSONAL TOUCHES
PROJECT 91 • SWAPPING TURN SIGNALS

Time: 2 to 4 hours

Tools: Wire stripper/crimper tool, shrink tubing, plastic conduit, multimeter, soldering equipment, and electrical tape

Talent: ▮▮

Tab: $ to $$

Tinware: Spare 16-gauge wire in yellow, white, black, and red; butt connectors; Scotch-Lock connectors; and spade connectors in various sizes

Tip: Think small, but brilliantly

PERFORMANCE GAIN: Increased visibility

COMPLEMENTARY MODIFICATION: Taillamps, head-lamps, and running lights that match

1 It would be silly to try to show you every conceivable turn signal trick or trick turn signal on the market. Instead, you must decide if you want a signal that can be identified as one like this one or one that is a bit more subtle.

2 Some turn signals are so subtle that they don't appear to be turn signals at all. Depending on state laws, you may or may not be required to have turn signals. If you want to keep the function without the fuss, it's hard to beat turn signals that are built into the license frame. They are unobtrusive until you need them; bright halogen lamps make them much more visible than you would expect.

Turn signals have many aliases, but the number of names pales in comparison to the number of turn signal styles available. That's because (and it's no secret) stock turn sigs are less than aesthetically inspired. But they follow one fairly important guideline—they're legal! Most replacement signals on the market are not DOT-legal and are intended to be used as decoration or marker lights only, in conjunction with, not instead of, "real" turn signals. Even if the law in your part of the planet is pretty slack about it, it pays to make sure you check your local laws and regulations and avoid the ticket-bait stuff before you make a decision.

The second consideration revolves around the flashing medium. Up until 1991, most Hogs employed automotive flasher units. These are relatively insensitive to changes in lamp amperage, or wattage. You might need to step up to a heavy-duty version, or surprisingly, down to a light-duty one for your specific application, but that's it. The 1991 and newer models don't have it so easy. That nifty self-canceling feature that was introduced that year comes with a little control box, a turn signal module that has a difficult time accommodating any bulb changes. There are aftermarket kits out there that usually consist of yet another module, fool-ing the factory unit into working. It's no great hardship to install one of these, but it just adds one more thing to cope with when swapping signals.

The final consideration is plain old visibility. Poor choices in lamps lead to not just illegal but invisible signaling. And size may not have much to do with visibility. Some very petite lights have very bright halogen bulbs; others, unfortunately, use the same bulb you have in your neutral light, and you know how dim that can be on a sunny day. The point is, don't sacrifice everything for the sake of style. Why bother with signals at all if they wind up being no more effective or law abiding than none?

Even something as simple as installing a flat lens in place of the stock one can add a custom touch. Just relocating the stock signals on a Springer can improve the looks. And it's true of other models as well. Kits are offered by all the major accessory houses, so it's not a major trick. A stock narrow-glide front end can have its signals mounted on either the upper or lower triple trees, and for late-model 39-millimeter forks, the aftermarket makes short versions of the stock stems that pull the lamps in nicely. Just ensure that there's no contact with the gas tank when you start moving signals around. It's no fun to have clean lamps and dings in the paint.

In the rear, the results of a signal swap can be dramatic. Lamps incorporated into the fender rails or built into a license plate frame are the cleanest of all, but they require more work to install. Some outfits make lamp assemblies that "blend" into the design of the fender rails. These are often as easy to deal with as stock signals, and though sporting a smaller reflector area, they are far brighter, if you get the right bulb design. It pays to check out other folks' setups for fit and candlepower before you commit to a change in yours.

Time: 1 to 3 hours

Tools: Wire stripper/crimper tool, shrink tubing, plastic conduit, multimeter, soldering equipment, and electrical tape

Talent:

Tab: $ to $$

Tinware: Spare 16-gauge wire in yellow, white, black, and red; butt connectors; Scotch-Lock connectors; and spade connectors in various sizes

Tip: Soldered connections are best; strive for quality bulbs, sockets, and ground connections; use dielectric grease in sockets

PERFORMANCE GAIN: Better visibility from the rear

COMPLEMENTARY MODIFICATION: Custom turn signals, running lights, and higher-powered headlamps

1. Since it's no surprise that there's nearly as much choice in taillamps as in turn signals, you should think of them as a team. Again, the question becomes do you want them to live apart, as on this stock setup with the factory "tombstone" lamp and DOT-legal lamps, or more closely together?

2. This aftermarket "beehive" lamp and yet another version of the license plate turn signals takes the "closer together" philosophy. The four most basic taillamp designs are the trusty tombstone (both old and new versions), the bumbling "beehive" (as shown), the cunning "cat's-eye" for bobbed Softail and Dyna rear fenders, and the tasty looking but unnamed fender filler you saw in the turn signal photo in the Project 91. But this just scratches the surface of what's available. Doss, Ness, and a dozen others have introduced new designs that are gaining popularity every day.

The taillight that comes stock on all new Harleys (except the Springer Heritage) dates from 1973. The one they used before that lasted from 1955 to 1972. Coming up with something new and different is up to you. That's okay because hanging a new taillight on your sled is one of the easier tricks you can do. The light is held in place by two tin speed-nuts, and you can get to them from underneath the fender (which is good, as they will occasionally loosen from vibration).

Okay, there is one taillight design, but four different rear fenders (again, not counting the reinvented "tombstone" light used on the Heritage Springer): standard FX and XL, Fat Bob, FL dresser, and custom.

So generalized steps for removing the one taillamp from any of the four fenders is to first disconnect the negative battery cable, and then loosen the mounting bolts but don't remove them. Carefully strip the plastic shrouding around the taillamp wires, allowing access to the individual wires. Before you start whittlin' on the wires, though, reach under the fender and loosen the harness from a few of the metal wire retainers to get some slack. Pull the slack through and make your cuts, leaving about 1 1/2 inches of wire

sticking out of the fender and taillamp, just in case you ever want to reattach the stock lamp. On all models except Dyna Wide Glides, you'll only have two wires to deal with. The Wide Glide has a third wire for ground. Now, take the mounting bolts out, lift off the taillamp, and you're ready to mount the replacement. But first you must choose your new light, and here are some recommendations.

STANDARD FENDERS

There are certain "old standbys," like the ever-popular tombstone, the old beehive, and the cat's-eye. But that's only the beginning. There are at least a dozen choices from Hot Top, Ness, CCI, Drag Specialties, and others, with more to choose from every month it seems. Some, usually the old standbys, will hook up in half an hour with no trouble. Others take longer, don't fit as well, or demand a little ingenuity to install.

The tombstone taillight kit uses a unique chrome-plated steel mount to allow the simplest installation on stock rear fenders. The kit comes with all the necessary hardware and two mounting gaskets. It's a bolt-on. A flush-mount taillight, as slick as it looks, is usually a major project to install. You need to whack the stock mounting bracket out of the fender to install it, and there may be additional cutting and grinding required to get the great fit. Use a Dremel tool and wear safety glasses.

FAT BOB FENDERS

The Softail-type Fat Bob rear fender is a perennial favorite, and certain taillamps make it look even better. The taillight and license bracket on a Fat Bob are the same as on other bikes, simply mounted upside down. What's different is the wire truss arrangement that's bolted on a Fat Bob fender by the four rearmost fender strut bolts. To remove it, reach under the fender, with the bike off the ground, and use a thin wrench. From there, nothing's tough to reach, and the whole assembly comes out easier. Again, you have a bunch of choices for replacement,

but the two that stand out are the cat's-eye and the one without a name that fills the entire contour and follows the flip of the fender. Both are easy to mount on Softail fenders. If you have a Dyna Wide Glide, you must find designs unique to that fender because Softail-types don't fit.

FL DRESSER FENDERS

Watch carefully which design you choose for these fenders, or you'll have problems with the aluminum bar that carries the rear turn signals. And it's not easy to work around this piece either. The dresser rear fender has indents and bulges made into the sheet metal that preclude some of the more popular choices of aftermarket lamps. Even if you remove the turn signal bar to make room for the taillight, you'll have those two indents where the bar was staring right back at you. And filling, then repainting, the rear fender, is a lot of effort and expense just to avoid looking at them.

CUSTOM FENDERS

You ready for this? There's not much help to be found here, aside from the common sense that says design the custom rear fender and taillight at the same time to be used together. Then fit the whole thing to the bike before you bother to paint or chrome any of it. Many's the time a setup looks good on the workbench, but once it's on the machine, something's too low, too high, crooked, or just plain ugly. Things are known to work loose, crack, or malfunction too, so even though choices are unlimited at this stage, make sure common sense isn't in short supply.

PERSONAL TOUCHES
PROJECT 93 • CHOOSING SISSYBARS AND RACKS

 Time: 1 to 2 hours

 Tools: Hand tools only

 Talent:

 Tab: $$$ to $$$$$

 Tinware: The rack or sissybar

 Tip: Keep the payload between the axles and don't overload

⚠ **PERFORMANCE GAIN:** Increased carrying capacity

COMPLEMENTARY MODIFICATION: Saddlebags

As Harleys have evolved from rigid frames to Softails, the sissybar has become more sophisticated. Most are mounted much more solidly, some look like an integral part of the bike, and detachable sissybars are out there as well. The pitfall is complexity, and most sissybars these days involve more than a couple of bolts to put them in service.

SISSYBARS

The key to choosing one of these lies with two questions: Will it hold any weight and will it fit with other accessories such as saddlebags? The detatchables that the factory sells are a lesson in parts picking unto themselves, with required attachment kits that the parts person may or may not be aware of, for certain models, years, and equipment. If you know what you need and can get it all from one source that provides integrated designs for future changes and additions, you did well.

A sissybar bag can give you a handy spot to put a few small items. Popular versions like the T-bag can be hung so the weight is on the passenger seat, allowing a bit more capacity, but don't overload a sissybar bag, no matter where it is hung.

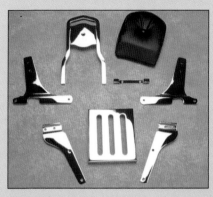

1 The new trend is toward detachable accessories, available for all models and owners who only have a need for such stuff on occasion. The rest of the time they can run around "clean" and unencumbered. There's still a lot to be said for permanent-mount accessories though, since they look good enough to leave onboard and usually are stronger so they can carry more weight. Style is one thing; payload is another. If you're contemplating a rack or sissybar, it helps to research the advantages and shortcomings of both types.

2 If you can't buy what you need, build it. If you build it and build it comfortable and stout enough, they will come—passengers, that is. Of course, with them comes the extra weight and baggage that so often overwhelms the store-bought stuff. This homemade contraption holds plenty, whether people or things, and has been beefed up accordingly. Even this monster has broken in service a couple of times when required to hold nearly 100 pounds.

LUGGAGE RACKS

If you're one of those people who tries to pack everything onto your bike, you need a luggage rack. The rack more than earns its keep even during jaunts to the store, let alone those long road trips. Keep in mind, however, that they are engineered with a weight limit of only 15 pounds. You choose to ignore that simple reality for long, and something's gonna give. It's not always the rack that breaks either—it's the alloy supports to which they are attached that sometimes break (usually when you're hauling a passenger), and those supports are all that hold the seat and fender off the rear wheel. Break them while riding, and you will crash.

A further reason for concern: Whatever you load on the rack is hanging off the back of the bike too. Not exactly textbook weight distribution. Realistically, then, there are limits. Overloading a rack is pulling the pin on a grenade—your steering gets so light it's unsafe, and stuff can break and fall off. If your expected payload will exceed prudent parameters, think about tank bags and racks.

PERSONAL TOUCHES
PROJECT 94 • DECODING HARLEY PAINT COLORS

Time: Several hours of work and several days of waiting

Tools: Harley paint, primer, base coat, and clear topcoat; sandpaper; buffer; chemical stripper; rubber sanding pad or block; paper towel; clean cloth towels; polishing compound; wax; assorted cleaners; and glaze

Talent: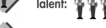

Tab: $ to $$$

Tinware: Plastic sheeting, scrap lumber, and heat lamp

Tip: Patience, cleanliness, and methodical preparation and execution are the keys to success

PERFORMANCE GAIN: Can make the eyes pop out of your head

COMPLEMENTARY MODIFICATION: Chromed, polished aluminum, stainless trim, and a nice soft motorcycle cover

Harley has done some memorable things with color. Basic black is a given, of course, and some form of red is with us every year as well. Past that, blue is next in the popularity polls, but what shade? From there, it's anybody's guess. Remember Candy Root Beer? The Khaki Green with Burnt Orange that graced the Shovelhead Heritage of 1981? Then there's the outrageous Black and Bright Orange, colors that have graced Harley's race bikes, as well as a few streeters, since time began. There is no end in sight either. How do you keep track of all these choices and combinations? Better yet, how does H-D manage it?

A favorite piece of Harley lore is that just a few years back, The Motor Company built a brand-new, high-tech paint facility at a cost exceeding the amount spent to buy the entire company from AMF in 1981. Not that the paint shop was a frivolous expenditure. The new paint plant was absolutely necessary to Harley's strategy for future growth, and an answer to an immediate problem.

Harley's resurgence required that they somehow increase the supply to keep up with burgeoning demand. The biggest single bottleneck to that increase was their somewhat antiquated and over-stressed paint process. In the early 1980s, conventional, labor-intensive painting techniques were okay. By the mid-1980s they weren't. Running the paint department two or three shifts a day, the company's color process still couldn't keep up with an assembly plant running only one 8-hour day shift. Something had to be done. Hence, the new high-capacity automated paint "factory."

As with any innovation, initially, there were a few bugs. You may recall that in 1992, the new Dyna Custom appeared with a silver frame in the brochures. As it turned out, there were only 200 machines made with frames that color. The rest had conventional black-painted frames. The reason? The metallic pigment in the silver would "magnetize" in the electrically charged paint bath and travel to the joints in the frame, thus leaving the corners dark and the middle of the tubes nearly white. The 200 silver-framed FXDCs that were shipped were hand-painted. Setting up the processes and the "flow" of the new hardware led to a few breakdowns and stoppages as well at first. And for a few months delays in shipping new units to anxious dealers were directly attributable to initial shortcomings of the new system.

That's history now, as Harley comfortably builds 100,000-plus bikes a year, each and every one of the new machines coated with the best paint in the business. Harley has also developed and applied powder-coat processes used on frames and black-wrinkle engines.

When it comes to paint and coatings, The Motor Company is the standard of the motorcycle industry. The quality is so good nowadays that owners should think very carefully before they haul off and repaint. The factory finish is a multiple-coat, positively-charged, electro-mechanically applied, baked-on wonder of unsurpassed durability. It resists ultraviolet breakdown and subsequent "sun-fade." Replacement parts are painted to an exact match, and a factory-painted spare can be cheaper than a good conventional repaint too. And the index of refraction (gloss) is something like 90 to 94 percent.

It's all done with a simple two-letter code. Presented here in all its glory, for what's probably the first time outside a dealership, is a list of all the codes for the last 10 years. Along with the current list of available "Air-Dry" paints from H-D, this might help you keep the factory paint on your Hog. It might also get you thinking about other possible combinations for any "genuine" custom paint work you may be considering. Heck, if nothing else, you can hang onto the list for the next couple of decades and win trivia contests or sell "secret codes" to high bidders who want an accurate restoration. A handy reference for some dandy decoration!

Okay, you've had your fun picking out a color scheme. Now, to work!

The first rule in painting is cleanliness. One speck of dirt in the middle of your fresh paint can ruin your day among other things.

First decision: to scuff or strip? With good original factory paint, all you may need to do is scuff it down a little so the new paint can adhere, but if it's old metal or a whole new plan, stripping may be required, if not preferred.

The time-honored method involves sandpaper, elbow grease, time, sweat, and persistence. A dual-action orbital sander makes it easier, but still you need commitment. Chemical stripping is easier on you and the sheet meal and often quicker. Spray or soak the part overnight, and then dip it in water to rinse it off. Wear gloves. After the water rinse it's into an iron phosphate solution for a couple of hours, which keeps the bare metal from rusting if it has to sit for more than a few days. The least recommended way to strip the metal is aluminum-oxide bead blasting. This method is useful enough, if you suspect bondo and filler, but done improperly, it can ripple the metal.

Speaking of such faux pas, the natural oil in your skin will sink into the metal and peel paint on its way back out. Wear clean rubber gloves when handling parts to be painted—clean, clean, clean! And use a degreaser on the part before applying any primer—self-etching primer. Apply each coat just thick enough to cover, yet thin enough to prevent runs. Allow to dry up to 24 hours before applying any primer surfacer. Scuff it a little, as required, with a Scotch Brite pad before the primer is bone dry. Afterwards, wipe the surface clean with a disposable paper towel to remove the dust. Rags might have slivers of metal or chemicals that can ruin your work, so stick with paper

for this stage. Next, apply the primer surfacer (fill primer) thick enough for block sanding.

Use a rubber block with #400 wet sandpaper to start, and use light, complete strokes—meaning all the way from one end of the part to the other, since smaller strokes create waves and swirls. When the surface is as smooth as the proverbial infant's fanny, it's time to apply the paint.

Hang sheets of thin plastic on a stick frame to "build" a small temporary spray booth in the cleanest draft-free area you can find. Apply as many *thin* coats as it takes to get the color you want. Finish up no thicker than a matchbook cover or the paint will probably crack. Rattle cans or a spray gun, doesn't really matter which, just go slowly and be thorough.

Apply any second color within 24 hours of the first. Masking and papering are an art unto themselves, so be sure the lines are symmetric (and where you really want them) before you proceed. Patience pays. You need to remove the tape and paper within an hour to prevent damage to the original color.

Once completely dry, dust with a damp paper towel and "final" wipe with a tack cloth before you apply clear coat. Don't go overboard with clear. A couple of coats should do; apply more, and it can run or turn cloudy. Give it three or four days to cure, and then wet-sand the paint with 1500-grit sandpaper that has been soaked in water. Go lightly, and rinse the sandpaper in water frequently. Lastly, secure the part, applying polishing compound with an electric buffer, gently, very gently; you want to remove marks not add any. The final phase is to protect the fresh paint. A high-quality glaze protects paint from stains but lets it breathe while it hardens. Two to three weeks later, apply a good non-abrasive carnauba wax, and then stand back. Gorgeous! And you did it yourself.

NOTE: Some colors require a base and final coat. These are indicated with "(bc)" after the color and the appropriate base coat is listed on the next line.

1987

Color	Touch-up	Aerosol	Quart
Arctic White	98600GY	98606GY	98603GY
Vivid Black	98600DH	98606DH	98603DH
Birch White	98600AV	98606AV	98603AV
Classic Cream	98600EX	98606EX	98603EX
Candy Crimson **(bc)**	98600HE	98606HE	98603HE
bc: Purple Metallic	98600HJ	98606HJ	98603HJ
Signal Red	98600GP	98606GP	98603GP
Silver Metallic	98600HB	98606HB	98603HB
Bright Candy Plum **(bc)**	98600HL	98606HL	98603HL
bc: Silver Metallic	98600HB	98606HB	98603HB
Dark Candy Plum **(bc)**	98600HL	98606HL	98603HL
bc: Slate Gray Metallic	98600GK	98606GK	98603GK
Candy Brandwine **(bc)**	98600HE	98606HE	98603HE
bc: Light Silver Metallic	98600FP	98606FP	98603FP
Candy Bronze **(bc)**	98600HH	98606HH	98603HH
bc: Brown Metallic	98600HI	98606HI	98603HI
Champagne Gold	98600GZ	98606GZ	98603GZ
Maroon	98600HK	98606HK	98603HK
Metallic Blue	98600HG	98606HG	98603HG
White Pinstripe	N/A		
Maroon Pinstripe	98600HP		
Red Pinstripe	98600FB		
Orange Pinstripe	98600HQ		
Silver Pinstripe	98600GT		
Gold Pinstripe	98600ES		
Blue Frame Paint	98600HD	98600HD	

1988

Color	Touch-up	Aerosol	Quart
Vivid Black	98600DH	98606DH	98603DH
Birch White	98600AV	98606AV	98603AV
Classic Cream	98600EX	98606EX	98603EX
Candy Crimson **(bc)**	98600HE	98606HE	98603HE
bc: Purple Metallic	98600HJ	98606HJ	98603HJ
Silver Metallic	98600HB	98606HB	98603HB
Bright Candy Plum **(bc)**	98600HL	98606HL	98603HL
bc: Silver Metallic	98600HB	98696HB	98603HB
Candy Brandwine **(bc)**	98600HE	98606HE	98603HE
bc: Light Silver Metallic	98600FP	98606FP	98603FP
Candy Bronze	98600HH	98606HH	98603HH
Champagne Gold	98600GZ	98606GZ	98603GZ
Metallic Blue	98600HG	98606HG	98603HG
Cadet Blue Metallic **(bc)**	98600HN	98606HN	98603HN
bc: Brown Metallic	98600HI	98606HI	98603HI
Bright Cobalt Candy Blue **(bc)**	98600HM	98606HM	98603HM
bc: Silver Metallic	98600HB	98606HB	98603HB
Red Pinstripe	98600FB		
Maroon Pinstripe	98600HP		
Silver Pinstripe	98600GT		
Gold Pinstripe	98600ES		
Orange Pinstripe	98600HQ		
Blue Frame Paint	98600HD	98600HD	

1989

Color	Touch-up	Aerosol	Quart
Vivid Black	98600DH	98606DH	98603DH
Birch White	98600AV	98606AV	98603AV

Color	Touch-up	Aerosol	Quart
Classic Cream	98600EX	98606EX	98603EX
Bright Candy Plum (bc)	98600HL	98606HL	98603HL
bc: Silver Metallic	98600HB	98606HB	98603HB
Candy Brandwine (bc)	98600HE	98606HE	98603HE
bc: Light Silver Metallic	98600FP	98606FP	98603FP
Candy Bronze (bc)	98600HH	98606HH	98603HH
bc: Brown Metallic	98600HI	98606HI	98603HI
Champagne Gold	98600GZ	98606GZ	98603GZ
Metallic Blue	98600HG	98606HG	98603HG
Cadet Blue Metallic	98600HN	98606HN	98603HN
Red Pinstripe	98600FB		
Maroon Pinstripe	98600HP		
Orange Pinstripe	98600HQ		
Silver Pinstripe	98600GT		
Gold Pinstripe	98600ES		
Blue Frame Paint	98600HD	98600HD	

1990

Color	Touch-up	Aerosol	Quart
Vivid Black	98600DH	98606DH	98603DH
Birch White	98600AV	98606AV	98603AV
Classic Cream	98600EX	98606EX	98603EX
Bright Candy Plum (bc)	98600HL	98606HL	98603HL
bc: Silver Metallic	98600HB	98606HB	98603HB
Champagne Gold	98600GZ	98606GZ	98603GZ
Black Pearl	98600JE	98606JE	98603JE
Bright Candy Hi-Fi Blue (bc)	98600JB	98606JB	98603JB
bc: Light Silver Metallic	98600FP	98606FP	98603FP
Dark Candy Hi-Fi Blue (bc)	98600JB	98606JB	98603JB
bc: Slate Gray	98600GK	98606GK	98603GK
Dark Candy Ruby Red (bc)	98600JA	98606JA	98603JA
bc: Black Pearl	98600JE	98606JE	98603JE
Fine Silver Metallic	98600HW	98606HW	98603HW
Bright Candy Ruby Red (bc)	98600JA	98606JA	98603JA
bc: Pink Metallic Base	98600JJ	98606JJ	98603JJ
Light Silver	98600FP	98606FP	98603FP
Red Pinstripe	98600FB		
Maroon Pinstripe	98600HP		
Orange Pinstripe	98600HQ		
Bright Orange Pinstripe	98600JG		
Pale Gold Pinstripe	98600JI		
Sky Blue Pinstripe	98600JH		
Silver Pinstripe	98600GT		

1991

Color	Touch-up	Aerosol	Quart
Black	98600DH	98606DH	98603DH
Birch White	98600AV	98606AV	98603AV
Dark Candy Ruby Red (bc)	98600JA	98606JA	98603JA
bc: Black Pearl	98600JE	98606JE	98603JE
Bright Candy Ruby Red (bc)	98600JA	98606JA	98603JA
bc: Pink Metallic Base	98600JJ	98606JJ	98603JJ
Bright Sapphire Metallic	98600JM	98606JM	98603JM
Candy Sapphire Sun-Glo (bc)	98600VT	98606VT	98603VT
bc: Bright Sapphire Metallic	98600JM	98606JM	98603JM
Dark Sapphire Metallic	98600DA	98606DA	98603DA
Turquoise	98600JZ	98606JZ	98603JZ
White	98600AZ	98600AZ	98603AZ
Vivid Yellow	98600JL	98606JL	98603JL
Wineberry Pearl	98600JN	98606JN	98603JN
Maroon Pinstripe	98600HP		
Red Pinstripe	98600FB		
Bright Orange Pinstripe	98600JG		

Color	Touch-up	Aerosol	Quart
Pale Gold Pinstripe	98600JI		
Sky Blue Pinstripe	98600JH		
Silver Pinstripe	98600GT		

1992

Color	Touch-up	Aerosol	Quart
Vivid Black	98600DH	98606DH	98603DH
Birch White	98600AV	98606AV	98603AV
Indigo Blue	98600GD	98606GD	98603GD
Dark Candy Ruby Red (bc)	98600JA	98606JA	98603JA
bc: Black Pearl	98600JE	98606JE	98603JE
Bright Candy Ruby Red (bc)	98600JA	98606JA	98603JA
bc: Pink Metallic Base	98600JJ	98606JJ	98603JJ
Dark Candy Sapphire Sun-Glo(bc)	98600VT	98606VT	98603VT
bc: Dark Sapphire Metallic	98600DA	98606DA	98603DA
Candy Sapphire Sun-Glo (bc)	98600VT	98606VT	98603VT
bc: Bright Sapphire Metallic	98600JM	98606JM	98603JM
Turquoise	98600JZ	98606JZ	98603JZ
White	98600AZ	98606AZ	98603AZ
Gold Pearl	98600KE	98606KE	98603KE
Light Poppy	98600KH	98606KH	98603KH
Red Voyage	98600KC	98606KC	98603KC
Silver	98600KG	98606KG	98603KG
Bright Orange Pinstripe	98600JG		
Pale Gold Pinstripe	98600JI		
Sea Coral	98600KM		
Red Pinstripe	98600FB		

1993

Color	Touch-up	Aerosol	Quart
Vivid Black	98600DH	98606DH	98603DH
Birch White	98600AV	98606AV	98603AV
Bright Victory Red Sun-Glo (bc)	98600KN	98606KN	98603KN
bc: Bright Victory Red Base	98600KU	98606KU	98603KU
Dark Victory Red Sun-Glo (bc)	98600KN	98606KN	98603KN
bc: Dark Victory Red Base	98600KV	98606KV	98603KV
Bright Wineberry Sun-Glo (bc)	98600KP	98606KP	98603KP
bc: Bright Wineberry Base	98600KW	98606KW	98603KW
Dark Wineberry Sun-Glo (bc)	98600KP	98606KP	98603KP
bc: Bright Wineberry Base	98600KX	98606KX	98603KX
Bright Auqua Sun-Glo (bc)	98600KR	98606KR	98603KR
bc: Silver	98600KG	98606KG	98603KG
Scarlet Red	98600LZ	98606LZ	98603LZ
Mandarin Orange (bc)	98600KS	98606KS	98603KS
bc: Mandarin Orange Base	98600KJ	98606KJ	98603KJ
Silver ('93 Anniversary) (bc)	98600KG	98606KG	98603KG
bc: Charcoal Satin Brite	98600KT	98606KT	98603KT
Charcoal Satin Brite	98600KT	98606KT	98603KT
Bright Orange Pinstripe	98600JG		
Pale Gold Pinstripe	98600JI		
Red Pinstripe	98600FB		
Silver Pinstripe	98600GT		
Sky Blue Pinstripe	98600JH		

1994

Color	Touch-up	Aerosol	Quart
Birch White	98600AV	98606AV	98603AV
Gold	98600BA	98606BA	98603BA
Auqua Pearl	98600BB	98606BB	98603BB
Vivid Black	98600DH	98606DH	98603DH
Silver	98600KG	98606KG	98603KG
Bright Victory Red Sun-Glo(bc)	98600KN	98606KN	98603KN
bc: Bright Victory Red Base	98600KU	98606KU	98603KU
Dark Victory Red Sun-Glo (bc)	98600KN	98606KN	98603KN
bc: Dark Victory Red Base	98600KV	98606KV	98603KV

Color	Touch-up	Aerosol	Quart
Burgundy Pinstripe	98600BC		
Red Pinstripe	98600FB		

Color	Touch-up	Aerosol	Quart
Silver Pinstripe	98600GT		
Bright Orange Pinstripe	98600JG		
Sky Blue Pinstripe	98600JH		
Pale Gold Pinstripe	98600JI		

1995

Color	Touch-up	Aerosol	Quart
Birch White	98600AV	98606AV	98603AV
Gold	98600BA	98606BA	98603BA
Auqua Pearl	98600BB	98606BB	98603BB
Nugget Yellow	98600BD	98606BD	98603BD
Burgundy Pearl	98600BE	98606BE	98603BE
Vivid Black	98600DH	98606DH	98603DH
Silver	98600KG	98606KG	98603KG
Bright Victory Red Sun-Glo**(bc)**	98600KN	98606KN	98603KN
bc: Bright Victory Red Base	98600KU	98606KU	98603KU
Dark Victory Red Sun-Glo **(bc)**	98600KN	98606KN	98603KN
bc: Dark Victory Red Base	98600KV	98606KV	98603KV
Charcoal Satin Brite	98600KT	98606KT	98603KT
Scarlet Red	98600LZ	98606LZ	98603LZ
Burgundy Pinstripe	98600BC		
Red Pinstripe	98600FB		
Silver Pinstripe	98600GT		
Bright Orange Pinstripe	98600JG		
Sky Blue Pinstripe	98600JH		
Pale Gold Pinstripe	98600JI		

1996 & 1997

Color	Touch-up	Aerosol	Quart
Birch White	98600AV	98606AV	98603AV
States Blue	98600BH	98606BH	98603BH
Patriot Red Pearl	98600BJ	98606BJ	98603BJ
Platinum Silver	98600BL	98606BL	98603BL
Mystique Green	98600BM	98606BM	98603BM
Violet Pearl	98600BN	98606BN	98603BN
Vivid Black	98600DH	98606DH	98603DH
Victory Sun-Glo **(bc)**	98600KN	98606KN	98603KN
bc: Platinum Silver	98600BL	98606BL	98603BL
Wineberry Sun-Glo **(bc)**	98600KP	98606KP	98603KP
bc: Charcoal Satin Brite	98600KT	98606KT	98603KT
Charcoal Satin Brite	98600KT	98606KT	98603KT
Burgundy Pinstripe	98600BC		
Green Pinstripe	98600BG		
Dark Gray	98600BK		
Red Pinstripe	98600FB		
Sky Blue Pinstripe	98600JH		
Pale Gold Pinstripe	98600JI		

1998

Color	Touch-up	Aerosol	Quart
Birch White	98600AV	98606AV	98603AV
Sinister Blue	98600BW	98606BW	98603BW
Lazer Red	98600BT	98606BT	98603BT
Mystique Green	98600BM	98606BM	98603BM
Violet Pearl	98600BN	98606BN	98603BN
Vivid Black	98600DH	98606DH	98603DH
Midnight Red	98600BX	98606BX	98603BX
Champagne Pearl	98600BV	98606BV	98603BV
Arctic White	98600GY	98606GY	98603GY
Burgundy Pinstripe	98600BC		
Pale Gold Pinstripe	98600JI		
Red Pinstripe	98600FB		
Sky Blue Pinstripe	98600JH		
Dark Gray Pinstripe	98600BK		
Green Pinstripe	98600BG		

Time: 1 to 3 hours

Tools: Extra cloths, squirt bottle of water, variable-speed drill, and wax

Talent:

Tab: $

Tinware: Paint repair kit (or equivalent) and clean diaper-type cloths

Tip: Test kits other than the factory repair kit and take your time

⚠ PERFORMANCE GAIN: Good looks

COMPLEMENTARY MODIFICATION: Clean and wax all chrome (especially brand-new exhausts; it helps against bluing) so they stand out as well as the paint

1 There are other similar kits on the market, but the genuine H-D paint repair kit (#H-D 39994) designed for use by dealers is the best of the bunch. Plus you can order replacement components: Hookit pads (#39994-4), buff pads (#39994-5), a rubber sanding plug (#39994-6), 1,200-grit sanding discs (#39994-7), cotton wipes (#39994-8), a bottle of Finishing Material (#39994-9), a bottle of Final Finish (#39994-10), and a bottle of Ebony Material (#39994-11). The kit isn't cheap at over $100, but compared to a repaint, the kit's a veritable bargain.

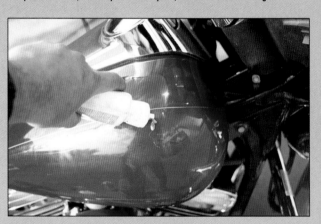

4 Apply a dab of the Final Finish, grab another clean towel, and rub it in by hand. Using a circular motion, begin with moderate pressure and then lighten up as you go. Let it dry to a haze and wipe clean. Then go at it one more time with the alcohol mix from the squirt bottle. If you're not happy with the results, you need to repeat the treatment—or it's not really such a minor blemish.

Nothing sets off a custom Harley like a trick paint job. By the same token, nothing bespeaks true loving care of a stock H-D like sparkling factory paint. These days a well-kept standard paint job is actually rarer than the custom stuff. A Hog that's a decade old and can't be told from a brand-new one by your average person on the street brings joy to the heart and an occasional tear to the eye.

Keeping your bike factory-perfect is not easy. Hours and hours of lavish care in washing, waxing, and protecting that thin layer of glossy pigment are the rule, not the exception, for perfect paint preservation.

No matter how much you scrub, something happens. Usually something stupid and irritating. You accidentally drop your keys right on top of the tank, swing a leg over the back fender and scratch it with your boot, or park where some dolt just can't resist admiring your scoot up close and personal and scuffs it up big-time with a belt buckle the size of Rhode Island, hanging off a belly the size of Texas.

The Motor Company recognizes that the slings and arrows or outrageous fortune can strike any-where. And where is such misfortune more likely than at the dealer's showroom? Every day down at the local shop, potential buyers bring potential ruin to shiny new paint. Any H-D that's sitting there can be sat upon and scratched umpteen times before the proud owner gets it home.

Harley-Davidson does not like buying a new tank or fender, under warranty, before the dealer even sells it. Owners don't much like taking delivery of a less-than-perfect unit either. And paint is a fragile thing, especially fresh paint. The factory thought about it long and hard and came up with a pretty fair solution.

It seems that about 90 percent of the claims weren't for big gouges and chips. Rather, it was tiny scratches, minor blemishes, dull spots, and other flaws that didn't really require a repaint. So the factory developed a paint repair kit, and it works extremely well on surface blemishes. If the wound in the paint is down to primer or bare metal, it won't really fix the problem. Otherwise, give it a shot. This kit and a tube of elbow grease can perform minor miracles.

2 If your paint has a blemish that can be seen but not felt, first spray the blemish with alcohol and water mixed in a squirt bottle.

3 Using only the diaper-like cotton towels in the kit, wipe the area clean and dry (don't ever use a paper towel on factory paint; it scratches like crazy).

5 If you can feel the blemish in the paint with your finger, the blemish is at least "medium." Start cleaning with the squirt bottle again and repeat the rubbing drill, but use a drop of the Finishing Material this time. Then repeat the whole sequence with Final Finish. If that doesn't get it, your paint is wounded. For this pass, you'll need a variable-speed drill, a Hookit pad, and a dab of the Ebony Material. The sequence is the same—squirt, buff, squirt, buff, squirt, buff—working your way back from the Ebony to the Final Finish. By now you should see the method in the madness, so hang tough until you get the results you need.

6 For blemishes that stand up, protruding from the paint surface, use the rubber sanding plug and a 1,200-grit disc. Usually this does the trick. Start with the squirt bottle again, but this time don't wipe or dry (never dry-sand Harley paint). Sand gently with the disc in linear strokes against the "grain" of the blemish. Smooth is the object of the game, so just take the blemish out, not the paint off!

7 Lastly, a word about using the drill. Wear safety glasses and buff or sand in a circular motion, rolling from the center of the blemish out, always coming off a corner or edge. Go lightly and let the drill and pad do the work. Once you're ready for the Finishing Material, realize that the stuff actually dissolves the clear coat slightly and redistributes it over the blemish. So the finished result should be protected with a nice layer of carnauba wax before you call it a day.

PERSONAL TOUCHES

PROJECT 96 • INSTALLING CHROME HANDLEBAR CONTROLS

 Time: 3 to 4 hours

 Tools: Allen wrenches; Torx wrenches; small Phillips screwdriver; 12 inches of fine stiff wire; 1/4x20-inch tap; Mity-Vac tool; small rat-tail file; and 3/8-, 1/2-, and 9/16-inch wrenches

 Talent:

 Tab: $$$ to $$$$

 Tinware: Chrome control housings, master cylinder (or chrome cover), and clutch and brake perches and levers; you might also need a master cylinder rebuild kit, electrical tape, solder and shrink tubing, new banjo washers for the brake hose, DOT 5 brake fluid, a 3/16- and 1/4-inch tap, and some new plastic handlebar wiring retainer clips

 Tip: Lay a blanket or towel over the gas tank area, and don't lose the little (metric) screws that hold the switch clusters in the housings

 PERFORMANCE GAIN: Improved appearance mostly; improved protection of cables

COMPLEMENTARY MODIFICATION: Different handlebars and internal wiring

1 Aftermarket kits come ready to install. As long as the quality is up to your standards, this is the easiest way to get chrome controls on your 1982 to 1995 Harley. Make sure your kit has the right size of master cylinder. Models from 1982 to 1983 with dual discs use a 3/4-inch bore; single-disc bikes have a 5/8-inch bore, and 1984 to 1995 models with dual 11-inch discs use an 11/16-inch bore. Aside from the housings, chrome switches are available, or you can use your old switches in the new housings. Either way, the "cleanest" way to wire them in is to go to the factory junction blocks in the main harness. It takes more effort, if not more time, but it beats having to splice, solder, and shrink wrap all those wires.

Harley used the same handlebar control housings that were used from 1982 through 1995, but the company never saw fit to offer them in chrome. If want chrome in this area, you have four options. One, have your existing housings chromed. Two, do a chrome exchange thing at a cooperative dealership. Three, buy aftermarket versions that are chrome in the first place. Four, you can swap to the 1996 and later version.

Having your own housings plated means down time, usually twice as long as they tell you when you drop the parts off, no matter what that time frame is. You may also suffer the proverbial loss or damage. This is especially likely if you are dealing with a chromer who doesn't know about aluminum or Harley parts in general. They tend to get chrome where it shouldn't be, like the mating surfaces and the small drillings in the master cylinder body. Or they get all the polishing perfect in places where you'll never see it and pit the surfaces that stare right at you.

The good news is, done correctly, there's not much chance that the parts won't fit back together well. They're your parts after all and should go back on as easily as they came off. That's not necessarily true in a chrome exchange situation. Pieces you get to make up the full set of housings may be from as many different bikes as there are pieces in the set. And, because each piece may have been buffed at a different time or by a different guy at the chrome shop, poor seams and joints may be the order of the day. Also, things like the master cylinder bore and the threads in the screw holes may need a little "completion" before you can use them. Look 'em over well before you swap your stock stuff away. Plan on tapping threads clean and sticking wire down the ports and drillings in the master cylinder, no matter which of these options you choose. And don't wait until you get back home to check the depth of the chrome in broad daylight.

If all this makes buying aftermarket chrome housings sound like a simpler better idea, rest assured there are pitfalls in that notion too. Most of the time it works out okay, but be aware that you need to inspect the parts in an aftermarket kit even more than genuine re-chromed stuff. It's not uncommon to see switch halves that don't mate up, shabby chrome, and even screw holes that aren't tapped at all. Then there's the issue of master-cylinder bore. The original version of this design used a 3/4-inch bore. By the time Evos came along, the single-disc bikes got a 5/8-inch bore, and the dual-disc models used 11/16-inch bores. That's good trivia to retain before you haul off and pop for a kit at the swap meet, only to get home and find the cylinder is useless to you.

No matter which way you go, when the time comes to install the goods, be methodical about it. Take all the fasteners and miscellaneous hardware out of one housing at a time and stick them in their own container. Use bungee cords, duct tape, or something else to hold errant cables and hoses and keep them out of your way. Once you get rolling, the most time-

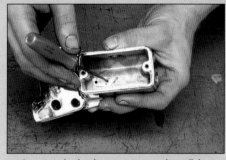

2 Don't be surprised if the toughest obstacle in the whole process is getting the little Torx screws to come loose. These screws are made of stuff only slightly stiffer than peanut butter and will round out the head at the slightest provocation. Don't provoke them. Use heat from a hair dryer, a little penetrating oil, a high-quality Torx bit, and patience to achieve victory. If that doesn't appeal to you, drill the heads of the screws off. Have some new ones on hand, just in case. Better to have them and not need them than need them and not have them.

3 Don't be shy about running a tap down all the screw holes before you start assembly and run those new chrome screws into the holes to make sure the holes aren't obstructed. While you're at it, take a probe or stiff wire and check the passages in the master cylinder. If they are blocked with crud or chrome, you'll never get the brakes bled.

5 Once you have the housings and their switches assembled on the handlebar, take a minute to ensure that everything works, especially the brake light switch. No leaks from the master cylinder and a firm lever pull mean you've got the sight glass and the lid gasket on properly and the brakes bled. Just don't overdo it when tightening the lid; as long as it doesn't leak, you're fine. If the rubber gasket is distorted, it's on too tight.

4 If you re-chrome your master cylinder, plan on rebuilding the cylinder after you've checked the bore to be sure no evil hides in there. Light honing is a last resort if there is chrome in the bore, but it's far better to select a chrome plater who knows how to keep the chrome off the inside so you don't have to fix a chromer's sloppy work.

consuming elements of the project are installing and correctly adjusting the throttle cables and bleeding the brakes. Be ready to spend an inordinate amount of time with brake bleeding if those little bleed holes in the bottom of the master cylinder reservoir are even mildly obstructed and if you don't own a Mity-Vac tool. Conventional bleeding techniques, as described in the shop manual, can have you pumping the lever from breakfast until dinner, without success. Use the Mity-Vac and pump "uphill" from the caliper to the cylinder, which is the direction air wants travel anyway. No sense defying physics, let alone logic.

The other thing that may distract you a bit is ensuring proper operation of the front brake switch. The little plunger doesn't have a lot of room to align with its hole in the switch housing in the first place, let alone when it's been chromed closed. A rat tail file will take care of it, but you need to lash the right-side housing up loosely and double-check that the brake works perfectly before you torque things down.

BAR BRIGHTWORK FOR 1996 AND LATER BIKES

H-D did a mighty re-think of handlebar controls for the 1996 model year. You get a strong first impression when you see a set of these sunk in an aquarium at the dealer show, working quite happily and reliably—underwater! These new controls are a very good design, and to keep us amateurs from messing them up (through either ignorance or expedience) in our never-ending pursuit of chrome, the factory did an unprecedented thing. They offered them in chrome as a genuine accessory, still waterproof, and much better looking.

If you've read the section on chrome housings for pre-1996 models and can take the hint, this means the factory's setup is the preferred one. Preferred and near, but not quite, perfect. Obviously, fit and finish are first class, and installation is simple, as it should be for factory parts. Harley cheated a little though. Fortunately, the factory cheated in your favor. Take the master cylinder. Harley figures that actually using a chrome one is a lot of unnecessary work, and potential brake performance problems are waiting to happen. So they don't go there. Instead, they offer a "second skin" chrome cover. As logical as that is, some of us don't like covers. We want the actual part to be shiny. That's okay, as long as you understand that this requirement doubles or even triples the grief and "agro" involved, not to mention the time and expense. You may surrender reliable function in a monsoon as well.

Be that as it may (or may not), it's not difficult to swap parts on 1996 and later housings. Use the factory instructions if you get the factory parts. And, much like the 1995 and older stuff, use a little common sense and a lot of caution if you chrome or chrome exchange your stockers.

PERSONAL TOUCHES
PROJECT 97 • CHANGING HANDLEBARS

 Time: 1/2 hour to 3 hours

 Tools: Torx wrenches, Allen wrenches, a long skinny screwdriver, WD-40, and the usual (toolbox) suspects

 Talent:

 Tab: $

 Tinware: A pair of new grips or an extra left grip (if you're not careful), a couple of #2508 handlebar switch housing screws for 1982 to 1995 models (unless you're careful), zip-ties or #56073-83 wire guides, 3M Weatherstripping Cement, and handlebars

 Tip: A handlebar is mounted by the book when the upright part of the bars is parallel to the fork tubes, as viewed from the side; angling them way forward or back affects steering characteristics more than you might think

⚠ PERFORMANCE GAIN: Better control and more comfort, but we all know it's really for looks

COMPLEMENTARY MODIFICATION: Internal wiring, cleaner routing of proper length control cables, and chrome handlebar controls

Handlebars are a very personal choice. For reasons of comfort, style, occasional damage, and perhaps just to be different, changing handlebars is a task we all face sooner or later, it seems. The choices are almost unlimited when it comes to the "bend" you can use, with new designs coming to market monthly. In broad terms, you can go with high bars, low bars, or medium bars. High bars, like "ape hangers," are great for stylin', but at 75 miles per hour or more you can feel a lot like a partially opened parachute. Most folks who ride lots of miles annually or ride hard at high speeds without a fairing or windshield opt for a low bar like the 883 or XLX/XR1000 bend. The most common medium bend is the so-called "buckhorn" bar, which is a surprisingly poor design. As popular as it is, the wrist angle is all wrong, and the height puts you in a "sit up and beg" posture that's an ergonomic disaster.

If you own a Springer model or an FL with rubber-mounted bars, other restrictions apply. Springers use unique "Dog Bone"-type risers and have the knurling in a different location than other Harley handlebars.

1 Handlebar swaps can offer up a couple of headaches. First you must determine what to do about the left grip: Trash it in favor of a new one, or try to remove and reuse it on the new bars. A liberal application of WD-40 and a screwdriver can allow you to work the original grip off intact, most of the time. Another concern is scratches on paintwork and chrome during the swap; towels and blankets draped as in the photo help prevent 'em. Also, whenever possible, the bars of your choice should be chosen not just for the bend but for the knurling. If the bars don't have knurling (and an amazing number of them don't), don't bother! Your safety and the ultimate usefulness of the bar often depends on considerations like these.

2 If the bike has a lot of time and mileage on it, now's a good opportunity to change the rubber mounts for the handlebars. You'd be surprised at how often people think their new bars are bent because old rubbers make things crooked when re-torqued. There are options here as well. Harley makes rubbers in two densities, soft and too soft. If keeping vibration at bay is a priority, opt for four of the #56158-73 rubbers, but be aware there will be a lot of flex at the bar. For folks with FXRs or Dynas, it not a bad idea to go with the firmer part (#53156-86) or even the aftermarket polyurethane type, which is a lot stiffer. Barnett even makes aluminum versions for racers, but there's a whole lot of "buzz" about rigid-mounted handlebars. They're no fun on long rides.

3 Installing taller-than-stock bars can be a lot of extra work, not the least of which is finding correct-length hoses and cables. Extra length on hoses and cables usually comes in 2-inch increments—plus 2 inches, plus 4 inches, and so on. A little too long is better than a little too short. Clever routing can hide extra length pretty easily, except in the case of brake lines. If you stay with rubber brake lines, remember they are premolded and one-piece on late-model Harleys. This means, for instance, that on a double-disc application of 16-inch ape hangers you may need a stock length hose to the brake junction from the calipers but plus 6 inches from the junction to the master cylinder. It makes sense to double-check what you need before you get home and strip the bike down.

4 If you do change cables, don't lose these little brass nipples for the throttle or the pin for the clutch cable. And once they are back in place, recheck your cable adjustments. It's almost too easy to wind up with a dragging clutch or a throttle that doesn't open all the way if you don't. Torque all the fasteners properly and swing the bars all the way from left to right to make sure there's no binding, pinching, or revving up going on without your knowledge. Test-ride cautiously until you can trust the brakes and all controls.

Rubber-mount FL dressers have a nacelle (shroud) of one sort or another over their two piece clamps, and that adds to the width of the handlebar below the first bend, and removing the nacelle to get at the clamps adds considerably to the fuss involved. It all amounts to fewer choices and more work for either.

MOUNTING SIMILAR BARS

If you install bars of the exact same bend or one that's close to the same rise and width, installation is a matter of following the process laid out in the service manual for your model. Briefly, that is as follows:

Always lay a thick clean towel or blanket over the tank and cover anything else you don't want to scratch.

Remove the handlebar control cluster screws until you can take the assemblies off the end of the bars.

Loosen the clamp fasteners, remove the clamps, and gently lift the old bars away.

Then lay up the new bars and check that the knurling matches, the cables and brake hose will reach, nothing fouls or hits, and you're happy with your choice.

Clamp the new bar down at the angle of attack you want, leaving the gap between top and bottom as even as possible. When in doubt about this angle of attack stuff, run the upright portion of the handlebar parallel to the fork tubes.

The only thing remotely tricky is saving the original left side grip to reuse with the new bars. Usually, a small screwdriver and some WD-40 will do the trick. Use the screwdriver to pry the grip slightly away from the handlebar. Squirt some lubricant in between the rubber and the metal and slowly "unscrew" the grip. Naturally, none of this is required if you have a new pair of grips handy.

Regardless, you need to "glue" the left grip in place when it goes back on. Some grips come with a small tube of the stuff when you buy them, if not, 3M Weatherstripping Cement (AKA "Gorilla Snot") works. Position the left side handlebar controls, then lay the new grip alongside to gauge final location. Don't tighten anything up just yet though. Clean the bar end with alcohol, run a bead of glue up the inside of the grip, and "screw" it back on.

Now, go to the right side controls while the glue dries and be sure you don't lose the little black plastic "shoe" for the throttle lock when you reinstall it.

Once lashed up, don't tighten anything on the right side until you've checked out the operation of the front brake switch. There's a small plunger running from the master cylinder to the switch housing that just loves to stick and bind on 1982 to 1995 models. Make sure yours doesn't. When you're sure, tighten everything down and then double-check.

MOUNTING LOWER BARS

If you choose to install lower bars, such as drag bars, be careful that your particular choice isn't going to bang dents into the gas tank when the bars are turned from side to side. Often you'll find that the stock cables and brake lines are a bit too long for use with the shorter bars. Sometimes, rerouting the cables and lines cures the problem. Clean routing is as much science as art in that no matter how stylish the look, it's pretty useless if there's a binding, kinking, sticking, hitting problem. Rarely will you need to replace any of the cables, but a shorter brake line might be in the cards. Quite often, you can gently bend the black metal tubing parts of a stock brake line to accommodate your lower bars. Don't just crank it around with a pair of pliers; instead "wrap" it around a "form," like a screwdriver handle or a tin can, by hand. No sharp bends!

MOUNTING HIGHER BARS

Mounting high bars (also known as ape hangers) is a mechanical anarchy of sorts. Virtually no rules apply when you go this route—except maybe to knurling. Without knurling (the striations cut into the bar where it is clamped down), a high bar simply will not stay put for long. One panic stop or a serious attempt at high speeds or wheelies, and floppo! Obviously, a bar that won't stay put is a serious safety hazard. Never buy a higher bar that lacks knurling.

If apes are in your future, you'll also need extended cables (clutch, throttle, and idle), along with a longer brake line. Most folks opt for braided stainless steel brake lines, which are fine, as long as you're aware that the metal braiding makes for pretty fair sandpaper and will leave its mark wherever it touches your tank, fork, or windshield. It's a good idea to sheath the braid in clear tubing where the stuff touches parts of the bike you don't want damaged. Purpose-built kits of clear thin wall "shrink tube" sheathing are available through most aftermarket suppliers that sell the stainless cables and lines. If you can't find a kit, clear aquarium tubing or even fuel line will work. It's not as clean an installation, however, because you must slit the hose lengthwise and then hold it on the braid with zip-ties.

Even if the bars are destined to be above the shoulder, you've got to be able to work the levers and see behind you. When taking handlebars to new heights, this simple fact often gets overlooked, if you'll pardon the pun, so pay attention to the angles of the clutch and brake levers. They should be angled so they don't give you wrist cramps or carpel tunnel before you hit the city limits, even if it means a 45-degree tilt. Also, you probably can't use the stock mirrors. Most serious ape-users have mirrors hanging down, instead of sticking up, if they use them at all.

PERSONAL TOUCHES
PROJECT 98 • HIDING HANDLEBAR WIRING

 Time: 2 to 4 hours

 Tools: Small hand-held rotary grinder (Dremel tool), bullet-nosed metal grinding bit, small rat tailed file, string or stiff wire, tape, aerosol lubricant, and sandpaper

 Talent:

 Tab: $

 Tinware: A set of handlebars, various colors of 16- to 18-gauge electrical wire, electrical-grade solder and soldering iron, shrink tubing, and electrical connectors (preferably Harley)

 Tip: Keep the holes as small as possible and de-burr the holes.

 PERFORMANCE GAIN: Cosmetic mostly, but it also water-proofs wiring to a degree and helps prevent accidental and vandal-generated damage

COMPLEMENTARY MODIFICATION: All the wiring can be routed more cleanly on any Harley, particularly under the gas tank and seat

One of the techniques that separates the artists from the hacks is the simple concept of hiding ugly electrical wires. Internal wiring is usually employed to clean up the aesthetic appeal of a gleaming set of ape-hanger handlebars, but that's not to say the concept is exclusive to handlebars. As a matter of fact, The Motor Company ran the main wire harness inside the frame tubes on bikes of the late 1960s and early 1970s as a factory exercise. Not a bad idea, but not without flaws, which may be why they no longer do it that way.

As with all modifications, hiding the wiring within the bars is a trade-off. On the plus side, it gives a sanitary, custom look and protects the wiring. On the negative side, the necessary holes weaken the handlebars, the edges of the holes can chafe the wiring, it's picky and meticulous work, and it all has to be redone to change the bars or switches. Running handlebar wiring internally takes more time than talent, but still, if you're going to take a crack at it, there are a few things to consider.

The holes you'll have to grind in the tubing should be as small as possible, be in an inconspicuous location, and must be thoroughly de-burred. The cuts and splices in the wire looms should be made at inter-

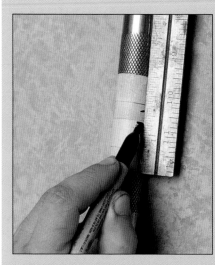

1 Mark the bar where you intend to make the hole. Try to center it in the knurling and tape the area.

2 Use a center punch to "pilot" the hole, clamp the works in a vise (one reason for the tape is to avoid marking up the bar), and drill a 5/16-inch hole.

3 Take your Dremel or rotary grinder, put on some safety glasses and gloves, and slowly start opening up the hole; make it just large enough to get the wires through. Repeat the process for the holes around the control clusters. Measure carefully since you only get one shot at lining up the control holes so they're hidden. Group the wires together with a little tape, attach them to a stiff wire with a little more tape, and pull or push the wires through the handlebar. From here on you reassemble just like the manual says.

vals of at least 2 inches, not all in the same place. In other words, you don't want to wind up with a golf ball in your garden hose, as you try in vain to stuff the wiring into the bars. Spacing out your wire cuts and splices and making them as petite as possible really helps. If you do it that way, there's less likelihood of a bulging "bottleneck" at the first bend in the bar. Needless to say, all the connections must be secure and clean and any splices soldered and insulated, preferably with shrink tubing.

Another (possibly better) approach if you don't go too high with the bars is to buy new switches. As a replacement part, these switches come with "unfinished" wires about 2 feet long. So you stick new switches in the housings and run the wire all the way through the bars to the main harness junction block. No splices, just clean runs of new wire. That's sanitary!

Speaking of which, putting a hole or three extra in a handlebar may not sound too techy, but some ways are better than others. Avoid just hack-sawing a chunk out where no one will see it. It will weaken the bar excessively and look primitive. Better to mark the spot with a dot from a black felt pen, gently cinch the bar into a soft-jawed vise with a wooden pad, then dimple and drill. Center punch the black dot, tape the drill bit about 5/8 inch up from the tip so you don't drill too far, and once the pilot hole is there, use the Dremel and bullet bit to carefully grind a narrow oval

hole parallel to the tubing. Stop as soon as the hole will accept all the wires. There's no point in making it any bigger, and if you do, the handlebar might make some nasty cracks, even if your friends won't. Take some time to properly de-burr the thing before you accidentally use it for a wire cutter.

Once that's done, tape the wire groups together; tie or tape them to a piece of stiff wire or string with a small nut tied to the end (whichever you think works best in your particular case) and start feeding it into the bars. Once it gets to the bottom hole, gently draw the wires on through, one at a time if necessary. If you hit a snag, don't be tempted to jerk on anything! Back and forth with doses of WD-40 and an occasional prod with a coat hanger will get it, eventually. From there on out, it's pretty much a plug and play proposition to reinstall everything. Just make sure all the switches function before you get to a spot where you have to undo what you've just done.

If you choose to go with non-spliced wire clear to the junction block, you'll probably need a special tool for removing and replacing the connectors in the block. The tool is available from Harley, Drag Specialties, Jim's, CCI, and others. If you insist on doing without it, you'll need a tiny "eyeglass" screwdriver or an ice pick and some extra connectors to replace the ones you might mess up without the tool.

PERSONAL TOUCHES

PROJECT 99 • MOUNTING FORWARD CONTROLS ON YOUR BIG TWIN

Time: 2 to 3 hours

Tools: 3/8-, 7/16-, 1/2-, 9/16-, 5/8-inch wrenches and sockets; screwdrivers; needle-nosed pliers; Allen wrenches; Torx wrenches; Loctite 242 (blue)

Talent: 👤👤

Tab: $$$ to $$$$$+

Tinware: Controls, cotter pins, and new Nyloc nuts

Tip: Double-check the shifter geometry; the lever must be comfortable to the boot, and the linkage must be logical to the tranny

PERFORMANCE GAIN: Comfort—and not having to worry about hitting pegs and levers when you put your feet down at stops

COMPLEMENTARY MODIFICATION: Make sure your saddle suits your seat when you put your feet up

Since regular XLs, Dynas, FXRs, and plenty of other stock Harleys have low seats and high mid-mounted pegs, you'd think there just has to be a better way to stretch those cramped legs, wouldn't you? Well, there is.

You can change to forward controls or rearsets. While rearsets solve the tailbone problem, they are even worse for legroom than stock controls. Besides, for most of us, Harleys are for cruisin' not bruisin', so why not spread out and relax? The Motor Company has a complete kit out to install the FXDWG factory controls on the other Dyna models, but most other models have to go with aftermarket controls. Fortunately, that's a big hardship because there are dozens to choose from!

Installing these forward controls is drop-dead easy; no sealed systems are opened up, and no special tools are needed. This is the kind of job that can actually be done in an afternoon.

GENERAL INSTALLATION TIPS

You may need to remove the exhaust to get the stock footpeg and brake pedal off. Typically, the brake pedal is secured to the footpeg mount with an outside snap-ring. You need to remove the pedal from the mount so you can unscrew the brake

1 There are literally dozens of forward control designs to choose from. Some things consider before you jump feet first into forward controls are the following: Will the master cylinder h to be relocated? If so, how and where? Will the stock master cylinder work with your choice, or do you need something different? Does the brake pedal run under or ove the footrest post? Does it matter to you? Can you operate the brake easily and effectively Do you want chrome, billet, or chromed billet? If you can, try to answer these questions b test-riding machines like yours that have forward controls before you lay down the mone If you get it right, nothing is more comfortable than feet-first riding. Get it wrong, and y feel like a bird on a perch at high speeds.

2 When installing forward controls you have to consid what you'd really like to re your feet on. Floorboards aren't just a Harley traditi They earned their populari for one simple reason: The are superbly comfortable. you bike wasn't born with them and no model in your bike's chassis family comes with them from the factory, you ca still relax. The aftermarket offers bolt-on and (usually) adjustable board kits for just abo every Hog ever made. Most work just fine with feet-first shifter and brake mechanisms.

pushrod from the master cylinder. The splined shaft, left sticking out of the primary case, gets a smooth cap. An O-ring under the cap can keep the old shaft from rattling. The master cylinder plunger is locked with two jam-nuts. This keeps the pushrod adjustment from changing while you are riding and allows minute changes in pedal height.

The front end of the shift rod is attached to the forward control shift lever with a bolt. Don't fully tighten this bolt until you've adjusted the shift rod to set the shift peg to fit your big foot. Also, to get crisp shifts and smooth action from the linkage, it's crucial that the two vertical levers (from the tranny itself and from where the shift lever attaches) must be as close to parallel as possible. If they're not parallel, they'll bind at the limit of their travel, sticking in first or hanging up in fourth, things like that.

Adjusting the foot pedals is a two-step process; first, the pedals are rough-adjusted on their splined shafts, and then they are final-adjusted using the shift and brake rods. To move the pedals on their shafts, the outer pivot cover is unscrewed, and then the nut is unscrewed off the pivot shaft.

After you have adjusted the pedals, levers, and such to your liking, tighten all the jam-nuts and put a drop of #242 Loctite (blue) on their threads. The shifter and brake pedal pegs are attached to their respective levers with various styles of fasteners. Give these the Loctite treatment as well.

PROJECT 100 • INSTALLING REARSETS AND FORWARD CONTROLS ON YOUR SPORTSTER

Time: 3 to 5 hours (pipes included)

Tools: Screwdrivers; 7/16-, 1/2-, 9/16-, and 5/8-inch wrenches and sockets; Allens and Torx bits; and a torque wrench

Talent: ♟♟

Tab: $$$ to $$$$$$$ (pipes and controls)

Tinware: Rearset or forward control kit

Tip: Rearsets work just fine with low 883-type handlebars, but real racers use clip-ons

PERFORMANCE GAIN: Control in high-intensity riding situations

COMPLEMENTARY MODIFICATION: Exhaust, either the flat-track flavor or a two-into-one

For those who pay homage to the "sport" part of the Sportster name, there's a way to improve the position of the stock footpegs, shifter, and brake pedal. The stock positioning of all the footpegs, shifter, and brake pedal goodies can leave many a rider feeling cramped, wishing for a way to stretch out a bit—as well as for a better angle of attack for instinctive access to critical shifting and braking at higher speeds. Anyone who spends much time at ticket-bait velocity on the twisty tarmac can attest to the superior disposition of shifting and braking offered by rearsets. To the forward-control crowd, this may seem alien. But the simple fact is rearsets do for those who boogie exactly what forward controls do for those who cruise—namely, improve rider comfort and vehicle control.

For the sport group, Bartels' Performance has just the ticket. And Storz Performance has two offerings—one with a "signature" reversed shift pattern characteristic of rearsets and one that allows the standard "down for low, up for go" pattern. These rearset kits come nicely packed, complete with hardware. To begin the installation, grab your shop manual and start pulling off the stock pipes. Since neither of these kits will work with the stock exhaust, it has to go.

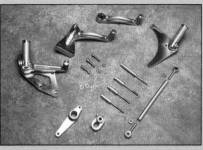

1 If you want rearsets on your Sportster, there are only two games in town (well, maybe two and a half): Bartels' Performance and Storz. If you noticed two shift levers in the photo of the kit, you get extra points. The extra shifter is the "half." You see, the one at the top, once installed, reverses the stock shift pattern, just like the Bartels' does. This is fine for real racers because they're used to it. But us street racers occasionally revert to "normal" shifting habits in the heat of battle. For us, Storz offers the more elaborate and damn clever version, which retains the stock pattern—down for low and up to go!

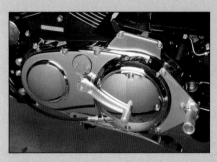

2 The left side of the bike with the racer shifter installed. Notice the clean mounting of the lightweight (and very trick) alloy footrests. Installation on this side takes all of about 20 minutes, using the instructions provided.

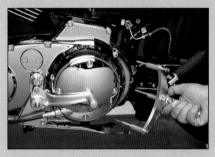

3 Here's the shifter for "the rest of us"— and the footrest about to go on. The long spacers are required to get your size-12 boots lined up with the lever, and all the hardware you need comes in the kit.

4 Okay, so the right-side installation is a bit more involved, but here are the brake lever and footrest in place. Stock shorty duals don't really work with rearsets, so you need to think in terms of a good two-into-one or some XR-replica pipes.

The shifter side of both kits are remarkably similar in design, and the procedure required to install them is identical:

Remove the stock footpeg—complete with bracket and shift lever—and the three screws at the rear of the primary case.

Using the provided spacers and screws, loosely mount the U-shaped bracket to the primary-case screw locations that were previously removed.

Next, fit the footpeg to the bracket, semi-tight for now.

Install the shift lever. Installing the shift lever on the Bartels' kit may prove a little tricky if you have a late-model Sportster with a separate derby cover; 1993 and later primary covers are wider in this area than older non-derby primary covers, so installation may require a little bending of the shift lever to clear the cover. Go ahead—it's okay. Once that's done, carefully tighten the shifter-lever pinch bolt. Do not over-torque it!

The brake side of the story is that there are more significant differences in design and execution between the Storz Performance and Bartels' Performance kits. However, both require removal of the stock brake pedal and the sprocket cover, so do that first.

The Bartels' kit requires that you remove the rear master cylinder, reverse it, and then gently reroute the brake line. The Storz kit, on the other hand, leaves the master cylinder in the stock location but backs it with a bracket plate. Bolting up the rest of the Bartels' Performance kit is pretty straightforward. Just be sure to replace all the cotter pins and install the snap-ring on the brake-pedal pivot like the instructions tell you to. Neither kit is difficult to install, and both work well. Choice really comes down to personal preference and price. Be aware, however, you've sacrificed passenger-carrying ability for the more aggressive stance that rearsets provide.

INSTALLING FORWARD CONTROLS ON YOUR SPORTSTER

Many people who buy Sportsters change the riding position by adding highway pegs, different handlebars, and risers, but not many seem to want the added expense or work of installing forward controls. Most riders overlook the advantages of moving not just the pegs, but the controls themselves, to a more comfortable "cruising" position. Partly, it's because there have been few choices of forward-control designs to choose from for five-speed XLs. That's changing. Custom Chrome (CCI), Drag Specialties, American Made, and others are coming on line (to

their senses?) with well-engineered kits that give the bike a great look and increased comfort.

In order to install the kit:

Start on the carb side and remove the exhaust system.

Remove both Allen-head screws that mount the rear master cylinder.

Remove the bottom oil line located under the right front of the engine, as it will have to be routed around the new forward control bracket.

Remove the master cylinder hose clip on the pulley cover and carefully move the master cylinder out of the way.

Remove the pulley cover, place it on a bench, and remove the footpeg and brake lever. Install the provided chrome cap, which covers the mounting hole for the peg.

Reinstall the pulley cover, master cylinder, and hose clip.

Remove the lower motor mount bolts.

Install the forward control assembly to the right side and install the crossbrace through the front hole in the right base.

Place the Oilite bushing into the brake linkage arm and install it by screwing the threaded end into the master cylinder and bolt it to the front control. Before you tighten it up, adjust the brake pedal by rotating the threaded rod in the arm into the master cylinder.

Before installing the exhaust system, check both gaskets to make sure they are in good condition; replace them if necessary. Now install the pipes and oil line.

Move over to the shifter side and remove the shift lever. The lever might need to be pried off; just remember to use care.

Remove the two Allen-head mounting bolts and remove the footpeg.

Install the shift assembly to the front motor mount.

Install the Oilite bushings into the shift linkage mount using the 2 3/8-inch bolts and Nyloc nuts, and bolt it to the shift arm and forward control.

Install the new shift arm by lining up the splines and sliding it on in position.

Tighten the Allen-head locking screw.

The shifter pedal is adjustable. It has detents machined into it and is easily adjusted by removing the peg and rotating the pedal to your desired position and then reinstalling the peg. (With CCI's kit, it's a good idea to pay special attention to the lever, keeping it tight, and using a light touch when shifting. If you don't, the fine splines on the lever and its bracket will strip, and you'll be left shiftless.

PERSONAL TOUCHES
PROJECT 101 • APPLYING COATINGS

 Time: Several days or weeks to have the work done by specialists

 Tools: Depends on what parts you're going to remove for coating

 Talent: and up

 Tab: $ to more than you should spend

 Tinware: Varies with intent and parts involved

 Tip: Check with the plater, coater, or technician regarding the suitability of the treatment to your pieces, and vise versa

 PERFORMANCE GAIN: Certain coatings can, in fact, improve performance and longevity, but most are for cosmetic enhancements

COMPLEMENTARY MODIFICATION: Custom paint, chrome, and so on

1 Modern coatings take many a form, some cosmetic, some functional. We all know about chrome and powder coat, which serve both masters to some degree, but look closely at this factory piston and behold the end of conventional break-in problems. No, you still have to use restraint and logic on fresh motors; it's just that this stuff layered and burnt into the skirt of the piston helps cover errors and protects not just from scuffing, but from long-term wear and tear.

We Harley-Davidson owners have a penchant for changing the condition and exterior coating of many a part on our hoss. Chrome brake calipers, highly polished brake discs, powder-coated cylinders and heads—on and on! Jeez, how we crave this "coat of many colors" cosmetic stuff. But how much thought do we give to its potential effect on the mechanical performance, or even composition, of the particular part in question? More importantly, just how much will we sacrifice function to the altar, and alteration, of form by the simple act of plating, polishing, coating, and chroming?

Two ways to cool off:

Take building a "hot" motor (literally), for example. In the eternal quest for more beans, we can easily screw up the fruits of our labor by ruining the heat dissipation qualities of our poor abused air-cooled engines. How? By chroming rocker boxes, by polishing head fins, by cutting fins off the bottom of the cylinders, that's how. Air-cooled engines cool by two methods: convection and radiation. Convection is when heat is transferred by movement or circulation, such as riding in the wind. This gives the hot parts of the engine a chance to shed their thermal burden in a hurry. Sitting still, the process oozes along, radiating heat into surrounding parts of the bike—like the engine cases or your pant leg if you give it a chance. Then maybe, eventually, into the still air around it. The factory is familiar with these two cooling methods. They go to great lengths to help the motor out by doing things like putting lots of fins on the cylinders and as many as possible on the heads. Then they leave them rough finished so all those little pores in the metal can spit up their share of the heat. Even the reason for black wrinkle finishes on H-D engines is similar. Forget that it looks pretty nice; it's there as much because a black finish dissipates heat really well as it is to dazzle your eye.

That's not cool:

Nothing like chroming a cylinder barrel to eliminate the fin's ability to shed heat by trapping it inside a layer of shiny insulation. And I've seen it done—even on engines that can ill afford to surrender what little cooling ability they have, like iron Sportsters or Knuckleheads. Think about this for a moment: Since you know that a running engine makes lots of heat and that heat cuts power (hence the expression "overheated"), why would you consciously want to keep it buried in the engine where it will cause trouble? Air isn't the greatest cooling medium known to man in the first place, but it's the only place besides your oil and other parts in the motor that heat has to go. And high horsepower generates even higher heat levels, crowding the limit more and more closely. The bottom line: If you can't feel mass quantities of heat coming from your engine, it's trapped inside. Not good for power or longevity. And by using improper finishes, you can easily screw up this delicate balance. Dumb, kids, just plain dumb—especially considering the last great frontier of engine tuning: thermal management.

Power from heat?

It is possible to create more power, as opposed to simply avoiding losing any, by using heat from combustion to make more power. One relatively well-known example of this is wrapping exhaust pipes in insulation to keep the heat in the cylinder head's exhaust port. It helps evacuate the charge. The flip side is keeping intake manifolds cool to improve the density of the incoming mixture. If you've been to the drags lately, you may have seen guys staging with bags of ice on the intake of their musclecars and asbestos blankets on their headers. Guess what, it works! Therefore, it stands to reason that doing the opposite doesn't. The fact is there's a company that's taking all this a step further. Bohacz Advanced Technology (BAT) specializes in application-specific coatings to just this end. They figure that if you can control where the 1,300-degree heat from combustion is allowed to go, you get more power. Things like cooler valves, complete with thinner seats, sharper valve jobs, cooler pistons to reduce detonation and allow more aggressive ignition timing, and better bearing and wrist pin life (especially in strokers), are a few of the benefits. They also offer a slightly different coating for moving parts—not for more lunge, but for longer life. And instead of polishing they stress relief by a special process known as Meta-Lax. This process allows up to three times the life in parts like valve springs that must work with high lift cams.

But never mind all that go stuff, let's think about whoa-ing for a minute.

Those of you who have opted to chrome your brake calipers, stay ahead of me if we go riding together, okay? If you ride behind, you may find yourself up close and personal (too personal, for my taste) in the event of a panic stop or two. It's all that heat that's generated by the brakes. Sure, the disc does most of the dissipating, but, oh, those poor pads.

Stuck inside a caliper running several times as hot as the wrinkle black heat-dispelling stock one, those poor pads have their work cut out for them. It can add up to much longer stopping distances, if not total fade, as the temperatures climb in a hard-pressed brake. Oh yeah, there's also an issue around the negative effect that chroming may have on the special bolts that hold the caliper on (not to mention other critical fasteners all over the bike, such as head bolts). Chrome plating in general involves polishing and dipping into molten vats of metals like copper nickel and the chromium itself. Sometimes, with several trips through this electroplating hell involved, it can change the temper of the base material. Do you really want a part this crucial to your well-being to be too soft to do the job safely? Or too brittle to trust not to snap when you least expect it?

Powder coat and chrome also have a nasty tendency to plug important holes, like oil holes or bushings in cam covers or crank/transmission cases. Some of these orifices have critical tolerances. It's not a great plan to dig excess shinola out of a hole of this caliber with your knife, sandpaper, or a rusty screwdriver, okay?

Powder coating (or as it's sometimes called, stove enameling) is a great invention. It offers a paint-like finish that's a whole lot tougher than paint. However, it's baked on at (can you see this coming?) 600 degrees! Some materials aren't gonna like that one bit. You give up a piece with solder on it or even some kinds of brazing, and if the part's not wrecked in the process, it's certainly not totally trustworthy afterwards. Be extra careful with parts like gas tanks to ensure that structural integrity is maintained. The rule of thumb should be to make slippery things even slipperier, things that are supposed to be sticky, stickier, and above all, control heat. Cool that which is too hot, and heat that which is too cool—whether it looks that "cool" or "hot" or not. Even a coating or finish that's guaranteed not to "chip, fade, peel, crack, or stink in hot weather" may have a huge hidden downside when applied to your Harley. So dote before you coat. You may not look as good sitting alongside the road, but it's more likely that you'll be sitting there by choice and will get home whenever you're darned good and ready. Besides, you'll be doing yourself and your Harley a favor—no sugar "coating" necessary.

Evolution Cams
103+ Cubic-Inch Engines

Company	Grind	Valve Timing	Duration at .053"	Duration at .020"	Valve Lift	Overlap at .053"	Lobe Center	Lobe Separation Angle	TDC Lift	Lifter Type	Spring Spacing
Andrews	EV9	36/60	276		.550	68	102	104		Hyd/Sld	Yes
		64/32	276		.550		106				
Andrews	EV88	34/70	284	318	.680	66	108	110	.288	Hyd	Yes
		76/32	288	322	.680		112		.264		
Carl's Speed Shop	CM6	36/60	276		.612	64	102	106	.244	Hyd	Yes
		68/28	276		.612		110		.228		
Carl's Speed Shop	CM780F	34/70	284		.774	64	108	110	.291	Sld	Yes
		74/30	284		.774		112		.267		
Crane	H314	26/54	260		.600	47	104	108	.219	Hyd	Yes
		65/21	266		.600		112		.184		
Crane	HEV0042	27/59	266		.600	50	106	110	.226	Hyd	Yes
		71/23	274		.576		114		.194		
Crane	HEV0034	37/59	276		.550	72	101	102	.281	Hyd	Yes
		61/35	276		.550		103		.263		
Crane	EVR0005	38/62	280	324	.731	73	102	106	.277	Sld	Yes
		75/35	290	332	.746		110		.238		
Head Quarters	HQ-28	23/63	266		.600	47	110	107	.199	Hyd	Yes
		52/24	256		.530		104		.186		
Head Quarters	HQ-27	26/60	266		.650	50	107	110	.221	Hyd	Yes
		70/24	274		.575		113		.198		
Leineweber	E-6	47/76		303	.560	86 at .020"	104.5	108.5	.285	Sld	Yes
		84/39		303	.560		112.5		.196		
Leineweber	E-7	43.5/73.5		297	.580	83.5 at .020"	105	106.8	.275	Sld	Yes
		77/40		297	.580		108.5		.227		
Powerhouse	620E	32/64	276		.620	56	106	110	.262	Sld	Yes
		72/24	276		.620		114		.215		
Powerhouse	620M	36/66	282		.620	66	105	109	.200	Sld	Yes
		76/30	286		.620		113		.200		
Red Shift	655	21/65	266		.655	37	112	114.5	.197	Hyd	Yes
		70/16	266		.655		117		.162		
Red Shift	625	33/58	271		.625	61	102.5	105.2	.250	Hyd	Yes
		64/28	272		.625		108		.216		
Red Shift	710	28/58	266		.705	49	105	108.5	.232	Sld	Yes
		65/21	266		.705		112		.190		
Red Shift	785	38/61	279		.785	65	101.5	107	.315	Sld	Yes
		72/27	279		.785		112.5		.243		
S&S	562	34/55	269		.560	63	100.5	103	.260	Hyd/Sld	Yes
		60/29	269		.560		105.5		.220		
S&S	563	32/64	276		.560	64	106	106	.250	Hyd/Sld	Yes
		64/32	276		.560		106		.220		
S&S	631	34/61	275		.630	63	103.5	106	.281	Sld	Yes
		66/29	276		.630		109		.221		
Sifton	142-EV	32/52	264		.540	62	100	102.5	.235	Sld	Yes
		60/30	270		.540		105		.226		
Sifton	147-EV	24/64	268		.640	54	110	109.5	.208	Sld	Yes
		66/28	275		.640		109		.240		
V-Thunder	3070	29/61	270		.608	60	106	106	.234	Hyd	Yes
		63/31	274		.608		106		.242		

Note: Valve lift with 1.63:1 rocker arm ratio.

Evolution Cams
89–93-Cubic-Inch Engines

Company	Grind	Valve Timing	Duration at .053"	Duration at .020"	Valve Lift	Overlap at .053"	Lobe Center	Lobe Separation Angle	TDC Lift	Lifter Type	Spring Spacing
Andrews	EV59	28/48	256	290	.560	52	100	103	.236	Hyd	Yes
		56/24	260	294	.560		106		.208		
Andrews	EV81	32/60	272	306	.610	62	104	106	.262	Hyd	Yes
		66/30	276	310	.610		108		.244		
Carl's Speed Shop	CM5	19/47	246		.580	35	104	105.5	.185	Hyd	Yes
		50/16	246		.580		107		.176		
Carl's Speed Shop	CM6	36/60	276		.612	64	102	106	.244	Hyd	Yes
		68/28	276		.612		110		.288		
Crane	H304	24/50	254		.600	49	103	104	.208	Hyd	Yes
		55/25	260		.600		105		.206		
Crane	H306	28/54	262		.500	51	103	108	.224	Hyd	Yes
		69/23	272		.510		113		.195		
Head Quarters	HQ-23	19/47	246		.600	43	104	104	.172	Hyd	Yes
		52/24	256		.530		104		.191		
Head Quarters	HQ-26	20/54	254		.600	42	107	106.2	.182	Hyd	Yes
		53/22	255		.530		105.5		.181		
Leineweber	E-5S	39/56		275	.544	65	98.5	105	.225	Hyd/Sld	Yes
		69/26		275	.544	at .020"	111.5		.132		
Leineweber	E-51	39/60		279	.540	72	100.5	103.5	.225	Hyd/Sld	Yes
		66/33		279	.540	at .020"	106.5		.168		
Powerhouse	560V	18/50	248		.560	36	106	107	.180	Hyd/Sld	Yes
		54/18	252		.560		108		.180		
Powerhouse	565VP	24/54	258		.565	44	105	107	.200	Hyd/Sld	Yes
		58/20	258		.565		109		.200		
Red Shift	575	25/54	259		.575	43	104.5	108.5	.225	Hyd	Yes
		63/18	261		.575		112.5		.162		
Red Shift	625	33/58	271		.625	61	102.5	105.2	.250	Hyd	Yes
		64/28	272		.625		108		.216		
RevTech	40	31/55	266		.560	58	102	104		Hyd	Yes
		59/27	266		.560		106				
S&S	561	32/40	252		.560	58	94	98	.252	Hyd/Sld	Yes
		50/26	256		.560		102		.210		
Screamin' Eagle	400	26.5/50.5	257	304	.500	58	102	102		Hyd	Yes
		55.5/31.5	267	314	.500		102				
Sifton	141-EV	29/41	250		.480	55	96	101	.232	Hyd/Sld	Yes
		58.5/26	264		.480		106.2		.184		
Sifton	146-EV	30/45	255		.500	54	97	101.5	.232	Sld	Yes
		56/24	260		.500		106		.200		
V-Thunder	3060	24/56	260		.585	53	106	106	.210	Hyd	Yes
		61/29	270		.585		106		.226		

Note: Valve lift with 1.63:1 rocker arm ratio.

Company	Grind	Valve Timing	Duration at .053"	Duration at .020"	Valve Lift	Overlap at .053"	Lobe Center	Lobe Separation Angle	TDC Lift	Lifter Type	Spring Spacing
Andrews	EV72	30/54	264	298	.560	58	102	104	.246	Hyd	Yes
		60/28	268	302	.560		106		.230		
Andrews	EV79	31/55	266	307	.560	63	102	104	.245	Hyd	Yes
		64/32	276	314	.550		106		.250		
Andrews	EV81	32/60	272	306	.610	62	104	106	.262	Hyd	Yes
		66/30	276	310	.610		108		.244		
Andrews	EV84	32/64	276	310	.640	62	106	108	.269	Hyd	Yes
		70/30	280	314	.640		110		.246		
Carl's Speed Shop	CM6	36/60	276		.612	64	102	106	.244	Hyd	Yes
		68/28	276		.612		110		.228		
Crane	H304	24/50	254		.600	49	103	104	.208	Hyd	Yes
		55/25	260		.600		105		.206		
Crane	H310	23/63	266		.550	51	110	110	.229	Hyd	Yes
		68/28	276		.550		110		.229		
Head Quarters	HQ-26	20/54	254		.600	42	107	106.2	.182	Hyd	Yes
		53/22	255		.530		105.5		.181		
Head Quarters	HQ-28	23/63	266		.600	47	110	107	.199	Hyd	Yes
		52/24	256		.530		104		.186		
Leineweber	E-5	45.5/70		295	.540	86.5	102.5	104.5	.272	Hyd/Sld	Yes
		74/41		295	.540	at .020"	106.5		.215		
Leineweber	E-4	49/74		303	.560	88	102.5	105.5	.297	Hyd/Sld	Yes
		76/39		295	.545	at .020"	108.5		.196		
Powerhouse	595E	24/60	264		.595	44	108	110	.215	Hyd/Sld	Yes
		64/20	264		.595		112		.191		
Powerhouse	620E	32/64	276		.620	56	106	110	.262	Solid	Yes
		72/24	276		.620		114		.215		
Red Shift	653	21/52	253		.653	37	105.5	108.2	.180	Hyd	Yes
		58/16	254		.653		111		.162		
Red Shift	654	21/59	260		.654	38	109	109.5	.192	Hyd	Yes
		57/17	254		.654		110		.162		
Red Shift	625	33/58	271		.625	61	102.5	105.2	.250	Hyd	Yes
		64/28	272		.625		108		.216		
RevTech	40	31/55	266		.560	58	102	104		Hyd	Yes
		59/27	266		.560		106				
S&S	562	34/55	269		.560	63	100.5	103	.260	Hyd/Sld	Yes
		60/29	269		.560		105.5		.220		
Sifton	142-EV	32/52	264		.540	62	100	102.5	.235	Sld	Yes
		60/30	270		.540		105		.226		
V-Thunder	3060	24/56	260		.585	53	106	106	.210	Hyd	Yes
		61/29	270		.585		106	.226			

Note: Valve lift with 1.63:1 rocker arm ratio.

Company	Grind	Valve Timing	Duration at .053"	Duration at .020"	Valve Lift	Overlap at .053"	Lobe Center	Lobe Separation Angle	TDC Lift	Lifter Type	Spring Spacing
Andrews	EV13	15/31	226	270	.485	28	98	102	.161	Hyd	Stock
		45/13	238	280	.495		106		.148		
Andrews	EV27	20/36	236	270	.495	36	98	101	.182	Hyd	Stock
		44/16	240	274	.495		104		.166		
Andrews	EV3	21/37	238	280	.495	36	98	101	.197	Hyd	Stock
		43/15	238	280	.495		104		.159		
Andrews	EV46	25/41	246	283	.495	42	98	102	.207	Hyd	Stock
		49/17	246	283	.495		106.5		.197		
Bartels'	BP20	18/36	234		.490	31	98	102		Hyd	Stock
		45/13	238		.495		106				
Bartels'	BP40	21/37	238		.495	41	98	101		Hyd	Stock
		48/20	248		.495		104				
Carl's Speed Shop	CM495F	19/47	246		.495	35	104	105.5		Hyd	Stock
		50/16	246		.495		107				
Crane	310	16/40	236		.490	35	102	102	.164	Hyd	Stock
		43/19	242		.490		102		.185		
Crane	H286	19/43	242		.490	43	102	102	.179	Hyd	Stock
		48/24	252		.490		102		.206		
Edelbrock	1740	19/43	242		.490	43	102	102	.177	Hyd	Stock
		48/24	252		.490		102		.204		
Head Quarters	HQ-24	20/36	236		.500	39	98	102.2	.174	Hyd	Stock
		52/19	251		.500		106.5		.166		
Leineweber	E-2	43/62		285	.470	80	99.5	102.4	.208	Hyd/Sld	Stock
		67.5/37		285	.470	at .020"	105.2		.182		
Leineweber	E3S	44/62		286	.502	80	99	103	.215	Hyd/Sld	Stock
		70/36		286	.502	at .020"	107		.170		
Powerhouse	500P	16/42	238		.500	32	103	103.5	.174	Hyd	Stock
		44/16	240		.500		104		.179		
RevTech	05	16/32	228		.465	33	98	100		Hyd	Stock
		41/17	238		.475		102				
RevTech	10	21/37	238		.475	39	98	102		Hyd	Stock
		50/18	248		.480		106				
Rivera Engineering	EV-100	27/43	250		.467	51	98	102.7		Hyd	Stock
		59/24	263		.467		107.5				
S&S	502	28/40	248		.500	52	96	99.5	.225	Hyd/Sld	Stock
		50/24	254		.500		103		.221		
Screamin' Eagle	406	16/48	244	282	.480	35	106	106		Hyd	Stock
		51/19	250	288	.480		106				
Sifton	143-EV	20/35	235		.500	34	97	101.5	.184	Hyd	Stock
		46/14	240		.500		106		.160		
Sifton	145-EV	28/42	250		.460	48	97	101	.200	Hyd/Sld	Stock
		50/20	250		.460		105		.176		
Sifton	140-EV	30/42	252		.450	57	96	100	.222	Hyd	Stock
		55/27	262		.450		104		.178		
V-Thunder	3010	15/39	234		.500	30	102	102	.156	Hyd	Stock
		39/15	234		.500		102		.156		
V-Thunder	3020	18/42	240		.500	36	102	102	.173	Hyd	Stock
		42/18	240		.500		102		.173		

Note: Pistons must have valve reliefs. Valve lift with 1.63:1 rocker arm ratio.

Evolution Cams
Modified 80-Cubic-Inch Engines

Company	Grind	Valve Timing	Duration at .053"	Duration at .020"	Valve Lift	Overlap at .053"	Lobe Center	Lobe Separation Angle	TDC Lift	Lifter Type	Spring Spacing
Andrews	EV35	21/37 52/20	238 252	280 295	.495 .500	41	98 106	102	.197 .182	Hyd	Yes
Andrews	EV51	28/44 54/22	252 256	286 290	.510 .510	50	98 106	102	.233 .195	Hyd	Stock
Andrews	EV59	28/48 56/24	256 260	290 294	.560 .560	52	100 106	103	.236 .208	Hyd	Yes
Bartels'	BP60	26/42 55/23	248 258		.495 .495	49	98 106	102		Hyd	Stock
Carl's Speed Shop	CM5	19/47 50/16	246 246		.580 .580	35	104 107	105.5	.185 .176	Hyd	Yes
Crane	H290	17/43 45/23	240 248		.581 .581	40	103 101	102	.169 .195	Hyd	Yes
Crane	H296	24/48 57/25	252 262		.490 .500	49	102 106	104	.200 .206	Hyd	Stock
Edelbrock	1741	20/46 52/22	246 254		.600 .600	42	103 105	104	.187 .180	Hyd	Yes
Head Quarters	HQ-25	18/38 42/14	236 236		.550 .550	32	100 104	102	.166 .150	Hyd	Yes
Head Quarters	HQ-29	20/36 51/19	236 250		.580 .500	39	98 106	102	.193 .162	Hyd	Yes
Head Quarters	HQ-23	19/47 52/24	246 256		.600 .530	43	104 104	104	.172 .191	Hyd	Yes
Leineweber	E5S	39/56 69/26		275 275	.544 .544	65 at .020"	98.5 111.5	105	.225 .132	Hyd/Sld	Yes
Powerhouse	530G	18/44 50/16	242 246		.530 .530	34	103 107	105	.184 .184	Hyd/Sld	Yes
Powerhouse	560V	18/50 54/18	248 252		.560 .560	36	106 108	107	.180 .180	Hyd/Sld	Yes
Red Shift	535	12/42 57/4	234 241		.535 .560	16	105 116.5	110.7	.138 .098	Hyd	Yes
Red Shift	560	18/44 58/4	242 242		.560 .560	22	103 117	110	.180 .100	Hyd	Yes
Red Shift	575	25/54 63/18	259 261		.575 .575	43	104.5 112.5	108.5	.225 .162	Hyd	Yes
RevTech	20	22/46 59/19	248 258		.480 .490	41	102 110	106		Hyd	Stock
Rev Tech	30	21/37 52/20	238 252		.495 .530	41	98 106	102		Hyd	Yes
S&S	561	32/40 50/26	252 256		.560 .560	58	94 102	98	.252 .210	Hyd/Sld	Yes
Screamin' Eagle	400	26.5/50.5 55.5/31.5	257 267	304 314	.500 .500	58	102 102	102		Hyd	Yes
Screamin' Eagle	433	23/47 56/24	250 260	286 299	.530 .530	47	102 106	104		Sld	Yes
Sifton	144-EV	27/46 56/22	253 258		.490 .490	49	99.5 107	103	.216 .166	Hyd	Yes
Sifton	141-EV	29/41 58.5/26	250 264		.480 .480	55	96 106	101	.232 .184	Hyd/Sld	Yes
V-Thunder	3030	16/44 44/16	240 240		.530 .530	32	104 104	104	.161 .161	Hyd	Yes
V-Thunder	3040	17/45 50/22	242 252		.510 .510	39	104 104	104	.164 .191	Hyd	Yes
V-Thunder	3050	22/50 50/22	252 252		.510 .510	44	104 104	104	.191 .191	Hyd	Yes

Note: Bolt-in cams also can be considered for this application level. Valve lift with 1.63:1 rocker arm ratio.

Evolution Cams
Stock Engines

Year	Grind	Valve Timing	Duration at .053"	Duration at .020"	Valve Lift	Overlap at .053"	Lobe Center	Lobe Separation Angle	TDC Lift	Lifter Type	Spring Spacing
1984–95	Stock-C	-15/03	168		.423	-30	99	99		Hyd	Stock
		03/-15	168		.423		99				
1984–87	Stock-V	-06/38	212		.472	-9	112	108		Hyd	Stock
		25/-03	202		.472		104				
1988–91	Stock-L	01/37	218	266	.495	3	108	111.5	.091	Hyd	Stock
		52/02	234	280	.495		115		.083		
1992–96	Stock-N	-02/30	208	250	.472	-11	106	108	.070	Hyd	Stock
		31/-09	202	242	.472		110		.049		
1995–96	Stock-Q	0/22	202		.472	-10	99	107.5		Hyd	Stock
		48/-10	218		.472		116				

Note: Valve lift with 1.63:1 rocker arm ratio.

Screamin' Eagle 1340 Camshafts Specs*

Description	Part Number	Lift at Valve Intake/Exhaust	Duration at .053 Intake/Exhaust	Timing at .053 Lift Open/Close	TDC Lift at Valve Intake/Exhaust
SE-C	25496-97	.505"/.505"	190°/190°	Intake: 12°ATDC/22°ABDC Exhaust:20°BBDC/10°ATDC	.043"/.053"
SE-1	25487-87A	.495"/.495"	244°/250°	Intake: 17.5°BTDC/46.5°ABDC Exhaust: 52.5°BBDC/17.5°ATDC	.177"/.170"
SE-2	25523-87A 25490-87 Kit	.516"/.516"	257°/267°	Intake: 28°BTDC/49°ABDC Exhaust: 55°BBDC/30°ATDC	.234"/.231"
SE-3	25422-97	.503"/.503"	236°/240°	Intake: 20°BTDC/36°ABDC Exhaust: 44°BBDC/16°ATDC	.185"/.169"
SE-4	25752-97	.505"/.505"	235°/240°	Intake: 20°BTDC/36°ABDC Exhaust: 46°BBDC/14°ATDC	.189"/.151"
SE-11	25753-97	.508"/.508"	246°/249°	Intake: 19°BTDC/47°ABDC Exhaust: 55°BBDC/14°ATDC	.181"/.153"
SE-54	25528-89A 25493-89 Kit	.546"/.546"	250°/260°	Intake: 22°BTDC/48°ABDC Exhaust: 55°BBDC/25°ATDC	.186"/.196"
SE-57	25754-97 25755-97 Kit	.575"/.575"	252°/256°	Intake: 22°BTDC/50°ABDC Exhaust: 56°BBDC/20°ATDC	.202"/.186"

*Theoretical. Based on rocker arm ratio of 1.65. Valvetrain components, operation temperature, and tolerance stack-up will affect actual lifts.

SOURCES

No, this isn't the 1-800 yellow pages for Evo goodies, but it is a good place to start. It offers brains to pick, people to solicit advice from, places to purchase tools and parts, and so much more. Frankly, this could turn out to be the most useful part of the book. The collective abilities, products, and talents represented in this section amount to the large tip of an iceberg of insight into Evolutions. The outfits listed here make their living knowing what to do and what to do it with—for H-Ds specifically, motorcycles in general, or the automotive universe as we know it. If they can't help, they'll know who can. If this book has taught you anything, call this part a "continuing education" program. Just remember—you won't know if you don't ask!

AAA SHOT PEENING
5245 S. Kyrene, Unit #24
Tempe, Arizona 85283
602-820-1283
Professional shot peening, magnafluxing, and performance engine building

ACCEL PRODUCTS
8700 Brookpark Rd.
Cleveland, Ohio 44129
216-398-8300
Flywheel shafts, ignitions, electrical systems, starter motors, and fuel injection components

ACCUTRONIX RACING PRODUCTS
17650 N. 25th Ave., Unit # 1
Phoenix, Arizona 85023
602-993-2675
Performance chassis components

AIR FLOW RESEARCH, INC.
10490 Hex Ave.
Pacoima, California 91331
818-890-0616
Cylinder head porting

AMP RESEARCH
1855 Laguna Canyon Rd.
Laguna Beach, California 92651
714-497-7525
E-Z Pull clutch

ANDREWS PRODUCTS, INC.
5212 Shapland Ave.
Rosemont, Illinois 60018
773-992-4014
Performance cams, transmission gears, and ignition coils

APE
P.O. Box 6998
1010 W. Oak St.
Burbank, California 91506
818-842-4952 or 800-824-1825
Leakdown tester

ARIAS PISTONS
13420 S. Normandie Ave.
Gardena, California 90249
310-532-9737
Racing pistons

ART, INC.
Rt. 360, Box 247
Burgess, Virginia 22432
804-453-3357
Multi-stage clutch systems, supercharging, and custom racing components

ASTRO-PEEN CO.
13732 Prairie Ave.
Hawthorne, California 90250
213-679-5288
Professional shot peening

ATLAS PRECISION
16091 Kamana Rd.
Apple Valley, California 92307
619-242-9111
Performance frames, parts, and accessories

AUTO METER INSTRUMENTS
413 W. Elm St.
Sycamore, Illinois 60178
815-895-8141
Performance tachometers and gauges

AUTOMOTIVE BALANCING SERVICE
10640 South Garfield Ave.
South Gate, California 90280
213-564-6846
Dynamic engine balancing, heat treating, and magna fluxing

AUTO WARE, INC.
7624 Verona N.W.
Albuquerque, New Mexico 87120
505-898-6444 or 800-647-2392
Computer software programs

AVON TIRE
Hoppe & Associates
407 Howell Way
Edmonds, Washington 98020
206-771-2115 or 800-624-7470
Performance tires

C. R. AXTELL
10949 Tuxford St., Unit #17
Sun Valley, California 91352
818-768-5595
Cylinder head porting and cams for Evolution motors only

AXTELL SALES, INC.
1424 S.E. Maury
Des Moines, Iowa 50317
515-243-2518
Big-bore cylinders, pistons, carbs, and cams

B & G RACING COMPUTERS
4213 N. 18th Place
Phoenix, Arizona 85016
602-274-2537
Performance tuning computers

B & K CYLINDER HEADS
104 W. Mill St.
Bloomington, Illinois 61701
309-827-0485
Cylinder head porting

BAISLEY HI-PERFORMANCE
5511 N. Interstate
Portland, Oregon 97217
503-289-1251
Cylinder head porting, valvetrain components, and oil system components

BANDIT MACHINE WORKS
222 Millwood Rd.
Lancaster, Pennsylvania 17602
717-464-2800
Performance Super Clutch

BARNETT ENGINEERING
9920 Freeman Ave.
P.O. Box 2826
Santa Fe Springs, California 90670
310-941-1284
Clutches and cables

BARTELS' PERFORMANCE PRODUCTS
3237 Carter Ave.
Marina Del Rey, California 90292
310-578-9888 or 800-747-1151
Exhaust systems, cams, valvetrain components, carbs, manifolds, and suspension components

BELT DRIVES LTD.
3080 E. La Jolla St.
Anaheim, California 92806
714-630-1433
Primary belt drive systems

BFZEZINSKI RACING PRODUCTS, INC.
N50 W23001 Betker Dr.
Pewaukee, Wisconsin 53072
414-246-8577
Flow-testing tools, porting tools, and digital burettes

BIG BOAR PRODUCTS
P.O. Box 369
Lenoir City, Tennessee 37771
423-458-8640
High Performance Starters

BIONDO RACING PRODUCTS
75 N. Corona Ave.
Valley Stream, New York 11580
516-825-0020 or 800-332-1320
Drag racing practice tree

BISAGO BROS. ENG.
P.O. Box 1029
Placerville, California 95667
916-622-1464
Heavy-duty transmission trap doors

Bohacz Advanced Technology (BAT)
201-227-6383
Manifold and other coatings

BOMAR MAGNETO SERVICE
2601 E. 28th St., Unit #304
Signal Hill, California 90806
310-424-4131
Magneto rebuilding service

BOSCH CORPORATION
2800 South 25th Ave.
Broadview, Illinois 60153
708-865-5381 or 800-937-2672
Spark plugs and heat-range guides

BRAKING USA
1331 India St.
San Diego, California 92101
619-239-0447
High-performance brake components

BRANCH FLOWMETRICS
5556 Corporate Dr.
Cypress, California 90630
714-827-1463
Cylinder head porting, valvetrain components, and carbs

BRC PISTONS
Rt. 3, Box 68
U.S. Hwy. 90 E.
Live Oak, Florida 32060
904-364-5623 or 800-522-7478
Custom performance pistons

BRUSH RESEARCH
MANUFACTURING CO.
4642 East Floral Dr.
Los Angeles, California 90022
213-261-2193
Cylinder honing tools

BSR PRODUCTS, INC.
7701 N. Tryon St.
Charlotte, North Carolina 28262
704-547-0901
Safety-wire pliers, spark plug tools,
aircraft fittings, and stainless steel
wire screen

BUB ENTERPRISES
22573 Meyer Ravine Rd.
Grass Valley, California 95949
916-268-0449
Performance Exhaust Systems

BUCHANAN'S FRAME SHOP
629 E. Garvey Ave.
Monterey Park, California 91755
818-280-4003
Frame straightening, wheels, rims,
and spokes

BW BILLETS
1334 W. Collins
Orange, California 92667
714-639-8750
Custom aluminum billet fork, triple
clamps, and accessories

CARL'S SPEED SHOP
390 North Beach St.
Daytona Beach, Florida 32114
904-258-3777
Performance engine building,
head porting, cams, billet carbs,
and racing components

CARRILLO INDUSTRIES
990 Calle Amanecer
San Clemente, California 92672
714-498-1800
Performance connecting rods

CHAMPION SPARK PLUG CO.
900 Upton Ave.
Toledo, Ohio 43607
419-535-2000 or 800-537-8984
Spark plugs and tuning charts

CHICAGO LATEX PRODUCTS
1030 Morse Ave.
Schaumberg, Illinois 60193
708-893-2880
Latex for cylinder head port molds

CHROME SPECIALTIES
4200 Diplomacy Rd.
Fort Worth, Texas 76155
817-868-2000 or 800-299-6256
Performance parts and custom
accessories

COMETIC GASKET
8767 East Ave.
Mentor, Ohio 44060
216-974-1077
Top-end gaskets

COMPETITION, INC.
8318 Braniff St.
Houston, Texas 77061
713-644-4922
Crankcases and big-bore pistons

COMPU-FIRE
20290 Carrey Rd.
Walnut, California 91789
909-598-5485
Performance ignition systems and
high-torque starter motors

CORBIN PACIFIC
11445 Commercial Pkwy.
Castorville, California 95012
408-633-2500 or 800-538-7035
(U.S.)
800-663-1016 (Canada)
Custom seats

CRANE CAMS
530 Fentress Blvd.
Daytona Beach, Florida 32114
904-258-6174
Performance cams and valvetrain
components

CUSTOM CHROME, INC. (CCI)
16100 Jacqueline Ct.
Morgan Hill, California 95037
408-778-0500 or 800-729-3332
Performance parts and custom
accessories

CUSTOM CYCLE ENGINEERING
CO.
629 S. Rancho Santa Fe Rd., Suite
309
San Marcos, California 92069
800-472-9253
Fork braces, fork trees, custom billet parts, and accessories

CV PRODUCTS
919 Finch Ave.
High Point, North Carolina 27263
910-883-4096 or 800-448-1223
Titanium valves, valvetrain components, and performance engine
coatings

CYCLE ELECTRIC, INC.
P.O. Box 81
Englewood, Ohio 45322
513-884-7300 or 800-523-2645
Manufacturers of generators and
regulators

D & S PERFORMANCE
2184 Rice Ave.
Lake City, Pennsylvania 16423
814-774-2591
Cylinder heads, frames, and
advance weight springs

D C COMPANY
P.O. Box 460
Loomis, California 95650
916-652-4751
Racing fiberglass components

DALTON DESIGNS
993-C S. Santa Fe, Suite 25
Visata, California 92083
619-726-1693
Fine Line thin-belt conversions

DELKRON MANUFACTURING
2430 Manning St.
Sacramento, California 95815
916-921-9703
High-performance crankcases

DEPARTURE BIKE WORKS
3091 Hull St.
Richmond, Virginia 23224
804-231-0244
Custom fabrication

DIAMOND ENGINEERING
1575 Aviation Center Pkwy., Suite
506
Daytona Beach, Florida 32114
904-254-4800
Polished stainless, titanium, and
high-strength fasteners

DILLS DEVELOPMENT
P.O. Box 369
Lenoir City, Tennessee 37771
615-458-8640
High-amperage batteries

DOUGLAS FILTER CO.
P.O. Box 131
Big Lake, Minnesota 55309
612-263-6615
Perf-Form quality oil filters

DRAG SPECIALTIES
P.O. Box 9336
Minneapolis, Minnesota 55440
612-942-7890
Performance parts and custom
accessories

DUNLOP TIRE CORP.
P.O. Box 1109
Buffalo, New York 14240
716-879-8258 or 800-548-4714
Performance tires

DYNATEK
164 South Valencia St.
Glendora, California 91741
818-963-1669
Manufacturers of Dyna electronic
ignitions

DYNOJET RESEARCH
200 Arden Dr.
Belgrade, Montana 59714
406-388-4993 or 800-992-4993
Carburetor jetting kits and
dynamometers

EARL'S PERFORMANCE PROD-
UCTS
189 W. Victoria
Long Beach, California 90805
310-609-1602 or 800-533-1320
Aircraft hose and fittings

EASTWOOD
Box 3014
Malvern, Pennsylvania 19355-0714
800-343-9353
Toys, tools, and memorabilia

EBC BRAKES USA
12860 Bradley Ave.
Sylmar, California 91342
818-362-5534
Kevlar brake pads

EDELBROCK CORP.
2700 California St.
Torrance, California 90503
310-781-2222
Performance cylinder heads

E.T.R. PRODUCTS
P.O. Box 31
Delphi, Indiana 46923
317-564-3946 or 800-245-5067
Oil pump pressure spring kits
EXTRUDE HONE
8800 Somerset Blvd.
Paramount, California 90723
310-531-2976
High-tech abrasive paste porting

50's Boy
2841 Saturn St., Suite L
Brea, California 92621
714-579-1957
Trick Gauges and Instrument
Packages

F & S HARLEY-DAVIDSON
7220 N. Dixie Dr.
Dayton, Ohio 45414
513-898-8084 or 800-783-2222
Performance engine building and
racing parts

FALICON PERFORMANCE
ENGINEERING
1115 Old Coachman Rd.
Clearwater, Florida 34625
813-797-2468
Flywheel and rod rebuilding,
Magnafluxing, polishing, heat
treating, and shot peening

FAST COMPANY
835 7th Ave.
Kirkland, Washington 98033
425-828-4130
Cylinder head porting, dyno testing, and performance engine
building

FERINA CARBIDE TOOL CO.
101 Chuck Sewell
P.O. Box 480
Marietta, Oklahoma 73448
800-233-1253
Carbide grinding burs

FERREA RACING COMPONENTS
2600 N.W. 55th Ct., Suite 238
Fort Lauderdale, Florida 33309
305-733-2505
Competition valves and piston
pins

FEULING R&D
2521 Palma Dr.
Ventura, California 93003
805-650-2598
Four-valve heads, custom exhaust
systems, dyno services, and engine
research

FLO DYNAMICS
1150 Pike Lane #2
Oceano, California 93445
805-481-6300
Cylinder head porting

FLORA RACING HEADS
3319 W. Sample St.
South Bend, Indiana 46619
219-233-0642
Cylinder head porting, custom
frames, and chassis components

FRAME ODDITIES
13001 Abbey Rd.
North Royalton, Ohio 44133
216-582-0240
Custom frame and metal fabrication

G & L PERFORMANCE TECH.
1042 Kitty Hawk Rd.
Kitty Hawk, North Carolina 27949
919-261-2986
Performance engine coatings

GEROLAMY COMPANY
3250 Monier Circle, Units G & H
Rancho Cordova, California 95742
916-638-9008
Cylinder head porting, balancing,
and porting abrasives

GREAT LAKES CYCLE
8567 Tyler Blvd.
Mentor, Ohio 44060
216-946-9600 or 800-522-4537
Performance engine building

GRIOT'S GARAGE
3500-A 20th St. E.
Tacoma, Washington 98424
800-345-5789
Specialty garage equipment and
tools

HANDCRAFTED AMERICAN
RACING MOTORCYCLES
9716 North Lima Rd.
Poland, Ohio 44515
330-549-9476
Publisher of monthly tabloid for
Harley racing events; Larry Smith,
editor

HARBOR FREIGHT TOOLS
Retail locations all over California,
or by mail order
800-423-2567
Tools and specialty equipment

HARLEY-DAVIDSON MOTOR
COMPANY, INC.
3700 W. Juneau Ave.
Milwaukee, Wisconsin 53208
414-342-4680
Screamin' Eagle performance parts

HAWAYA RACING
1122 Husband St.
Baker, Louisiana 70714
504-774-5384
Performance engine building and
racing parts

TOM HAYDEN ENTERPRISES
2727 Calle Olivo
Thousand Oaks, California 91360
800-664-6872
M6 primary chain tensioner

HEAD QUARTERS
Warehouses in Ontario, Canada,
and Buffalo, New York
519-289-5229 or 519-289-5990
Cylinder head porting, cams, valvetrain components, carbs, and
exhaust systems

HEMI DESIGN
3147 South Austin Blvd.
Cicero, Illinois 60650
708-652-1033
Cylinder head porting

H/E/S, INC.
4156 Mildred Ave.
Los Angeles, California 90066
310-397-3195
Custom machining

HIGHWAY ART CORP.
17516 Von Karman Ave.
Irving, California 92714
714-756-9201 or 800-398-0222
Carlini torque arms

HIGHWAY CHOPPERS
6723 W. Glendale Ave.
Glendale, Arizona 85303
602-939-9083
Engine balancing

PETE HILL MOTORCYCLES
1401 W. Blue Ridge Dr.
Greenville, South Carolina 29611
803-271-0528
Performance engine building

HOLESHOT PERFORMANCE
320 Babe Thompson Rd.
La Selva, California 95076
408-761-2808
Electric power shifters

HOT SHOT MOTORWORKS
555 S. Warpole
Upper Sandusky, Ohio 43351
419-294-1997
Performance engine building,
cylinder head porting, and
crankcase repair

HOUSE OF HORSEPOWER
600 South Sunset St., Unit D
Longmont, Colorado 80501
303-776-4421
High-performance crankcases and
fuel-injection pump drives

HPC
550 W. 3615 South
Salt Lake City, Utah 84115
801-262-6807
Performance engine coatings

JOE HUNT MAGNETO
11336-A Sunco Dr.
Rancho Cordova, California 95742
916-635-5387
Dual- and single-fire magnetos
and alternators

HYPERFORMANCE
5152 A, N.E. 12th Ave.
Pleasant Hill, Iowa 50317
515-266-6381
Big-bore cylinders, pistons, and
cylinder head porting

IMI PERFORMANCE PRODUCTS
10065 Greenleaf Ave.
Santa Fe Springs, California 90670
310-944-9265
High Performance Starters

IMPARTS LTD.
9330 Manchester Rd.
St. Louis, Missouri 63119
800-325-9043
Specialty tools and tidbits

JACOB'S ELECTRONICS
500 N. Baird St.
Midland, Texas 79701
915-685-3345 or 800-627-8800
Performance ignition components

JAN'S CYCLE GASKETS
12 Edgeboro Rd.
East Brunswick, New Jersey 08816
908-613-4494
Quality gaskets

JAY BRAKE ENTERPRISES
720 Cayuga St.
Lewiston, New York 14092
716-754-9092
Brake and shifter controls

JC WHITNEY
(Motorcycle accessories and parts
division)
2319 S. Troop St.
P.O. Box 8410
Chicago, Illinois 60680
312-431-6102
Parts and accessories

JE PISTONS
15312 Connector Ln.
Huntington Beach, California
92649
714-898-9763
Racing pistons

JIM'S MACHINING
555 Dawson Dr.
Camarillo, California 93012
805-482-6913
Performance engine parts and
special tools

JOHNSON CYLINDER HEADS
P.O. Box 5546
Santa Maria, California 93456
805-922-3569
Performance billet cylinder heads

K & N ENGINEERING
561 Iowa Ave.
Riverside, California 92507
909-684-9762 or 800-858-3333
Performance air filters

KARATA ENT. CO.
3 River Rd.
Conshohocken, Pennsylvania
19428
610-825-2070
Belt-drive kits and magnetos

KATELEY PERFORMANCE PROD-
UCTS
P.O. Box 25271
Anaheim, California 92825
714-534-0564
Performance cams and valvetrain
components

KB PERFORMANCE PISTONS
4909 Goni Rd.
Carson City, Nevada 89706
702-884-1299 or 800-560-4814
High-performance pistons

KECK ENGINEERING, INC.
3888T Taylor Pkwy.
North Ridgeville, Ohio 44039
216-327-2715
Billet aluminum crankcases, cylinders, and motorcycle lifts

KENNY BOYCE PRO STREET
CHASSIS WORKS
11295 Sunrise Gold Circle, #F
Rancho Cordova, California 95742
916-852-9116
Frames and chassis components

KERKER/SUPERTRAPP
4540 W. 160th St.
Cleveland, Ohio 44135
216-265-8400
Performance exhaust systems

KINSLER FUEL INJECTION
1834-A Thunderbird Rd.
Troy, Minnesota 48084
810-362-1145
Fuel injection systems

K-LINE INDUSTRIES, INC.
315 Garden Ave.
Holland, Minnesota 49424
616-396-3564 or 800-824-5546
Engine and cylinder head repair
tools and supplies

KLOTZ
P.O. Box 11343
Fort Wayne, Indiana 46857
219-749-0489 or 800-242-0489
Synthetic lubricants, octane boost-
0ers, and gasoline additives

KORN'S CYCLE SERVICE
9440 Breckenridge Rd.
St. Louis, Missouri 63114
314-423-5455
Performance engine building and
custom machining

KOSMAN RACING
55 Oak St.
San Francisco, California 94102
415-861-4262
Custom racing frames and suspension components

KT COMPONENTS/KENDON
INDUSTRIES
3711 E. La Palma Ave.
Anaheim, California 92806
800-847-8618
Sofspension, trailers, and Buell
exhausts

KURYAKYN USA
448B Hwy. 35/64
Somerset, Wisconsin 54025 or
P.O. Box 37
Stillwater, Minnesota 55082
715-247-5008
Hypercharger air cleaner and cus-
tom accessories

LAKE SHORE HARLEY-DAVIDSON
1424 Belvidere Rd.
Waukegan, Illinois 60085
708-662-4500
Performance engine building

LARSON MACHINE
P.O. Box 693
Belton, Missouri 64012
816-322-1007
Five-speed auto transmissions

LEINEWEBER ENTERPRISES
P.O. Box 335
Yucca Valley, California 92286
619-364-4432
Performance cams and valvetrain
components

LOCKHART OIL COOLERS
151 CaiJe IgJesia
San Clemente, California 92673
714-498-9090
Oil coolers and thermostats

LOCTITE CORP.
4450 Cranwood Pkwy.
Cleveland, Ohio 44128
216-475-3600 or 800-321-9188
Adhesives, sealants, and retaining
compounds

LOS ANGELES (L.A.) SLEEVE
12051 Rivera Rd.
Santa Fe Springs, California 90670
310-945-7578
Cylinder liners

LOVETT ENTERPRISES
6 Maplewood Dr.
Petal, Missouri 93465
601-545-1093
Goodyear racing tires

MAC PRODUCTS
43214 Black Deer Loop, #113
Temecula, California 92590
800-367-4486 (U.S.) or 800-423-
5501 (Canada)
Exhaust systems

MAC TOOLS, INC.
S. Fayette St.
Washington Court House, Ohio
43160
614-335-4112
Quality hand tools

MACKIE ENGINEERING
2065-H Sperry Ave.
Ventura, California 93003
805-658-6969
Cylinder head porting

MAGSEARCH CO.
3065 Powell Rd.
Kent, Ohio 44240
216-673-0342
Racing weather stations and computers

MANLEY PERFORMANCE
PRODUCTS
1960 Swarthmore Ave.
Lakewood, New Jersey 08701
908-905-3366 or 800-526-1362
Valvetrain components and
engine-building aids

MASTER PERFORMANCE
3707 Roctiamteau Dr.
Williamsburg, Virginia 23185
804-566-0544
Performance engine building,
rods, crankcases, and fuel-injection
pump drives

MC ADVANTAGES
P.O. Box 22225
Des Moines, Iowa 50325
515-987-5826 or 800-726-9620
Power Arc single-fire ignition

MC IGNITION CO., INC.
2518 N.E. 102nd Ave.
Ankeny, Iowa 50021
515-964-7608
Manufacturer of Power Arc ignition

MCCI/JET-HOT COATINGS
55 E. Front St.
Bridgeport, Pennsylvania 19405
610-277-5646 or 800-432-3379
High-temp metallic-ceramic coatings

MERCH PERFORMANCE
R.R. 2
Red Deer, Alberta T4N 5E2
Canada
403-346-1221
High-performance crankcases

METZELER TIRES
4520 107th St. S.W.
Mukilteo, Washington 98275
206-348-4000
Performance tires

MICHELIN TIRES
1 Parkway S.
Greenville, South Carolina 29602
803-458-6053
Performance tires

MID-USA
4937 Flyer Ave.
St. Louis, Missouri 63139
314-351-3733
Powerhouse cams, motorcycle
parts, and accessories

MIKE'S PRECISION MACHINE
4588 E. 2nd St., Unit M
Benecia, California 94510
707-747-1711
Crankcase repair

MIKUNI AMERICAN
8910 Mikuni Ave.
Northridge, California 91324
818-885-1242
Carburetors

MILMEYER PRECISION
17370 McBride Ave.
Lake Elsinore, California 92530
909-245-9664
Copper head gaskets

MMI
2844 W. Deer Valley Rd.
Phoenix, Arizona 85027
602-869-9644
Certified mechanic/technician
training

MOROCCO RACING PRODUCTS
13001 Abbey Rd.
North Royalton, Ohio 44133
216-582-5801
Billet crankcases and custom street
and racing bikes

MOROSO
80 Carter Dr.
Guilford, Connecticut 06437
203-453-6571
Spiral-core spark plug wires

MORRIS MAGNETOS, INC.
103 Washington St.
Morristown, New Jersey 07960
201-540-9171
Performance magnetos and gear
covers

MOTION SOFTWARE, INC.
535 W. Lambert, Bldg. E
Brea, California 92821-3911
714-255-2931
Automotive simulation computer
software

MOTORCRAFT
3000 Schaefer Rd.
Dearborn, Michigan 48121
313-322-3000
Spark plugs and heat-range guide

MOTORSPORTS RACING
570 Bell Rd.
Conyers, Georgia 30208
404-929-3723
Cylinder head porting and valvetrain components

MOUNTAIN CYCLE
7455 Wileytown Rd.
Middlegrove, New York 12850
518-882-9863
Performance engine building and
Slipper clutches

MOUNTAIN MOTORS
Rt. 23
E. Windham, New York 12439
518-622-8225
Performance engine building,
machine work, flow testing, and
needle-bearing rocker arms

M.R.E.
625 Pinellas St.
Clearwater, Florida 34616
813-443-5330
Transmission services and gear
back cutting

MSD IGNITION
1490 Henry Brennan Dr.
El Paso, Texas 79936
915-857-5200
Performance ignition systems and
controls

MUSTANG SADDLES
Box 29
Terryville, Connecticut 06786
203-582-9633 or 800-243-1392
Custom seats

NEIDENGARD'S
284 Canton Rd.
Wintersville, Ohio 43952
614-266-6188
Performance engine building

NEMPCO
P.O. Box 311
Guilderland Center, New York
12085
518-861-6949
Performance parts and custom
accessories

NGK SPARK PLUGS, INC.
8 Whatney
Irvine, California 92718
714-855-8278
Spark plugs and heat-range guide

NIPPON DENSO
3900 Via Oro Ave.
Long Beach, California 90810
310-834-6352
Spark plugs and heat-range guide

NITROCYCLE
2100-8 Arctic Ave.
Bohemia, New York 11716
516-567-7320
Performance engine building and
custom machining

NITROUS OXIDE SYSTEMS
5930 Lakeshore Dr.
Cypress, California 90630
714-821-0580
Nitrous oxide fuel systems

ORANGEBURG CYCLE SHOP
1389 Five Chop Rd.
Orangeburg, South Carolina
29115
803-534-9804
Performance engine building,
external starting systems, and custom fabrication

ORION INDUSTRIES
5170 Northwest Hwy.
Chicago, Illinois 60630
312-282-9100
FluoroPlate performance engine
coating

OZMO
601 E. Calvert Hill Rd.
Columbia, Missouri 65202
314-442-1560
Cylinder head porting

PATRICK RACING
10925 Kalama River, Unit E
Fountain Valley, California 92708
714-965-2957
Performance billet cylinder heads

PATTERSON RACING
920 Industrial Rd.
Augusta, Kansas 67010
316-775-7771 or 316-775-6045
Custom piston machining, lightening, and dome profiling

PERFECTION CYCLE
8666 Tyler Blvd.
Mentor, Ohio 44060
216-974-1133
Performance engine building

PERFORMANCE MACHINE
P.O. Box 1739
15535 Garfield Ave.
Paramount, California 90723
310-634-6532
Wheel, brake, and suspension
components

PETERSON RACING PRODUCTS
1817 Houret Ct.
Milpitas, California 95035
408-263-3778
Mechanical tach, tach-drive units,
and external starting systems

PINGEL ENTERPRISE
2076-C 11th Ave.
Adams, Wisconsin 53910
608-339-7999
Gas valves, carbs, wheelie bars, super starter motors, electronics, and race accessories

POLYMER DYNAMICS, INC.
4116 Siegel
Houston, Texas 77009
713-694-3296
Performance engine coatings

PORT-A-TREE INDUSTRIES
594 Blackstone St.
Box 206
Uxbridge, Massachusetts 01569
508-278-2199 or 800-541-7613
Drag racing practice tree

POWERHOUSE PRODUCTS
3402 Democrat Rd.
Memphis, Tennessee 38118
901-795-7600 or 800-872-7223
Precision engine assembly tools

PRECISION MACHINING
580-H Crespi Dr.
Pacifica, California 94044
415-359-4704
Black Diamond valves and valve-train components

PRECISION MEASUREMENT SUPPLY
P.O. Box 28097
San Antonio, Texas 78228
210-681-2405
Precision tools, spring testers, weather stations, and cc burettes

RAY PRICE H-D, INC.
1126 5. Saunders St.
Raleigh, North Carolina 27603
919-832-2261 or 800-394-2753
Racing transmissions, performance products, and machine-shop facilities

PROGRESSIVE SUSPENSION
11129 G Avenue
Hesperia, California 92345
619-948-4012
Fork springs, shocks, and suspension components

PRO-ONE PERFORMANCE
1715 Corrigan Ct.
La Verne, California 91750
909-596-4711
Frames and chassis components

PRO-TRONICS
P.O. Box 1185
Erick, Oklahoma 73645
405-526-3777 or 800-255-7707
Drag racing practice tree

QWIKSILVER II, INC.
13465 Nomwacket Rd., Unit A
Apple Valley, California 92308
619-247-1714
QwikSilver II carburetors

R & D MOTORSPORTS, INC.
935B Harborlake Ct.
Safety Harbor, Florida 34695
813-725-2446
Transmission rebuilding, blueprinting, and gear undercutting

RACEPAK COMPETITION SYSTEMS
17502 Studebaker Rd.
Cerritos, California 90701
310-403-7128
Onboard racing computers

RACE TECH
3227 Producer Way #127
Pomona, California 91768
909-594-7755
Suspension upgrades, fork springs, and Gold Valve emulators

RACE VISIONS
350 Hinman Ave.
Buffalo, New York 14216
716-875-9010
Custom racing frames

RACING SYSTEMS ANALYSIS
P.O. Box 7676
Phoenix, Arizona 85011
602-241-1301
Racing computer software

RAM JETT RETAINER
Box 1521
Santa Maria, California 93456
805-934-5833
Performance computers, intake manifolds, and clutch components

RAT'S WHOLE PLACE
2777 N. Woodford
Decatur, Illinois 62526
217-875-7223 or 800-421-7287
Performance engine building

R. B.'S PERFORMANCE TECHNOLOGY
Rt. 1, Box 38A
Beecher City, Illinois 62414
618-487-5885
Carbon-fiber products, race frames, and performance engine coatings

RC COMPONENTS
140 Hunters Ct.
Bowling Green, Kentucky 42103
502-842-6000
Billet aluminum race wheels, pulleys, and stainless rotors

RED LINE SYNTHETIC OIL CORP.
3450 Pacheco Blvd.
Martinez, California 94553
510-228-7576 or 800-624-7958
Synthetic motor and gear lubricants

RED SHIFT CAMS
8040 Washington Blvd.
Jessup, Maryland 20794
410-799-9451
Performance cams and valvetrain components

RICH PRODUCTS CO.
12420 San Pablo Ave.
Richmond, California 94805
510-234-7547
Performance exhaust systems and Evo cams

RIMAC Tools
69 Armour Pl., Box 98
Dumont, New Jersey 07628
201-384-7600 or 800-932-0513
Valve-spring testers and special-purpose tools

RIVERA ENGINEERING
12532 Lambert Rd.
Whittier, California 90606
310-907-2600
Carbs, cams, valvetrain parts, clutches, belt drives, exhausts, ignitions, and four-valve heads

ROBERTSON'S CYCLE
R.D. 2, Rt. 8
Centerville, Pennsylvania 16404
814-694-3225
Performance frame components

ROMINE RACING
70960 M-66 [S.
Sturgis, Minnesota 49091
616-651-9081
Performance engine building

ROSS RACING PISTONS
12901 S. Yukon Ave.
Hawthorne, California 90250
310-644-9779
Racing pistons

ROWE U.S.A.
P.O. Box 7409
Santa Maria, California 93456
805-349-1932 or 800-531-9901
Valves, valve guides and seals, rings, and rebuilding tools

ROYAL PURPLE SYNTHETIC LUBRICANTS, INC.
2006 Wilson Rd.
Humble, Texas 77396
713-446-1000
Synthetic lubricants

RPM CYCLE
436 W. 8th Ave.
National City, California
619-474-8451
Dyno testing and performance work

RUSSELL PERFORMANCE PRODUCTS
2645 Gundry Ave.
Signal Hill, California 90806
310-595-7523 or 800-394-1120
Braided stainless brake lines and fittings

S & S CYCLE, INC.
Rt. 2, County G, Box 215
Viola, Wisconsin 54664
608-627-1497
Big-bore stroker kits, cylinder heads, crankcases, flywheels, rods, carbs, oil pumps, cams, and valvetrain components

SAM'S PERFORMANCE SPECIALTIES
7634 South Railroad, Unit A-4
N. Charleston, South Carolina 29420
803-569-0252
Cylinder head porting, flow testing, manifolds, and carbs

SCHIRRA SLIDER CLUTCHES
R.D. 2
Velencia, Pennsylvania 16059
412-898-0029
Slider clutches, performance engine building, and machine work

SCHULTZ & SHREVE
19700 Crystal Rock Dr.
Germantown, Maryland 28074
301-694-0602
Race-frame fabrication and chassis components

THE SERVICE DEPARTMENT COMPANY
12907 Valimar Rd.
New Port Richey, Florida 34654
813-856-1264
Special engine assembly tools

SHUMAKER RACING COMPONENTS
11037 Van Wert-Decatur Rd.
Van Wert, Ohio 45891
419-238-0801
Billet aluminum crankcases, cylinders, and cylinder heads

SIFTON MOTORCYCLE PRODUCTS
943 Bransten Rd.
San Carlos, California 94070
415-592-2203 or 800-227-1962
Performance cams and valvetrain components

SNAP-ON TOOLS
2801 80th St.
Kenosha, Wisconsin 53141
414-656-5372
Quality hand tools

SOUTH COAST HARLEY-DAVIDSON
345 E. St.
Chula Vista, California 92101
619-420-7000
High-performance work and custom bike building

SPECTRO OILS
P.O. Box 993
Brookfield, Connecticut 06804
203-775-1291 or 800-243-8645
Premium-quality lubricants

SPLITFIRE, INC.
9 N. Broadway
Des Plaines, Illinois 60016
800-477-5847
Performance spark plugs

SPROCKET SPECIALISTS
P.O. Box 265
Palermo, California 95968
916-533-0802
Sprockets

SPUTHE ENGINEERING, INC.
11185 Lime Kiln Rd.
Grass Valley, California 95949
916-268-0887
Crankcases, big-bore cylinders,
cylinder heads, carbs, and transmission components

SPYKE
(See MC Advantages)
High Performance Starters

STAGE 8
15 Chestnut Ave.
San Rafael, California 94901
415-485-5340 or 800-843-7836
Locking safety bolts

S.T.D. DEVELOPMENT CO., INC.
9601 Cozycroft Ave., Unit 10
Chatsworth, California 91311
818-998-8226
High-performance crankcases,
cylinder heads, and transmission
cases

STORZ PERFORMANCE
239 Olive St.
Ventura, California 93001
805-641-9540
Carbs, cams, exhaust systems,
front ends, and suspension components

SUMAX
337 Clear Rd.
Oriskany, New York 13424
315-768-1058 or 800-654-5546
Frames, powder coating, suspension components, exhaust systems, and ignition wires

SUPERFLOW CORP.
3512 N. Tejon
Colorado Springs, Colorado 80907
719-471-1746
Flowbenches and dynamometers

SUPERTRAPP/KERKER
INDUSTRIES
4540 W. 160th St.
Cleveland, Ohio 44135
216-265-8400
Performance exhaust systems

SWAIN TECH COATINGS
35 Main St.
Scottsville, New York 14546
716-889-2786
Performance engine coatings and
exhaust insulating wrap

TAYLOR CABLE PRODUCTS
301 Highgrove Rd.
Grandview, Missouri 64030
816-765-5011
Ignition wires and components

TECH LINE
P.O. Box 2113
Waxahachie, Texas 75165
214-923-0752
Performance engine coatings

TECH PRODUCTS
511 W. Mahoney
Mesa, Arizona 85210
602-649-3901
EZ-Tyme degree plate and high-
powered starter motors

THERMO-TEC
P.O. Box 946
Berea, Ohio 44017
216-243-9997 or 800-274-8437
Exhaust insulating wrap and heat-
retention coatings

THORN MICROSYSTEMS
799 Holt Rd.
Webster, New York 14580
716-872-4810
Drag racing practice tree and electronic racing equipment

THREE BOND AMERICA
20815 Higgins Ct.
Torrance, California 90501
213-320-3342
Gasket sealers and adhesives

THROTTLE UP, INC.
P.O. Box 601
Blairstown, New Jersey
510-825-1926 or 888-590-7546
Fuel Stat Performance Pollution
Control

TORCO INTERNATIONAL
9916 Pioneer Blvd.
Santa Fe Springs, California 90670
310-942-8480
High-performance lubricants

TOTAL SEAL
2225 W. Mountain View, #6
Phoenix, Arizona 85021
602-678-4977 or 800-874-2753
Gapless piston rings

TRETT'S SPEED & CUSTOM
Rt. 1, Box 1715
Demorest, Georgia 30535
706-754-3784
Performance engine building and
fuel injection units

TRICK RACING FUEL
1189 Morena Blvd.
San Diego, California 92110
800-444-1449
Racing fuels

TRIPOLI MFG., LTD.
R.R. 1, Box 45, Site 14
Red Deer, Alberta TN4 SEI
Canada
403-347-8810
Performance frames and acces-
sories

TROCK CYCLE SPECIALTIES
13 N. 417 French Rd.
Hampshire, Illinois 60140
847-683-4010
Transmission parts, cylinders, float
bowls, specialty tools, and custom
machining

TRUETT & OSBORN
3345 E. 31 St. S.
Wichita, Kansas 67216
316-682-4781
Flywheels, pistons, valvetrain components, frames, and performance
engine building

VANCE & HINES
14010 Marquardt
Santa Fe Springs, California 90670
310-921-7461
Exhaust and fuel injection electronics

V-M-O PRODUCTS, INC.
218 N. State St.
Marion, Ohio 43302
614-383-2396
Performance engine building,
dyno engine testing, research and
development, and inventor of
Velva-Touch lifters

VP RACING FUELS
20846 Lamm Rd.
Elmendorf, Texas 78112
210-621-2244
Racing fuels

V-THUNDER by COMPETITION
CAMS
3406 Democrat Rd.
Memphis, Tennessee 38118
901-794-2833 or 800-967-1066
Performance cams, valvetrain components, and Velva-Touch lifter kits

V-TWIN MANUFACTURING
9 Scobie Dr.
Newburgh, New York 12550
914-565-2806
Performance parts and custom
accessories

WAG'S U.C.T.
8858 S. Painter, Suite D
Whittier, California 90605
310-907-0660
High Performance Starters

WALTERS TECHNOLOGY
P.O. Box 451
Richland Center, Wisconsin 53581
608-643-4777
Performance billet cylinder heads,
billet racing carbs, Mikuni Pro Back
carbs, cams, and engine-simulation
software

WATERMAN RACING
COMPONENTS
37250 Church St.
P.O. Box 148
Gualala, California 95445
707-884-4181
Fuel injection systems

THE WAX SHOP
P.O. Box 10226
Bakersfield, California 93389
805-397-5274 or 800-323-9192
Paint, polish, and hygiene products

WESTERN MANUFACTURING
P.O. Box 130
Marshalltown, Iowa 50158
515-752-5446 or 800-247-7594
Air and electric cycle lifts

WHITE BROTHERS
24845 Corbit Place
Yorba Linda, California 92687
714-692-3404
Cams, carbs, exhaust systems, and
suspension components

WHITE STAR/DUKE VIDEO
195 Hwy. 36
West Long Branch, New Jersey
07764
800-458-5887
Automotive and motorcycle videos

WISECO PISTON, INC.
7201 Industrial Park Blvd.
Mentor, Ohio 44060
216-951-6600 or 800-321-1364
Performance pistons

W. L. GORE & ASSOCIATES
100 Airport Rd.
P.O. Box 1010
Elkton, Maryland 21922
410-392-3200
Gore-Tex RT form-in-place gasket
material

WORKS PERFORMANCE
8730 Shirley Ave.
Northridge, California 91324
818-701-1010
Suspension components

XRV PERFORMANCE PRODUCTS
10428 Burbank Blvd.
North Hollywood, California 91601
818-762-5407
Performance engine building

YOST PERFORMANCE
PRODUCTS
P.O. Box 33408
Minneapolis, Minnesota 55433
612-755-0398
Powertube carburetor fuel atomizer

ZIPPER'S PERFORMANCE
8040 Washington Blvd.
Jessup, Maryland 20794
410-799-8989
Performance engine building,
carbs, Thunderjets, Red Shift cams,
valvetrain components, cylinders,
pistons, Pro Flow oil pumps, ignitions, exhausts, and transmissions

INDEX